The Second Industrial Divide

THE SECOND INDUSTRIAL DIVIDE

Possibilities for Prosperity

MICHAEL J. PIORE

&

CHARLES F. SABEL

Basic Books, Inc., Publishers   New York

Library of Congress Cataloging-in-Publication Data

Piore, Michael J.
  The second industrial divide : possibilities for
prosperity

  Bibliography: p. 309
  Includes index.
  1. Industrialization. 2. Mass production.
3. Corporations. 4. Economic policy.
I. Sabel, Charles F. II. Title.
HD2329.P56 1984   338'.06—dc19   83—46080
ISBN 0–465–07562–2 (cloth)
ISBN 0–465–07563–0 (paper)

For

Nora and Emanuel Piore

and

Lillian and Joseph Sabel

CONTENTS

ACKNOWLEDGMENTS

THIS BOOK is the product of the community in which we live and work. The research on which it depends was financed in large part by the German Marshall Fund of the United States and the Center for Advanced Studies at Princeton. Subsidiary funding was provided by the International Labor Organization, the John D. and Catherine MacArthur Foundation, and the U.S. Department of Labor. Its argument was framed by discussions with colleagues in the Program in Science, Technology, and Society and the Industrial Relations Section of the Sloan School at M.I.T. The list of our debts to individuals is too long to reproduce here. But without the combined help of the following persons, this book would have been literally unthinkable: Arnaldo Bagnasco, Suzanne Berger, Robert Boyer, Ted Brand, Sebastiano Brusco, Vittorio Capecchi, Franca Chizzoli, Paul Church, Martha Cooley, Benjamin Coriat, Sheila Emmerson, Steven Fraser, David Friedman, Peter A. Govrevitch, Steven Graves, Elizabeth Hagen, Gary Herrigel, Helen Hershkoff, Albert O. Hirschmann, George Hoberg, Hilary Horton, Harry Katz, Carl Kaysen, Carla Kirmani, Peter Katzenstein, Heinz Kienzl, Thomas Kochan, Steven Krasner, Charles Maier, George Marcus, Egon Matzner, Deborah Meinbresser, François Michon, Robert McKersie, Christina Duckworth Romer, Jack Russell, Michele Salvati, Annalee Saxenian, Werner Sengenberger, Harley Shaiken, Jean-Jacques Silvestre, Peter Temin, Silvio Trevisani, Roberto Mangabeira Unger, Howard Wial, Peter Weitz, Jonathan Zeitlin, and Robert F. Zevin. Finally, we have drawn throughout upon the intellectual heritage of our parents, to whom the book is dedicated.

The Second Industrial Divide

CHAPTER

1

Introduction

THE TIMES are troubled indeed when the good news is almost indistinguishable from the bad. Economic downturns no longer seem mere interruptions in the march to greater prosperity; rather, they threaten to destroy the world markets on which economic success has depended since the end of World War II. Meanwhile, upturns avert disaster without solving the problems of unemployment and slow growth, which have become chronic in almost all the advanced countries. No theory seems able to explain recent events, let alone predict what will happen next. National leaders play their economic hunches in bold, sometimes desperate attempts to regain control of events. Even the Japanese—whose economic triumphs have won them the envy of their trading partners—are as worried by the fragility of their success as they are gratified by its magnitude.

But amid the confusion, two things are generally counted as near-certainties. First, disruptions in the supply of natural resources—primarily, sources of energy—are seen to have slowed economic growth. And second, the modern welfare state's efforts to control the pace and consequences of growth are seen to have obstructed industrial development (surprisingly enough, there is agreement on this across political lines). However they differ in their analyses and prescriptions for improvement, most theoretical efforts to explain our economic difficulties draw on these two ideas, singly or in combination.

This book takes a different tack. We argue that political intervention in the economy—ranging from the formation of a cartel of oil exporters to the operation of the welfare state—has at worst aggravated a crisis that has other, deeper causes. These causes lie in the economies of the advanced capitalist countries. Our claim is that the present deterioration in economic performance results from the limits of the model of industrial development that is founded on mass production: the use of special-purpose (product-specific) machines and of semiskilled workers to produce standardized goods. We argue that the technologies and operating procedures of most modern corporations; the forms of labor-market control defended by many labor movements; the instruments of macroeconomic control developed by bureaucrats and economists in the welfare states; and the rules of the international monetary and trading systems established immediately after World War II—all must be modified, perhaps even discarded, if the chronic economic diseases of our time are to be cured. If we are right, then the analysis of the distant origins and hidden logic of current economic practice is a precondition to detailed plans for economic reform. Most fundamentally, we argue that to understand the choices we face today, we must clarify the choices made in the past.

These convictions rest on a growing body of research that depicts economic development as a gigantic, centuries-old collective experiment in productive organization. In this picture, rare breakthroughs in the use of labor and machines are followed by periods of expansion, which culminate in crises signaling the limits of existing arrangements. Such crises are of two kinds.

One kind of crisis, easily visible, is marked by the realization that existing institutions no longer secure a workable match between the production and the consumption of goods; these institutions must be supplemented or replaced. We refer to the institutional circuits that connect production and consumption as regulatory mechanisms; we call the disruptions of these circuits regulation crises.*[1] The two major

* The term "regulation" is borrowed from the French *régulation*. But—as will become apparent in the text—the concepts of historical change and economic crisis with which we associate it differ from those concepts in the French theory. More precise English translations of *régulation* are "balancing mechanism" and "equilibration." These terms too, however, imply something different from our argument: they are closely associated with the market mechanism as understood in neoclassical economic theory, and a critical point in our argument is that the market—and neoclassical theory as a whole—is but a specific solution to more general economic problems. Our usage, furthermore, should not be confused with the everyday use of "regulation" as a shorthand for "government intervention in private markets." Rather, we are using the word in its most extended sense: in some economic systems the government might play a critical role in regulating markets, yet the system as a whole would be self-regulating.

regulation crises in the epoch of mechanized production are associated with the rise of the large corporations, in the late nineteenth century, and of the Keynesian welfare state, in the 1930s.

The second and less visible kind of crisis does not concern the flow of income and the distribution of power associated with a given system of industrial technology, as does the first kind of crisis. The second kind of crisis concerns the choice of the technology itself. Industrial technology does not grow out of a self-contained logic of scientific or technical necessity: which technologies develop and which languish depends crucially on the structure of the markets for the technologies' products; and the structure of the markets depends on such fundamentally political circumstances as rights to property and the distribution of wealth. Machines are as much a mirror as the motor of social development.

The brief moments when the path of technological development itself is at issue we call industrial divides. At such moments, social conflicts of the most apparently unrelated kinds determine the direction of technological development for the following decades. Although industrialists, workers, politicians, and intellectuals may be only dimly aware that they face technological choices, the actions that they take shape economic institutions for long into the future. Industrial divides are therefore the backdrop or frame for subsequent regulation crises.

In our view, the first industrial divide came in the nineteenth century. At that time, the emergence of mass-production technologies—initially in Great Britain and then in the United States—limited the growth of less rigid manufacturing technologies, which existed primarily in various regions of Western Europe. These less rigid manufacturing technologies were craft systems: in the most advanced ones, skilled workers used sophisticated general-purpose machinery to turn out a wide and constantly changing assortment of goods for large but constantly shifting markets. Moreover—in contrast to mass production—economic success in these industries depended as much on cooperation as on competition: unless the costs of permanent innovation were shared among firms, and between capitalists and workers, those who stood to lose from change defended their interests by blocking it. And the sharing of costs depended, in turn, on institutions that protected the vulnerable in the name of the community as a whole.

Under somewhat different historical conditions, we argue, firms using a combination of craft skill and flexible equipment might have played a central role in modern economic life—instead of giving way, in almost

5

all sectors of manufacturing, to corporations based on mass production. Had this line of mechanized craft production prevailed, we might today think of manufacturing firms as linked to particular communities, rather than as the independent organizations—barely involved with their neighbors—that, through mass production, seem omnipresent.

This book's central claim is that we are living through the second industrial divide. Extrapolating from current developments, we see two potentially contradictory strategies for relaunching growth in the advanced countries. The first strategy builds on the dominant principles of mass-production technology; but it requires a dramatic extension of existing regulatory institutions, including a redefinition of economic relations between the developed and the developing worlds. The second strategy veers sharply from established technological principles and leads back to those craft methods of production that lost out at the first industrial divide. This second strategy requires the creation of regulatory mechanisms whose association with bygone forms of economic organization apparently discredits them as instruments of modern industry.

It appears that either of these two strategies could be enacted in a variety of ways—resulting in strikingly varied consequences for the long-term position of labor and capital in any one country, and for the position of entire national economies in the world order. Resolving the question of what kind of industrial world we will inhabit does not automatically resolve the question of which nations and social groups will control it; we find, for example, craft production sometimes dominated by entrepreneurs loyal to communist parties and trade unions, and at other times dominated by entrepreneurs with ties to the Catholic church. There are plausible versions of an international mass-production economy that connect small islands of prosperity in a sea of misery, whereas others presuppose general well-being.

Our overarching purpose is not to predict the outcome of the current struggles to impose order on production. Rather, we attempt to clarify the preconditions and implications of these possible forms of economic reconstruction. Even when technology is not fundamentally in flux, it is hard to grasp the operation of the economy, and harder still to predict either the general line of its expansion or the range of political institutions with which it will be compatible. The succession of regulation crises during the last hundred years demonstrates how slowly we collectively learn about the economy in relation to the larger society: however obvious the solutions to regulatory problems appear in retrospect, the disruptions that led to their discovery is proof that they were almost unthinkable until the moment that they began to work. The possibility of a radical, politically contentious redirection of technological development further complicates the problem of economic reconstruction, and correspondingly reduces the range of foresight.

The stakes are high. Prolonged confusion in the advanced world increases the risk of international economic collapse. Paralysis in any one country can mean national economic disaster—a danger, we argue, that is acute for the United States. And once made, decisions are likely to be fateful. The choices of the coming years could define the way we work long into the coming century—just as the outcome of the early-nineteenth-century war of economic worlds gave shape to the economy during the hundred years that followed.

The choices that are made will be of particular importance to blue- and white-collar workers in the advanced countries. They will probably bear the largest share of the costs of adjusting to the new economic order, whatever it is; and they will have to live day by day with the new technologies of production. But though any of several strategies could lead to a viable economic order, these workers often lack the resources even to conceptualize the solution that is most favorable to their interests. Nevertheless, if they and their leaders do not make the most of the scarce opportunities they have to shape the economic order to their wants, only luck will preserve the gains that these people have made in the last decades. Prosperity of a kind could come again yet pass them by.

This view of technological and institutional change in history differs radically from prevailing views of both the Right and the Left. It implies that even the most insightful elaborations of reigning doctrines will prove poor guides to understanding the coarse facts of our times. To clear a space for our argument, therefore, we next set out and then criticize the major theories of the current disorder.

The Surprising Convergence of Neoclassical and Neo-Marxist Views

What is most striking about the well-developed views of the current crisis is their similarity. Liberals and neo-Marxists agree that the disruptions of the 1970s are the sign of a fundamental incompatibility between market capitalism and political democracy, at least in their existing forms. They argue that it is political intervention in the economy that has slowed growth and deterred investment. Had it been possible to protect firms from the state, and given the existing organization of the world market—they argue—there is no reason to think that competition among them would have produced an economic logjam.

The liberal variant of this theme has, as we show in chapter 2, a long but straightforward genealogy. Ever since Adam Smith attacked mercantilist meddling in the eighteenth-century British economy, thinkers in what is now called the neoclassical tradition of economics have held that the competitive markets are the optimal form of exchange: as a rule, restrictions on competition are purchased at the price of a decline in economic performance.

The upshot of these views is that liberals have only three justifications for political intervention in economic activity. The first—and only legitimate one, from a strictly theoretical point of view—is the desire to protect or restore the free-market regime in those areas where it is not self-regulating. State control of monopolies (which are a natural impediment to competition) and regulation of the money supply (a precondition, not a consequence, of orderly markets) are two well-known examples of such intervention. The second justification of political intervention is to temper the formally defined efficiency of the system with substantive equity, by redistributing some of the fruits of victory from the winners to the losers in the struggle for economic success. The third conceivable justification of state intervention, in the liberals' view, is mismanagement. Shortsighted, self-seeking, or simply ignorant officials may use their public power to influence economic developments to essentially private ends, or to experiment with hopelessly impractical utopian projects, or to apply quack cures to business ailments.

Liberal views of crisis in general and of the current crisis in particular are compounded of these elements. The most narrowly economic accounts focus on direct political disruption of markets. Thus, one line of neoclassical commentary on the current situation stresses the disruptive effects of skyrocketing fuel prices.[2] The price increases, in this argument, have slowed growth rates directly and indirectly: directly, by taxing the wealth of the advanced countries and reducing the funds available for investment, and indirectly, by forcing the write-off of energy-intensive capital equipment and increasing inflation, thereby making potential investors cautious.

A related line of commentary maintains that the state's attempts at macroeconomic management have involuntarily contributed to costly economic disorder, because they are based on unrealistic or contradictory assumptions about market behavior. The influential McCracken report on the slowdown of growth in the 1970s, for example, argues that the provision of unemployment insurance and other social-welfare benefits— which serve to sustain effective demand during business downturns— actually undermined the effect of much state economic policy. By making the loss of a job more tolerable, said the report, these programs reduced workers' willingness to accept wage cuts during a recession, thus reducing the government's capacity to control inflation.[3]

These economic analyses shade into and are complemented by more sociological arguments. Such arguments hold that state activity that is (or was) legitimate in liberal eyes was perverted into behavior that is not. One central figure in these arguments is the power-hungry welfare bureaucrat, who puts the state at the service of politically influential clients, in return for their allegiance. The bigger the program, and the larger the number of dependents, the easier it becomes to browbeat the state into further concessions. A second figure, the political entrepreneur, operates by a parallel logic but allegedly subverts the state from without, not from within. This is the huckster, the candidate who buys votes with promises of benefits that cumulatively would cost more to fulfill than society can afford to pay.[4]

Carried to their logical conclusions—as they were in the late 1970s— these arguments broaden into a profound condemnation of mass political participation and government's attempts to control economic development—or even to ameliorate its effects through redistribution. Often unwillingly, liberals have been drawn by the structure of their arguments to conclude that mass participation leads to impossible demands on the state's budget—and that both welfare and macroeconomic control retard growth by paralyzing markets. These liberals are trapped between the idea that democracy and capitalism need each other and the conviction that they cannot coexist. Thus, people who once thought they knew how to balance economic equity and efficiency are now demanding democracy just for the elite and welfare for the moribund.[5]

Many of these themes appear in the work of such leading neo-Marxists as Claus Offe, Samuel Bowles, and Herbert Gintis.[6] These writers have abandoned the orthodox Marxist idea that market competition and technological change, the "logic of capital," determine the trajectory of economics and political developments. They argue, instead, that politics constrains economic activity, controlling its pace if not its direction. It is to the logic of the politics of the welfare state—its origins and effects on the economy—that they turn their attention.

In the neo-Marxist view, the Keynesian welfare state is the political expression of a stalemate between the bourgeoisie and the working class. The latter has not proved strong enough to impose socialism, and the former is too weak to defend successfully all the principles of market capitalism. The result is a situation in which the working class has used its political power to redistribute income in its own favor, to secure minimal guarantees of its welfare, and—by such measures as health-and-safety legislation—to circumscribe capital's rights to dispose of property. The economy has been slowly and partially democratized, in the sense that the right to vote can be used to control the market in limited ways.

The current economic difficulties, the neo-Marxist argument continues, are simply the belated outcome of this imposition of alien, proto-socialist forms of exchange on a capitalist economy. Inflation, high unemployment, and slow growth are all, one way or another, the result of state interference in the economy, at the behest of the subordinate classes. At this point, the conclusions of neo-Marxist analysis coincide with those of liberal argument: democracy is a threat to capitalism. The neo-Marxists hope, of course, that the collapse of capitalism will clear the way for socialism, whereas the liberals hope that the collapse of socialist pipe dreams will clear the way for the reconstruction of capitalism. But having lost faith in any underlying logic of economic development, even the neo-Marxists admit that this is only hope against hope.

To understand the overlap of liberal and neo-Marxist views, it is necessary (anticipating another theme from the next chapter) to see that neo-Marxism is joined to its orthodox parent just at the point where the latter touches liberal doctrine. Marx no less than Smith believed that survival in any economic system imposes severe constraints on the survivors: to endure, they must adopt the unique form of social and technical organization that is most suited to the conditions of the moment. Groups—even nations—that deviate from this ideal are threatened by extinction at the hands of those who conform to it; and this threat is enough to ensure the long-term triumph of efficiency. Smith believed, of course, that the competitive market is the ideal system of exchange, and the firm that uses special-purpose machines is the ideal unit of production: everything that went before this optimal social and technical organization was a prelude to it, and it would have no successor. Marx thought of the market and the modern factory as a way station to socialism. Both agreed that the track of human progress—the "natural path of opulence," as Smith called it—is narrow and unique.

These ideas echo in the school of neo-Marxism. The neo-Marxists, too, define markets as the most efficient form of exchange in a system of private ownership of the means of large-scale production. From this starting point, the idea becomes unthinkable that there can be various equally efficient ways of organizing systems that are dominated by a private investor class. Conversely, any disruption of mass production is regarded as wasteful, in that it does not contribute to the transformation of the property order into something higher. For the liberal, the choice is between capitalism and chaos. For the neo-Marxist the choice, in moments of despair, looks tragically similar.

Some Counterevidence

The liberal and neo-Marxist theories of the crisis seem validated by the paralysis of efforts to redirect the economy through politics. The advanced countries' incapacity to control the spending of the welfare state and the privileges of the corporation—despite dramatically changed economic conditions—gives credence to the view that political stalemate explains economic decline. But why should the failure to find a political solution to the economic problem be taken as proof of its political origin? Indeed, the logjam of politics might be the effect of conflicts touched off by the deteriorating advanced economies—not the cause. To exclude these possibilities, the liberals and neo-Marxists would have to demonstrate a clear relation between political intervention in the economy—however defined—and the slowdown in economic activity. This they cannot do.

Suppose, for example, that government spending on social programs (such as pensions, health and unemployment insurance, family allowances, and aid to the poor) significantly slows economic growth, by creating disincentives to work. In that case, we would expect an inverse relation between the level of welfare spending as a percentage of gross national product and the rate of economic growth: the higher a nation ranks in the league tables of welfare spending, the lower it should rank in the league tables of growth.

TABLE 1.1

Social-Security Expenditures and Gross Domestic Product per Capita
in Selected Industrial Economies in the 1970s

	Total Expenditures of Social-Security Schemes* as Percentage of GDP (1977)	Growth of Social Expenditures: Percentage of GDP (1973–79)	Average Annual Percentage Rate of Growth of Per-Capita GDP (1975–79)
Austria	21.1	2.7	3.8
France	25.6	4.7	3.4
West Germany	23.4	4.9	4.0
Italy	22.8	0.3	3.0
Japan	9.7	5.8	4.3
U.K.	17.3	2.5	2.4
U.S.A.	13.7	1.6	3.7

SOURCES:
International Labor Office, "The Cost of Social Security: Tenth International Inquiry, 1975–77" (Geneva: ILO, 1981); *United Nations Yearbook of National Accounts Statistics*, 1980, vol. 2, International Tables (New York: UN, 1982); Manfred G. Schmidt, "The Welfare State and the Economy in Periods of Economic Crisis: A Comparative Study of Twenty-three OECD Nations," *European Journal of Political Research* 11 (1983): 1–26.
* Social-security schemes include medical-care benefits, cash benefits, and benefits in kind other than for medical care (social-welfare schemes for the aged, disabled, children and housewives, et al.).

In fact, however, the statistics show nothing of the sort.[7] In the mid-1970s, social-welfare expenditures as a percentage of national income were roughly one-and-a-half times as high in such countries as Austria and West Germany as they were in the United States; yet of these economies, the American was the slowest-growing. Table 1.1 juxtaposes the social-welfare spending and average growth rates of selected advanced industrial countries during this period.

Other ways of construing the thesis that politicization of the economy retards development fare no better. It has been argued, for example, that it is not welfare spending but government's attempts to regulate labor markets, police the environment, and influence investment patterns that are at the root of the crisis. But here, too, the facts are discomfiting. Firms in high-growth countries such as West Germany, for example, must bargain with unions to fix compensation for workers affected by plant closings; by contrast, American law does not even require managers to inform workers that their plants are about to close.[8] The French *inspecteurs du travail* (government officials who supervise the administration of rules and regulations regarding the labor market) have the power to intervene in labor-management disputes, which is unthinkable in the United States.[9] By different means, the French and Japanese governments exercise pervasive control over domestic credit markets;

their use of this power to shape industrial investment would scandalize American—and West German—business executives.[10] Yet, as table 1.1 shows, France and Japan are among the great economic success stories of the 1960s and '70s. Or take—as a final example of these incongruities— the fact that no one in Japan argues that the national environmental regulations have burdened industry, even though these regulations are among the strictest that exist.[11] In sum, it is easy to find instances of botched state intervention in the economy; but it is extremely difficult to argue that state intervention always leads to disaster.

More rigorously studied than the claims about welfare spending or regulation—and all the more decisively discredited—is the idea that economic shocks to the advanced countries—in the form of oil-price increases—account for the slowdown in growth. The fact is that outlays for energy are only a small fraction of total manufacturing costs (in 1977, energy expenses came to less than 2.5 percent of the total cost of inputs in U.S. manufacturing, up from 1.5 percent in the years before the first oil shock, in 1973). From this, Ernst R. Berndt, one of the most careful students of the subject, concludes that "variants in energy prices or quantities will not weigh very heavily in productivity calculations in U.S. manufacturing."[12] Moreover, even if energy amounted to a greater fraction of manufacturing costs, it appears that, at least in the United States, productivity began to slow down in the early 1960s— well before the first dramatic increases in the price of oil.[13]

Outline of an Alternative View

By focusing on the relation between the government and the economy, liberal and neo-Marxist analyses distract from a central fact of the current crisis: confusion about the future course of economic activity. Forecasting models that in the prosperous 1950s and '60s could predict the development of national economies within a narrow band now cannot foretell even the direction of change in economic indicators from one month to the next. Uncertainty about changes in national economies is matched by confusion about the prospects of individual markets. Business executives are unsure of which products to make, which technologies to use to make them, and even of how to distribute authority within their firm. Anyone who speaks with industrialists or reads trade journals will probably conclude that even without government interference, many firms would still have trouble mapping a comprehensive strategy for the future.

Uncertainty is a natural—even a defining—feature of any economic crisis; but the current confusion has novel aspects. The current crisis differs most obviously from the Great Depression of the 1930s. In that period, fascists, communists, and capitalists around the world all strove to emulate the technological example of one country: the United States. Ironically—at a time when society as a whole seemed most fragile and mutable—no one seemed to doubt the necessity of just those principles of industrial organization that today seem the most debatable.

The current confusion over how to organize technologies, markets, and hierarchies is evidence of the breakdown of crucial yet poorly understood elements in the familiar system of economic development. And whenever the familiar suddenly becomes mysterious, it is because assumptions have ceased to hold.

To grasp the special features of the post-1973 crisis, it is therefore necessary to examine the familiar: to look at the history of industrial capitalism, from two perspectives. First we must retrace this familiar ground to gain a deeper general understanding of the workings of capitalist economies—from the beginnings of extensive mechanization, in the early nineteenth century, to the present. We need to know how a particular technology came to dominate industrial production; what kinds of regulatory crises could develop, given this apparently unchangeable technological choice; and how the current economic instability could reopen debate about the alternative possibilities of technological advance. This reexamination of the past—together with a survey of the contradictory changes now in progress—illuminates the preconditions for the survival of any of the emerging economic alternatives.

But the view of mass production as a system of markets, technologies, and institutions gives only half the picture. The other half concerns the development of single nations, and the way their struggles for advantage both shaped the general conditions of competition and were shaped by them. Turning backward, we need to know why the United States took the lead in developing a particular variant of the mass-production system—and how this nation's preeminence influenced rival countries' attempts to imitate the American success. Turning forward, we need to know how differences in national efforts to build a mass-production economy are influencing the major capitalist economies' response to the crisis—disposing some to cling to habits of technological development formed at the first industrial divide and others to embrace craft principles of production. The organization of our argument follows from the double aim of presenting a model of mass production both as a general type of economy and as a historical creation of competing nations—nations whose particularities influence not merely their own fates but also the rise of the system as a whole.

Our starting point is the first industrial divide: the early-nineteenth-century victory of mass production over craft production as the dominant form of industrial organization. Chapter 2 therefore sets out the technological foundations of both systems, in relation to their respective markets and the various social worlds in which they prospered. The outcome of the contest is then explained, by reference to a model of technological change built on the assumption that there is no "natural path" to economic success. In this model, the triumph of a technological breakthrough over competing adaptations depends on its timing and the resources available to its champions—rather than on its intrinsic superiority. In this view, competition guarantees only that the weak must follow the lead of the strong, not that the strong have found the uniquely correct solution to common problems. Progress, we will show, is best described not as the narrow track of Smith and Marx, but as a branching tree—yet the limbs of this tree thrive or wither according to the outcomes of social struggles, not some natural law of growth.

Chapters 3 and 4 focus on two consequences of the Americans' discovery that the profitability of investment in mass-production equipment depends on the stabilization of markets. The first of these consequences was the construction, from the 1870s to the 1920s, of giant corporations, which could balance demand and supply within their industries. The second consequence was the creation, two decades later, of a Keynesian system for matching production and consumption in the national economy as a whole. Our aim here is to show how American institutions were reshaped to provide a nationally specific solution to the problems of any economy that is based on mass production.

To capture what is distinctively American in the U.S. system of mass production, we call attention to alternative solutions to various aspects of the general regulatory problem. One way to do this is to show how different outcomes might have occurred under slightly different historical circumstances in the United States; another way is to demonstrate that these potential variants did emerge in those countries where the appropriate conditions prevailed. In chapter 3, for example, we show how the distant, adversarial relation of American corporations to banks and the state originated in the precocious development of the corporations and the delayed development of banks and the state. Chapter 4 emphasizes how, in the absence of a state policy of demand stimulation, the American system of collective bargaining became an instrument for increasing demand for industrial goods in step with the expansion of supply.

Chapter 5 completes the analysis of American developments. It looks at the two extremes of economic organization: the microscopic world of shop-floor industrial relations and the macroscopic world of international trade, as they each relate to the corporation and Keynesianism. Here, too, history made a difference. We argue, for instance, that the timing and duration of the Depression may well have blocked the emergence in the United States of a system of shop-floor industrial relations that today is associated with Japan and West Germany. Chapter 6, finally, looks at mass production and its American variant from the perspective of other advanced capitalist countries: France, Italy, West Germany, and Japan. The obstacles to pervasive mass production in these countries before the 1960s—and the institutions they developed to overcome them—reveal the special conditions that prevailed in the United States, and the constraints imposed by product-specific technologies.

Then comes the crisis of the 1970s. Chapter 7 tells the tale of the post-1973 dislocations twice: once as a series of shocks to the economy, exacerbated by political responses that ignored the institutional foundations of stability in a mass-production economy; and a second time as the consequence of the dramatic spread of mass production and the resulting exhaustion of the possibilities for further growth within the regulatory system that was created after World War II. Our point is that these lines of argument are complementary. Were it not for the shocks, the slowdown in growth might have come much later or—in an optimistic view of the powers of collective foresight and the capacity for farsighted reform—not at all. And were it not for the increasing competition among mass producers for limited markets, the shocks could probably have been absorbed without shaking the foundations of the regulatory system and the dominant modes of technological development. In any event, we will argue, as the shocks undermined already fragile institutions, and these crumbling institutions redoubled the effects of the shocks, firms that were accustomed to stability suddenly found themselves struggling for survival in an ever less certain world.

Chapters 8 and 9 describe the reactions to the growing disorder. They compare the divergent behavior first of competing firms, then of competing national economies. Chapter 8 distinguishes two major company-level responses to the crisis. One—favored by the American automobile firms—aims at extending the mass-production model. It

16

does so by linking the production facilities and markets of the advanced countries with the fastest-growing third-world countries. This response amounts to a use of the corporation (now a multinational entity) to stabilize markets in a world where the forms of cooperation among states can no longer do the job.

The other major company-level response we call flexible specialization. It is seen in the networks of technologically sophisticated, highly flexible manufacturing firms in central and northwestern Italy. Flexible specialization is a strategy of permanent innovation: accommodation to ceaseless change, rather than an effort to control it. This strategy is based on flexible—multi-use—equipment; skilled workers; and the creation, through politics, of an industrial community that restricts the forms of competition to those favoring innovation. For these reasons, the spread of flexible specialization amounts to a revival of craft forms of production that were emarginated at the first industrial divide.

Chapter 9 sets these company-level developments in the context of their national economies. Its argument is that whether firms drift toward flexible specialization or maintain existing practices depends on their country's adaptation to mass production. On the one hand, the United States follows the familiar path, because of the accident of its system of shop-floor industrial relations; France, too, because of the state's powers and past success with mass production, is doing the same. On the other hand, vestiges of the craft tradition in Italy, West Germany, and Japan encourage a shift in the direction of flexible specialization.

Chapter 10 is the first part of a double conclusion. It focuses on the politics of the world economic order. This chapter presents the respective conditions under which mass production or craft production could serve as the framework for future prosperity. Its import is that if we are to make a conscious choice between these two worlds, we must be able to imagine the alternatives as vital wholes. Such visualization is an act of emancipation from the prevailing view of historical development.

This analysis of global alternatives is complemented in chapter 11 by a discussion of the economic choices facing the United States. The first part of the chapter depicts American firms that are attracted to the strategy of flexible specialization; yet these firms are so attached by their heritage to the mass-production model that they cannot create the requisite communitarian institutions. The second part of the chapter draws an analogy between this dilemma of U.S. firms and the confusion of contemporary public debates regarding the future of the U.S. economy. It argues that even programs to encourage industrial flexibility—by redefining the role of the firm and the workers' rights within it—are too attached to the concept of the mass-production corporation to succeed.

To see how a system of flexible specialization might operate in the United States, we must look past the current debates. We need to examine the ideas and industrial communities of the nineteenth-century American artisans, and of their heirs among the Populists, the twentieth-century craft workers, and even some modern unions. The small-holder democracy that these people have practiced and defended shows a way to reconcile individual autonomy—at the core of American politics—with the restricted competition that is essential for flexible specialization. If this is so, then to remake our economy we must return to and elaborate an older conception of the polity. To shape our future, we will have to change our ideas, not just of how history happens, but of our own past.

2

Mass Production as Destiny and Blind Decision

THROUGHOUT the nineteenth century, two forms of technological development were in collision.[1] One was craft production. Its foundation was the idea that machines and processes could augment the craftsman's skill, allowing the worker to embody his or her knowledge in ever more varied products: the more flexible the machine, the more widely applicable the process, the more it expanded the craftsman's capacity for productive expression. The other form of technological development was mass production. Its guiding principle was that the cost of making any particular good could be dramatically reduced if only machinery could be substituted for the human skill needed to produce it. Its aim was to decompose every handwork task into simple steps, each of which could be performed faster and more accurately by a machine dedicated to that purpose than by a human hand. The more specialized the machine—the faster it worked and the less specialized its operator needed to be—the greater its contribution to cutting production costs. The visionaries of craft production foresaw a world of small producers, each specialized in one line of work and dependent on the others. The visionaries of mass production foresaw a world of ever more automated factories, run by ever fewer and ever less skilled workers.

By World War I—at the latest—it seemed clear which had been the truer vision. Manchester cotton goods, Waltham clocks, Lynn shoes, Colt revolvers, Yale locks, McCormick reapers, Singer sewing machines, Remington typewriters, American Tobacco cigarettes, U.S. Steel, and Standard oil—industry after industry came under the domination of giant firms using specialized equipment to turn out previously unimagined numbers of standard goods, at prices that local producers could not meet. When, in 1913, Ford's Model T rolled out of his Highland Park, Michigan, plant, it was the culmination of a century's experience with mass production: the machinery for making the parts was so precise that no hand-finishing was necessary, yet it was so easy to operate that workers just off the farm could run it; and the final assembly of the product—paced by an endless circulating chain that moved the work in progress from one station to another—required no more traditional craft skill than the operation of the automatic equipment that the engineers privately called farm tools.[2] The indisputable contribution of these techniques to the American success in World War I made mass production a matter not just of commercial prudence, but of national survival. By 1936 the industrialized world recognized its present and future in the bitterly comic movie about an assembly-line worker entitled *Modern Times*.

Yet the victory of mass production never proved so complete as its early triumphs suggested it would be. Despite waves of concentration and rationalization in all the industrial powers in the 1880s and '90s, the 1920s, and the 1950s, some firms in almost all industries and almost all firms in some industries continued to apply craft principles of production. By the 1980s, if there is any relation between industrial concentration and economic success, it is the reverse of the one Henry Ford expected: Japan, with its substantial small-firm sector, flourishes; Great Britain, with its highly concentrated economy, languishes.[3] Indeed, in many cases the progress of mass production seems to depend on coexistence with its technological counterprinciple.

From the perspective of late-twentieth-century scholarship, moreover, even the successes of mass production seem less the outcome of mechanization than of an interplay of social and political forces. The historians' assault on the popular understanding has many motives: a professional passion for detail; suspicion that technological development has been manipulated to serve powerful interests; perplexity at the persistence of diverse national styles of machine operation in the face of competitive pressures for uniformity; curiosity about the possible antecedents of new forms of craft production. But regardless of its motives, the research has uncovered preconditions for the success of mass production (and the concomitant decline of craft production) in the politically defined interests of producers and consumers—rather than in the logic of industrial efficiency. Thus, not only do craft and mass production appear to be complements, but also, under slightly different historical conditions, the former might have been a more equal partner of the latter. The exponents of craft production begin to look more like realists with a fighting chance than romantic apologists for artisan pride; and society seems to have blindly chosen its technology through a myriad of local conflicts—but chosen nonetheless.

This chapter looks twice at modern industrial structure. First it tells the story of mass production as we and most readers of this book learned it and—a thousand qualifications aside—repeat it. Then, in a widening circle of criticism, we confront this view with counterevidence: we amend and then we abandon the notion of mass production as the unique path of technical progress, so that we arrive at a picture of technology as a refractory yet periodically malleable expression of the distribution of power in society.

Mass Production as Modern Times

Mass production has come to mean modern times because it is the expression of a web of ideas that promise to explain how industrial society works, where it came from, and why it has to be as it is. As elaborated by the classical political economists from Ferguson to Smith to Marx, these ideas offer a theory of economic growth relating changes in the market to changes in the use of technology and labor. They also offer a story about the end of feudalism and the rise of industrial capitalism and an object lesson on the constraints of nature and humankind's freedom to overcome them. These ideas have passed into our collective self-conception because they illuminate crucial features of the way current industrial economies work. They plausibly account for the startling economic success of the leading industrial powers, and they theoretically second our everyday experience of the limited plasticity

21

of technology. Nonetheless, we will argue, these partial truths do not corroborate the classical synthesis in its entirety. On the contrary, the successes of the industrial pioneers can be better understood in light of other ideas of historical transformation. But to see why, it is necessary first to examine the existing understanding of mass production as a whole.

The core of the classical theory of economic development is that increases in productivity (output per unit input) depend on the increasingly specialized (product-specific) use of resources. For Adam Smith— observing in the 1780s a pin factory that his analysis made famous,— the crucial source of increased productivity was primarily the increasing division of labor, understood in the narrow sense of the continual subdivision of manual tasks. According to Smith, a top-of-the-pin maker and a bottom-of-the-pin maker working together produce more pins in an hour than two workers each making whole pins. The reason he gives is that the partial-pin makers' concentration on a narrower range of tasks allows them to perfect their skills faster and waste less time switching operations than the whole-pin makers. The increase in efficiency did, however, have a cost in increased rigidity: the more tasks were subdivided and connected in a precise sequence, the more difficult it became for the network as a whole to produce anything but pins.[4]

Marx, writing a half century later—and extending a leitmotiv in the *Wealth of Nations* that had been taken up in turn by David Ricardo, Charles Babbage, and Andrew Ure—integrated this argument about the subdivision of tasks with an argument about the role of machines.[5] To Marx, the specialization of manual work—whatever its immediate impact on productivity—was decisively important because it led to the introduction of special-purpose automatic machinery. Once a human task had been decomposed into its elementary motions, it became possible to build a device that would perform these motions automatically; and as one step of a manufacturing process was thus mechanized, the preceding and following steps had to be correspondingly reorganized, to keep pace with the new machinery. Thus, the introduction of automatic equipment also increased the rigidity of production, making it ever harder to switch resources to alternative uses.

It was the spread of these dramatically productive task-specific devices (Marx's illustration was the self-acting mule, a machine for spinning cotton) that reversed the traditional relation between the worker and the instruments of production—thereby making mechanization revolutionary. Although the subdivision of tasks had led to an ever more restrictive, specialized use of the handworker's tools, those tools remained an adjunct to artisanal skill; they facilitated the worker's translation of his or her idea of a product into an actuality. With the introduction of automatic machinery, the roles of artificer and instrument were reversed: the worker became the adjunct of the machine—whose purpose, far from translating human skill into action, was to make human involvement in the production of a good superfluous. Whereas the worker had once defined the product, the product now defined the worker. To Marx, it was this subordination of the worker to the product that marked the transition from the use of tools to the use of machines.[6]

There was, however, a crucial qualification to the idea of a progressive increase in efficiency through the product-specific use of resources: the dynamic of specialization could be activated only by growth in demand. Obviously, it made no sense to rearrange the production setup to increase output if there was no market for the increase and the rearrangement made it expensive to switch the resources to some alternative purpose. In Smith's phrase, the division of labor was therefore limited by the extent of the market.[7] Progress in the efficient use of resources was blocked unless the market for a good could be increased (by such means as reducing tariff barriers and taxes; decreasing transportation costs; redistributing income to those too poor to buy what they want; and consolidating demand for closely related goods into demand for a single standard product). Once the division of labor was freed from restraint, however, its advance was theoretically self-sustaining. Increases in efficiency themselves enlarged the market by lowering production costs, thus bringing goods within the reach of those previously unable to afford them.

This connection between the market and the division of labor was linked to the second great theme of classical political economy: the transition from the agrarian world of a small-holder peasantry paying dues to feudal lords to the industrial world of capitalism—specifically, the emergence of Great Britain and the United States as industrial powers. Despite their different perspectives, both Smith and Marx interpreted this transition as progress from autarky to specialization. And for both, the moral of the story was that economic interests would reshape political institutions according to the requirements of increasing efficiency. The most that states could do was to obstruct the progress of specialization temporarily; to put it the other way around, freedom— the absence of state interference in the self-organization of the economy— expedited economic development.

In Smith's view, Western feudalism had been undermined by an alliance between the crown and the merchants—the latter being concentrated in towns, surrounded by the autarkic feudal manors yet independent from them. In return for tax exemptions, the merchants sided with the crown against the feudal lords, who preyed with equal delight on the king's tax revenues and the traders' profits.[8] To Marxists, the crucial political alliance was between the peasants and the urban merchants. The peasants could always threaten to flee to the cities, beyond the lords' jurisdiction (according to the German saying, *Stadtluft macht frei*—city air emancipates); this threat increased the peasants' bargaining power in the struggle to enlarge their share of the feudal estate's economic surplus. This bargaining power—augmented by the plagues' decimation of the labor force—allowed the peasantry in time to capture control of the proceeds of its labor.[9] Both alliances, however, had the effect of loosening legal restrictions on the producers' ability to profit from investment and thereby encouraging the expansion and specialization of production. This expansion became self-sustaining as the wealth it created drew new social groups, in ever widening circles, into the market—empowering them to attack the remaining restrictions on free exchange and specialization.

The first step toward specialization was the putting-out, or *Verlag*, system. Merchants and successful peasant entrepreneurs bought raw materials such as wool or flax and circulated them to spinners, weavers, and dyers—all paid by the piece—and then marketed the finished product. The natural next step was to concentrate these operations in a single building, or manufactory. The purpose was to reduce pilferage, control quality, lower the costs (in time and money) of transportation, and—most important—oblige the workers to put in longer, more regular hours than they had done when employed at home: as outworkers, they had regarded an industrial income as a convenient supplement to their agricultural earnings. The third step toward specialization, begun in Smith's day and well under way in Marx's, was the mechanization of production, which the decomposition of tasks in the preceding period had made possible.

These developments contributed to and were accelerated by political transformations. There was the abolition of mercantilist restrictions on trade, foreseen by Smith (and, he hoped, hastened by his writings).[10] Parliament's complicity in the landlords' attack of small holders' property rights made it possible, according to Marx, to drive the peasantry from its traditional holdings—thus creating both an industrial proletariat and a market for its products.[11] That these shifts in economic and political power took place in Great Britain rather than elsewhere was, to the classical writers, a matter of historical luck. For complex historical reasons, there were fewer barriers to free exchange in Great Britain than on the Continent, so British markets expanded first; the social transformations that the markets wrought brought down the rest of the archaic restraints. But neither Smith—with his belief that the division of labor was rooted in an innately human propensity to truck and barter for advantage—nor Marx—with his belief in the inevitable development of the technological forces of production—had any doubt that efficiency would have triumphed elsewhere even if the way had been blocked in Great Britain.

This idea of the inevitability of progress through specialization was the third great, metahistorical theme of the classical writers. To both Smith and Marx, the triumph of mass-production capitalism was proof that humankind was constrained to play out a paradoxical drama in history. The struggle to survive and prosper in a world where every satisfaction created new wants led to the constant improvement of productive efficiency; yet the constant improvement of efficiency subjected individuals to ever greater restrictions, according to the logic of divided labor and mechanization. The price of human liberation was thus subjugation (a subjugation that Marx—trusting to the liberating powers of the automated factory—thought would be temporary) to the inhuman logic of specialization. Progress was both inevitable—in that political interference could retard but not stop it—and uncontrollable—in that it required the elimination of skill and the product-specific automation of manufacturing. Competition assured that those who did not bow to these necessities were crushed by those who did.[12]

This classic synthesis—whether or not acknowledged as such—continues to serve as the matrix not only for broad-gauge treatments of industrialization, but also for detailed programs of research. Thus, a standard textbook on European industrialization (David Landes's *The Unbound Prometheus*) attributes Great Britain's early lead both to an open social order—which encouraged entrepreneurship by recognizing nobility in wealth—and to a state that did not impose internal barriers to trade, or enforce guild restrictions on production or sumptuary restrictions on consumption; in this view, once Britain had made its breakthrough, the rest of the story was about competing nations' race to catch up. Similarly, recent discussion of proto-industry—the period between the emergence of the putting-out system and the consolidation of the factory—merely supplements the classic view by considering the role of demographic changes (provoked by the spread of industry to the countryside) in subsequent developments.[13]

As a last example, the pioneering study of the modern corporation by the American historian of business Alfed D. Chandler, Jr., also follows the classic pattern.[14] To Chandler, the unification of the vast American market through the construction of the railroads—themselves the product of antecedent technological development—leads directly and indirectly to the modern form of business organization. The railroads allowed the aggregation of previously fragmented demand, thus clearing the way for the introduction of mass-production technology (this was a commonplace view in the nineteenth century; Marx thought the British had opened the way to the industrialization of India by constructing a railroad there). Moreover, the solution of the scheduling, accounting, and operating problems of the new common carriers led to the elaboration of administrative techniques that proved widely applicable outside the transportation industry.

The persistence of these themes is not surprising. British success in the nineteenth century and American success in the twentieth have vindicated the classical views of the connection between specialization and efficiency, of the relation between state and economy, and of the inevitability of progress. What is more convincing than a prophecy come true?

Yet under this smooth surface of acceptance, intellectual countercurrents were forming. They flowed from persistent reports of economic experiences that could not be reconciled with the idea of an inevitable, unitary, all-inclusive logic of technological development.

The Limits of the Classical View: Industrial Dualism

Among the most discordant facts about the mass-production economy is the persistence of small firms and short production runs. In the 1970s, roughly 70 percent of all production in the metalworking sector in the United States consisted of small batches—not a result that the view of Smith and Marx would lead one to expect after a century and a half of intensive mechanization.[15] Indeed, throughout modern industrial history observers have been repeatedly struck by the persistence of small firms despite increasingly confident predictions of their disappearance. Thus, although it is difficult to completely discredit any very long-term prediction, by the 1960s it had begun to seem implausible that the small-firm sector would ever vanish; instead of dismissing it as a historical vestige, observers started to look for systematic reasons for its continued vitality.

The attempt to explain the persistence of small firms led to a theory of industrial dualism.[16] The theory was developed through interviews with engineers and business executives. Thus—like the view of the classical economists—it was an abstraction of existing practice, an explication of the principles that were being applied to the organization of production. Its central theme was that (paradoxically) a second and contrary form of production is inherent in the logic of mass production.

Mass production, as we have seen, means the creation of general goods through specialized resources. The more general the goods, the wider the variety of uses to which they can be put, the more extensive is their market—but the more specialized the machines and finely divided the labor that go into their production. Yet an economic system organized according to this master principle cannot be composed of mass-production firms alone—because the general goods they produce cannot be specialized enough to meet the needs of the firms engaged in mass production. In other words, the special-purpose machinery required for mass production cannot itself be mass-produced.

Mass-production machinery must, in fact, be built according to a logic that is the mirror image of mass production: the production of specialized goods through general resources. Because the product is a specialty, with a limited market, production must be continually reorganized; and workers must have the range of skills and general understanding of the process that are classically attributed to preindustrial artisans. Thus industrialization should, according to the dualism theory, revitalize at least part of the craft sector—reorienting it toward its own ends.

A similar logic applies whenever fluctuation in or constantly low levels of demand create markets that are too uncertain or small to encourage mass production. At the fringe of almost every industry, therefore, small firms survive by supplying a changing variety of oddments or responding to surges in demand. In exceptional cases—for example, women's garments—most of an industry consists of such firms.

In this way, dualism interprets modern craft production as a necessary complement to mass production. In this interpretation, technological progress in industrial society continues to be dominated—as in the classical theory that predicted the disappearance of the crafts—by mass production. Although craft production may, in this view, share innovations generated by mass production (and occasionally come up with a technique on its own), it is not expected to generate the flow of technological progress that marks industrial society and drives economic growth. Mass production is seen as the technologically dynamic form, and specialty production its subordinate. Industrial dualism thus saved the classical rule by providing it with an exception.

The Limits of Industrial Dualism: Flexible Specialization

But however accurately industrial dualism depicts the current economic structure, it does not do justice to that of the most famous industrial districts of the nineteenth century. Silks in Lyon; ribbons, hardware, and specialty steel in neighboring Saint-Étienne; edge tools, cutlery, and specialty steel in Solingen, Remscheid, and Sheffield; calicoes in Alsace; woolen and cotton textiles in Roubaix; cotton goods in Philadelphia and Pawtucket—the history of all these industries challenges the classical view of economic progress. Small firms in these industrial districts (the term is Alfred Marshall's, who applied it to Lancashire and Sheffield) often developed or exploited new technologies without becoming larger; large firms that from the start used sophisticated technology did not produce standardized goods.[17] The technological dynamism of both these large and small firms defies the notion that craft production must be either a traditional or a subordinate form of economic activity. It suggests, instead, that there is a craft alternative to mass production as a model of technological advance.

This alternative form of production also had its visionary exponents. In one form or other they propagated the idea of a republic of independent craftsmen linked by dependence on one another's skills. A typical figure was Pierre-Joseph Proudhon, the French philosopher who advocated a mutualist social revolution that would transcend individualism yet not lead to etatist collectivism.[18] A second was Terence Powderly, the leader of the American Knights of Labor and sponsor of producers' cooperatives (some of the largest of which, founded as independent municipalities, were named after him.)[19] Yet a third was Hermann Schulze-Delitzsch, who organized a system of cooperative banks at the service of German artisans.[20] Unlike Smith or Marx, these exponents of craft production were enmeshed in the lives of the working class: Proudhon, trained as a typographer, was familiar with and influenced by the semiclandestine world of trade fraternities and mutual-aid societies that had survived the Revolution and flourished in France before 1848; Powderly became a skilled mechanic in the sophisticated Philadelphia machine shops; and Schulze-Delitzsch, a lawyer, entered the artisans' world during the abortive March Revolution of 1848 as the rapporteur of the committee of the Frankfurt National Assembly charged with responding to reform petitions from the artisans—the *Handwerker*. These three men gave voice to the workers' movements that arose through the 1880s; and—again in contrast to Marx (and Engels), who had little popular following until late in the century—their ideas inspired projects of cooperative production.

Yet precisely because of their attachment to particular communities and epochs, all three craft exponents presupposed knowledge of a context of political idioms and conditions of production that the writings of the well-schooled theoreticians of mass production do not. As the progress of large-scale industry and changes in political vocabulary destroyed that context, the ideas of this alternative tradition came to seem utopian, if not incomprehensible; its themes now stand out more clearly in the mirror of its opponents' scorn than in the original manifestos. But as modern research restores that context, some of the ideas that were seen as utopian now provide clues to an astonishingly viable economic system. To Marx, and even latter-day mutualists, Proudhon's claims that competition and productive association were complementary, and that machinery could extend human skill, were patently false. Today these ideas draw attention to the inner workings of the successful industrial districts.[21]

These districts were defined by three mutually dependent characteristics. The first, most obvious characteristic was the districts' relation to the market. The districts produced a wide range of products for the highly differentiated regional markets at home and abroad; but—more important—they also constantly altered the goods, partly in response to changing tastes, partly to change tastes, in order to open new markets. (Producers in the industrial districts could never say which was the reason; the Lyonese, like today's garment makers of New York and Milan, never decided if they were the masters or the slaves of fashion.)[22]

This relation to the market encouraged and depended upon the second and third characteristics of the industrial districts: their flexible use of increasingly productive, widely applicable technology and their creation of regional institutions that balanced cooperation and competition among firms, so as to encourage permanent innovation (just those conditions that Proudhon took so much for granted that he felt no need to elaborate on them, and that Marx regarded as contradictions in terms). Technology had to be flexible in both a narrow and a broad sense. It had to permit quick, inexpensive shifts from one product to another within a family of goods, and it had to permit a constant expansion in the range of materials worked and operations performed, in order to facilitate the transition from one whole family of products to another. Institutions had to create an environment in which skills and capital equipment could be constantly recombined in order to produce a rapidly shifting assortment of goods. As a precondition of this, firms were discouraged from competition in the form of wage and price reduction, as opposed to competition through the innovation of products and processes.

A spectacular example of technology that reduced the costs of shifting products was the Jacquard loom, the precursor of modern numerically-controlled machine tools. It was perfected for industrial use between 1800 and 1820 by Lyonese silk weavers as a means of reasserting their traditional dominance in markets for fashionable fabrics against increasing competition from England, Germany and Italy. The loom wove complex *façonnées* or brocaded patterns according to instructions on perforated cards which automatically raised and lowered the threads of the warp in the appropriate sequence. The use of perforated cards as a control mechanism substantially reduced the time it took to set up the loom for a new pattern, because—like the program of a modern computer—the cards could be quickly altered. The Jacquard mechanism, furthermore, eliminated the need for the drawgirls who had previously raised and lowered the warp threads by hand. This cut labor costs and increased precision of operation, thus allowing designers to realize many previously unobtainable effects. For these reasons the new loom substantially reduced the costs of producing textiles in batches too small to pay back the costs of dedicated mass-production equipment.[23] The ribbon makers in Saint-Étienne subsequently attached the Jacquard programming system to the Zurich ribbon loom, thereby creating a device capable of producing up to twenty-five patterned ribbons simultaneously; their efforts to embroider ribbons by machine produced a device similar to the sewing machine—not to be developed until twenty years later.[24]

The centers of textile production also pioneered the development of new fibers, dyes, and printing techniques. From the 1880s through the 1950s, the Lyonese helped develop or found fashionable applications for, first, mixtures of silk and other natural fibers, and then such artificial fibers as rayon, nylon, and Tergal. Until recently the area was, as a modern observer remarked, a giant "laboratory for experimentation with new fibers." The Lyonese and the Alsatians at Mulhouse also developed a wide range of dyestuffs, and they perfected techniques for printing elaborate multicolored designs on cloth to achieve effects previously attained only by weaving different-colored threads.[25]

Similar experimentation with flexible techniques and new materials occurred in the metalworking districts. The Birmingham hardware trades, for example, pioneered the development and application of metal stamps and presses, drawbenches, electroplating, and diesinking, while they learned to work iron and then copper, brass, steel, and enamel into products that ranged from buttons to bedsteads to bicycles to small arms.[26] In Sheffield, the cutlery industry developed silver-plating and led the way—together with the Remscheid firms in the edge-tool industry—in the production of crucible and specialty steels and the industrial use of electric-arc furnaces. Saint-Étienne became a center of precision forging and specialty steels.[27]

A further indication of the technological vitality of these districts was the speed and sophistication with which they adapted power sources to their needs. The large Alsatian textile firms not only made early use of steam power but also became—through their sponsorship of research institutes—the nucleus of a major theoretical school of thermodynamics.[28] Small firms in Saint-Étienne experimented with compressed air in the middle of the nineteenth century, before turning, along with Remscheid and Solingen, to the careful study of small steam and gasoline engines. After 1890, when the long-distance transmission of electric power was demonstrated at Frankfurt, these three regions were among the first industrial users of small electric motors.[29]

The institutional framework that made such flexibility possible varied according to the particularities of each industry. Three systems can be distinguished that encouraged permanent innovation through the re-shuffling of resources: municipalism; welfare capitalism, or paternalism; and an entrepreneurial use of kin relations that we will call familialism. Any given industry might move from one system to another as it adopted new technologies and entered new markets.

MUNICIPALISM

Municipalism was a form of territorially dispersed production centered on and coordinated by an urban seat. It predominated when productive units were small and capital requirements modest. Nineteenth-century observers, following the French engineer and social scientist Fréderic Le Play, called such districts *fabriques collectives*.[30] The most famous example was the Lyonese silk industry. Others were the Saint-Étienne ribbon, hardware, and bicycle industries—until the middle of the twentieth century—and substantial sectors of the Solingen cutlery and

Remscheid edge-tool industries—until at least World War II. These industries were confederations of small shops, each specializing in a phase of production, such as weaving, polishing, and forging. Before the widespread use of electric motors, these shops might be grouped in large buildings that housed a steam engine and a system of belts; the belts transmitted torque to workrooms that could be rented by the day, thus offering small producers an efficient source of power.[31] Typically, the movement of work in progress was coordinated by either a merchant-manufacturer or a large firm: the merchant-manufacturer, as in the days of the putting-out system, supplied credit and raw materials to the subcontractors and took charge of selling the final product; the large firm not only performed the merchant's tasks but also assembled the final product.

The variability of demand meant that patterns of subcontracting were constantly rearranged. Firms that had underestimated a year's demand would subcontract the overflow to less well situated competitors scrambling to adapt to the market. But the next year the situation might be reversed, with winners in the previous round forced to sell off equipment to last year's losers. Under these circumstances, every employee could become a subcontractor, every subcontractor a manufacturer, every manufacturer an employee. A sign of the fluidity of this situation was that business dealings were by parole contract, and that *intuitus personae*—judgment, acquired by long experience, about the character of potential partners—was seen as a prerequisite to success.[32] The constant reorganization of production was possible only on the condition that everyone knew, and was known to abide by, a long list of rules of fair behavior: had these rules required formal application, they would have prohibitively delayed shifts from one grouping of firms to another.

It was up to the municipality in these small-unit systems to guarantee the mobility of resources. It did this in several ways: by protecting the firms against paralyzing shocks from the market; by providing access to any skills and knowledge that the firms lacked; and by policing competition, through forbidding the sale of inferior goods under the local trademark and overseeing the wage-stabilization system, which eliminated wage cutting and ruinous price wars.

Thus the Lyonese created a system of *caisse de prêts* (loan banks) to provide credit to weavers during downturns, while in Saint-Étienne municipal taxes were among the highest in France, to finance unemployment insurance that would keep skilled workers attached to their trade during slack times. Remscheid, Solingen, and Saint-Étienne, to name just a few, established vocational schools to train workers both in manual skills and in design. In the late 1920s, Remscheid created a research institute that helped acquaint firms with the latest in metallurgy. Most of these regions also had equivalents of Lyon's *conditions des soies* or Saint-Étienne's *banc d'épreuve* (both descendants of Old Regime institutions), which guaranteed the quality of locally produced silks and arms, respectively.[33]

Similarly, the municipalities were drawn into the complex relations between small subcontractors and their employees, and between manufacturers and their employees. Although all parties liked the idea of avoiding price wars by taking wages out of competition (through the imposition of uniform rates and working conditions), in hard times the temptation to undercut competitors was strong. Political institutions therefore played an important part in stabilizing the industry. In Saint-Étienne at the turn of the century, the ribbon weavers acted through a Socialist municipal government to control the length of the workday, by regulating the hours at which the municipal power station supplied current to the looms.[34] The municipal governments in Remscheid and Solingen, responding to the political strength of the Social Democratic work force, played an active role in improving health and safety conditions in the metalworking industry. In Lyon, a board of arbitration—another descendant of the Old Regime system of corporations—mediated disputes between weavers (*canuts*) and merchants (*fabricants*).[35]

WELFARE CAPITALISM, OR PATERNALISM

At the opposite extreme was production that occurred in large factories. This was the case when operations, though flexible and requiring skill, also required expensive equipment, which individual artisans could not afford. From afar, this type of large steel, engineering, or textile firm could be easily confused with mass-production factories, owing to the popular view that increasingly associated large plants with mass production. But close examination shows that these firms were really groupings of artisans' shops under one roof, rather than assembly-line factories. An observer in the 1930s, for example, called the specialty-steel plants of Saint-Étienne "veritable metallurgical pharmacies"; and a historian of nineteenth-century Lyonese industry writes, "one could multiply examples which reveal the factory not as the articulated organism of the twentieth century, but as a simple aggregation of individual trades in which everyday work preserved its artisanal appearance."[36] Another indication that diversified production in large factories was a persistent but perplexing fact are the remarks, in the 1920s, of the historian of the J. A. Henckels firm—the largest Solingen cutlery manufacturer (employing 1,000 workers). He wrote that a late-nineteenth-century commentator had been correct to detect a traditional work organization beyond what seemed to *his* contemporaries a modern facade; that the firm could now truly be called a factory because it used the most advanced machinery in every phase of production; and that the company turned out more than 10,000 different products, suited to every cutlery task and every national taste.[37]

When firms of this sort dominated a locality, they adopted a program of welfare capitalism, or paternalism. Such a program provided many of the same institutions that the small producers provided through the municipal government. The calico printing firms at Mulhouse are the classic example. Already in 1822 the leading firms had founded, at their own expense (though with the approval of the municipal council they controlled) a course in chemistry and a research laboratory, later to become the École Nationale de Chimie. And in the 1850s—in order to train and retain a skilled work force (whose indispensability was publicized in the *Bulletin de la Société Industrielle de Mulhouse*)—the industrialists created an extraordinary network of social institutions: schools for mechanized weaving and spinning, the École Supérieure de Commerce, a savings society, an old-age home, public baths, worker housing, a society for maternity care, and associations to prevent and investigate industrial accidents.[38] The purpose was to make the company town into a community in which artisan skills, scientific knowledge, and artistic imagination were continually regenerated and advanced.

FAMILIALISM

The third institutional means of securing the flexible use of resources was based on the family. This system typically emerged in intermediate cases, in which production was neither so concentrated as in the case of paternalism nor so dispersed as in municipalism. In this case, production required a loose but reliable alliance of medium- and small-sized firms specializing in the component manufacturing operations. The idea of using family ties to create the alliance was conceived by a prominent cotton-textile manufacturer in Roubaix, France: Alfred Motte. In the 1850s, after a failure to gain ground against established and better-situated mass producers, Motte switched his strategy; he began to construct a confederation of firms owned by different members of his family, which would jointly produce fashionable fabrics. The *système Motte* was to pair each family member who had come of age with an experienced technician from one of the family's firms; provide these two with start-up capital (most of which was held, of course, by the family member), and have them establish together a company that specialized in one of the phases of production that was still needed. The new firms often found markets outside, as well as inside, the family, but their financial and emotional ties to the lineage made them dependable partners, even in difficult times. This common loyalty to the family freed the companies to make the realignments dictated by changing fashions, while ensuring against extreme fluctuations in the demand for particular processes, and providing the necessary trust to maintain a system of common financial reserves, marketing, and purchasing.[39]

But if—as this section has depicted—industrial districts allowed the extension of flexible technologies on craft lines, why have these districts not survived? And why were they not more numerous and influential in the early phases of industrialization? The answers to these questions lead to a stylization of the history of mechanization—and, beyond that, to an understanding of technological change in history—that breaks with the saga of mass production.

The Survival, Submergence, and Self-suffocation of the Craft Economies

The individual histories of the industrial districts underscore the technological vitality of the craft economies. Indeed, some of these districts continued to innovate, preserving their craft structure and flexible relation to the market, up until after World War II; at this point, national governments—attending more to general prophecies for economic development than to the performance of specific regions—encouraged the firms' conversion to mass production. But other firms, tempted by their own discoveries, decided to convert to mass production—at the cost of permanently changing both their structure and their environment. In still other cases, the institutional supports of flexibility gave way and became obstacles—rather than props—to innovation. Most significant, however, the search for ever more productive and flexible machines never proved fruitless: those who looked, found.

STATE-IMPOSED MASS PRODUCTION

Lyon was one of the most successful of the industrial districts, surviving crisis after crisis—only to fall victim, after 1960, to the French state's campaign of economic modernization.[40] An early crisis was an epidemic of *pebrine* in the 1850s, which decimated the French silkworm industry and sent the cost of raw silk sky-high; the Lyonese responded by developing dyeing techniques that increased the weight of the precious raw silk and allowed the creation of styles based on vivid colors rather than intricate weaves. When, in the 1870s and '80s, the Victorian taste for these bright but expensive and stiff *unis* gave way to the desire for cheaper, less formal fabrics of silk wastes and cotton—manufactured by the Swiss and Germans—the Lyonese again met the challenge: they mixed their fabrics with Asiatic silks (whose durability made machine-powered weaving possible) and developed new forms of printing and dyeing, which gave rise to more competitive styles. During the 1930s Depression, the Lyonese used their vast experience with artificial fibers to discover—in collaboration with small silk-throwing firms of the Ardèche—new methods of working acetate and viscose fibers, thus launching an international demand for artificial crepes, which sustained them until the late 1940s. And this discovery was but the prelude to a whole series of innovations in artificial fibers that carried them through the next decade.

In the 1960s, however, the French state (for reasons to be examined in chapter 6) sponsored a campaign of mergers and restructuring that recast the district's organization of production. Local firms came under the control of French-based multinationals, such as Rhône-Poulenc and the Alsatian group Dolfuss, Mieg et Cie, or of foreign firms, such as Burlington and J. P. Stevens.[41] In this way, the district's loose confederations of specialists were broken up, and the components of production that they had provided were integrated into the divisional structure of new corporate parents pursuing mass-production strategies in the world market. Another outcome, however, also occurred: specialty production moved across the border to the Como district of Italy, where today it flourishes as part of the renaissance of flexible production in that country. We will look at this phenomenon in detail later.[42]

SELF-IMPOSED MASS PRODUCTION

A different story from that in Lyon took place in other areas. Some craft producers lost their capacity for innovation or else they were drawn into mass production by what they saw as its attraction—rather than being pushed in that direction by the government.

A clear example of stalled innovation is the fate of the Sheffield cutlery industry. Between 1830 and 1870, employment in that industry doubled. But from the early 1860s, the firms began to concentrate on a slow-growing, almost luxurious segment of the market; moreover, domestic tastes had stabilized. Meanwhile, by 1870 foreign competition had become a threat. Given their narrow market, the Sheffield manufacturers were reluctant to mechanize, for fear of lowering quality standards and thereby encouraging foreign competition. Some of the most dynamic firms therefore abandoned the cutlery industry for the production of specialty steel.[43] The tendency to rigidity was reinforced by the numerous local guilds, each organizing a narrow trade and powerful enough to protect the existing division of labor.[44]

In this case as in Lyon, there was nothing inevitable in this outcome. British observers noted that the Solingen metalworking industry was able to modernize while maintaining specialized production. It established factories to house machines (such as mechanical forges) that offered great economies of scale, and it provided electric power to outworkers who used modern equipment. Here a federated labor movement pressed employers to innovate, to raise productivity, and to pay high wages— rather than defending the existing organization of production.[45]

The attraction to mass production is illustrated by the Birmingham metalworking shops. This craft sector responded to the 1890s' explosion in the bicycle market, by—eventually—amalgamating into mass production. In this district, as in Sheffield, tastes and production methods had become quite fixed after midcentury; hence the hardware shops, looking for new markets, were willing to become subcontractors for the early bicycle firms. But the more these shops concentrated on pressing, stamping, and casting for the large assembly companies, the more standardized their own output became. Then the growth in the production of automobiles and electrical equipment drew the shops ever more closely into the orbit of mass producers. Finally, as in Saint-Étienne, the small firms were sapped of their autonomy, to the point that—far from pioneering new products—they all but lost the capacity to produce anything unless blueprints were provided by the dominant firm.[46]

The obstacles to the progress of mechanization on craft lines lay, then, not in some self-blockage of this model of technological development. Rather, they lay in the unfavorable environment—political, institutional, economic—with which craft production had to contend. Recent American experience shows that a mass-production economy can become paralyzed; history suggests that—under different circumstances—the craft sector could have played a stronger role in economic development. The following section examines that possibility, in connection with a reassessment of our understanding of technological change in history.

Branching Points, Markets, and Technology

In the narrow-track view of technological development, the vitality of the industrial districts appears (if seen at all) a violation of the laws of progress. To make sense, therefore, of this vitality, and to orient a discussion of its origins, we must conceptualize a world in which technology can develop in various ways: a world that might have turned out differently from the way it did, and thus a world with a history of abandoned but viable alternatives to what exists.[47]

A first postulate of such a world is that any body of knowledge about the manipulation of nature can be elaborated and applied to production in various ways; some of these ways are more flexible than others. A further postulate is that the technological possibilities that are realized depend on the distribution of power and wealth: those who control the resources and the returns from investment choose from among the available technologies the one most favorable to *their* interests. A third postulate is that technological choices, once made, entail large investments in equipment and know-how, whose amortization discourages subsequent different choices.

The role of politics and of competition in this conceptualized world contrasts with their role in the classical world of mass production. In the classical view, politics—except when it slows growth by limiting the market—is extraneous to economic development. In the world we are now envisioning, both the rate and the direction of growth depend on the distribution of economic entitlements; and because this distribution is connected to the state's power to privilege and penalize groups and activities, this amounts to saying that economic development reflects politics.

This contrast in turn is paralled by the contrasting roles of competition in the two systems. In the classical view, competition drives humankind to discover the best of all currently possible worlds; the victor of every contest is also a hero of universal efficiency. In the world of all possible worlds, competition pits one potential way of combining machines and skills against another; the way that succeeds—the technological breakthrough—does so because of the conditions of the moment—not because it is necessarily the one best way. Thus, an advance in a particular direction can choke off promising experiments with alternatives, since threatened competitors choose to emulate a proven approach, rather than risk failing to find one more suited to their needs. There is, therefore, no guarantee that competition drives society to the frontier of its productive capacities; ironically, even the victors in this kind of competition cannot be sure they have hit on the approach that best serves their interests.

The upshot is that in the world of possible worlds, relatively short periods of technological diversification punctuate longer periods of uniformity. The technical knowledge that is accumulated during the interludes of diversity creates the possibility of divergent breakthroughs: branching points. At these technological divides, the different political circumstances in different regional or national economies moves technology down correspondingly different paths. But competition eliminates some of these technological experiments, and bends others toward a common goal. Growing investments in the dominant technology reinforce the constraints of competition, by giving even those who may once have opposed its introduction a stake in its perpetuation. The tendency toward uniformity is reversed only when some combination of developments in the market and in the capacity to control nature makes it economically feasible to disregard the sunk costs and technically feasible to strike out in new directions. If in the world of classical political economy the history of technology is pictured as a narrow track, in this other world, an apt metaphor is a zigzagging path or branching tree.[48]

Although a branching-tree world may seem odd, given our habits of thought, its principles frame most of the current discussions of innovation in certain industries. Less directly—but unmistakably—these same principles inform much of the analysis of comparative economic history. Therefore, even a brief look at both the recent pattern of industrial innovation and that of the nineteenth century will establish the empirical plausibility of the many-worlds model; it will also indicate how this model accounts for the rise and fall of the industrial districts we have just surveyed.

Consider first the microcosm of innovation in particular industries. Detailed studies show that in the formative stages of the automobile, aircraft, and computer industries—to take some notable examples—the abundance of competing possible solutions to technical problems was so great as to actually block progress. Each variant was potentially better on some dimension than the others; its advantages reflected the particular circumstances and favored the interests of its sponsor over the other competitors. No producer was willing to abandon its proposal, for fear of playing into the hands of the competition; yet each was leery of proceeding with its favorite solution, for fear of failure, or that its pioneering mistakes would teach others how to construct a superior model.

Typically, an exercise of economic power ended the impasse. Some firm or group of firms with enough control over the emerging market to assure a minimum of demand for its solution, and enough capital to cover the costs of its mistakes, pressed ahead and imposed its plan. (A classic example is IBM's imposition of its designs on the computer industry; once its products had been established, competitors had reason to emulate them more or less completely.)[49] The development, then, of promising alternative designs was costly, and the prospects that costly innovation would be rewarded were diminished as customers became habituated to existing solutions.

Growth in the automobile, aircraft, and computer industries proceeded, therefore, along the lines determined by the established solution. Firms could improve their position by refining the existing designs. Only a sudden shift in the conditions of competition—such as the discovery of a new technology, a change in the price of raw materials, or a realignment of demand—reopened debate on the definition of the product. Thus, although the winning design had to meet some minimum performance standard, the sweep of its success was not a proof of unrivaled technical superiority, nor of the existence of a narrow track of progress: other variants could have served as well. Power in the market, not efficiency (in the sense of a uniquely appropriate application of technology), decided the contest.

By an analogous logic, economic developments in the United States, France, and Great Britain in the nineteenth century can be interpreted as competing attempts to elaborate a distinct variant of industrial technology suited to the particularities of national circumstance. Political factors in each country gave domestic markets a distinctive form; profit-maximizing firms adapted the emergent machine technology to local conditions; the pattern of adaptation then explains why industrial districts, although found in all the major industrial countries, occurred more frequently in some than in others; and, finally, the constraints of competition obstructed the full development of flexible systems of production—leading, as in the case of industrial innovation, to the otherwise inexplicable abandonment of evidently viable alternatives.

Of the three countries, the United States, as we have seen, moved furthest in the direction of a mass-production factory system. In the early nineteenth-century, labor, especially skilled labor, was in short supply; there were no guilds to restrain the reorganization of production;

and an affluent yeomanry—whose ancestral diversity of tastes had been erased by transplantation to the New World—was willing and able to purchase the crude standard products that early special-purpose machine tools turned out. Raw materials such as wood were abundant enough to make the inefficiency of the machines economically inconsequential. Because employers needed labor-saving machinery and because customers bought the machine-made goods, the American turn in the direction of mass production was natural.[50]

The French pattern, despite some superficial similarities to the American, was different. Like American yeomen, French peasants had control of their land: during their Revolution they had been able to block (as they had done in previous centuries) the efforts of nobles and wealthy commoners to dispossess them. But the French peasants subsisted on small plots (a result of subdividing land among heirs, according to the rule of partible inheritance), which were largely outside the cash economy. Thus in France the demand for manufactured goods came from regionally based groups of nobles, as well as the bourgeois merchants and officials and the few rich peasants in each province who aped them. Tastes and markets therefore differed from region to region. In addition, France had guilds—revitalized as of the late sixteenth century—which kept alive traditional canons of excellence and enforced standards. Yet the guilds' control over production was lax enough in the countryside to permit experimentation with new products and processes; and the Parisian court exempted its favorite artisans from guild restrictions, in order to encourage production of such new products as naval chronometers (useful in shooting wars) and porcelain (useful in the battle for international prestige). Under the circumstances, the French economy began to specialize in the production of a wide range of high-quality goods by means of the technologies and organizational techniques discussed in the preceding section of this chapter.[51]

Great Britain at this time was an intermediate case. On the one hand, because many English peasants had lost control of their land and were forced to migrate to cities (as a result of the reorganization of agriculture that had begun in the fifteenth century), there was a mass urban market for cheap consumer goods. Moreover, colonial markets demanded the same kind of products. Handicraft producers, encouraged by the government in the seventeenth century (in an effort to reduce national dependence on imports), subsequently escaped state and guild control by putting out work to the countryside, and began to reorganize production accordingly. Growth thus proceeded in part along the lines of the narrow-track model.[52]

On the other hand, British tastes were more variegated than tastes in the United States. Because industry provided employment in the rural areas, population thickened in the countryside, and this thickening helped stabilize provincial tastes. There was, furthermore, an abundant supply of skilled and unskilled labor, so that entrepreneurs—unlike their American counterparts—were not driven to look for labor-saving devices. Thus, Great Britain developed some mass-production industry (in such sectors as cotton spinning, food processing, and brewing), but its economy, as seen in the examples of Sheffield and Birmingham, remained in many respects more like the French than the American.[53]

No wonder, then, that Marx, comparing Great Britain with the Continent, could see the former as a pioneer of automatic production, and that the French could regard the English as a homogeneous mass of factory drudges with uniform (and bad) taste. Nor was it surprising that British engineers who inspected American techniques for manufacturing such products as locks and small arms (at London's Crystal Palace exhibition, in 1851, and later on tours of American factories) spoke of the "American system of manufacture"—underlining the difference between the Americans' concerted use of special machines to produce interchangeable parts and the residues of craft tradition in the British practice.[54]

Our analysis of the relation between markets and the evolution of technology reveals a coherence among diverse national developments, which the classical theory denies; but this analysis also obscures a crucial aspect of technological evolution. So far, we have assumed a direct correlation between the distribution of economically relevant interests and the orientation of technology toward either craft or mass production. In this view, machine makers respond immediately to the commands of the market. But the idea that technology somehow arises spontaneously from market transactions is empirically untenable—as shown by two (of many possible) examples from among the American developments.

First, many of the special-purpose metalworking machines that characterized American manufacture were inspired by a vision of design that had originated outside the American market. During the American Revolution, French ideas on the virtues of producing interchangeable parts for firearms were transmitted to the United States and became— through France's influence in the creation of the military academy at West Point—a goal of the U.S. Army's ordnance department. It was thus at federal armories (primarily the one in Springfield, Massachusetts) that mass-production technology first took shape. Many of the mechanics who were trained in this effort would later apply the technology to various branches of private industry.[55]

It might, of course, be argued that even in the absence of armory practice, the American market would in time have called forth special-machine technology. But this argument fails because of a second counterexample to the idea that markets directly beget technology. In the 1840s, waves of immigration to the United States made labor conspicuously less scarce than it had been in the preceding decades. The notion of market determination suggests that this influx of cheap hands would provoke substitution of labor for capital—and thus block the drive to mass production. But it did not. If anything, it seems more plausible to argue that the technology shaped the use of labor (in, for example, such industries as steel and shoes), rather than that the availability of labor shaped the use of technology.[56]

One way to reconcile the branching-tree model to the facts of the American case is to argue (as Paul A. David and others have done) that once a constellation of market forces has switched a national economy onto a particular technological track, the unchanging logic of the chosen technology—rather than the shifting balance of market forces—dictates further development. In this view, there is not one but many forms of technological determinism, and which one(s) a society is bound to endure over long periods is fixed at crucial moments by historical happenstance.[57]

But though this argument stands market determinism on its head, it suffers from an analogous flaw: just as markets fluctuate in time—giving conflicting signals as to the direction of technological development—so the development within any national economy of any one line of technology constantly unearths clues as to the possibility of progress in others. The London Crystal Palace, in which the British admired the accomplishments of American special-purpose machines, had itself been built with the help of ingenious domestic special-purpose machines;[58] conversely, the small textile mills of southern New England pioneered flexible machinery that seems more the offspring of French textile firms in Roubaix than of the mass-production firms in Lowell, Massachusetts. National technology is no more likely to give unambiguous indications of the best course of future development than do national markets. To understand how the often-attested national styles of technological progress persisted despite the underlying instabilities of material interests and inspirations, we must look at the ideas of the machine designers themselves: to adapt a phrase from the historian of science Thomas Kuhn, we must look at the designers' *technological paradigms*.

Mass Production as a Technological Paradigm

The dictionary defines a paradigm as a "model or pattern; in grammar, an example of a conjugation or declension showing a word in all of its forms."[59] But in Thomas Kuhn's work, the word takes on the larger meaning of an understanding of the world embodied in or defined by an explicit theory about nature: for example, the concept of a heliocentric universe as portrayed in Copernicus's theory of planetary motion. For Kuhn, a scientific revolution occurs when proponents of a new paradigm oust the advocates of orthodoxy from university chairs and editorial boards of professional journals.[60]

In analogy to scientific revolutions, technological branching points— or divides—mark not just the moments at which political contexts and their associated markets push industrial development down a divergent path; they also mark the consolidation of new visions of efficient production—new technological paradigms, or trajectories. As with a revolutionary scientific theory, a new technological paradigm imposes order on the confusing practical activity of the preceding period; and in the process of distinguishing the relevant from the irrelevant in conflicting tendencies, the paradigm creates the preconditions for a new orthodoxy. This new orthodoxy is exemplified in model machines and factories whose producers and owners never tire of advertising them, and its structuring principles are propagated in technical schools by textbook and example. At best half aware that their imagination has been circumscribed by convention, technologists push down the new path; they ignore the hints of alternative possibilities that are constantly unearthed by their experience with markets and machines—so long as the economy they are building meets the (frequently lax) test of international competition. In this way, the constellation of factors that prevailed at the branching point of a national economy's technological history continue to shape developments—even when those factors start to change and technological progress itself creates the possibility for a divergent line of development.[61] Here, then, is an explanation for the coexistence of distinct, stable national types of technology in the nineteenth century.

But the shock of war, on the battlefield or in the market, strips local practice of its aura of inevitability. It pits technological paradigm against technological paradigm, in a gladiatorial enactment of scientific debate. The weak—unable to untangle the complex relation between the practices and the theory of the strong—try to survive by slavishly emulating the former and learning the latter by rote. In any case, victor and vanquished soon see the abandoned paradigm not as a viable alternative to the now dominant one, but as a misstep: a flawed or out-of-date theory that could not have succeeded. This, then, is a fuller explanation for the eclipse of craft production as a coherent system of resource deployment, to which we referred in the discussion of Proudhon and Powderly. But it is also—as the other side of the same coin—an explanation for the surprise that met every rediscovery of craft production's continued practice.

The recent historiography of technology clearly documents the vision of automatic machine production as a structuring principle of Anglo-American, particularly American, technological development. One piece of evidence of this vision is the role of French ideas in the development of American armory practice. Another is the enthusiasm with which, from the early nineteenth century on, proponents of mass production seized on one new piece of equipment or organizational technique after another. To them, these innovations meant that skill—the active participation of labor in controlling the flow of production—would soon be superfluous in the factory.

In 1830, to begin with a famous case, the Manchester engineering firm of Sharp, Roberts & Company introduced the self-acting mule, and promised its customers that the new equipment would allow the substitution of unskilled machine operators for skilled cotton spinners—thus putting an end to the spinners' union in the mills. Ure, a political economist and industrial consultant, popularized this claim as a statement of fact; Marx (who called Ure the Pindar of the factory) accepted this account and, as we saw, made it a starting point for his reflections on the decisive role of special-purpose machinery in modern industry.[62] Yet the cotton spinner's role in production—part supervisor, part recruiter of labor—was far more complex, and management's grip on the shop-floor activity far more limited, than the machine maker, the consultant, and the theorist imagined. The spinners' (now called minders') union not only survived but gained extensive control over the use of the new technology.[63]

In midcentury, to take an obscure but similar example, many British observers were convinced that the increasing use of the slide-rest lathe meant the end of a whole class of skilled metalworkers—only to discover that although the new machine could automate some of the work, it proved most valuable in the hands of craftsmen who used it to shape metal in previously impossible ways.[64] At the turn of the century, the

American industrial engineer Frederick Taylor attracted attention with his schemes to routinize production by transferring skill from the shop floor to a central planning bureau; but modern historians find that employers made little of his ideas for redeploying labor, even in those plants whose reorganization he personally supervised.[65] In the 1960s and '70s, finally, the manufacturers of numerically controlled machine tools advertised—yet again—the end of metalworking skills; and though many observers took them at their word, it soon became clear that—as with the slide-rest lathe—the new machines were often used to augment skill rather than to replace it.[66]

The point, to repeat, is not that machine makers, consultants, and theorists were fantasists—blind to the reality of their times. If machine makers tried to build automatic equipment and exaggerated their success, it was because they were correctly convinced that many manufacturers wanted such equipment. If theorists accepted the advertising as truth, it was because what they had already seen convinced them that the claims were plausible. And despite the exaggerations, they were right. Measured not by the boosters' claims but by current practice, successive efforts (particularly in the United States) to apply the mass-production paradigm did transform the factory along the prophesied lines.

These transformations were mirrored both in the reports of industrially versed visitors to the United States and in the debates on the future of craft production in the industrial districts of France, Great Britain, and Germany. These observers' bafflement at change within mass production was as indicative of an attachment to a distinctive technological paradigm as the mass producers' persistently premature self-congratulations.

The most sober accounts of the consolidation of mass-production practice in the United States were written by the British engineers who toured American plants after 1850. They define a characteristically American technique for manufacturing such products as locks and small arms.[67] Like today's American automobile executives touring the plant of a Japanese competitor, the British engineers were aware that the ex-colonials' technology derived from familiar principles, yet these principles were applied according to a logic they could not define. For example, upon visiting the English subsidiary of Samuel Colt's pistol company, James Nasmyth (a celebrated English machine maker) commented that the Americans' "acquaintance with correct principles has been carried out in a fearless and masterly manner," but among the English mechanics "there is a certain degree of timidity resulting from traditional notions, and attachment to old systems, even among the most talented persons."[68]

As viewed, at still greater distance, by the Continental industrial districts, the mass-production paradigm seemed first like a dangerous competitor, then the inevitable heir to craft techniques. In the late 1890s, for example—long after the midcentury tide of mutualism and cooperation had ebbed—the German Franz Ziegler could still point to promising examples of the technological renovation of decentralized production in Remscheid, through the introduction of flexible machine tools, powered by small electric motors.[69] A decade later, his son wrote *The Emergence of the Large Factory in Remscheid Batch Production,* in which, despite substantial evidence of the persistence of small shops, the eventual disappearance of small-scale production was a foregone conclusion.[70]

By the 1920s, the sheer material success of mass production made it almost irresistible as a paradigm. Leading industrialists the world over— we will see in chapter 6—were mesmerized by it. But the real measure of its attraction was not its fascination for those to whom it promised wealth and power; rather, it was its appeal to those schooled to detest mass production: workers raised in the craft tradition. Few demonstrations of this appeal are so convincing as the story of a leader of the reformist French Socialists, a skilled metalworker and a mutualist, who in the inter-war years visited Detroit, worked in automobile factories, and returned to France a convert to Fordist techniques. It was as if Proudhon himself had awakened from a fifty-year sleep to discover not merely that the world had enacted the ideas of his opponents, but that he, Proudhon, approved of what they had done.[71]

Mass production won out in the realm of ideas as it won out in the realm of practice. The second victory augmented the first. In Remscheid, Saint-Étienne, and Lyon, regional geographers and business people still pointed to the vitality of craft production; but the successes of mass production diminished their capacity to explain this vitality—peevishly or wistfully, they spoke of their own experience as a fortunate but inexplicable exception to modern developments. And the less coherent their defense of the craft model, the easier it became for "modern" bureaucrats, engineers, and industrialists to promote the conversion of industry to mass production.

The experience in the industrial districts was emblematic. Although craft production persisted here—as it did even in the heartlands of mass production—it was a discredited paradigm. As a model it was invisible—a practice without a name, by definition incoherent. In this void, industrialization became synonymous with mass production, and the mass-production paradigm became self-evident truth. Because, after the nineteenth century, mass production was never challenged by craft heterodoxy, there was no need to defend it as industrial orthodoxy. But like so much apparently commonsensical truth, the mass-production paradigm had unforeseen consequences: it took almost a century (from about 1870 to 1960) to discover how to organize an economy to reap the benefits of the new technology. It is to the logic of this discovery, and the historical conflicts through which it was elaborated, that we turn next.

CHAPTER

3

The Corporation

WHETHER CRAFT production could have survived as a technologically dynamic, productive form is a matter of conjecture; the technological dynamism of mass production is a matter of fact. Mass production offered those industries in which it was developed and applied enormous gains in productivity—gains that increased in step with the growth of these industries. Progress along this technological trajectory brought higher profits, higher wages, lower consumer prices, and a whole range of new products. But these gains had a price. Mass production required large investments in highly specialized equipment and narrowly trained workers. In the language of manufacturing, these resources were "dedicated": suited to the manufacture of a particular product—often, in fact, to just one make or model. When the market for that particular product declined, the resources had no place to go. Mass production was therefore profitable only with markets that were large enough to absorb an enormous output of a single, standardized commodity, and stable enough to keep the resources involved in the production of that commodity continuously employed. Markets of this kind, like markets in general, did not occur naturally. They had to be created. In the United States, the modern corporation was organized for this purpose.

The first of the new, mass-production corporations emerged after the Civil War; from the late nineteenth century on, this organizational form spread rapidly. Almost all of the fifty largest American corporations in 1917 appear in the financial pages today.[1] By 1930, half of the manufacturing output of the American economy was produced by these giants.[2]

The Corporation and Microeconomic Coordination

The modern corporation is one solution to a problem faced by every social system: the need for microeconomic regulation. Every economy must have mechanisms to coordinate the actions of the separate decision-making units of which it is composed. Those mechanisms must balance supply and demand in individual markets—they muster available resources to produce and distribute the market basket of goods that society wants and can afford to consume.

In the capitalist countries, the most familiar form of microeconomic regulation is the price system, as described in neoclassical economic theory. Prices in such a system perform a double function: they signal when scarce resources are inadequately employed and they induce a redeployment of those resources to allow those with money to get more of what they want.

But though the price system is often seen as a universal solution to the problem of microeconomic regulation, this system works in anything like its paradigmatic form only under certain conditions. At one extreme—in the autarkic communities of preindustrial society—price coordination is irrelevant, because a market hardly exists: extended families produce goods mostly for themselves. Coordination within the family occurs informally, and collective relations with outsiders are regulated by custom. At the other extreme—where resources are very highly specialized—price coordination is impossible. A piece of modern machinery dedicated to the production of a single part cannot be turned to another use, no matter how low the price of that part falls, or how high the price of other goods rises.

The early-nineteenth-century American economy probably came close to the model of price regulation envisaged in neoclassical theory. Most resources were general-purpose. The typical carpenter, for example, was able to build houses and cabinets, machinery and carriages, and this person moved readily among these alternatives as demand shifted and prices varied. In the shoe industry, firms could put out work to farmers when demand for footwear rose and there was little to do on the farm—thus allowing industrialists and agriculturalists to adjust to price movements.[3] Firms using the most specialized resources were generally small, and many were founded and went out of business each year. Adjustment to shifting demand could thus take place through normal turnover. As equipment wore out and skilled workers retired, they could be replaced by machines and labor suited to the new, more marketable tasks.[4]

But as the century wore on, these forms of adjustment were increasingly foreclosed: by the growing size of new productive units in relation to their markets and by the increasing specialization of resources associated with this change in the scale of manufacturing. In the cigarette industry in the mid-1880s, for example, the output of about thirty machines could saturate the market.[5] Henry Ford found that the unit cost of the Model T declined continually with output; thus, had he been able to control the market for automobiles (and we will see in a moment why he could not), he could have satisfied the entire demand. Similarly, although there was no such possibility in such industries as sugar and petroleum refining, steel, electrical equipment, and meat processing, units of production here, too, were so large and built at so nearly the same date that these markets could not react to changes in demand by attrition and replacement.[6]

Moreover, the growing specialization of resources raised the cost of redeploying them. When screws and files were made with special-purpose machinery, instead of all-purpose tools, the machinery owners became screw or file makers, not manufacturers of hardware; and the value of the screw or file machine outside the screw or file factory was what it fetched as scrap metal. And as workers became more specialized, their earning ability depended increasingly on their industrial job: as machines became more and more dedicated to the production of a particular product, skills came to mean familiarity with the idiosyncrasies of a particular plant's equipment. A worker was thus paid for exercising discretion based on this familiarity—detached from this specialized job, he or she was suddenly an unskilled laborer.

In sum, as mass-production technology developed, it presented a growing problem for the coordination of supply and demand in individual markets. To understand how entrepreneurs came to see the corporation as an effective response to this problem, we must shift perspective and examine microeconomic coordination from the point of view of the individual productive unit: the business firm.

The Corporation and Mass Production

Within the firm, the distinction between general and specialized resources is seen as a distinction between variable and fixed costs. Variable costs are costs that the firm incurs only if it is producing; they rise and fall with the level of output. The profit-maximizing firm produces only so long as the price it gets for its goods covers these costs; if the price falls below the average variable cost, the firm is obviously better off not producing at all. Fixed costs, by contrast, are independent of output; whether or not it produces, the firm must pay them. These are largely the sunk costs of the specialized plant and equipment that the firm has already bought, and the specialized labor that it has already trained. These costs, therefore, do not influence the firm's decisions about output in the short run.

Although in the long run no costs are truly fixed (because worn-out equipment and retiring employees must be replaced), the distinction between fixed and variable costs is nevertheless crucial to business decisions. Fixed costs are viewed before the fact as investments: the firm incurs these costs only on the assumption that during the life of the resources they obtain, product prices will remain high enough to repay them. Decisions about fixed costs thus require predictions of medium- and long-term market developments; by contrast, decisions about variable costs do not.

Variable costs apply to general resources because these resources are purchased on an as-needed basis (since they are used in a variety of processes, these resources are usually readily available). Note that even a plant and equipment—which we think of as fixed costs—can, if general enough, be treated as variable costs (for example, in the garment industry, where the basic equipment and work space are a sewing machine and a storefront, everything the firm needs to go into business can be rented; an investment need not be made). Mass production introduced rigidities in this situation, owing to the increased unresponsiveness of output to variations in price. These rigidities appear as a rise in the ratio of fixed to variable costs.

The situation is depicted in figures 3.1 and 3.2. In figure 3.1, cost is measured on the y-axis, output on the x-axis. The curves show the way in which average unit cost varies with output. The curve $a'b$ represents the variable-cost technology; it can be thought of as the craft antecedent of mass production. The mass-production alternative is represented by the curve $c'd'e$: the initial fixed costs are indicated by the point c, where

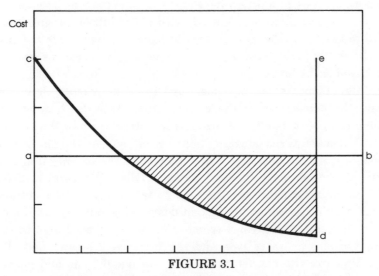

FIGURE 3.1

Cost Structures of Mass Production and Craft Production

the curve intersects the x-axis (although these costs are shown here, in true mass production they would be so high as to be way off the diagram). Unit cost then drops rapidly as output expands, until capacity is reached, at which point further expansion is blocked. Figure 3.2

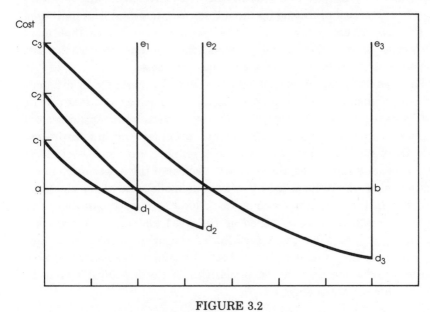

FIGURE 3.2

The Development of the Mass Production Cost Structure

shows how, as mass production develops, the gap between these curves becomes more and more pronounced, with $c'd'e$ shifting progressively outward to the right. The shaded area in figure 3.1 represents the cost savings of shifting from craft to mass production, provided the level of output sustains the latter.

These developments can be understood from the perspective of the firm and the perspective of the society as a whole. So long as the prevailing technology is $a'b$, the firm has no interest in how the market behaves; if demand turns down, it simply moves out. As the alternative $c'd'e$ emerges, so too does the firm's interest in the organization and structure of the market. Whenever demand falls below point d, firms already committed to the new technology try to restore the optimal level. But even if fear of fluctuations in demand has initially forestalled such commitments, the savings represented by the shaded area in the diagram provides an incentive—and a progressively greater one—for firms to organize the market so as to avoid fluctuations and permit investment in the new technology. This was the central goal of the modern corporation; and, as we shall see, there were several strategies for achieving it.

But the savings depicted do not accrue only to the firm; they represent real gains for society as a whole, as well. The shaded area in the diagram permits a reduction in the resources required for production of the commodity in question, making these resources available for other purposes. The cost of freeing up these resources, however, is proportional to the risk of unemployment of the specialized resources that mass production entails. The social problem, then, is how to organize the market so as to reduce that risk and lower the cost.

This general logic of specialization unfolded differently in different industries in nineteenth-century America. Two major variants can be distinguished, each associated, but not exclusively, with certain sectors of manufacturing. The first is typical of older continuous-process industries, such as sugar and petroleum refining, iron and steel, basic chemicals, and explosives; the second is typical of the newer mechanical industries, of which the automotive was the model, and of the electrical industry. In the next two sections, we follow the footsteps of these two types of industries as they discover the need and means for market stabilization. The subsequent sections of the chapter then show how the solutions they found reflected both the general economics of specialized production and the particularities of the historical setting in which these solutions emerged.

Stabilizing the Continuous-Process Industries

In the continuous-process sector, industrial development clearly preceded the emergence of the corporation. The market—in the loose sense of a large group of customers familiar with a well-defined product and accustomed to purchasing it on a regular basis—was of long standing. Most of the technological basis for mass production had already been established, under competitive market conditions. Economies of scale grew slowly, through the gradual improvement of the new technology by trial and error; and firms that initially thought of themselves as small in relation to the total demand were not concerned with market organization or control. As the minimum size of an efficient plant became larger and larger, however, these industries became increasingly unstable, and this instability increasingly troublesome to individual producers. The corporation emerged out of efforts to control this new instability.

These efforts at control can be seen as a series of organizational experiments that ultimately led to the corporate solution. In almost all cases they began as pools: agreements among producers to fix prices or to limit output. The pools were at first relatively simple constructions, but in the face of successive failures they became increasingly elaborate. Eventually the pools included provisions for the exchange of production and sales data among companies, and fines for violations of the agreement. When fines imposed after the fact failed to ensure compliance, member companies were, in effect, required to pay for their breaches in advance, by making contributions to a common fund. In the case of violation, the payments were forfeit and distributed to other members. Some of these schemes eventually included provisions for the stronger producers to compensate the weaker ones for reducing production, an elaboration amounting to a primitive form of financial integration.[7]

When even the most sophisticated pooling arrangements failed, the companies finally turned to more direct integration, through horizontal mergers; from this strategy it was only a short step to the modern corporation. Once the mergers had occurred, power soon shifted to the central management, which then moved to consolidate the organization, by closing down the weaker facilities and (most important for our purpose) organizing the market itself, to stabilize production.

The stabilization strategies differed according to the technical properties of the product and the geographic contours of the market in

55

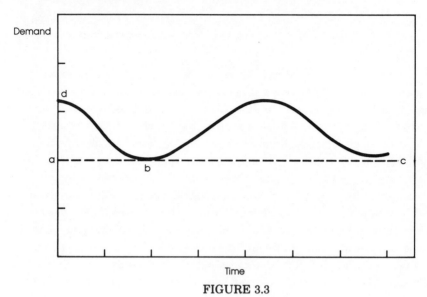

FIGURE 3.3

Market Segmentation

which it was sold. All of the strategies, however, reflected the desire to obtain economies of a high-fixed-cost technology by sustaining high levels of capacity utilization. This was clearly understood by the executives directing company policy, and it was articulated in both internal communications and public statements. Two basic approaches stand out: segmentation and varying inventory.

SEGMENTATION

One approach to stabilization was segmentation. The strategy was to divide the market, retain the base level of demand for the corporation's mass-production plants, and leave the rest for smaller producers (which presumably used more flexible resources and production techniques, whose cost characteristics approximated those of the craft technology). This strategy produced a dual industrial structure of the kind discussed in the last chapter. Its logic is depicted in figure 3.3, which shows the variation in demand (measured on the y-axis) over time (measured on the x-axis).

This dualistic strategy in effect draws a baseline under the fluctuations (*abc*) and captures that level of output, leaving the rest to other producers. A letter from a Du Pont executive to Coleman du Pont at the beginning of this century contains a clear explanation of the strategy:

If we could by any measure buy out all competition and have an absolute monopoly in the field, it would not pay us. The essence of manufacture is steady and full product. The demand for the country for powder is variable. If we owned all therefore when slack times came, we would have to curtail production to the extent of diminished demands. If on the other hand we controlled only 60% of it all and made that 60% cheaper than others, when slack times came we could still keep *our* capital employed to *the full* and our product to this maximum by taking from the other 40% what was needed for this purpose. In other words you could count upon always running full if you make cheaply and control only 60%, whereas, if you own it all, when slack times came you could only run a curtailed product.[8]

A more complex strategy of segmentation, resting on the same logic, was evident in electric-light manufacture. There, a high-fixed-cost technology was associated with the production of high-quality, long-lived bulbs; even with long production runs, the unit cost of these bulbs was relatively high. At the same time, standard light bulbs could be produced much more cheaply in smaller production facilities, although the product was considerably less durable and the defect rate much higher. The bulb market was therefore segmented by the sophistication of the customer. The Edison firm (one of the companies that eventually merged to form General Electric) and Westinghouse organized a national market of sophisticated commercial customers, who purchased in large quantities; these customers made the long-run cost calculations that showed that the higher initial cost of high-quality bulbs was repaid by their longer life. Production was centralized in plants large enough to obtain the available economies of scale and the product was shipped to local marketing organizations. The remainder of the market was left to a wide variety of regional producers, which made low-quality items in smaller plants, close to their customers.[9]

VARYING INVENTORY

An alternative to market segmentation as a strategy for stabilizing production was to meet demand fluctuations by varying inventory. When demand fell off, output was stored; when demand rose again, the stored output was put on the market. This approach is feasible when there is a standard, storable product, whose value is unlikely to decrease because of sudden changes in taste or technology, or a rapid fall in the cost of raw materials.

This was the strategy of the sugar-refining industry. As a sugar executive testified in 1894 to a committee of the U.S. Senate:

Now it happened last September . . . that there was in this country a sugar famine. The country had been afraid by reason of the panic [i.e., the panic of 1893] to buy anything: the grocers and all wholesale dealers were unable to raise the money to carry the stocks of sugar they had been able to carry previous to the month of August. The question came to us whether we should stop our refineries, and some of our people felt as though we ought not to accumulate large quantities of sugar. But we did run our refineries until we had a stock of nearly 400,000 barrels of sugar, and in one week we had a call from the country for the entire 400,000 barrels. Under the old system of refineries, with sixteen [independent firms], the refiners would not have been found who would have dared to have accumulated any such stock of sugar with the possibility of a decline in raw sugar which we faced.[10]

The Edison firm pursued a similar strategy in the electrical-equipment industry, by inducing its customers to sign long-term "future delivery" contracts, under which they had to buy specified quantities of Edison products at regular intervals over ten years. By assuring the demand for output, these contracts enabled the company to invest in large plants; the contracts also transferred some of the inventory costs—which in the sugar-refining industry were borne by the producer—to the consumer. In markets where demand was stable, the agreements created a barrier against potential competition. As one Edison executive explained:

It is essential in order to make lamps at a minimum cost that the factory should be run constantly at as uniform an output as possible. Our future delivery plan in lamps has been very successful [in this regard]. . . . It is very expensive work changing from one rate of production to another in factories. . . . The benefit of the future delivery plan is apparent since we can manufacture to stock knowing that all the stock is to be taken within a certain time.[11]

Still another example of the way in which production economies were affected by market organization is meat cutting. In this industry, the critical technological innovation was the invention of the refrigerated car. These cars involved enormous fixed-capital cost, and the development of large-scale organization in the meat-packing industry is usually explained by the economies of this form of transportation, together with the necessity of organizing production and marketing to keep this equipment fully employed.

What this explanation overlooks, however, is that the crucial effect of refrigerated shipping was to stabilize demand for cut meat in Chicago. Before refrigeration, meat had been slaughtered and shipped from Chicago only in winter, when the weather provided natural refrigeration; in the warmer seasons, cattle were instead shipped on the hoof—a costly passage, during which many lost valuable pounds and some died of disease—and slaughtered at the destination. This seasonal pattern permitted an elaborate division of labor that economized on butchery skills, but obstructed mechanization. Semiskilled laborers could be laid off at the end of the cold season, but special-purpose butchery equipment could not be; hence, there was no point to installing it in the first place. The introduction of the refrigerated car led to a rapid increase in mechanization in meat cutting because special-purpose machines could now be employed the year round.[12]

As some of these examples suggest, the organization of the market that was necessary to realize the economies of mass production was often extensive, involving not only horizontal but also vertical integration. Alfred D. Chandler, Jr., in his recent history of the modern corporation, has emphasized the integration of mass marketing and mass production as the basic organizational innovation in the creation of the modern corporation.[13] But this form of integration seems, in fact, to be only one instance of a broader class of institutional reforms—all rooted in the high fixed cost of mass-production technology—that cleared the way for the corporation. For example, some sugar refiners did eventually create their own retail brands, but these were a late and apparently minor development in their corporate strategy. The key to the inventory policy in sugar refining was, not mass marketing per se, but the development of a network of warehouses. The stabilization of production in that industry was always threatened, as we have seen, by a fall in the price of raw sugar; therefore the organization of the raw-sugar market—which in this case preceded the integration of production—was a necessary element of the final industrial structure.[14]

The economies of meat packing required integration from production through wholesale distribution. In this case, moreover, the development of the new technology led to extensive reform, not only of the transportation and production systems, as we have seen, but also of the distribution and marketing systems. Unlike sugar, butchered meat could not be stored for long periods, so marketing had to be organized to ensure sale as soon as possible after the product had arrived at its destination.[15]

An especially clear example of the requirements for vertical integration is the electrical industry. Early techniques for manufacturing electric lights could not produce lamps that operated at the same voltage; the manufacturing process yielded a batch of lamps adapted to various voltages distributed in a statistically predictable way above and below a target value. Electricity-generating equipment, on the other hand, had to be built to produce a single voltage. As a result, the full economies of scale in the manufacture of electric bulbs could be achieved only if power-generating capacity was planned to coincide with the distribution of lamps produced by the manufacturing process. The strategy, therefore, of General Electric in the late nineteenth century involved the coordination of its electrical-equipment division and the power-generating companies under its control, so as to match generating capacity with the composition of the output of its lamp-manufacturing facilities.[16]

Stabilizing the Newer Mechanical Industries

Most of the first generation of corporations developed in order to organize a market that already existed. Even the electrical industry, which utilized a wholly new technology, was designed to capture the market for artificial lighting that had been created by natural-gas companies. Thomas Edison used the cost of gas lighting as a measuring rod for his inventive efforts and as a standard in pricing the product. He also modeled his distribution and sales systems on the organization of the gas-lighting industry, utilizing the legal entities, underground rights of way, and metering principles that industry had originally developed.[17]

But a second important territory for these new organizational forms was markets for products that were themselves new. In these cases, the corporation not only organized the market, but created it. Some examples appear early in corporate history: the Singer Sewing Machine Company and McCormick Harvesting Machine Company.[18] But the most important case is the automobile industry, and particularly Ford's development of the Model T.[19]

FORD AND GENERAL MOTORS: TWO MARKETING STRATEGIES

If the impetus behind the first group of corporations was the need to stabilize a market, in Ford's case it was the need to have a market—to ensure the market's expansion, in the classic Adam Smith sense of the term. Ford set out to produce a reliable form of transportation at a price accessible to the average consumer, and he believed that if he could do so, the market would then materialize. To realize this goal, Ford believed that he had first to create an automobile that was both reliable and easy to operate. He thought that he then needed to reduce costs enough to open up the mass market, by elaborating a manufacturing technology based on interchangeable parts, an extreme division of labor, and a moving assembly line and, finally, build a sales network that would organize the market for a single standardized product.

The last was the easiest—Ford could simply imitate the sales and service organizations pioneered by Singer and McCormick. Ford's system of manufacturing, though less revolutionary than it appeared to his contemporaries, was in fact innovative; and his developments in production—often described as his decisive achievement—did drive the price of his product low enough to make it accessible to many people who could not afford his competitors' automobiles. But Ford's success was equally dependent on his product innovations, such as the Ford clutch and gearshift, which transformed what was initially something of a toy into a simple, reliable, useful vehicle.

Once the basic product design had been fixed, Ford relied on what he saw as infinite economies of scale to expand the market. Nevertheless, he dimly perceived that the spiral he envisioned, of lower costs–increased demand–lower costs–increased demand, might not be self-sustaining. His decision to raise his workers' wages to five dollars a day can therefore be interpreted as, among other things, a primitive attempt at a second marketing strategy based on increasing aggregate purchasing power through the redistribution of income, rather than the reduction of production costs. In any event, Ford's ambition was checked, not by the saturation of the market for automobiles, but by the different marketing strategy of his major competitor, General Motors.

The GM strategy was to replace the single standardized product with a series of different models, ranged across a price spectrum, from a basic car to a luxury product.[20] The different models in fact shared many components, so as to maximize economies of scale in production, but they were presented as different—often with little more than the cosmetic touches that the industry today calls nameplate engineering—so as to maximize the size of the market. Ultimately, the market was further extended by the creation of the General Motors Acceptance Corporation, which provided installment financing to low-income customers, and by annual model changes, which regularly created "new" products.

From the beginning, GM—in direct contrast to Ford's preoccupation with production and product technology—focused on marketing. The key elements of the strategy were developed through trial and error (later they were codified in company handbooks and operating procedures). Originally, GM was a large conglomerate of different automobile and automotive-parts firms, assembled by William C. Durant to no clear purpose. Together the welter of companies that made up the new firm produced numerous models, ranging from the most expensive to the relatively low-priced—although there were too many models to achieve long production runs comparable to those of the Model T, and even GM's least expensive cars were luxurious compared with Ford's. This ramshackle structure was taken over by a group of Du Pont executives, who purchased the company partly because of a decline in demand for Du Pont's older product lines.

The new management realized that the demand for basic transportation, on which rested the success of the Model T, would increasingly be met by used cars; hence the Du Pont group's strategy was to fashion from Durant's collection of companies a single, integrated firm that would displace the Model T in the new-car market by building a somewhat costlier and better-equipped model. In a sense, therefore, GM sought only to win for itself the economies of scale in the production of a single mass-consumption item that had previously been captured by Ford. The rest of its product line, inherited with the old Durant package of companies, was seen as a means of assuring that no firm would subsequently do to it what it was planning to do to its competitor: invade the mass market from above.

The production side of the GM strategy emerged as part of this preemptive marketing plan. Upon finding a critical hole in its model line directly above the low-priced Chevrolet, GM quickly moved to plug the hole by creating a new product, the Pontiac. In deciding where in the organization to place responsibility for development of the Pontiac, GM president Alfred Sloan realized that additional economies of scale could be obtained by integrating the design and production of variously priced models, so as to standardize the parts used in all GM cars. This component of GM's strategy was fully developed only in the Great Depression, when the market could not be further extended by enlarging the total demand for automobiles—the only way to reduce costs through economies of scale, therefore, was to homogenize, subtly, the products for the existing market. In this way, what started out as a marketing strategy became a production strategy, as well.[21]

The product-design component of the original Ford strategy is less salient in the GM story, but still not negligible. The strategy of differentiating models by price and year often depended on superficial variations on the standard design, but some of them (such as the automatic gearshift) made the car more accessible to technologically inexperienced drivers.[22]

In sum, the strategies of the automobile industry, though more complex than those of older industries, all had a simple goal: to organize and maintain a market that permitted the realization of the economies of mass production. Moreover, these strategies are distinguishable from those of the first generation of corporations only in one important aspect: whereas the first corporations aimed to create a market sized to fit a preexisting technology, the automobile corporations—foreseeing long-term increases in economies of scale—wanted not just to create a market of a predetermined size, but also to ensure its continual extension. In this sense, they, even more than their predecessors, grasped and tried to implement the principles promulgated by Adam Smith.

Labor Relations

The large corporations' concern with stabilization extended from the product market to the input markets, as well. It led to various forms of backward integration and control. The symbol of this policy was Ford's River Rouge site in Michigan: iron ore and coal were fed into a steel mill at one end of this vast complex, and finished automobiles rolled out the other. Similarly, the independent steel companies integrated backward into coal mining, and the railroads went into warehousing. As we have seen with sugar refining, one motive for backward integration was to prevent, through inventory accumulation, the sharp price fluctuations that prevent stabilization of production. Often, however, backward integration was designed simply to ensure a steady supply of raw materials of the requisite quality. Among the various inputs that the large corporations sought to stabilize was labor.

American corporate strategies in this regard have been widely misunderstood. The formative period of corporate history in the United States was marked by extreme labor strife. This strife was provoked by the determined efforts of the new corporations to destroy existing unions and prevent new ones. The unstable labor relations were thus the product of corporate policy. But this policy's chief motive was not, as is commonly thought, to create an open market for the determination of wages and working conditions. Rather, the corporations attacked labor organizations in order to maintain tight control over their own internal operations. As one railroad executive put it in discussing a labor dispute: "We should show at once that the row is not a question of money but as to who shall manage the road."[23]

Seen this way, the corporations' labor strategy was an extension of the basic principles of mass production. The decomposition of production into discrete operations made sense only if the separate operations could be reintegrated into a whole—a process that placed a huge premium on managerial coordination. Hence, anything that threatened the authority necessary for this coordination was suspect; from this point of view, American corporations were no more resistant to union organization than they were to outside financial control. It almost killed Henry Ford to sign a union contract in 1937, but he went to his grave without selling equity on the open market.[24]

This corporate insistence on internal control over the production process was very different from an interest in the competitive market determination of wages and working conditions, which unions aim to prevent. The new companies knew that their profits depended on the expansion of the market and the concomitant innovations in production. They were thus prepared to use violence against any opposition to the introduction of special-purpose machines—as Andrew Carnegie's 1892 assault on the iron puddlers' union at Homestead, Pennsylvania, showed. But gains made by simply sweating labor—driving wages down to the subsistence minimum in the absence of technological change—were decidedly secondary. Efforts to benefit in this way were, at best, a diversion from the primary source of profit; at worst, they were a source of precisely the kind of instability that mass production needed to avoid. In short, although the corporations were clearly opposed to unions, it was because the unions represented a check on managerial discretion. As we will see, the corporations were in fact willing to pay relatively high, stable wages—and improve working conditions and stabilize employment—in order to avoid the managerial intrusion of unions.[25] The one industry in which corporations used their new power to increase profits through sweating was meat packing, and that policy was short-lived.[26]

Nevertheless, there was an obvious conflict between, on the one hand, the corporations' determination to avoid union organization and thus maintain internal control and, on the other, their desire for stability, which union busting disrupted. Before the 1930s, the conflict was resolved in two ways: one by accepting unionization, the other by attempts to supplant it.

The railroad industry—eventually—took the former route, and it is here that railroads differed most from the rest of American industry. In doing so, the railroads developed a system of collective bargaining that was designed to minimize both the disruption caused by labor strife and the interference of labor in management efforts at coordination and control.

Many forces acted upon the railroads to take this path in the development of labor relations.[27] Among the most important was the transportation system's centrality to the national markets upon which other mass-production industries depended—labor strife in the railroads threatened the whole emergent mass-production economy. Therefore, as early as 1889, national legislation was passed to foster industrial peace through collective bargaining. That legislation was supplemented repeatedly, in 1898, 1920, and finally 1926, through the Railway Labor Act.[28]

Outside the railroad, American industry moved increasingly to forestall union organization by providing unilaterally what collective bargaining provided in the railroad industry. There were numerous variants of this policy. Probably the best known is Henry Ford's, which combined the much heralded wage increases of the five-dollar day with the creation of a "sociological department," to supplement welfare services for the workers and protect them from such subversive influences as unions and liquor.[29] By World War I, as we will see, this approach to labor relations had coalesced into a widely discussed managerial philosophy known as the American Plan—of which Ford's system became a brutal caricature.[30] The important point about these efforts was management's attempt, by stabilizing wages and employment, to insulate the cost of a major element of production from the flux of a market economy.

Infrastructure and Structure: The Railroads and the American Corporation

From our account so far, the nineteenth-century American corporation seems a kind of demiurge, able singlehandedly to organize the economy according to its needs. But the corporation's capacities were limited, and its success depended on the environment in which it moved. At the most general level, this environment was the distribution of wealth, taste, and power that, as we have seen, predisposed the United States, more than other countries, to take the path of mass production. Much more particularly, the environment consisted of such developments as the growing willingness of the courts to facilitate the formation and respect the autonomy of joint-stock corporations, as well as the creation of financial instruments that could sustain a vast circulation of goods. But if any single external factor was crucial to the corporation's success, it was the railroads. One cannot fully understand either the logic by which the mass producers operated or the way they applied that logic without considering the corporations' connection to the rail lines that from 1859 on crisscrossed the American continent.[31]

First, the railroads were critical to the mass producers because they aggregated a homogeneous but geographically dispersed demand.[32] Note that the railroads did not *create* this demand: as the French—with their regionally differentiated markets and their autarkic peasantry—discovered in the 1870s, the construction of a rail network did not by itself produce a mass demand for standard goods.[33] But in the American context of an existing mass demand, the railroads enabled a regional center of manufacturing (such as the New England shoe industry) to supply the nation.

Second, it is arguable that the railroads' policy of favoring their largest customers, through rebates, assured the survival of sugar- and petroleum-refining trusts during their formative years.[34] Although these trusts undoubtedly profited from the economies of scale permitted by combination and market stabilization, such increased efficiency would not necessarily have guaranteed the survival of the new organizations in the absence of favorable treatment from the railroads. Indeed, seen in this light, the rise of the American corporation can be interpreted more as the result of complex alliances among Gilded Age robber barons than as a first solution to the problem of market stabilization faced by a mass-production economy. But looked at more carefully, the rise of the corporation, as related to the railroads, supports both the model of technological change introduced in the last chapter and the model of market stabilization discussed in this one.

THE RAILROADS' DEVELOPMENT AND ITS EFFECT ON CORPORATIONS

The railroads' start-up costs were huge—securing rights-of-way, preparing roadbeds, and laying track—and the returns on this investment were far from assured. It is unlikely that railroads would have been built as quickly and extensively as they were but for the availability of massive government subsidies.[35] These ranged from straightforward (if often illegally obtained) concessions regarding rights-of-way to revisions of tort and contract law: the new common carriers, for example, were exempted from responsibility for many kinds of physical damage caused by their operation, as well as from liability for infringing the turnpikes' monpoly rights to transport goods and passengers between certain points.[36]

But even disregarding the need for subsidies, modern economic historians are divided on whether the American railroads were the unique solution to the problem of expanding the nineteenth-century system of transportation.[37] Robert Fogel, for instance, has argued that the nation's economy would have been as well served by an extension of the canal system, and that the decision, instead, to build railroads cannot be explained on narrowly economic grounds. If the railroads were the matrix of mass-production industry, then this matrix was itself shaped—as suggested by our earlier discussion of the branching-tree view of history—by political forces.

In any case, once the railroads were in place, the complexity of their political origins became irrelevant. The railroads were themselves an industry, using a high-fixed-cost technology, so the logic of their operations (such as the rebates policy) was determined by their cost structure, not their history. Because of their huge investment in rights-of-way, roadbeds, and rolling stock, the railroads had a tremendous incentive to use their capacity in a continuous, stable way. This incentive meant, in turn, that they had an interest in stabilizing the output of their principal customers—an interest that extended to protecting their customers from competitors who were served by other railroads. It is therefore not surprising that the railroads promoted merger schemes that had this effect, nor that they favored the resulting corporations or trusts with rebates. The rate concessions were motivated by the same technological logic at work within the mass-production industries; or, to phrase it usefully for our later discussion, the logic of the extra-firm infrastructure helped shape the intra-firm structure of economic organization.

The railroads' influence was not limited, however, to areas where they had a direct economic stake in, and intimate commercial contact with, emergent corporations. Because the cost structure of the railroads presaged the cost structure of mass-production technology, they pioneered American thinking about the technical and organizational problems that had to be solved in order to make that technology effective. Many of the solutions later adopted in other industries were obviously modeled on railroad practice.[38] Examples of this influence extend from the legal structure of the corporation to such, now basic, American labor-relations institutions as the use of seniority in promotion and layoff, and collective bargaining. The railroads also made critical contributions to the development of the capital markets through which the new organizational entities were financed, and to the scientific and engineering know-how upon which many of the new industries were based.[39] In sum, the railroads' prominence in American industrial development—as an actor and as a model—undoubtedly hastened the emergence of mass production in general, while it imparted a particular shape to the corporations that exploited the new high-fixed-cost technologies.

Disaggregation and False Necessity

One way to understand how the rise of the American corporation represented the solution to a general problem of microeconomic regulation while it reflected the particularities of the historical setting is, as we have done, to examine the connection between infrastructure and structure. Another way is to study the process by which inventor-entrepreneurs conceptualize products and industries as discrete physical and organizational entities.

From the point of view of the inventor-entrepreneurs (though not that of their rivals, or subsequent observers), new industries are created by a visionary, ineffable synthesis of technology and organization. So blinding is this vision that neither the visionaries nor their executors can make out just which parts of it are contingent and variable, and which are indispensable to the realization of the insight. Similarly, the mass-production corporation, especially in the new industries, was seen by its creators as created whole: the action of creation—protracted and halting in fact, yet recollected as exhilaratingly sudden—obscured the relation among the parts.

Great ideas in industry no less than in science are, of course, always in the air. They are the extension of precedent technological and social developments, and in this sense collective, not individual, creations. Ford was not the only person to conceive of a mass market for cars. Refrigerated shipment of meat was developed by at least three entrepreneurs working independently.[40] Edison was not alone; Westinghouse and a half dozen European inventors had technological conceptions that would undoubtedly have produced the electric-light industry.[41] The fact that these ideas were incipient in the technological and social environment was surely a precondition for the inventors and entrepreneurs who realized them to attract any following at all.

Nonetheless, the ideas were initially only vague conceptions, inchoate approximations of goods that only later would become so well defined as to be called commodities—and thus assimilated to the world of apparently natural products, such as wheat and beef. It took extraordinary determination to translate these visions into salable reality; the visionaries could hardly even communicate their ideas to collaborators and subordinates. They themselves did not fully grasp the implications of their intuitions, learning what they meant only as they put their conceptions into concrete form. Thus even a sycophantic account, by his collaborator, of Ford's role in the development of the automobile industry rejected the notion that Ford initially had anything in mind as coherent as the system he eventually created. And modern historical research attests that the assembly line was the end point of ad-hoc innovations in production, not a deduction from a master idea.[42]

Sloan, to take another example, claims in his autobiography that the GM strategy was all written down in a 1921 corporate memo. To the extent that he is talking about the company's strategic vision, that is true. Yet he describes the decision to assign the Chrysler engineering division the responsibility for the Pontiac motor—the critical decision establishing the principle that different models would use the same basic parts—as something he did not arrive at until late 1924.[43] Edison, for another example, hired a mathematician with a doctorate from Princeton to solve equations critical to the development of electric light, but this employee could not understand the significance of his task.[44]

Once a corporation and its product were in the market, however, the inchoate vision acquired a clarity and self-evidence that made its earlier unintelligibility hard to understand or recollect. In his autobiography, Ford presents himself as a methodical philosopher of mass production. Sloan viewed his one-page memo of 1921 as a concise statement of the thousands of pages of company policy that were circulating by 1955. Edison's mathematician was amazed by his own obtuseness: "I cannot imagine," he writes, "why I could not see the elementary facts in 1878 and 1879 more clearly than I did. I came to Mr. Edison a trained man, a postgraduate at Princeton; with a year's experience in Helmholz's laboratory; with a working knowledge of calculus and a mathematical turn of mind."[45]

Clarification through realization of the initial vision had two contradictory effects on the organization of production. On the one hand, it made it possible to see that some of the operations that the corporation performed for itself (because, lacking a sense of the ultimate product, no one else had thought to perform them) could in fact be delegated outside the organization: a sense of the whole revealed the marginality of some of the parts.[46] The refrigerated cars that Chandler views as the critical innovation in meat packing—and which the packers originally built and owned themselves—were subsequently sold to the railroads, and the packers contracted for their use, as any shipper contracted for freight cars. Edison power stations were freed in the late nineteenth century to buy Westinghouse equipment. The automobile producers relied more and more on subcontractors to supply components.

On the other hand, clarification—realization—of the unity of technology and organization, product and procedure, made it hard to see that many aspects of standard practice were not dictates of the logic of production—that they were merely expedients that had been adopted under the pressures of the moment. The very consolidation of practice that showed some activities to be peripheral made all the others seem essential. This situation is most apparent in the American corporation's relation to capital markets and to the state.

The early American entrepreneurs developed a fetish about self-financing. Even when, pressing on all fronts to expand, they were hamstrung by shortages of capital, they resisted any form of outside financing, seeing it as a dilution of their personal control. Henry Ford was the extreme example: he never sold. The firm's entire expansion was financed without public sale of equity and without bank loans.

The rationale for this attachment to internal financing is easy to understand given the experiences of the early entrepreneurs. Edison, for example, made his initial electrical inventions in a laboratory heavily dependent on outside financial backing. When his board of directors, unable to grasp his plans, blocked the ideas' commercial development, he was able to proceed only by wresting control of the laboratory patents in a bitter fight with his early financers. But this commitment to internal financing has persisted long after the entrepreneurial phase of corporate development. American corporations have a resistance to bank financing that is unknown in other industrial nations, where, as we will see, banks often played a major role in establishing and organizing relations among large firms. And in recent years, when internally generated funds have exceeded the requirements of the corporations' activities, they have invested this money in internal diversification, through conglomeration, rather than lending it or making other kinds of arm's-length investments.

Similarly, relations between the large American corporations and the state have been enduringly shaped by the circumstances in which they began—circumstances that were largely adversarial. European and Japanese corporations (as we will see in chapter 6) often grew under the tutelage of, or were modeled after, the state. But American corporations grew up at best indifferent, at worst opposed to the national government. Conflicts between corporations and the state arose when, for example, firms that had been disadvantaged by the railroads' preferential treatment of mass producers successfully advocated government restraint of the corporations.[47] Even if the new organizations might have benefited by collaborating with the state, their sophistication and size—compared with the dwarf government of the day—made it seem pointless to do so.

The resulting distance between government and economy was particularly evident regarding the expansion of foreign trade in the late nineteenth and early twentieth centuries. American mass producers of reapers, sewing machines, cash registers, elevators, cigarettes, matches, breakfast cereals, canned goods, roll film, butchered meat, and petroleum products had no need of government help to export their products, or to establish subsidiaries in Europe and Latin America.[48] The organizational advances that had allowed them to unify the American market facilitated their expansion abroad; and the economies of scale obtainable in the United States often gave them an edge over the competition they encountered abroad. Paradoxically, the successes at home led mass producers to regard foreign trade as no more than an important adjunct to their domestic strategy.

The only firms that did look to the government for assistance in opening foreign markets (when, as in the 1890s, business slumped at home) were in precisely those sectors that could not take advantage of the stabilization policies of the mass producers: labor-intensive industries, such as apparel, furniture, lumber, and textiles; industries making simple mechanical products, such as laundry wringers or shears, that required little start-up capital; and the segment of the machine-tool industry that made specialized products, often to customer specification, by craft methods. Because these firms could not collectively solve the problem of surplus capacity, they had to find foreign outlets for it; but lacking the organizational capacity to resolve the first problem, they were unable to manage the required export drive by themselves. While the large firms went their own way, therefore, the small ones formed lobbies (such as the National Association of Manufacturers) to pressure the government for help in selling their products abroad. But without the support of the mass producers, these efforts brought only minor results. The upshot of these early developments was to isolate small producers from international markets and to keep foreign-trade policy in the United States—in contrast to many of its foreign competitors—largely a private affair of the giant corporations.

Thus, as it turned out, the structure of the American corporation was as marked by the creation of mass production as it was by mass production itself. This structure was thus a special case—responsive to the peculiarities of a particular historical time and space—of a more general class of solutions to the problem of microeconomic regulation. In countries where mass-production corporations developed later, they were outwardly similar to those of the United States (since they sought to imitate American success), but were organized and functioned very differently.

This specificity of the American corporation is, however, apparent only in comparative retrospect. In the 1920s, American corporations viewed themselves, and were viewed by others, as explorers who had discovered the narrow path to progress: what they did was what *had* to be done. And what could be more natural, given this success, than that they applied their proven strategies to the next problem faced by economies moving along the mass-production trajectory—the problem of macroeconomic regulation?

CHAPTER

4

Stabilizing the Economy

HE CORPORATION was a so-
lution to the organizational problems created by the rise of mass-
production technology. But it was at best a partial solution. It asserted
control over the market for its own products and for its immediate
supplies of resource inputs. But these markets were ultimately dependent
on the prosperity of the national economy, and this was beyond the
control of the new corporate enterprises. The Great Depression of the
1930s revealed the limits of corporate control. Out of the Depression
and the world war that followed emerged a new macroeconomic structure
that overcame, at least for a time, those limits.

At the height of the postwar prosperity, it was generally believed that
the key to macroeconomic stability was Keynesian economics. Keynes's
argument was that an economy in which decisions about savings and
investment are made privately can fall into an underconsumption trap:
demand will not absorb the output of aggregate productive capacity;
output will fall; and no automatic mechanism will restore economic
activity to its previous level. If this happens, Keynes's practical recommendation was for government spending on public projects to be used
temporarily to put the idle resources to work, setting in motion a self-
reinforcing process that will return the balance of supply and demand
to the higher level of output. After 1946, policymakers in the United
States took this advice and tried to use federal control over taxes, the

interest rate, and the national budget to compensate for shortfalls in private demand. By 1954—when the conservative Eisenhower administration reacted to a recession by lowering interest and tax rates and contemplating an expanded program of public works—it was clear that a form of Keynesianism, originally associated with the Left, had become a tool of prudent statecraft, if not an explicit principle of good government.[1] In time the American version of Keynesianism, like the American model of the corporation, had been raised to a high level of theoretical sophistication and graced by success; it thus became a model for foreign emulation.

The political appeal of this understanding of macroeconomic stabilization is easy to see. A minimum of state intervention apparently guaranteed the prosperity of a competitive market economy; a maximum of efficiency proved consistent with virtually undiminished respect for the rights of private property holders to buy and sell as they chose. But, we argue, in the United States and elsewhere the steady growth of the economy depended far more on the creation of mechanisms that replaced free markets than on discretionary government policies operating through them. Like microregulation, macroregulation in mass production worked through institutional coordination.

In the United States the most critical macroregulatory institutions were the industrial unions in mass-production industry—specifically, the rules and procedures that the unions imposed for setting wages. Together, those rules ensured an autonomous expansion of private purchasing power at the same rate as the expansion of capacity. They operated, however, by freezing relative wages and prices. In so doing, they curtailed the ability of wages and prices to signal to private decision makers where resources were needed and induce their redeployment. The economy thus became dependent instead on an allocative system that relied on, among other things, the large internal labor reserves in the rural South; on-the-job training of semiskilled production workers in mass-production industries; and the surpluses of basic commodities accumulated under federal agricultural price-support programs.

The stabilization of aggregate demand was also fostered by the enormous expansion of government spending, which supplemented private demand, and by the creation of the Social Security system, which also augmented private demand and automatically increased consumer purchasing power whenever private incomes turned down. The institutional complex as a whole actually did much of the work of safeguarding national economic prosperity. It thus minimized the need for overt use of Keynesian policies of stabilization.

To appreciate the need for these institutional forms and to understand how they arose and came to play the role that they did, it is necessary to examine in more detail the Great Depression and its relation to mass production and the corporation.

The Great Depression and Macroeconomic Stabilization

The cause of the Great Depression and the nature of the reforms that sustained the postwar prosperity are subjects of enormous controversy.[2] In fifty years of debate it has proved impossible to distinguish the effects of fortuitous shocks to the international order, amplified by the blunders of policymakers (whose definition, of course, is highly controversial), from the effects of structural flaws in the organization of national economies and world markets. But whatever the factors immediately responsible for the crisis of the 1930s, our argument is that its fundamental cause was the structural fragility of the economy that was associated with the rise of the mass-production corporation. The postwar prosperity, in turn, can be traced to the institutional reforms that remedied the defects of the mass-production economy that were brought to light by the crisis.

As we said in the last chapter, the pre-corporate American economy approximated—as much as any economy ever has—the neoclassical model of self-stabilization through competitive prices. It therefore serves here, too, as a useful point of historical reference for the changes in the form of stabilization that took shape in the 1930s.

In the early-nineteenth-century United States, unemployment in the modern sense was unknown. The term existed, but it referred to unpaid activities: people said they were "unemployed" when they were engaged in productive activity that was outside the market, or in leisure pastimes. As the economic structure changed over the century, the implications of the word "unemployment" also changed, taking on its modern meaning of enforced idleness, the inability to find a job. By World War I, the word was used exclusively in this way, having completely lost its original meaning.[3]

The original meaning reflected the character of the household economy and the polyvalence of so much of its work force. Even the specialized shoemakers in early-nineteenth-century Lowell, Massachusetts, worked at home, where they also produced much of their own food and clothing. In the most extreme economic depression, when the demand for shoes fell so low that master shoemakers were "unemployed," the household still could turn to farming, spinning, weaving, and home repair.[4]

Even this kind of unemployment, however, must have been rare. Competitive markets of the kind that linked first the household producers and then the early factories are self-equilibrating. Private investment varies so as to produce an automatic balance between aggregate demand and productive capacity. Investment is sensitive to the rate of return, the difference between the revenue earned from the sale of a commodity and the cost of the basic inputs necessary for its production. The natural reflex of a competitive economy to any decline in demand is a decline in wages and in the rate at which funds can be borrowed. This will, in turn, increase the rate of return, producing an expansion in investments. The expansion of investment increases income; the increase in income leads to an expansion of consumption; and the expansion of consumption further increases income, producing a chain reaction that restores full employment. If this reaction goes too far and demand rises above capacity, wages and interest rates rise, and investment declines. The process is reversed, and balance is restored as these adjustments press down on aggregate spending.

The development of mass production and its spread in the course of the twentieth century led to two changes in the structure of the economy that disrupted this process of macroeconomic stabilization.

First, as we saw in the last chapter, the rise of mass production made investment especially sensitive to the level of demand for the product. Individual productive units became so large relative to the total market that the propensity to invest in manufacturing plants was determined by the prospective level of capacity utilization, rather than by changes in the costs of inputs. Producers thus required assurances that the market would expand to absorb the enlarged output called forth by their investments.

By itself, however, this first change in the economic structure would not have materially affected the process of macroeconomic stabilization described in competitive market theory. So long as the corporate sector is small, or centered in new industries whose demand is expanding faster than national income, or centered in semifinished goods used to make final products sold in competitive markets, the demand that it faces will not depend directly on the expansion of aggregate demand.

But here the second important structural change intervened. Mass production became increasingly concentrated in consumer durables—most notably automobiles—and in industries linked to consumer durables, such as steel, rubber, and plate glass. As this occurred, the whole economic system became extremely sensitive to the level of consumer purchasing power: it became a mass-consumption as well as a mass-production economy.

In a mass-consumption economy, the natural response of prices to many kinds of disturbances has the perverse effect of producing contradictions of economic activity, rather than relaunching growth. Investment is not directly responsive to declining wages and interest costs as long as industry already has substantial excess capacity; and the fall in wages under the pressure of unemployment undermines the demand for consumption goods, creating exactly the kind of excess capacity that deters the revival of investment spending. Because investment is so sensitive to consumer income, it is thus possible that the mass-production, mass-consumption economy will respond to a wage decline in a fashion precisely opposite to that of a competitive economy.

The long-term planning and strategic perspective of the corporations operated to compensate for this tendency within a certain range of demand fluctuations. Corporate managers, we have seen, understood that demand would not expand in an even pattern, so in planning their productive capacity they anticipated some instability. Part of their strategy in this regard was to build only for the sustainable portion of demand and to subcontract nonsustainable increases to smaller producers that were not powerful enough to insulate themselves in this way, but that sometimes also used a more flexible technology. But corporate planners also geared investment to long-run market projections, anticipating temporary shortfalls and discounting them in advance.

Their long-term investment in plant and equipment was thus relatively insensitive to the "normal" business cycle. It slowed in a recession, but it could be postponed for only a relatively short time without running the risk that the company's existing plant would be inadequate to meet demand in the next upturn—which might turn out to be large and very sudden. Given that the corporate-based industries were oligopolies dominated by a handful of firms, and that economies of scale grew with time, the penalty for being caught short could be severe: a tardy firm would probably face competitors that used newer, more specialized, and therefore more efficient, equipment. In the best case, this firm would cede some share of the market to the more modern, low-cost producers. In the worst case, the cost differential would be so great that the laggard's absolute output might decline, augmenting its unit costs and exacerbating its competitive disadvantage.[5]

As we have seen, the corporate sector attempted to stabilize wages and employment in much the same way that it sought to stabilize long-term investment. This effort also acted to sustain consumer purchasing power in an economic downturn and to forestall the perverse interaction among declining wages, consumer spending, and investment spending to which the corporate sector was vulnerable.

Under the corporate regime of the 1920s, however, the stabilization of investment and wage levels depended completely on managerial expectations for the course of business cycles. There was no independent institutional regulation of economic activity—regulation that would have stabilized investment activity both directly, through its effect on markets, and indirectly, by reinforcing expectations of continuity. If a recession was more prolonged than expected or demand fell below the anticipated level, long-term investment could be postponed indefinitely; and nothing prevented the corporation from attempting to restore profits through the exercise of its dominant position in the labor market—by sweating its workers. These two policies were, moreover, likely to coincide. The postponement of investment was most likely to occur when there was an extreme excess of capacity; when the expansive strategy of cost cutting through technological innovation was temporarily checked; and when the only available means of restoring profits (or, more accurately, cutting losses) was through draconian reductions in the price paid for inputs, of which wages were obviously a major component.

A reaction of this sort seems to explain the length and severity of the Great Depression. Despite the drama of the stock-market crash that accompanied it, the downturn in 1929 was first perceived as just another recessionary trough in the waves of economic activity that periodically move across an ocean of prosperity. It was only in early 1931—when the recession extended beyond the accustomed period, and the downward slide of economic activity, which had seemed to end earlier in the year, resumed—that business began to perceive this downturn as qualitatively different from others. Firms started canceling long-term investment projects that until then had been only slowed or postponed. Deep wage cuts, initially confined to competitive labor markets, were extended to the corporate sector. The effect was to push the economy off the cliff.[6] The cuts in investments further reduced income, which reduced consumption yet again and lessened still more the incentive to invest. And these effects on consumption, and then investment, were aggravated by the cuts in corporate wages.

Institutional Transformation:
Postwar Macroeconomic Stabilization

The Depression initiated two decades of institutional transformation in American society. The transformation began with attempts to respond to the economic collapse and to cushion its impact. But it was prolonged by World War II and the effort, first, to convert the economy to war production, then to manage it under the pressure of war demand, and finally to reconvert the productive apparatus and prevent the society from falling back into a postwar depression. By the end of the 1940s, however, the remnants of these diverse institutional experiments and reforms had coalesced into what—at least in retrospect—can be seen as a new and relatively stable structure of macroeconomic regulation. As in the last chapter, we will first examine the components as the logical building blocks of a system that solves a general problem of regulation in a mass-production economy; then we will consider the components as the outcomes of uniquely American historical developments.

The centerpiece of postwar macroeconomic stabilization was the system of national wage determination that resulted from the rise of trade unions in mass-production industries and the concomitant spread of collective bargaining. Whereas industrial unions had played a negligible role in American industrial labor relations before the Depression, they were crucial to the organization of labor after World War II. Union members, it is true, remained a minority of the total labor force; but by 1946, almost 70 percent of production workers in the major manufacturing industries were covered by union contracts. In the agricultural-implement, aircraft, electrical-machinery, meat-packing, nonferrous-metals, rubber, shipbuilding, and basic-steel industries, rates of unionization ranged from 80 to 100 percent. In machinery, steel products, and petroleum, the range was 30 to 60 percent.[7]

The system of wage determination in these industries was defined by five principal elements: the model automobile-contract formula, established in a 1948 United Auto Workers–General Motors agreement; pattern bargaining, which spread the automobile settlement to the rest of the unionized sector; federal labor legislation, which facilitated unionization and thus forced nonunion employers to increase their wages at the collectively bargained rate, or else run the high risk that their firms would be organized; minimum wage legislation, which forced up wages at the bottom of the labor market in step with wages at the top; and wage-setting mechanisms in the public sector, which linked the movement of salaries paid by the government to that of union workers.

The keystone of the whole system of macroeconomic stabilization was the wage-setting formula negotiated between General Motors and the United Auto Workers in 1948.[8] The formula established as the standard for wage setting the long-run, economywide increase in labor productivity plus the change in the consumer price index; wages, it was agreed, should rise by this amount every year. Given that labor productivity adjusted for price changes is a measure of productive capacity, consistent and uniform application of the formula to all wages and salaries would ensure that private-consumer purchasing power would expand at the same rate as national productive capacity. The complex of labor-relations and wage-setting institutions generalized the formula in precisely this way.[9]

Within the mass-production industries, the automobile settlement was spread through the institutional links between the major national unions. Each of the industries—and within them, most companies— conducted separate negotiations; but the negotiations were tied together in "orbits of coercive comparison," which forced all unions to follow similar patterns. Because the industries were large and important in the national economy—and strikes, therefore, of great consequence— the negotiations received wide press coverage and the settlements were highly visible. Rank-and-file union members used these highly publicized settlements as a measure to judge their union leaders: settlements in one industry became a standard that other union leaders had to meet in order to prove their prowess at the bargaining table. Competition among the leaders for power within the labor movement—and in the larger arena of national politics—further heightened the importance of matching one another's achievements in negotiations. Because the automobile industry was a major customer of several of the other large mass-production industries—steel, rubber, and plate glass—the latter industries' ability to pay and capacity to resist strike pressure rose and fell with automobile demand. This meant that the economic pressures reinforced the institutional pressures, causing contract settlements in different industries to move in step.

Outside mass-production manufacturing, there were strongholds of union organization in such industries as construction, trucking, large retail establishments, mining, and communications. Economic conditions in these other industries were not closely tied to those in mass production, nor were the unions, historically or institutionally, closely tied to the mass-production unions. Nonetheless, because mass production was the focus of public attention, and because it had a pervasive impact on the national economy and many local labor markets, its settlements set standards for virtually every contract. The result was that, despite substantial short-term differences, the rest of the union sector in the long run followed the lead of the unions in mass production.

The relatively large nonunion component of the private sector was forced, by the threat of organization, to follow the union wages. The importance of this threat is difficult to appreciate in the 1980s, when unions are so much on the defensive, struggling to hold the members they have. But postwar attitudes were highly colored by memories of the 1930s, when mass-production unionism arose suddenly, apparently from nowhere. The National Labor Relations Act protected the right to union membership and provided effective mechanisms by which a majority of workers in any unorganized shop could vote to form a union local whenever their employer stepped out of line. Union membership expanded rapidly from the late 1930s through World War II, and it continued to grow, though at a slower pace, into the mid-1950s: memories of a militant, expanding labor movement lingered well into the 1960s. Although only a few employers (such as Du Pont, IBM, and Texas Instruments) met the union threat by paying wages equal to those in the organized sector—so there was a substantial differential between union and nonunion establishments—the nonunion sector nonetheless agreed to match the rate of change of the union wages. Had it failed to do so, the differential would have risen, making nonunion firms an increasingly attractive candidate for a union election under the auspices of the prounion (or at least not antiunion) National Labor Relations Board.

At the bottom of the labor market, the pay rate was governed by the nationally legislated minimum wage.[10] This legislated minimum was periodically amended, so the lowest legal wage rose along with other wages in the private sector. These adjustments were motivated in part by concern about the welfare of workers. But such legislation was also understood by the trade-union movement—the major group to lobby for it—to be part of a broader strategy, whose micro- and macroeconomic aspects were conceived along the lines of this book's presentation of the wage-determination system.

The macroeconomic case for the minimum wage, as elaborated in repeated Congressional hearings, was to maintain consumer purchasing power. At the microeconomic level, those unions whose wages were relatively low saw the minimum wage as the principal constraint on their nonunion competitors—it was a precondition of these unions' ability to follow the wage movements of the pace-setting industries (such as automobiles) without losing business to nonunion firms. Thus unions were motivated to use their extensive political power to ensure that as time went on, the minimum wage was raised in step with the contract settlements that they felt compelled to follow.

In the public sector, workers were mostly not union members, they did not have the right to strike, and they had to accept wages set by legislation and civil-service procedures; nonetheless, their pay was linked to the wage-setting movements in the private sector. Many public-sector wage-setting procedures relied on surveys of wages in comparable private jobs to establish standards for periodic wage adjustments; and the legislative process by which wages for government employees were increased assured that wage rates in the private sector—particularly the highly publicized settlements in the mass-production industries—were taken into account.

Viewed together, these different institutional mechanisms tied wages throughout the economy into a single structure. Though there were always a few deviations from the pattern, these were generally short-lived. Through the UAW-GM agreement, wages were keyed to productivity plus inflation, and consumer purchasing power to the expansion of productive capacity. This was Keynesian income policy without a Keynesian state.

The impact of these institutional changes can be seen in figures 4.1(a), (b), and (c). The figures show relative movements in the wages across all sectors and within manufacturing industries from 1901 to 1978. The best cumulative indicator of the extent to which wage rates shifted with respect to one another is the variance in the rate of change of average hourly earnings; the variance measures the degree to which the rate of change of wages differs in different industries. When the variance is large, wage increases and decreases vary greatly from one industry to the next, and it is impossible to speak of pattern bargaining; when the variance is small, the rate of change is roughly the same in all industries, and the common rate is, de facto, a pattern. As can be seen in the diagram, before 1948 the variance fluctuated widely from year to year, but after that year it fell dramatically and remained extremely low relative to the earlier observations. The result holds for almost all of the available wage series. And the patterned stabilization of wages is part of the larger pattern of macroeconomic stabilization in this period, as shown by the movements of the prices of goods and services in different sectors, graphed in figure 4.2(a), (b), and (c). The variance in the rates of change is stable from 1948 to 1972; when fuel and food prices are removed, it remains stable between 1973 and 1980, as well.[11]

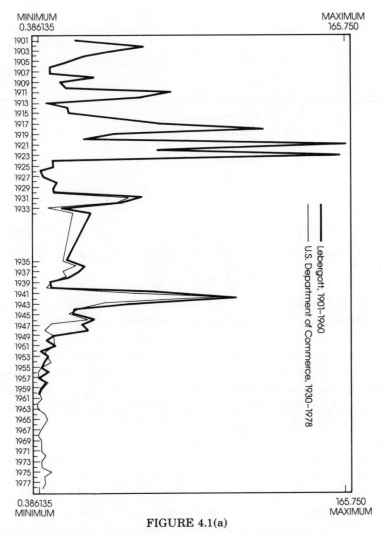

MINIMUM
0.386135

MAXIMUM
165.750

Lebergott, 1901–1960

U.S. Department of Commerce, 1930–1978

0.386135
MINIMUM

165.750
MAXIMUM

FIGURE 4.1(a)

Variability of Relative Wages, All Industries, 1907–1978

SOURCES: Stanley Lebergott, *Manpower in Economic Growth* (New York: McGraw-Hill, 1964), table A–18; U.S. Department of Commerce, *The National Income and Product Accounts of the United States, 1929–74: Statistical Tables* (Washington, D.C.: U.S. Government Printing Office, 1977), table 6.9; U.S. Department of Commerce, *Survey of Current Business* (July 1977), table 6.9, and (July 1979), table 6.9.

Economic Adjustment Given Structural Rigidities

The wage-setting mechanisms just described maintained consumer purchasing power, but they did so by making wages and prices so rigid that they could no longer serve as an effective means of allocating resources.

83

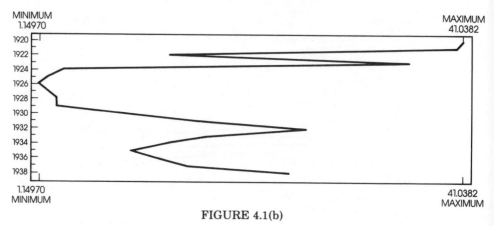

FIGURE 4.1(b)

Variability of Relative Wages, Manufacturing Industries, 1920–1938

SOURCE: Simon Kuznets, *National Income and Its Composition, 1919–1938*, vol. 2 (New York: National Bureau of Economic Research, 1941), tables M–10 and M–27.

The institutional structure that tied wages in one industry to those in the others was such that any highly publicized, sustained wage increase would have become the target for other settlements. Any major attempt to attract workers from one location in the economy to another by means of wage hikes was therefore likely to be self-defeating, because it would raise the level of all wages. Worse still, a general rise in wages or in the price of any other input would lead to a self-reinforcing rise in the general price level, owing to the link between wages and the cost of living created by the GM formula. Wages are the major component of costs. If wages rise, prices rise; and in a system in which wages are implicitly indexed to prices, this rise touches off a spiral of wage and price increases. If prices rise because of increases in the cost of inputs other than labor, wages rise, and the result is the same.

The viability of the whole system thus depended on institutional mechanisms to forestall unsettling price increases. There were a number of such mechanisms in the postwar economic structures—so many, in fact, that it is not possible to identify all of them here. Several, however, eventually broke down. Because their breakdown plays a part in the crisis of the 1970s, we will set the stage for later discussion by using them as illustrations of the system's operation.

LABOR RESERVES

In the American labor market, one key element was the reserves of workers who were exempted from minimum-wage legislation. The largest group of those exempted worked in the agricultural sector, particularly

84

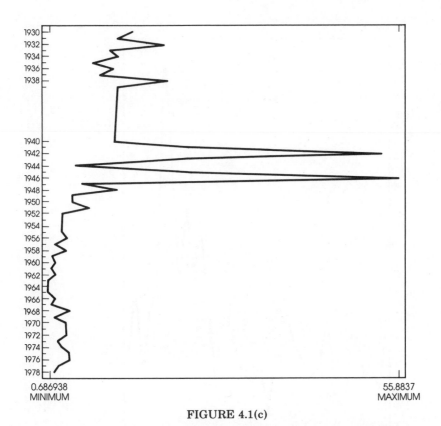

FIGURE 4.1(c)

Variability of Relative Wages, Manufacturing Industries, 1930–1978

SOURCES: U.S. Department of Commerce, *The National Income and Product Accounts of the United States, 1929–74: Statistical Tables* (Washington, D.C.: U.S. Government Printing Office, 1977), table 6.9; U.S. Department of Commerce, *Survey of Current Business* (July 1977), table 6.9, and (July 1979), table 6.9.

in the South, where the standard of living was substantially below that of the rest of the country. By sanctioning this differential, the minimum-wage legislation created—for reasons we will take up later—a large pool of labor that was available on call to the manufacturing sector at the prevailing industrial wage rate.

The decomposition of tasks associated with mass production also contributed to the smooth functioning of the labor market. As we saw in chapter 2, the advance of mass production leads to the increased substitution of specialized low-skilled workers for craftsmen. In the United States, these mass-production workers are called semiskilled, but many of their skills are trivial—much of what they do can be learned on the job through repetition of their assignment and tips from more experienced co-workers. In time, a reserve accumulates, at the

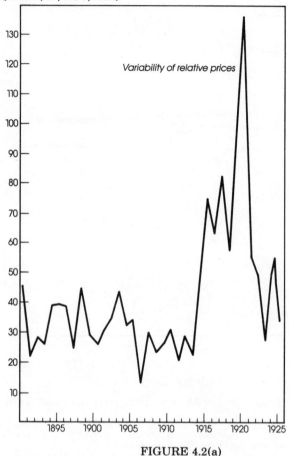

Variance of relative price change
(percent per year, squared)

Variability of relative prices

FIGURE 4.2(a)

Variability of Wholesale Prices, 1891–1926

SOURCE: Stanley Fischer, "Relative Shocks, Relative Price Variability, and Inflation," *Brookings Papers in Economic Activity,* 1981, no. 2, p. 390.

bottom of the blue-collar hierarchy, of trained low-skilled workers who are capable of moving up to slightly more demanding jobs. Moreover, because the equipment and skills for even relatively sophisticated mass-production jobs are so highly plant- or company-specific, the employer has an incentive to train its own people to fill jobs.

This structure of jobs and training made it possible to draw untrained workers from the rural labor reserves directly into mass production, at the bottom of the job hierarchy, and to fill higher-level jobs through internal promotion. In this way a firm was able to increase its labor

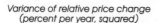

Variance of relative price change
(percent per year, squared)

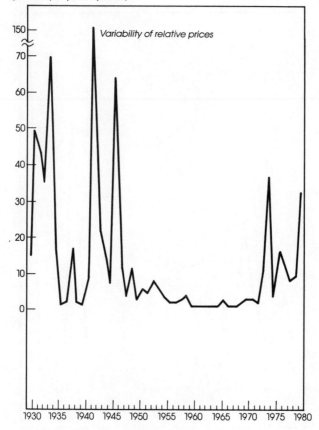

FIGURE 4.2(b)

Variability of Relative Prices, Personal Consumption Expenditure Deflator,
1930–1980

SOURCE: Stanley Fischer, "Relative Shocks, Relative Price Variability, and Inflation," *Brookings Papers in Economic Activity,* 1981, no. 2, pp. 393–94.

force without the need of high wages to attract workers from elsewhere in the industrial sector.[12]

The national commitment to universal elementary and secondary education and the independence of the educational system from the requirements of the economy also contributed to the flexibility of the labor market, despite the rigidity of wages. For most of the postwar period, the educational system produced an oversupply of generally trained workers at virtually every level. There was, of course, still an undersupply of certain specialized professionals, particularly in science

87

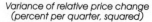

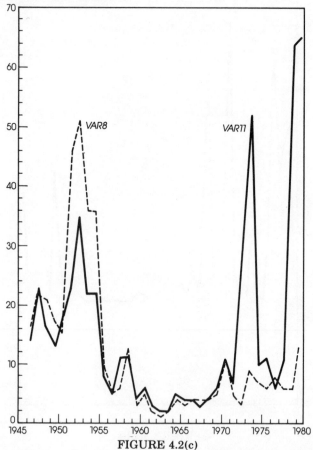

FIGURE 4.2(c)

Variability of Relative Prices, Including (VAR11) and Excluding (VAR8) Energy and Food Prices, Personal Consumption Expenditure Deflator, 1947–1980.

SOURCE: Stanley Fischer, "Relative Shocks, Relative Price Variability, and Inflation," *Brookings Papers in Economic Activity*, 1981, no. 2, pp. 393–94.

and engineering in the late 1950s (when the United States sought to respond rapidly to the challenge of the Soviet space program); yet, as with uneducated labor, industry's basic requirements could be met without changing relative wages.[13]

PRODUCT-PRICE STABILIZATION

Product prices were stabilized by analogous mechanisms. The most elaborate of these was the agricultural price-stabilization program. Under this program the government accumulated large reserves of basic agricultural commodities in order to prevent wide price fluctuations: when large harvests threatened to drive prices down, these stocks were expanded; and in poor crop years, when prices would have risen, the stocks were released onto the market. The government also maintained strategic reserves of a number of militarily critical raw materials, which it utilized in a similar way to stabilize markets in such metals as copper and uranium.[14]

The United States' colonial and neocolonial economic relationships with underdeveloped countries, especially in Latin America, played much the same role as domestic surpluses and strategic reserves in stabilizing prices. The underdeveloped countries provided effectively unlimited supplies of basic commodities ranging from sugar to oil, which were available on call to the American market at their prevailing prices. Because these countries were poor, they had to spend virtually all of their export earnings to cover the cost of imports; and their political and economic ties to the United States meant that the export earnings followed the exports to North America. Thus, the subordinate position of the commodity exporters in the world economy not only helped prevent price shocks in the U.S. markets, but also contributed to raising the level of aggregate demand there.

Finally, as we will see in the next chapter, the dominant position of the United States in the postwar trading system enabled it to run a long-term trade deficit without devaluing its currency and thereby raising the price of imported goods. In this way, yet another potential disruption of the domestic price system was for a long time neutralized.

THE GOVERNMENT'S ROLE

The function of the wage-determination system in sustaining purchasing power was supplemented by changes in governmental activity. Especially after World War II, the federal government played a triple role in the economy, a role that was both quantitatively and qualitatively different from the roles it had played before.

First, government expenditures as a percentage of total economic activity increased enormously. The proportion of gross national product consumed by government expenditures was 3 percent in 1929, but in the post–Korean War decade (1954–64) it averaged 18 percent, and in the post–Vietnam War decade (1972–82), 22 percent. Table 4.1 indicates that the rise in this percentage is significant regardless of the year used as a base for comparison.

Military expenditures associated with the cold war account, of course, for a large share of this increase in state activity. Military outlays rose

TABLE 4.1

Federal Expenditures as a Percentage of Gross National Product, 1920–1982

Year	Gross National Product ($ B)	Federal Government Total ($ B)	Expenditures: % of GNP
1920	69.6	5.1	7.3
1925	93.1	2.9	3.1
1929	103.1	3.1	3.0
1930	90.4	3.3	3.7
1935	72.2	6.5	9.0
1940	99.7	9.6	9.6
1945	211.9	95.2	29.6
1950	284.8	43.1	15.1
1955	398.0	68.5	17.2
1960	503.7	92.2	18.5
1965	691.1	118.4	17.1
1970	992.7	196.6	19.8
1975	1,549.2	324.2	20.9
1980	2,633.1	576.7	21.9
1982	3,057.5	728.4	23.8

SOURCE: United States Bureau of the Census, *The Statistical History of the United States: From Colonial Times to Present,* Series Y (New York: Basic Books, 1976), pp. 457–65.

from 2.1 percent of GNP in 1929 to 12.5 percent between 1955 and 1965; the average for the whole postwar period is even higher.[15] On the one hand, the growth of military spending increased the stability of the private economy by removing a large portion of economic activity from the direct control of what remained of competitive markets; on the other hand, military expenditures were themselves volatile, fluctuating widely in response to the events of the cold war—their net effect on the economy is thus hard to assess. Although influential government officials in the 1950s stressed the potentially stabilizing effect of military spending on employment (as in the famous National Security Council Memorandum Number 68, of 1950), a massive military budget was hardly a necessary precondition of macroeconomic stability—other countries were able to obtain comparable results without spending proportionally as much on armed services as the Americans.

The remainder of the increase in government spending went to the social-welfare programs of various kinds. Here there was a double effect. First, another significant portion of effective demand was rendered independent of variations in private activity, further raising the minimum level to which economic activity could fall. Second, most social-welfare spending was countercyclical and thus automatically compensated for recessionary declines and expansionary booms in private spending.

The reorganization of American living space reflected and reinforced those processes. Government policies promoting the construction of housing and highways spurred the suburbanization of the population. In the 1930s, Congress encouraged the growth of the house-ownership market by creating such institutions as the Federal Housing Administration and the Federal National Mortgage Association. The federal government also financed 90 percent of the costs of the interstate freeway system.[16] These policies directly stimulated the construction industry, and simultaneously boosted demand for cars and for a wide range of consumer durables, appliances, and other household commodities.

The last and most celebrated change in government activity associated with the welfare state was the adoption of Keynesian countercyclical fiscal and monetary policy. The state became committed to dampening fluctuations in aggregate demand by varying interest and tax rates to encourage or discourage investment and consumption, and so to offset forecast variations in private spending. If monetary and fiscal policy seemed unlikely to smooth the business cycle sufficiently, the state could resort to increasing or decreasing its own expenditures. Democratic presidents and their advisers were more explicit and dedicated to this commitment to intervene in the economy than were Republicans. But, as the Eisenhower administration's response to the recession of 1954 showed, even conservative administrations that disavowed association with Keynesianism were prepared to accept periodic budget deficits in order to assure the long-term growth of the economy. This abandonment of a commitment to balance the budget in each and every year was for many business conservatives a "fiscal revolution." It cleared the way for postwar "commercial Keynesianism," with its emphasis on perhaps the least intrusive of the available forms of state intervention in the economy: monetary policy.[17]

American Macroregulation as a Historical Construction

A description of the postwar macroeconomic organization as a coherent system suggests that the institutional system was a conscious creation: a deliberate response to the diagnosis of the Depression as we outlined it at the beginning of the chapter, put in place as a rational whole. This is, however, a misleading view, not only of how the society responded to the crisis of the 1930s, but also, more generally, of the relation between a crisis of an institutional order and the reforms through which it is (or is not) resolved. As we saw in the case of the creation of the corporation, general problems are solved only through experiments that always yield an indissoluble compound of the structurally necessary and historically contingent. There are *only* particular answers to the general problems posed by any set of fixed background conditions; in other words, any given success story might have turned out somewhat differently from the way it did. As we saw with the corporation, the historical reconstruction of institutions—entities that seem to be defined by the exigencies of the system they form—typically reveal possibilities for varying some of their parts. A comparison of different systems responding to the same problem often shows the foregone possibilities of one to be the reality of another.

A backward glance reveals the jerry-rigged character of the American solution to the problem of macroeconomic regulation, a character that was obscured by our initial exposition. Many features of the postwar macroeconomic organization, it is true, are embodied in pieces of legislation and court decision. But the legal framework is best understood as the residue of successive uncoordinated programs of vast social experimentation undertaken in the Depression years—programs partially or radically modified by shifts in the unsteady balance of political power and by the historical idiosyncrasies of an American state that gave opponents of reform extraordinary powers of disruption. The remnants, moreover, of these diverse and unpredictably transformed experiments fused into a single, more or less coherent institutional structure only during and immediately after World War II—long after the initial legislation had occurred[18] Finally, crucial elements of the new system, especially in the area of industrial relations, emerged as unwritten practices in the shadow of the ramshackle legal structure. It is hard to discover the workings of conscious design in habits of thought that escaped definition, if they were perceived at all.

The first and in many ways boldest of these programs of reform was defined by the National Industrial Recovery and Agricultural Adjustment Acts, both passed during the famous hundred days after President Roosevelt's inauguration in 1933—the high noon of what historians later called the first New Deal. Although the bills were subtly different in inspiration, both were seen as part of what Arthur Schlesinger calls an effort at "affirmative national planning," whose ultimate aim was to "rebuild America through the reconstruction of economic institutions in accordance with technological imperatives."[19] Neither survived its original form, but their ruins became the most important parts of the legislative foundation of the postwar system.[20]

The Agricultural Adjustment Act (AAA) was by far the more successful of the two efforts. It was premised on the view that overproduction was the chief problem of the economy in general and of the farm sector in particular. Its aim was to raise the ratio of the prices of agricultural products to those of industrial goods back to the level that had prevailed during the pre–World War I period of agricultural prosperity. Substantial progress toward this goal was rapidly made through a system of production controls and commodity stockpiles administered within the established, extremely well informed United States Department of Agriculture in collaboration with committees of local farmers and regional farmers' associations. Although the AAA was declared unconstitutional by the Supreme Court in 1936, it was quickly reconstructed along its original lines and its successors were able to reduce fluctuations of agricultural prices to levels that facilitated the larger program of macroeconomic stabilization.[21]

The National Industrial Recovery Act (NIRA) fared much less well in practice; and it too was ultimately a victim of the conservative Supreme Court. To its most sophisticated architects and supporters, the NIRA was a way of solving what they saw as the twin problems of overproduction and underconsumption through a radical extension of the principles of economic stabilization that had been developing in the American economy since the late nineteenth century. The act provided for industry committees that were empowered to promulgate "codes of fair competition," which would control prices, wages, and conditions of production in their own markets. Firms were thus encouraged to stabilize their market shares by forming pools or trusts of the kind that had served as way stations on the road to the mass-production economy. But at the same time, the law aimed to limit a decline in—and to eventually increase—the purchasing power of workers, both by requiring the codes to establish minimum wages and maximum workweeks, and, more important, by guaranteeing the right of labor to "organize and bargain collectively through representatives of its own choosing." The high-wage, regular-employment policies with which many large firms had begun to experiment in the 1920s were to be reinforced and generalized, albeit indirectly, through government support for unions; the unions would then presumably force all employers to do what some had done unilaterally.[22]

But this vision of industrial reorganization presupposes both a consensus between capital and labor and a capacity for self-coordination among capitalists, which simply did not exist. Only a small group of businessmen and intellectual technicians held the elegant conception of the NIRA as a way out of the Keynesian underconsumption trap through self-organization of the economy, rather than state spending for public works (relegated to Title 2 and viewed more as poor relief than as demand stimulation). This small group included Charles Frederick Roos, director of research at the National Recovery Administration (the NRA, established under the NIRA), and Gerard Swope, head of General Electric—they were close to the centers of power, yet hardly able to impose their will on events. Outside this circle, the NIRA was viewed differently and less systematically: politicians, especially the president, saw it as a desperate effort to try all plausible economic remedies in the hopes that one or some combination of them would work. Capital and labor each saw it as a license to pursue their separate pre-Depression strategies, often at the expense of the other.

For industry, the attraction of the law was the freedom it granted to fix prices and eliminate underbidding; few managers, including many who saw the need for generally high wages, were willing to recognize unions. Labor, meanwhile, saw government protection of organization primarily as a chance to regain the influence in national affairs that it had held under federal aegis in World War I. (This was a plausible enough hope, given that the administration itself compared the efforts at economic recovery to wartime mobilization, and that the head of the NRA was General Hugh Johnson, who had played an important role in coordinating the mobilization of the civilian economy during World War I.) No wonder, then, that by 1935 the two prospective parties to a regime of collaborative planning were at each other's throats.

Finally, even where business had its way, it was unable to establish effective pooling arrangements, for many of the reasons already familiar from the story of the corporation. As the history of the cotton-textile industry in this period shows, production could not be stabilized unless information about market developments and decisions about capacity utilization were centralized: centralized in a way that, at best, destroyed the autonomy of individual firms, and at worst exposed the industry as a whole to comprehensive government regulation.[23] Had trade unions been better established at that time, businessmen differently organized, and the government as well equipped to deal with the problems of industry as it was with agriculture, all these conflicts might have been resolved and a "business commonwealth" established. But it is clear that when the Supreme Court declared the NIRA unconstitutional (in the Schechter Poultry Corporation case of 1935), it toppled an extremely unstable structure.

But this failed effort to promote cooperative industrial recovery produced, among its fragments, two central pieces of the postwar system of wage determination. The first was the Wagner Act, which reasserted and extended the protection of organization and the duty to bargain collectively, as defined in Section 7(a) of the NIRA. The second was the Fair Labor Standards Act, of 1938, which prescribed minimum wages, required premium pay for overtime, and defined permissible uses of child labor; it was an outgrowth of the early attempt to regulate work conditions on an industry basis. That these remnants of the NIRA survived challenges to their constitutionality was due partly to a clarification of the later statutory language, but mostly to a shift in the Supreme Court's canons of judgment. The court modified its standards in the sphere of economic regulation in response not only to political pressure but also to popular sentiment, which—as the Depression wore on—increasingly favored state action to counter economic distress. The Wagner Act was tested in a different legal world from that of the NIRA.

The second wave of reform with important consequences for the postwar macroregulatory system concerned social-welfare legislation: legislation that provided insurance for the old, the unemployed, the disabled, and the mothers of dependent children. Here the historical gap between legislative intent and ultimate practice was even greater than the one separating the designs of the first New Deal from its eventual application. Whereas the principal architects of the NIRA had addressed the problem of raising effective demand (though not as the Keynesians suggested), Roosevelt and those he appointed to draft the Social Security Act, of 1935, were determined to secure a bill that would give relief to the needy and provide a convenient form of insurance to the working classes, yet which could not be used as a mechanism for redistributing wealth in favor of consumers.[24]

There were a number of schemes that saw such insurance as a way out of the underconsumption trap (the widely discussed Townsend Plan called for payment of 200 dollars per month to each retired person over sixty, provided the recipient spent the money during the same month, to speed economic recovery). But Roosevelt drew his inspiration from the Progressive Party's ideas of social welfare, pioneered in Wisconsin and New York. The Progressive view of social security was as a form of obligatory self-insurance, rather than as a collective recognition of each citizen's right to a subsistence income, or as an instrument of economic policy. It had complex roots in the reaction of nineteenth-century advocates of "good" government against the expansive uses to which the system of old-age pensions for Civil War veterans had been put. It was the distant shadow cast by these earlier disputes—rather than the equally distant gleam of a stable economy of the future—that caught the government's eye in this matter. In fact, the Social Security Act's immediate effect was to diminish demand—since it taxed payrolls, beginning in 1937, for an insurance pool that would not start to disperse equivalent amounts in benefits for decades.

The third wave of reform is associated with the large expenditures for public works in 1937–38. These measures came to define the second New Deal, which runs by historical convention from 1935 to 1940. If the aim of the first New Deal was to replace the market, the aim of the second was to regulate it. The second New Deal was both more and less radical than the first: less radical because it accepted the idea of a competitive economy as fundamental, more radical because it declared the necessity of periodic government intervention in that economy, in a way that the NIRA, for all its etatist potential, did not.[25]

Roosevelt's acceptance of Keynesian arguments in the face of the economic slump of 1937 (industrial production fell by one third with respect to the preceding year) and Congressional approval of a 6.5-billion-dollar spending program were only the beginning of a long battle that ended with the emergence of the commercial Keynesianism of the postwar period.[26] Southern conservatives intolerant of federal spending that would disrupt their control of local patronage; businessmen worried by the idea of unending budget deficits; farmers already well served by the new system of price supports and unwilling to spend tax dollars on programs for industrial workers—all these groups combined in opposition to the second New Deal. Allying themselves in various ways from the late 1930s through the early 1950s, these groups attempted to limit the application of Keynesian ideas to the fiscal and monetary measures— supplemented in dire circumstances by an increase in direct public spending—that in the postwar period became the substance of the state's discretionary macroeconomic policy.

Ironically, however, the same alliances of interest groups that formed to reduce the state's capacity to stabilize the economy also shaped the social-welfare and labor-standards legislation in ways that created labor reserves essential to the institutional equilibration of demand and productive capacity. There was simply no majority in the United States Congress for either social-security or minimum-wage legislation unless workers in agriculture and a large portion of small business were exempted from coverage. Defense of the status quo in these sectors thus created an essential precondition for drastic changes in wage determination in manufacturing (even though no one at the time seemed to realize the connection in theory between innovation and conservation).

By themselves, however, these legislative building blocks did not constitute a coherent system of regulation. Their fusion into an integrated whole depended on the rise of mass industrial unionism: a social movement encouraged by, yet not reducible to, the changes in the legal order. The chief expression of the new labor militancy was a series of factory occupations, beginning in the Akron, Ohio, rubber industry in 1935 and spreading rapidly during the following year to automobile plants in the Midwest.[27]

For those who lived through it, the period verged on anarchy. The major corporations initially resisted the occupations as a usurpation of their property and held out against the unions. But they ultimately retreated as they came to see the situation as a choice between concessions and open revolution, and so they recognized and bargained with various worker organizations. A turning point in the relations between the corporations and the labor movement was marked, in the spring of 1937, by General Motors' recognition of the UAW and U.S. Steel's recognition of the Steel Workers Organizing Committee. The legal obligation of collective bargaining imposed by the Wagner Act (and the validation of the act by the Supreme Court in 1937) provided corporations that were holding out—including the smaller steel companies and Ford—with a face-saving pretext for acknowledging the unions' right to exist in their plants. But even in the companies that based their acceptance of the unions on the New Deal legislation, the new law did not dictate either the form or the substance of the unions.

The sit-down strikes of the mid-1930s transformed not only labor-management relations, but also the labor movement itself. Before 1935, American labor had been organized in craft unions and dominated by the American Federation of Labor. Experience dictated that only craft unions could survive in American industry, so the AFL strongly resisted attempts to organize unskilled workers or to combine workers in a single industry into unions that crossed craft lines. In response to the industrial militancy of the 1930s, the AFL leadership organized blocks of the new members, and then broke these blocks down into separate craft units, each affiliated with an appropriate national craft union. This strategy was opposed by younger organizers within the AFL and by the workers themselves; the consequent disputes over organizing strategy finally led to a split within the AFL and the formation in 1936 of the rival Congress of Industrial Organizations (CIO). In the event, of course, the industrial-union structure proved so successful in attracting and holding members that the AFL quickly abandoned its commitment to craft unionism. By 1937 the whole labor movement had shifted to organizing within the new industrial format.

Although the major industrial unions that would dominate industrial relations in the postwar period were organized outside the Wagner Act, they played a critical part in the way the law ultimately functioned. These unions provided money and dedicated manpower to help in the organization of other workers under the act's election procedures; their example powerfully advertised unionism giving many workers the courage to vote against management in representational elections. Moreover, the successes of the new unions kept the image of near anarchy before the employers' eyes, forcing industrialists, at least in the North, to meet their legal obligations in collective bargaining. Finally—and ironically, given that the act was passed with craft unions in mind—it was the practices of the new industrial unions, as emblemized in the 1948 GM-UAW agreement, that came to define collective bargaining as understood by the National Labor Relations Board and the courts.

Many writers in the American radical tradition have interpreted those practices as the expression of an "accord" between labor and management.[28] But the notion of an accord is misleading: it is misleading either if taken in the strong sense of a peace treaty setting out the rights and responsibilities of each party or if taken in the weak sense of a cease-fire freezing the positions obtained during past battles and subject to violation whenever the balance of forces changes. There was neither a peace treaty nor a cease-fire; rather, there was a shared set of understandings about the continuation of the struggle. Within the unions, these understandings seem to have been as much the product of a spontaneous, un-self-conscious evolution as they were of the original organizing drives.[29]

The initial recognition of the unions in 1937 was only the first step in the establishment of the postwar industrial-relations system: it was a big step up in the long history of ups and downs of American industrial unionism. Historically, employers have accepted worker organization during periods of prosperity and worker militancy (which typically, though not always, coincided), when the cost of industrial warfare was high; they then repudiated this acceptance when the balance of power shifted back in their favor. It thus appeared in the late 1930s as if the rise of the unions and the collective bargaining they forced on employers might be merely a temporary victory for labor in a continuing war.

Nor did labor, moreover, have a clear strategy of collective bargaining in the late 1930s. It is now conventional in historical writing to distinguish those labor leaders who accepted the existing system and saw collective bargaining as a means for improving labor's position within it from those labor leaders who saw worker organization as a means of changing the very system of property relations. But this view projects onto the past a distinction that emerged only as individual labor leaders—unsure of what they wanted and of what was possible in the chaos of the times—placed their bets on the course of future developments. For example, the Depression transformed John L. Lewis from an autocrat willing to let his union dwindle so long as he held the power into an autocrat willing to gamble everything on the success of the early organizing drives. And defeat in a critical strike against General Motors transformed Walter Reuther of the UAW from a labor statesman ambitious to control the investment and pricing decisions of automobile firms to a labor statesman willing to acknowledge a sphere of management rights. Collective bargaining became what it became by the same process in which the labor leaders evolved.

The Depression had called into question the viability of capitalism, and the possibility of basic change was widely debated both inside and outside the labor movement. The government had experimented with such change in the National Industrial Recovery Act. The established labor unions had little experience with industrial collective bargaining— the old American Federation of Labor remained opposed to it until it was a fait accompli. Nothing was settled: not the unions' attitude toward the industrial giants, nor the procedures of collective bargaining, nor the range of permissible weapons, nor even the range of admissible demands and topics of discussion.

The sit-down strike was symbolic. This was an apparently indispensable weapon in the initial campaign of industrial organization, but its legitimacy was suspect from the start; and ultimately it was rejected, not only by the Supreme Court (which declared it illegal in 1939), but also by those who had pioneered it and who owed their positions to its success. The place of industrial unionism in American society was similarly transformed. The emergence of industrial unions in the 1930s represented such a radical break with the past that it could be seen as a rejection of capitalism and a major first step toward an alternative. If in the postwar period industrial unionism proved compatible with capitalism, it was because of the way it had been shaped by events since its emergence—the most critical being World War II.

During the war, industrial relations were monitored by war-production boards, which were appointed by the government and composed of representatives of the unions, management, and the public. The purpose of these tripartite boards was to foster production through the preservation of industrial peace. To this end, they sought to maintain an equitable system of compensation and work practices—often by imposing their conditions on both management and labor—without impairing an enterprise's productivity. The boards played a crucial role in generalizing the idea of binding arbitration (introduced, from the needle trades, to the mass-production industries by the UAW-GM contract of 1940) and of the stepped-grievance procedure.[30]

The wartime experience also taught a generation of business executives, labor leaders, and "neutral" arbitrators to accept one another, as well as to reconcile equitable industrial relations with the demands of economic efficiency. Their collaboration exemplified a system of industrial relations that presupposed yet circumscribed conflict, by focusing on the development of a "rational" structure of wages, salaries, and job definitions, as against other kinds of worker demands. Thus, the new unions entered the war period without a clear model of collective bargaining, and the war experience provided them with the crucial elements for building such a model.

Although the details of the war-production-board system are more pertinent to the theme of shop-floor control (taken up in the next chapter) than to this discussion of macroeconomic organization, it is important to explain here how the postwar synthesis of this system became rule-driven: dependent on rule making and rule enforcement, rather than on a direct contest for power. Under the production pressure imposed by the war, these boards developed a theory of the division of labor between union and management. The role of management was to assume responsibility for production; an extension of that responsibility was the freedom to organize the production process, including the disposition of labor, as management saw fit. Management's conduct in this regard was circumscribed by a set of rules and customs established and enforced through collective bargaining. The role of the union was, first, to negotiate the rules, and, second, to monitor the employer's compliance.

With strikes and lockouts illegal, the boards pushed the parties to adopt wage-determination formulae that would make contract negotiations less contentious and to use grievance and arbitration machinery to eliminate the need for militant action during the terms of collectively bargained agreements. In return for their pledge to forswear strikes and discourage wildcat walkouts, the unions received the right to collect dues through automatic payroll deductions, called checkoffs. Issues of ideology were in this way reduced to disagreements about the formulation and application of specific rules. Thus, each party could discuss and eventually agree on the rules without abandoning its global interpretation of long-term developments and possible strategies.

The wartime production and political pressures also led to blurring of the line between labor and management rights. In 1942, for example, the War Production Board urged joint management-labor committees at the plant level, as part of the effort to increase productivity. Such committees were formed most frequently in firms in the steel, engineering, and electrical-equipment industries, which had experience with the works councils discussed in the next chapter. Although the main activity of the new consultative bodies consisted in posting suggestion boxes, many labor leaders saw these committees as a first step toward establishing the workers' influence over the shop and the unions' right to information about significant plant decisions. Thus, Clint Golden, of the steel workers—an influential CIO advocate of collaboration with management—could write in 1944:

Labor in the post–war world expects to sit down with management and government to work out the estimated levels of production by private enterprise. It expects to participate in the establishment of industry-wide councils to promote the fullest use of our major productive resources, technology, and know-how. It expects an equal place on a national economic council.[31]

Furthermore—quite apart from the state's advocacy of cooperative industrial relations—labor's shop-floor control was increased by economic conditions. Companies operating under cost-plus contracts (which guarantee producers profits equal to an agreed percentage of their actual costs of production) were more attentive to the quantity of output than to its unit cost; workers, in short supply, could set their own pace; foremen, often newly promoted off the shop floor and sympathetic to the new unions, were unwilling to impose stiff discipline. The result was that in some companies—Packard and Allis-Chalmers are prominent examples—production decisions were arrived at through consultation between foremen and union shop stewards, and the distinction between management's right to act and the union's right to challenge actions was irrelevant: "If any manager in this industry tells you he is in control of his plant," one automobile executive told an interviewer, "he is a damn liar."[32] At the end of the war, it was unclear whether wartime theory or wartime practice would shape postwar industrial relations.

A series of strikes in 1945–46—of which the most important was the UAW strike against GM—settled the issue in favor of a restrictive interpretation of labor's rights. The UAW demanded a 30-percent wage increase, as a means of protecting purchasing power in time of reduced working hours and rising inflation; a freeze on GM's price increases, justified on related grounds; additional guarantees of the union's security as an organization; and an increase in the union's control over work organization, including abolition of piecework and bonus systems, stricter seniority rules to govern intra-firm labor mobility, an end to management's unilateral power to set production standards, and an increase in the numbers and powers of the union's committee members. The UAW thought it could rouse the country against the giant, profitable company—it reckoned that GM would not dare take the risk of letting its competitors gain an advantage in the race to supply the coming boom market for cars. But as the election of the conservative Eightieth Congress in 1946 showed, the country wanted peace and quiet; and the erratic supply of automobile parts in the early postwar months meant that no one could retool for the coming boom. The UAW lost. Defeat put an end to all vague hopes for a cooperatively managed economy. And it set the stage for the model 1948 agreement regularizing relations between the union and the company. In short, defeat for the UAW meant victory for the war boards' official interpretation of the role of labor and management, and for its determination to limit strikes through wage formulae and grievance procedures.[33]

The formula for the 1948 UAW-GM contract originated with Charles Wilson, president of GM; he arrived at it during a stay in the hospital that freed him to ponder the labor problems that were promising to be the chief postwar obstacles to company expansion. His principal motive was to assure the stability of production. The details of the formula were in some ways less important to him than its acceptability to labor—since increases in efficiency depended on a stable environment, labor's agreement to obey well-specified rules would be valuable in itself. But the specific provisions of Wilson's formula were, not surprisingly, appealing to GM in that they obliged the company merely to do something that had proved historically easy: to keep pace with the national increases in the level of productivity and prices. The alternative of linking wages to either auto prices or auto productivity must have occurred to GM and been rejected, as inadmissibly postulating the union's right to inspect company data on production costs.

Why the head of the UAW, Walter Reuther, accepted this formula is less clear. The defeat in 1946 must have been a major cause: a formula that guaranteed wage increases, in combination with various clauses indicating the company's willingness to tolerate the union (as, for example, by not testing its right under the new Taft-Hartley Act to make the UAW liable for damages caused by its members' wildcat strikes) must have seemed more welcome than the prospect of continual conflict. The removal of wage determination as an issue, moreover, left the UAW free in subsequent negotiations to seek health insurance and the guaranteed annual income—the welfare-state reforms that it had to obtain at the sectoral level, because it lacked the political power to enact them nationally. Both parties, in any case, seem to have been vaguely aware of the implications of such formulae for the maintenance of aggregate purchasing power. This awareness may have helped make the formula seem equitable and enhanced its aura of legitimacy, but there is no evidence that such considerations moved them to agree.

The way in which the UAW-GM formula was extended throughout the economy can also be attributed to the desire to find rules and formulae that would resolve disputes arising in the negotiation of the agreements. Pattern bargaining, the role of private-sector wages as a reference point for the public sector, the periodic readjustment of the minimum wage in response to movements in supra-minimum wages, and the like—all are examples of such formulae.

The False Dichotomy of Monetarism and Keynesianism

The history of economic institutions in the 1930s and '40s suggests that the postwar structure of macroeconomic stabilization fell into place. Only as the shape of major pieces of the structure was determined, by the vagaries of politics, did it become possible to divine the shape of complementary, supporting elements. If the final result was no accident, in that it meshed with the microeconomic institutions of the corporation, neither was it the product of a design.

Probably for that reason macroeconomic stabilization was not well understood as a systematic whole by those charged with its daily operation. Perhaps because it lacked institutional integrity (what could social security have in common with the agricultural-price-supports system?), the American system of stabilization existed in fact but not in theory. There were no figures corresponding to Ford or Sloan, practitioners theorizing about the practice from the inside. Perhaps, if either of the New Deal reform programs based on underconsumptionist ideas—the NIRA or the spending program of 1937—had survived whole, such figures would have emerged as bearers of an institutional under-standing at once abstract and concrete, scientific and political. Certainly this is what happened in countries such as Sweden, where Keynesian principles were adopted as part of a national agreement (the famous "Cow Deal," of 1933) to boost simultaneously the purchasing power of farmers and of workers.[34]

But whatever the reason, there was no American equivalent of the Swedish minister of finance, Ernst Wigfoss; and the task of producing a theoretical understanding of macroeconomic stabilization in the United

103

States fell to two contending and still-current schools of university economics: the Keynesians and the monetarists. The absorption of each with the defects of the other and the detachment of both from the institutional mechanisms of allocation made it impossible for either to understand the process of stabilization.

The Keynesians view the economy as inherently unstable: wage rigidities render precarious any balance between aggregate demand and national productive capacity, and discretionary government monetary and fiscal policy is required to maintain long-term stability. In the monetarist view, the private economy, left (almost) to itself, would be optimally regulated by neoclassical wage and price adjustment; the observed instability is the result of precisely the kinds of discretionary government actions that the Keynesians advocate. To eliminate the instability, the monetarists favor withdrawing the government from many of the economic activities in which it is engaged, limiting its role to those areas where rigorous proof demonstrates that the market cannot regulate itself (a classic example is the control of the money supply, which monetarist authorities would exercise subject to strict rules). But despite their opposition, the two schools do agree on the undesirability of interference with the price system in individual markets. Both condemn the minimum wage, agricultural price supports, and the commodity stockpiles, and both favor a strong antitrust policy.

The discussion of macroregulatory institutions in this chapter suggests that neither school is right; or, more precisely, that each is correct in the criticism of the other but both are wrong in their understanding of how the economy actually works. As we have seen, the private economy has been self-stabilizing, as the monetarists maintain; but, as the Keynesians assert, prices and wages are too rigid to serve as the stabilizing mechanism. During the prosperity of the 1950s and '60s, stability was produced by the institutions of wage determination embedded in the private economy, and wage and price rigidities were the by-product of those institutions. The minimum wage, agricultural price supports, and the other "imperfections" that both schools deplored propped up a system in which relative wages and prices were not free to allocate resources in individual markets. As we shall see in subsequent chapters, the failure of these props—and not a hidden flaw in one school and unsuspected truth in the other—are in large measure responsible for the crisis of the last decade.

CHAPTER

5

The Global and the Microscopic

THE LAST THREE chapters have presented the history of the American economy as a chain of discoveries about the central properties of a mass-production–mass-consumption technology. These properties are: its technological trajectory; its need to stabilize individual markets through microregulatory institutions, such as the corporation; and its need to match aggregate demand to productive capacity, by coordinating the stabilization of individual markets through macroregulatory institutions such as the wage-determination system. The American innovations in this progression of economic activity were colored by local circumstance; nonetheless, they served, as we shall see, as a model for increasingly successful, if inaccurate, foreign emulation. And Americans admired in themselves what foreigners admired in them. The assembly line, the corporation, and the loose, conflictual, yet cooperative relations among big business, big labor, and the Keynesian state made up the epitome of the modern industrial economy that the United States had proudly pioneered.

There were, however, two critical aspects of American economic organization that remained largely invisible to domestic observers and all but inimitable for foreign ones. The first of these neglected aspects of economic organization was the U.S. position in the international system of trade. In the years after World War II, the United States established a regime of international commerce that, intentionally or not, limited American freedom of action less than that of other nations in the global economy. To most Americans—for whom world markets were in any case an invisible adjunct to domestic economic activity—this was an irrelevant technical fact. But to America's foreign competitors, it appeared, at least for a time, as an almost inevitable precondition of the reconstitution of world trade—a kind of globally enveloping economic atmosphere.

The second neglected aspect of the American economy was the organization of relations between labor and management in the smallest unit of the productive structure, the work place. If the U.S. position in the world-trade order escaped attention because Americans ignored it as remote and foreigners took it for granted, American shop-floor relations were disregarded for just the opposite reasons. To foreign eyes, the complexities of the American common law of the shop were too remote, too rooted in national political, judicial, and trade-union experience, to seem universally applicable—unlike American machines, corporate-organization charts, and textbooks on macroeconomics. And to Americans, domestic industrial-relations practices were unremarkable because they were omnipresent—shrouded by the oblivion of everyday experience, so as to be an indistinguishable part of the larger institutional background to economic life.

In the early postwar decades, neither the U.S. role in international commerce nor the distribution of authority on the shop floor seemed directly connected to national prosperity. Only in the past few years of crisis has the relation of these two factors to the core of the American mass-production system—and their part in shaping its response to change—come to light. Because of this connection, we will complete our characterization of U.S. industrial organization by examining, in this chapter, its operation at the global and the microscopic level. Despite their difference in scale, we will discover that in these two realms—no less than in the others thus far surveyed—political struggles produced rules that limited the freedom of even those who thought they had imposed their will on events.

The Global: The American Role in International Trade

The system regulating international trade in the postwar world was created in reaction to the two major strategies that the world's industrial powers had pursued since the breakdown of world markets as of 1929.[1] The first of these strategies was a beggar-thy-neighbor policy: by breaking with the longstanding regime of fixed exchange rates, and devaluing the national currency while simultaneously raising tariffs, each power had hoped to increase its share of world trade while reducing its expenditure on imports.

The second strategy aimed at securing national autarky: economic self-sufficiency, independent of the increasingly chaotic international economic order. This strategy was pursued partly by restricting the exchange of national for foreign currencies, to ensure that domestic restabilization policy would not be held hostage to conditions in foreign financial markets. When the British government, for example, reduced interest rates to encourage domestic investment, it also blocked the flight of capital to countries offering a higher rate of return. A complementary policy was to enter into bilateral trade agreements. These were, in effect, barter arrangements in which two nations exchanged a combination of goods deemed of equal value; thus trade between them, by definition, was always in balance, eliminating the danger that one could not cover a deficit with the other for want of a profitable exchange with a third party—such an exchange was typically necessary in open, or multilateral, trade.

These policies had helped to spread the Depression from one country to another and had greatly aggravated the overall decline—on this there was general agreement (despite serious individual differences) among the small groups of British and American government officials, university economists, and bankers who laid the foundations for the postwar trade order at Bretton Woods, New Hampshire, in 1944. Their aim, therefore, was to design an open trading system, which would encourage expansion of international commerce by blocking competitive devaluation and attempts at national autarky. The principles of the new system were set out in 1946 in the Articles of Agreement, which created the International Monetary Fund (IMF), a kind of supra-national bank. Other negotiations beginning in that year led to the General Agreement on Trade and Tariffs (GATT), which created a forum for the negotiation of tariff reductions and trade rules.[2]

THE INTERNATIONAL MONETARY FUND

The key elements of what came to be called the Bretton Woods system were de-facto fixed exchange rates and the free convertibility of one currency to another. To join the IMF, a country had to forswear discriminatory currency practices and peg the value of its currency to gold or the U.S. dollar (which, in continuation with prewar practice, was convertible to gold at the rate of thirty-five dollars an ounce); the country's central bank was obliged to defend this par value in actual trading by buying the national currency with foreign currencies (in practice dollars) at a price not more than one percent above or below the pegged rate of exchange. Member nations were allowed to re- or devalue their currency, but only—in the language of the Articles of Agreement—"to correct a fundamental disequilibrium," and "after consultation with the Fund." At its discretion, the IMF could lend its own reserves of foreign currencies to central banks that were unable to defend par values on their own.

How much this return to the prewar system of fixed exchange rates would restrict member nations in setting domestic economic policy depended on the amount of the Fund's reserves and how it would use its discretionary powers; and it was in this connection that controversy emerged among the architects of the Bretton Woods system. Under a fixed-rate exchange system, the chief means of balancing export income and import expenses is adjustment of the domestic price level; this adjustment in turn affects the level of domestic economic activity. If, for example, imports exceed exports, a reduction of the domestic price level relative to foreign price levels can balance trade by making national products cheaper in world markets and increasing the cost of foreign goods. But unless a country takes the politically difficult route of wage and price controls, it can reduce its domestic price level only by raising interest rates to choke off consumption and investment. The crucial question under the fixed-rate system is how quickly deflation then occurs. The greater a country's reserves of foreign currency or the easier the terms on which foreign reserves can be borrowed, the longer the country with a trade deficit can defend the par value of its currency— postponing restrictive measures and giving domestic industry a chance to cut costs through reorganization. The IMF's capacity and willingness to provide buffer stocks of money to countries with deficits would therefore be a crucial determinant of domestic policymakers' freedom to pursue expansionary, full-employment policies.

Opinions on the IMF's role as a supra-national lender of last resort not only divided the British from the Americans, it also created factions within the American government. The British, foreseeing the possibility that their country would show a long-term deficit, wanted to provide the Fund with a generous pool of resources, available on easy terms, and to oblige countries with persistent trade surpluses to revalue their currency. They were supported, at least in the first part of their proposal, by American officials who either feared the political consequences of a return to Depression-level foreign unemployment, or simply wanted to ensure markets for the vastly increased exports of the giant American economy that had emerged from World War II. On the other side were American officials and bankers who wanted to defend the United States' interests as the world's largest creditor, by denying debtor nations the chance to continually postpone settlement of accounts through appeal to the Fund.

The creditors' faction won out. The Fund was provided with such meager reserves that it had to be exiguous in its dealings with deficit-ridden members. In the short run, the problem of financing the American export surplus and laying the foundation for a European reentry into world markets was solved by two measures: the four-year Marshall Plan loan of 17 billion dollars, beginning in 1948, and the inducement, in the late 1940s, of the European countries to set par values for their currencies so low that their exports would attract American customers. In the long run, members of the Fund were on a short tether—with the exception of the United States.

The unique position of the United States had two causes; one cause was temporary, in that it was linked to the extraordinary circumstances of World War II, and the other cause was more enduring and structural, in that it was linked to the role of the dollar in the Bretton Woods system. The temporary cause of the United States' freedom from international monetary constraint was simply the good fortune that had allowed the American economy, alone among the industrial powers, to survive the war intact. All other nations were thus dependent on American products for their postwar reconstruction. The result was an enormous U.S. balance-of-trade surplus and a corresponding demand for dollars, which together made the Fund's operations irrelevant to American domestic policy.

This early U.S. trade surplus was, however, self-limiting. As American efforts to encourage reconstruction succeeded, other countries became less dependent on U.S. supplies and they entered world markets as competitors. By the late 1950s, the American surplus had been virtually eliminated.[3] Nevertheless, American macroeconomic policy even then was not subjected to the deflationary discipline automatically applied to other nations.

The structural cause of the United States' freedom from international monetary constraint was the dollar's role as the medium of international exchange. Other countries held reserves in dollars and balanced accounts among themselves with dollar payments. The reason they did this was the dollar's convertibility to gold: by the end of World War II, most of the world's gold reserves had accumulated at Fort Knox, so there was a long period in which the dollar really was as good as gold, despite the absence of any legal convention formally regulating convertibility.

Ultimately, of course, the dollar's role as a medium of international exchange and as a source of liquidity also proved self-limiting. As the U.S. deficit accumulated, some countries' central banks became sufficiently concerned about the security of their holdings to sell dollars or to trade them for gold; their actions induced others to follow suit. But until that happened (under conditions that we will examine later), the international monetary regime simply validated the results of the American system of macroregulation through collective bargaining.

The application of the GM-UAW formula had raised wages at a rate above the rate of productivity increase, causing the general price level to rise slightly, for reasons discussed in the last chapter. By itself, the wage formula would have produced price stability but for the fact that the UAW added a variety of fringe benefits, whose effect did not spread throughout the economy as evenly and rapidly as did that of the direct wage increases; nevertheless, the probable effect of the fringe benefits was to allow purchasing power to grow more rapidly than private productive capacity. Assuming that public-sector policies offset the excesses of the private sector, this effect would not have made any difference. But insofar as the expansion of private purchasing power was not counterbalanced by other measures, the United States' position in world trade meant that it could dissipate that excess purchasing power through imports, thus minimizing the internal strains. Macroeconomic stabilization was also helped by the dollar's role as a reserve currency, to the extent that the prices of many imports were denominated in dollars rather than foreign currencies.

THE GENERAL AGREEMENT ON TRADE AND TARIFFS

The GATT, the second element in the Bretton Woods trading system, was an institutional embodiment of the postwar commitment to free trade. The signatories agreed that they would create no barriers to trade other than tariffs; that, through international agreements, they would periodically reduce the level of tariffs; and that they would respect a most-favored-nation policy, subjecting all imports to the same tariffs, whatever their country of origin. Over the first three postwar decades, the GATT probably contributed to a general expansion of trade. But its chief significance for our purposes is the restrictions it placed on the signatories' capacity, in response to crises, to close off their domestic markets and limit international exchange.

The Microscopic: American Shop-Floor Control

The other unrecognized dimension of the United States' postwar institutional structure was the system of shop-floor control over the work process. If there is one undisputed finding of industrial sociology, it is this: In every known society in which the division of labor is not fixed by custom, workers doing related tasks attempt to gain control over their workplace. This struggle for autonomy concerns every aspect of productive activity: the way tools and machines are used, and by whom; the determination of wages and income; patterns of recruitment and promotion; standards of satisfactory performance and penalties for failing to meet them; and so on. The written and unwritten rules of the contest for power between, on the one hand, the work group and, on the other, its superiors, subordinates, and confederates at other work sites constitute a system of shop-floor control.

Because it meshes with the organization of production, the system of shop-floor control is delimited by the prevailing use of technology, as well as by the micro- and macroregulatory institutions associated with it. For example, the more product-specific the machinery and the less variable the product, the more likely it is that managers can formulate and consistently apply a comprehensive set of task assignments; conversely, the less likely it is that workers will have discretion in organizing the flow of production. The more determined a corporation is to ensure a target level of capacity utilization through stabilization of its environment, the more likely it is to regularize all its procedures, from labor recruitment to the setting of production goals; hence, the smaller the margin of maneuver for the workshop. Finally, the greater the role of national macroregulatory institutions (such as unemployment and old-age insurance), the smaller the chance that corporations or, *a fortiori*, work groups will be able to devise systems of work allocation suited to their particular circumstances. Thus, patterns of shop-floor control in all mass-production economies are generically similar yet distinguished according to the historical peculiarities of the corporation and the macroregulatory institutions of the nation.

But a technological paradigm and its armature of stabilizing institutions delimit the forms of shop-floor control without completely defining them. Just as the predictability of commercial transactions can be assured through either the Anglo-American common law or a Continental civil code, so too the regularization required by engineers, corporate executives, and public administrators can be met by more than one system of shop-floor organization. For example, among three workshops of comparable performance, one may be run according to a rule book, itemizing the results of bargaining between labor and management; one by informal consultation between supervisor and work team; and the third according to the customs of the work group, as sanctioned by their nominal superiors. Thus, the system of workshop control—a system spread by unions and the movement of labor and managers from plant to plant—is linked to, yet distinct from, other economic institutions. Its distinctive features, we will see, help explain the differences in the ways different national economies react to common changes in the environment.

But so long as (in the language of American manufacturing) the iron is getting out the door, and the company and national economy are meeting the prevailing standards of competition, the features of a given shop-floor system are likely to be ignored. At best, they are dismissed as customary practices, or else declared an inevitable outcome of modern development—in any case, irrelevant. Consequently, unions, workers, supervisors, and corporate industrial-relations departments are left to settle shop-floor accounts as they see fit.

So it was in the United States throughout most of the postwar period. In the 1940s, academic observers and authors of handbooks for foremen[4] did define key elements of shop-floor organization, describing them as contingent, imperfect, and changeable products of the Depression upheavals, suited to some kinds of industry and economic conditions but not others. But by the 1960s, these elements were taken for granted, as part of an indisputably successful system of industrial production. From the late 1960s on, the subject of American shop-floor control was treated primarily by foreigners, struck both by the singularity of American institutions and by the Americans' conviction that their methods were universally applicable (with which the foreigners did not agree).[5]

In retrospect, the American observers of the 1940s and the foreign observers of the '60s were right: the American system of shop-floor control was neither historically necessary nor uniquely efficient. In the 1950s and '60s—the starting point of our discussion of the origins and evolution of American work-site organization—craft systems of shop-floor control existed uneasily alongside institutions thrown up by the seismic changes in mass-production industry in the 1930s.

The Mass-Production Model of Shop-Floor Control

The predominant American system of shop-floor control solidified in the mass-production industries in the 1950s. It depends on two central concepts:[6] a job is a precisely defined aggregate of well-specified tasks; and seniority—understood as length of service in a particular company, plant, or shop—is a criterion in the allocation of jobs. Workers' income, employment security, and degree of autonomy all depend on the definition of their jobs and on seniority. Hence, the struggle for control on the shop floor is a struggle over task classifications and allocative rules; this struggle, in turn, reinforces these two central concepts as structuring elements of American workshop life.

Wages in this system are set according to the characteristics of jobs, not the individuals who hold them. Jobs are broken down into their component tasks: each task is rated on the basis of a list of underlying characteristics (reflecting the required level of dexterity, exposure to hazards, degree of responsibility, and so on). The ratings are cumulated to form point totals, and then grouped on the basis of these totals into labor grades. Wages are attached to labor grades, so that the job, through the labor grade to which it belongs, determines the individual's current income.

Jobs are also grouped into hierarchical "lines of progression" or "seniority districts" that involve progressively more skill and higher pay. Workers move along these lines of progression in an order determined by the application of seniority rules, which typically give those who have the longest service in the productive unit priority in filling higher-paying vacancies. As a result, income from employment in the firm comes to be governed by seniority.

Seniority rules also govern job security. If the work force is reduced, a chain reaction is set off in which workers with more seniority "bump" (displace) workers in their district with less seniority from their jobs; those with so little service that they cannot bump anyone are laid off. When business picks up, workers on layoff are rehired in the order of their seniority. All former employees must be offered a chance to resume working before workers with no previous attachment to the firm may be hired.

Because so much turns on the subtleties of job classification and seniority rules, their interpretation leads to constant disputes, any one of which might provoke a strike. To limit this threat, a judicial system capable of assessing the extremely detailed circumstances of particular disagreements was created to compose differences. Under this grievance system (to which we referred in the last chapter), a worker with a complaint typically asks a shop-floor representative of the union to present his or her case to the foreman. If no agreement is reached during this first consultation, and if the union is convinced that the case merits the effort, the grievance is passed upward to committees composed of successively higher-ranking company and union officials. If no agreement is reached through such negotiation, it is resolved by the binding decision of a neutral arbitrator, chosen by a procedure acceptable to both labor and management. All final decisions become precedents for the judgment of subsequent disputes. In return for its acceptance of binding arbitration, management insists that the union renounce its right to strike during the term of the contract.

The grievance procedure, like most common-law judicial institutions, tends to ratify accepted practice in those areas where precedents are silent. If, for example, workers in a company have not traditionally been penalized for moderate tardiness, arbitrators are likely to acknowledge the workers' right to arrive late, rather than uphold an unprecedented attempt by management to punish for failure to clock in at the officially posted but previously unenforced times. Defense of existing practice thus creates new rights, so proposed revisions of plant operation must be negotiated between management and labor when collective-bargaining contracts are renewed.

The logic of the system of job classifications and seniority rights, and the judicial process by which they are supervised, operates to ensnare ever more of factory life in a net of rules with an ever finer mesh. Both the managers and the workers have strong motives for making seniority districts and job classifications narrower, and seniority rules more precise. Management wants to narrow seniority districts to minimize the movement—and the associated retraining—that occurs whenever a vacancy arises or a job is eliminated; the more narrowly jobs are defined, the easier it is to block workers' attempts to widen seniority districts (and thereby broaden bumping rights) by their appealing to similarities in task description. Workers, for their part, have an interest in seconding restrictive job definitions, because it gives them greater control over management practice. But the more narrowly jobs and seniority districts are defined, the more bargaining is required to shift workers from location to location when production is reorganized, and the more likely it is that disadvantaged workers will try to redress their situation through grievances—thus setting the rule-making machinery in motion again.

No wonder, then, that by the 1970s workers in, for example, the steel industry possessed a bundle of rights to promotion, transfer, and recall based variously on their seniority in the plant, in a particular division, or even in a single shop. The modern American system of shop-floor control in mass production had produced a parceling of de-facto rights to property in jobs that would bring a smile of recognition to the lips of any historian who had studied the struggles between lords and peasants in medieval Europe.[7]

The Craft Model of Shop-Floor Control

The mass-production model of American shop-floor control was the predominant but not unique model in the early 1950s. Labor in the craft sector was organized according to contrary principles. The organization of the construction industry, then and now, is a first example of these counterprinciples in operation.[8]

In the construction crafts, wages are linked to the worker's skill, not to the job he or she happens to be performing. Job security is controlled by limiting the access to skills. A form of industrial democracy is achieved through the close collaboration of craftsmen and union officials with management in the organization of production.

A construction craft is in theory a community of equals, each able to perform an endless variety of tasks by the application of common principles mastered through long experience with particular materials. Carpenters work with wood; masons with brick and concrete; operating engineers with steam. The sign of a skilled carpenter or mason, for example, is the ability to solve problems posed by the use of wood or cement that he or she has never before encountered.

The construction crafts generally recognize only two skill levels: that of the apprentice and that of the journeyman. All journeymen within a craft are considered to possess the same basic skills, and they receive a single, standard rate of pay. Apprentices are learners who, for want of experience, have yet to intuit the general principles of their craft; they are either paid a single rate or else advanced in two or three steps until, at the end of the apprenticeship, their pay equals that of the journeymen. In this craft, the wage progression represents the accumulation of skill, not an increasing work load.

Short-term employment security is provided not by seniority rules, as in mass production, but rather by the hiring-hall system. In this system, a full-time union official serves as the business agent, assigning craftsmen to particular jobs. Because construction work is often of short duration yet requires specialized, scarce skills; and because both the high capital costs of construction and the necessity of skilled work occurring in fixed sequences put a premium on the right workers' being on site at the right time, the hiring hall serves the employer as well as the worker. It serves the employer by ensuring that the requisite skills are always on call. It serves the worker by ensuring that available work is rationed equally among the members of the community—under conditions that make allocation of work by seniority meaningless. This principle of equal allocation of work is modified only by communally sanctioned judgments of equity: in periods of adversity, workers with large families, extraordinary medical expenses, or other exceptional needs may be given priority in job assignments.

The construction work force obtains long-term job security by carefully rationing its skills. Craftsmen monopolize the skills in their trade, and the craft is perpetuated by transmission of these skills from one generation to another on the job, through apprenticeship. Limitation of the number of apprentices and of what is taught to outsiders is the craft community's best long-term defense against scarcity of work. Indirectly, through the market, this limitation upon entry into the trade also facilitates the craft's control of wages; but in the craftsmen's view, such control is at most a secondary effect.

Construction work is governed by far fewer procedural rules than is mass-production work. The mass-production plant's grievance procedure, with its parent concept of a formal industrial jurisprudence, is foreign to the ethos of the construction industry. In construction, differences are resolved by debating and eventually agreeing on substantive outcomes, rather than by formally interpreting rules: the parties agree on what, consistent with their individual ideas of rights and responsibilities, ought to be done to solve a given problem—rather than on what any rules affecting that problem might say.

This focus on substantive as opposed to procedural justice can be explained partly by the particularities of the industry. Construction projects are too short-lived, firms too unstable, employment too ephemeral for the time-consuming process of grievance arbitration. Moreover, construction projects vary too much to justify—for either labor or capital—a precedent-based arbitration system: neither side has a motive to fight for elaborate judgments that are unlikely to bear on the facts of future conflicts.

There are in construction, furthermore, ways to resolve or avoid disputes without even articulating them. No employer, for instance, is obliged to accept a particular craftsman assigned by the hiring hall, and no craftsman is obliged to accept a particular job. Personal differences of the kind that in mass production might lead to grievances are resolved in construction by separations. Those who violate the norms of the craft community may be informally but effectively disciplined: the employer who sends back too many workers referred by the hiring hall will begin to receive only the poorest craftsmen; the worker who refuses too many assignments will end up at the bottom of the list for jobs. If provoked, the craftsmen will simply pick up and walk off the job as a group; their capacity to do so always stands silently behind their voiced complaints.

Thus, part of the tradition of substantive resolutions is explained by the obstacles to establishing procedural rules in construction. But another and larger reason for substantive negotiation is the nature of the work process in this industry. Unlike mass production, where management and production are clearly separated, construction work requires collaboration between managers and workers. Since construction is always based on a unique design (or the unique adaptation to local circumstances of a standard design), the organization of the work has to be defined each time *de novo;* with their technical knowledge, the workers are integral to the drawing up of the plan, just as they are essential for solving the inevitable problems that arise in its execution. Because of this collaboration between management and labor, questions about the respective responsibilities of bosses and workers often become indistinguishable from substantive questions about the layout of the work—the system of responsibilities and rights is built along with the building. Whenever formal contracts do touch on work organization, the business agent negotiates their provisions or "discusses their application" according to the needs of the given project.

The collaborative character of construction work and the substantive resolution of disputes are reinforced by the mobility of individuals between management and labor. Because work sites are constantly being created and dissolved, because entry into the industry is as easy for firms as it is difficult for workers, and because so much work is performed by subcontractors (who may be organized for a particular job), individuals are constantly changing places in the organizational hierarchy. Construction foremen are typically craftsmen and union members, who on the next job may return to their craft. The employer-contractor is also often a craftsman and a union member, who, if things do not work out, winds up an employee. A subcontractor's independence is so limited that he or she may share the perspective of once-and-possibly-future workmates, more than that of the contractor in charge of the job. The upshot of this confusion of roles is that the substantive negotiations that are rooted in the work process also appear ethically natural to the bargaining parties—who have good reason to see themselves as part of a single community.

A related model of shop control is found in the women's-garment industry.[9] This industry, like construction, is a craft industry. The frequent changes in fashion in women's clothes[10] require the same redeployment of skills and materials as does the construction worker's shift from one building site to another. But despite this similarity, wage determination in the women's-garment industry is a hybrid of craft and industrial principles.

Payment within each garment-making craft is based on output. Every operation required to produce any garment has been identified and assigned a price; a garment is "priced" by translating its manufacture into a list of these basic operations. Workers are then paid according to the type and number of operations they perform. Because skill is a major determinant of a worker's pace, the piecework system rewards craft experience. But this system makes pay much more sensitive to individual skill differences than it is in construction, and so the piecework system accords such factors as intensity of effort a role in determining earnings—factors that are not considered in the building industry.[11]

Historically, the garment industry resembles construction in two major respects other than their similar flexibility of skills and materials. First, job security is controlled through work sharing, rather than seniority. The entry and exit of firms is easy and constant in the clothing industry (for all the reasons cited regarding the nineteenth-century regional economies); firm-based seniority is therefore meaningless. Second, labor and management are both more concerned with substantive, as opposed to formal, resolution of disputes than is the case in mass production. Again, this is partly because formal grievance systems, apart from that governing piece rates, are both inconvenient and superfluous in this craft industry; but it is also because the collaborative character of the work (as reflected in the fluidity of both industrial organization and individual careers) makes substantive deliberation seem an outgrowth of production itself.

The wage-determination system in garment making is by itself a deterrent to the creation of nonwage grievance machinery. Since workers are paid by the piece, management is disposed to leave the workers free to decide how to work. Given this indifference to rules, the workers are correspondingly less concerned with protecting themselves against the arbitrary exercise of managerial discretion.

At the same time, the high birth and death rates of garment-making firms means that many people in the industry pass from being workers to being supervisors to being employers and back to being workers. There is also substantial subcontracting, which places even the employers in a subordinate role, and the hierarchy of contractors shifts from year to year. The winners in the year's competition for fashion become the contractors; they then subcontract to the losers the market share that they have not geared up to meet, out of fear that they cannot duplicate this year's success next year.

Like construction, garment making's mutable work roles and variable production reinforce the sense of community that includes all those in the craft—regardless of their current position in the hierarchy. It makes possible a collaboration between labor and management that is unthinkable in American mass production. For example, the International Ladies' Garment Workers maintains an industrial-engineering department, which the employers regularly consult for technical advice on production. In some cases, union engineers even lay out an employer's whole plant—confounding the roles of employer and employee beyond the distinguishing power of any analysis based on the idea of production as a war between social classes.[12]

Many features of shop-floor control in construction and garment making reflect the peculiarities of those industries. Yet the critical elements of both are typical of the craft sector in general: the link between wages and skill; the control of short-term job-security through work sharing; the defense of long-term job security through monopolization of skill; and collaboration between labor and management in the organization of work. To take a well-studied example, print-shop work is also organized along these lines.[13] But the most striking proof that such shop-floor control is associated with craft production occurs in mass production: in those enclaves in mass-production plants where the use of machines approximates the craft model—even though the rest of the plant is organized on mass-production principles.

Thus, for example, work in the skilled trades of the American automobile industry is organized by skill grades rather than job classifications. When the responsibilities of the skilled trades are routinized, the work assigned to each skill grade is so sharply delimited that this system is almost indistinguishable from one based on narrow job classification. But when the workers make specialty items—as in the Ford tool-and-die shop that Harley Shaiken studied—the skill categories are broadly defined and designate true craftsmen, as they do in construction.[14] Similarly, the scope of activity that is controlled by procedural rules and grievance machinery is much reduced. Above all, jobs are not precisely specified and the craftsmen determine how the work is to be done. Moreover, seniority plays a much smaller role: because wages are based on skill, and the skill hierarchy is short, the assignment of work has little influence on income; and since these workers' skills are so scarce, management does not want to lay off these people in a downturn. Clearly, broad job classifications and worker autonomy found in the hostile environment of seniority rules, narrow jobs, and grievance machinery are evidence of the significant (though not all-determining) link between technology and regulatory institutions, of which we spoke earlier.

The Eclipse of Craft Control in the Mass-Production Economy

Our comparison of the postwar American models of shop-floor control in mass and in craft production helps clarify each type of control; but it obscures a crucial aspect of the organization of labor during this time: the deterioration of the model of craft shop-floor control under the weight of the mass-production system. The mass-production system dominated thinking about shop-floor industrial relations, and so the legal and legislative context of shop-floor industrial relations came more and more to presuppose the mass-production model. In so doing, the deviant craft cases were reshaped in its image.

For example, the unemployment-insurance system was designed on the presumption that workers would be laid off in an economic downturn. Put the other way round, it did not recognize the system of work sharing through part-time work (what the French call partial unemployment) that prevailed in the women's-garment industry. As a result, this industry, too, moved to a system of layoffs, so that its workers could draw unemployment insurance.

For another example, the courts began to read no-strike clauses into collective agreements, and they pushed the contracting parties toward formal grievance procedures, with binding arbitration, such as prevailed in mass production. This development directed attention on the shop floor away from substantive concerns to procedure, which could be reviewed in arbitration. The courts also generalized the strict demarcation between the rank-and-file and supervisors, which had been established in mass production in the 1940s as part of upper management's efforts to maintain discipline on the shop floor.[15] This action cast another shadow on the collaborative relations between capital and labor in garments and construction. The elaboration of a doctrine of managerial prerogatives had a similar effect.

The mass-production concept of the "shop" as the site of a permanent "work community" came to predominate; in so doing, it assailed the concept of community in the craft industries, where the shop was merely the transitory expression of a larger, more enduring craft community. In mass production, workers in a given shop were presumed to have a collective interest, which sometimes justified the abridgment of their rights as individuals. (This was the rationale for allowing a majority vote to determine the bargaining status of the group as a whole, and for allowing a single bargaining agent to make agreements binding all those it represents.) Because the interests of workers outside the shop were not accorded the same legitimacy, they were not allowed to impose their will on others. This logic led the courts to limit the forms of outside, or "third-party," pressure that craft workers at a site not involved in a dispute had traditionally used in support of embattled co-workers. The effect of such limitations was to choke off expressions of solidarity that maintained the balance of power between capital and labor in dispersed craft industries. It thus undermined a precondition of collaborative work-place relations.

The legal provisions had only a limited effect. The garment industry was in fact excepted from some of the secondary boycott provisions of the National Labor Relations Act. Most construction unions continued to operate exclusive hiring halls, omitting the telltale records needed to document their illegality. A number of garment shops operated part-time while their employees collected unemployment; the workers were paid in scrip, which they redeemed after exhausting their eligibility for unemployment benefits. Since record keeping in the piecework system is normally by means of chits, which workers redeem only periodically, this system was hardly disruptive. Nonetheless, each of these intrusions from mass production weakened the craft model as both a practice and a conception of shop-floor control.

More subtly, the crafts were also weakened from within, as they sought to adjust to technological change. They used strategies that were borrowed from traditional practice yet which resonated with the prevailing model of shop-floor control in mass production. When technological change threatens to displace craftsmen in a particular industry, the craft typically pursues a two-step strategy: First, it uses whatever market power its skills represent to oblige management to freeze the existing division of labor. Then it trades its right to continue working with the old technology for the right to the best jobs available with the new, plus compensation for those who cannot be accommodated by reorganization.

This system assures both the suppleness of the craft system of control and the historical relationship between a craft community and a particular group of firms, so long as the imposition of rigid labor division is seen as an exceptional condition, justified by tactical considerations. In the postwar period, however, two mutually reinforcing tendencies often turned the exception into the rule. First, as the pace of technological change increased, skilled workers began to fear—sometimes correctly—that there would be no place for their skill if they allowed the introduction of new techniques. Second, the narrow job classifications of the mass-production sector made the specification of tasks seem a normal part of the contractual relationship between labor and management.

The fate of the American typographers is a classic example. In the 1950s and '60s, the printing trades wrote provisions into their contracts stipulating that work be done in the traditional way. In the long run, these provisions proved to be self-defeating, as such major employers of typographers as newspapers eliminated the trade altogether, by switching to computer typesetting. But in the short run, for most of the postwar period, the provisions did maintain printers' jobs. They did so, however, by reshaping labor relations in the printing industry on the mass-production model.

In the construction industry, the defense of job security against technological change also recast the industry in the mass-production image—but for a quite different reason.[16] Construction unions have difficulty imposing a specific division of labor on management. This is because the different materials and processes that originally distinguished the construction crafts are, at the margin, substitutable. Thus the crafts come into competition, giving the employer the opportunity to play one off against another. That opportunity is enhanced when technological change involves new materials and processes that lie outside traditional craft lines.

Before World War II, the American labor movement met this challenge by chartering new crafts. Unions of electricians and operating engineers took their place beside the ancient trades of carpenter and mason. After the war, however, the construction unions reacted to change by expanding traditional jurisdictions. This strategy is consistent with the craft model when there is a clear relation between the materials or procedures used in the new work and those used in the old—when, for example, electronic work is assigned to electricians. But in construction, the response seldom took this form. Instead, the assignment of new tasks was adjudicated case by case and resolved so as to apportion the work equally among the different crafts. For example, rather than creating a new union of plastic workers, or expanding the jurisdiction of carpenters to include plastics, each new plastic material was assigned as though by rota to a given union—some to carpenters, some to masons, some to ironworkers. The method of distribution was modeled on the grievance procedure in mass production; its goal was to avoid the wildcat strikes over jurisdiction disputes that plagued the construction industry, just as the aim of the grievance machinery had been to limit the disputes over work rules that plagued manufacturing during and after World War II.

The long-term effect of case-by-case adjudication of jurisdiction was to transform the nature of the crafts themselves. Considerations of job security and industrial peace came to eclipse the logic of the work process, making the craft jurisdictions increasingly resemble manufacturing jobs—a collection of tasks rather than a generically related application of principles. As this has happened, the basis of the craft form of shop control has been undermined. The more the crafts consist of heterogeneous tasks, the greater the danger that craftsmen lose their capacity to solve problems, which underpins their shop-floor power—

they no longer understand what they are doing any more than the semiskilled worker in mass production. And as production has increasingly to be planned by those who do understand the process, management loses the incentive to collaborate with the work force. Workers must then protect their jobs and income by further elaboration of detailed rules, and this in turn undermines the remaining integrity of their work, opening the way for still further incursions by management into job organization.

The disruptive influence of the mass-production system of job control on craft methods of shop-floor control is analogous to the corrosive influence of mass production on flexible specialization in the late nineteenth and early twentieth centuries. Just as the successes of mass production made flexible specialization appear archaic and disorderly, so the dominance of seniority rules and narrow job classification made craft control appear a haphazard, untidy collection of traditional practices. And the more legislators, judges, arbitrators, managers—and craftsmen—borrowed elements from the dominant model to solve the problems of labor organization in the craft sector, the more craft practice actually became as hodgepodge as it had first appeared to be.

In sum, the decline of the craft model of shop-floor control in the United States is surely associated with the rise in mass production of seniority rules and narrow jobs. But it is not clear that these rules and jobs were an inevitable result of the rise of mass production. As we saw in the last chapter, the dominant pattern of industrial relations in postwar America is a relatively recent institutional development—one that grew up as part of the accommodation between labor and management that produced the regime of macroeconomic regulation described in chapter 4. In the early twentieth century, however, mass production was associated with a very different model of industrial relations: welfare capitalism and the American Plan.

The American Plan: An Alternative Form of Shop-Floor Control in Mass Production

The American Plan, as it was defined in the 1920s, was a system for assuring the workers' loyalty and dedication to the firm by offering them the opportunity to purchase the firm's stock at favorable prices and to participate in company-sponsored health and pension funds, social programs, and recreational and vacation facilities. The Plan also provided for a system of dispute resolution designed to prevent any hardening of the lines between labor and management. Most of the evidence about the American Plan consists of managerial declarations of its intent. We know little about how the Plan was administered. Moreover, our knowledge is colored by the experience of the 1930s, when the Plan collapsed under the Depression and management reneged on the prosperity-based promises it had made to labor. The disparities that then emerged between what was practiced and what professed still influence debate about the Plan's operation—so much so that today it is hard to determine how it functioned in the economic climate for which it was designed.

The dominant interpretation sees the spread of welfare-capitalism institutions as management's effort to forestall union organization and to extend employers' control over the work process. In this view, welfare capitalism was designed to dupe the work force into tolerating increased oppression; as such, it was bound to give way to something like the union system as soon as adversity gave the labor force a keener sense of its interests.[17] There is, however, an alternative view of the American Plan; in this view, best argued by David Brody, welfare capitalism was more than a screen for exploitation and a shield against unionization.[18]

Brody writes that welfare capitalism grew out of management's inchoate realization that it had an interest in a healthy, prosperous, collaborative work force. To this end, Brody claims, many firms made concessions and commitments to their employees that cannot be dismissed as drapery for employers' unilateral control of the work place and absolute freedom to hire and fire. In fact, Brody believes that the American Plan was successful enough even under adverse conditions to suggest that, had the Depression been briefer than it was, the collaborative forms of shop-floor control emerging under welfare capitalism—and not the system of procedural justice associated with the CIO unions—might have become the matrix of plant-level industrial relations in the United States. In short, the American Plan was the victim of bad historical timing, not of capitalists' incapacity to make concessions to labor.

Managers espoused welfare capitalism as a paying proposition for two reasons. First, managers' awareness was growing that the mass-production labor force also constituted the market for what it produced; hence, the prosperity of an industry depended on the prosperity of its workers. Insofar as individual businessmen thought they could assure their markets by how they treated their own work force, they were clearly wrong—as we have just seen, market stabilization had to be worked out through national economic institutions. But many corporate executives saw the American Plan as part of a national business movement of which they were the leaders, and so they saw their labor policies as models that would be widely followed; and, to the extent that this is so, their ideas made sense as a roundabout form of macroeconomic policy. The NIRA can be seen as a fumbling attempt to make an institution of their sentiments.

The second reason managers espoused welfare capitalism was their conviction that productivity could be increased by cooperation between labor and management. This theme surfaces even in the works of Frederick Taylor and Henry Ford, who of course are justly known as advocates of a rigid separation of the conception and the execution of tasks; and it appears frequently in the comments of other businessmen about the American Plan.[19] The desire for collaborative plant-level industrial relations was reflected in the creation of shop-floor institutions to facilitate consultation between labor and management, as well as in policies aimed at guaranteeing the job security on which the vitality of such institutions depended.

Under the American Plan, labor-management consultation was advanced through so-called works councils, or shop committees. Most historians see these bodies as company unions or company grievance machinery, and there is an important sense in which this is true. Many of the councils were formed in response to government pressure during World War I for employee representation during working hours; employers hoped thus to avoid independent union organization. And many works councils focused on grievances regarding company policy. Nevertheless, their structure and mandate made these councils more concerned with the substantive resolution of production problems than is today's industrial grievance committee.

For example, at the Lynn, Massachusetts, plant of General Electric, the works councils comprised equal numbers of managers and workers. Worker representatives were elected by secret ballot; foremen and group leaders were excluded. These councils had a hierarchy, and problems that could not be resolved in the shop were referred to a higher level, as in the modern grievance procedure. But the Lynn system did not culminate in binding arbitration, nor—more important—were the councils' discussions restricted to the issues that are "grievable" in a contemporary American industrial plant.[20]

The broad scope of the Lynn works councils was typical of the consultative bodies founded under welfare capitalism. A survey of industrial-relations practices in the 1920s by the National Industrial

Conference Board (an obvious advocate of the American Plan) described a works council as

... a meeting place, where management and working force can consider calmly, on the basis of accurate information rather than rumor, their respective positions and problems.... Beyond the settlement of grievances and, better, their prevention, is the broader and more constructive accomplishment of employee representation in welding together management and working force into a single, cohesive productive unit.[21]

This description was echoed in the statements of business leaders. Gerard Swope, of GE, lectured his foremen: "You are constantly being hounded to increase your output. One of the ways of getting it is to have your workers cooperate with you." Charles Schwab claimed that Bethlehem Steel's employee-representation plan promoted "constructive cooperation along the lines of increased efficiency, elimination of waste, and improved methods and quality and quantity of products." And C. B. Seger, of U.S. Rubber, admonished managers that intelligent leadership "presupposes that leaders will keep those whom they lead informed and it presupposes also that they will be responsive to those led.[22]

Despite the puffery of such declarations, it is clear from employment practices that management was willing to go to some lengths to build a long-term relationship with its work force. The major companies in the 1920s heavily favored wage and employment stabilization; when employment stabilization was not possible, work sharing was generally instituted—resort to layoff and recall was almost unknown. Companies with stable or expanding markets actually guaranteed employment: the Procter and Gamble plan in 1923 promised forty-eight weeks of full-time work a year to most of its employees;[23] IBM's employment guarantees date from this period. Even companies that could not promise continuous employment (such as General Electric and Bethlehem Steel) made efforts to reduce their variability. And a number of firms introduced unemployment-insurance schemes.[24]

Corporate training policies were also used to achieve the twin ends of stabilized output and stabilized employment. By broadening the skills of its work force, a company could move workers from one job to another. And the greater the possibilities for redeploying the work force, the greater the possibilities for meeting shifts in demand or overcoming bottlenecks in the flow of production—rather than having to replace employees with new ones trained in the requisite tasks, or to lay off workers until shortages are overcome. The Joseph and Feiss Company, of Cleveland, Ohio—one of the nation's largest producers of men's clothing—devised an elaborate incentive scheme to encourage its seamstresses to learn several jobs: when a worker had fulfilled her production quota for the day, she was free either to go home or to earn more money by moving to another department, where production was behind schedule. Goodyear Tire and Rubber Company, of Akron, Ohio, formed a flying squad of 500 workers (5 percent of the work force), trained the squad members in a variety of skills, and rotated them as necessary throughout the plant. The company's aim was not merely to fill gaps in production lines, but also to use this squad's breadth of experience to identify problems in the organization of manufacturing operations. As part of its plan to guarantee employment, Procter and Gamble established a "utility department," which supplied workers to shops that were short-handed. All of these measures were supplemented, in these firms and others, by efforts to schedule production so that the work load was spread as evenly as possible throughout the year, avoiding seasonal bursts of activity and hiring, followed by slack times and layoffs.[25]

The corporations' adjustment to the early Depression in 1929–30 is perhaps the best evidence that they were committed to their work force. The major manufacturing companies tried to maintain both wage and employment at previous levels; when that proved impossible, they shifted to work sharing. U.S. Steel and Ford abandoned wage maintenance only in the fall of 1931, and most of the major corporations followed suit.[26] Work sharing, however, continued into 1932. Up until October of that year, U.S. Steel employed 85 percent of its normal work force, even though production had fallen 90 percent.[27]

Seen from this perspective, the failure of the American Plan of works councils and job sharing, and the rise of a system of layoffs and procedural justice, was largely an accident of economic history. If the recovery had come more quickly, welfare capitalism might have emerged strengthened from the Depression, and its shop-floor practices validated. If the NIRA had succeeded, the result might have been the same. But when the corporations broke their promises, and could not redeem them even with the government's help, the entire system was discredited. Hence workers, disillusioned and bitter, looked to the new unions to defend their jobs.

The new labor movement did not have a clear solution to the problem of job security. Ideally, it would have liked to guarantee workers their jobs. But this was simply not possible in the midst of the Depression. Thus, labor sought instead some equitable system of work allocation, one that would limit management's playing favorites with workers and using job allocation to divide the rank and file and break the union. In the late 1930s, the labor movement experimented with a variety of means to this end, ranging from work sharing to layoff based on either seniority or need, or some combination of these. Increasingly, the debate about job security pitted union member against union member, placing the leadership—and the union—in an untenable position. This, as David Montgomery observes, "stimulated the desire of the union's membership to return control to management's hands, provided it could be limited by clearly formulated seniority rights in the contract."[28] For Frederick H. Harbison, an academic commentator writing in 1940, the seniority principle's appeal had become self-evident:

In the face of widespread unemployment . . . employees in the mass-production industries desired above all job protection. Consequently, the leaders of the new unions pressed for the acceptance of seniority rules as a means of demonstrating to the workers that organization would provide job protection and security of employment. The appeal was well timed, for many employers . . . that were hit by the depression had been laying off workers in a haphazard and not unbiased fashion.[29]

Despite the debate, once the new system was in place, the unions were obligated to defend it—regardless of their reservations about rules that pitted workers against one another, with predictably unpleasant consequences for labor leaders. If there was a margin for modifying the system in the 1940s (Harbison thought both labor and management could benefit from less formal regulation of job security), it was reduced in the postwar period: provisions of unemployment compensation and the grievance machinery reinforced the framework of the Depression settlement.

For the reasons discussed earlier, the new seniority rules probably contributed to the narrowing of job classifications, to increased attention to job evaluation, and to a tighter link between wages and job definition. But historical documentation shows only a loose association among seniority-rule changes in these different realms; it does not show precisely how rule changes in one realm affected the others. For example, Slichter, Healy, and Livernash date the widespread adoption of job evaluation from the late 1930s, and attribute it to the rise of industrial unions. Management, in their account, found that in organized shops, job evaluation served to stabilize labor relations; in the absence of unions, it provided a way of controlling wage inequities that were conducive to organization. Unions themselves did not favor job evaluation, but few actively opposed it.[30]

In any case, job narrowing and job evaluation—as prompted by the seniority rules—were sped along by numerous undercurrents of industrial practice. In some instances (such as the steel industry), job-evaluation plans were abstracted from the existing wage structure in a way that suggests wages had been attached to jobs for some time.[31] And there had apparently been a gradual movement toward job-related wages throughout the twentieth century, as encouraged in the work of Frederick Taylor. The growing number of formal job descriptions in hiring and promotion also favored this trend, as did the development of civil-service classifications and the salary standardization of the 1920s.[32] Had the American Plan not broken down, however, these undercurrents might today appear as perturbing factors in a system of broad job classifications, instead of precursors of a system of narrow ones.

Accidental Combinations: Deconstructing Shop-Floor Control

Against the backdrop of the narrow jobs and the seniority rules that dominated U.S. shop-floor relations in mass-production industry after World War II, the American Plan stands out for two reasons. First, by separating the resolution of disputes from the definition of tasks, it made shop-floor control independent of the technology: welfare capitalism, taken at its word, obliged the firm to employ its work force continuously—at high wages and under bearable if not attractive conditions—and it obliged the work force to resolve its differences with the firm amicably, through discussion of the substance of its complaints. Given a stable economic environment, tasks in a mass-production firm under the American Plan might well be as subdivided as those in a firm operating under current principles; however, the work-place jurisprudence of the former firm would not translate the division of labor into a distribution of rights, as it would in the latter firm. Every reorganization of production or redisposition of labor would not, therefore, require a renegotiation of responsibilities. Put another way, the American Plan was compatible with craft systems of shop-floor control in large firms in that it permitted workers to exercise autonomy without threatening the rights of workmates or undermining their collective position against management. And the Plan was compatible with craft control in dispersed industries in that it supplied neither actionable precedents nor invidious comparisons to undermine existing practices.

The second distinguishing feature of the American Plan was that it kept out unions and the state. It was as though American managers could relax their control over the work place only so long as the work place was cut off from the larger society. From labor's point of view, this led at best to corporate syndicalism, in which workers and managers in a company joined together to defend their interests against those of competing companies. At worst, it meant exploitation under the cover of paternalism—as denounced in the dominant interpretation of the American Plan and later prohibited in laws against company unions.

The lesson conventionally drawn from American labor history is that where there are unions, disputes are resolved through procedural rules rooted in the narrow jobs of mass production: unionization and formalization of shop-floor life necessarily go together. American radical writers saw this connection as a stage of industrial development dictated by the laws of motion of capitalism; American industrial-relations experts saw it as evidence of the maturation and stabilization of the simultaneously conflictual and cooperative relations between labor and capital. For many business and union leaders, this apparently self-evident connection made partnership seem practicable, if not inevitable, so long as industry followed its nineteenth-century technological trajectory; this partnership then became (as we shall see) a contradiction in terms when it began to experiment with more flexible uses of its resources: given what had gone before, a return to craft practices meant a return to a world without unions.

But the conventional lesson of the connection between unionization and job control is deceptive. It results from the same kind of confusion of the specific and the general that caused American corporations to see in their relations to banks and to the state the expression of universal principles, rather than historical contingency.

From the vantage point of the early 1920s, a professor at the Tuck School of Business Administration—who was both an advocate of the American Plan and close to the labor movement—foresaw a day when welfare capitalism, the stabilization of employment, and substantive dispute resolution could be combined with unionization. His model for a union that would be compatible with this regime of shop-floor control was the United Mine Workers; the jurisdiction of the UMW covered all workers employed in and around coal mines, skilled or not, and regardless of craft differences. When he asked whether the UMW would block the use of the same worker as a carpenter, an electrician, and an operating engineer, he was told by the union's secretary-treasurer:

Men employed to do carpenter work, electrical work, or engineers' work in and around coal mines are hired without interference, and we require only that they belong to the United Mine Workers of America. There is no interference with the assignment of men to do this work by the mine management. The mine management determines who is to do the carpenter work, electrical work, and the engineers' work, and our union has no objection to men who do carpenter work doing other classes of work if the mine management wishes them to do so. An agreement is in effect in some districts under the jurisdiction of the United Mine Workers of America providing for a schedule of wages for blacksmithing, electrical work, carpenters, enginemen, etc.

The union's chief purpose is to see that men employed in each of these classifications receive the union scale as agreed to between the miners and the operators. We are interested in securing the scale for the men employed and allow the management to employ men to work at the different classifications.[33]

The idea of combining flexible welfare capitalism and industrial unionism appealed not just to academic reformers but also to influential industrialists. In 1926 Gerard Swope and Owen Young, of General Electric, met secretly in New York with William Green, the leader of the American Federation of Labor; they proposed that the Federation organize their company by winning control of the works-council system. By inviting the union into the plant, Swope hoped that the company would avoid the conflicts that turned labor into a long-term adversary. He wanted, he recalled later, "an organization with which we could work on a businesslike basis." But precisely for that reason he insisted that the prospective union be organized on industrial principles; from experience, he believed the company would be "intolerably handicapped" if the employees were organized in "competing craft unions." This condition was apparently unacceptable to Green, who never pursued the proposal.[34]

Outside the United States, history took a different course. In some countries, mass production, unionization, and craft systems of shop-floor control became associated in a way that American experience makes hard to conceive. The next chapter completes our discussion of the world of mass production by showing how other countries emulated the American model while recombining some of its features. This recombination recalls lost possibilities of U.S. development. It may also—if our subsequent arguments are correct—contain clues for the successful adaptation of American industry and labor to changed conditions of competition.

6

The Pieces Repositioned: Mass and Craft Production Abroad

FROM the late nineteenth century (when the rigidities of Britain's economy were becoming evident) through the mid-1970s (when the shortcomings of American factories became a subject for the daily press), American ways of using technology, organizing corporations, deploying labor, and, finally, controlling macroeconomic fluctuations defined the standards of industrial efficiency. Large, industrializing countries ranging from France, Germany, and Italy, in the West, to Russia and Japan, in the East, emulated the United States. In some measure they were forced to do this by the military superiority of American technology. But most countries were also attracted by the rising standard of living that the American model offered; they therefore tried to create a civilian as well as a military economy like the one in the United States. In the process, they borrowed not only specific components from U.S. industrial technology, but also numerous features of American regulatory institutions. As a result, the economic structures of the major industrial countries came to exhibit a broad family resemblance.

But when other countries tried to duplicate American techniques and structures, they never succeeded totally. This inability reflected these countries' reliance on world markets—which distinguished them as a group—and the historical vicissitudes that gave each country's corporate organization and system of shop-floor control a distinct cast.

Until the 1970s, as we have seen, American industry was largely independent of foreign markets. Numerous prosperous family farms, the willingness of an immigrant population to experiment with machine-made products, the absence of sumptury laws or class barriers restricting consumption, and unlimited natural resources—all of these factors produced a mass market large enough for American manufacturers to obtain critical economies of scale without depending on exports. By contrast, outside the United States the turn to mass production required the conquest of foreign outlets.

In France and Japan, in the nineteenth century, most potential consumers were peasant small holders subsisting at the edge of the national market. In (southern) Italy and (eastern) Germany, agriculture was controlled by latifundia. The day laborers and sharecroppers of these economies were scarcely in a position to buy sewing machines or bicycles, let alone automobiles. Thus, before the Depression, the mass-production sector in these countries survived only by exporting most of its output. It was only the collapse of world markets during the Depression that prompted—often through military spending—experiments with autarky and stimulation of the domestic market (enlarged sometimes by imperial preference zones or "co-prosperity" spheres). Chapter 5 showed how the outcome of World War II and Bretton Woods encouraged a return to export-based growth after the years of autarky. Even in the 1960s—when the expansion of domestic markets, the success of the European Economic Community, and ample labor and raw materials allowed these countries to adopt some of the American techniques of demand management—their history of vulnerability to the flows of world trade dampened enthusiasm for policies that are indifferent to the international economy.

Beyond this common dependence on the world market, each of the countries was distinguished by its individual system of shop-floor control and corporate organization. In these economies, various forms of coop-eration between industry and the state that would be unthinkable in the United States became second-nature. Work-place relations that to Americans join incompatible elements evolved in some countries as integral wholes; even work-place regimes that seemed similar to the American model operated by a different logic.

But by the height of the postwar prosperity, these differences among national systems seemed unimportant. The growth of the separate domestic markets promised to make Keynesian control over domestic business cycles universally applicable. The persistence of national styles of management and shop-floor regimes was interpreted as "functional equivalence": the translation into national idioms of a single solution to the common problems of all mass-production economies. Americans thus saw likenesses of themselves when they looked abroad at their competitors.

This chapter surveys the industrial development of France, Germany, Italy, and Japan. By comparing these major mass-production systems, it reinforces the claim put forward in our discussion of buried historical possibilities of the American economy: the advance of mass-production technology and regulatory institutions does not, by itself, determine the organization of shop-floor control or managerial hierarchies.

France

The country that went furthest toward the U.S. system is France. This is paradoxical, because in the nineteenth century France, of all the countries, had seemed the most committed to the opposite production principles. But after World War II, the emergence of a dominant mass-production sector in France depended on an alliance between the state and large firms, both of which were imitating the American models. The system of shop-floor control, however—although also suggesting American influence—was the result of a peculiar mesh of French management traditions with the syndicalist and socialist politics of a labor movement that was weak at the plant level.

Between the end of the nineteenth century and the onset of the Depression, large metalworking, chemical, automobile, and electrical-equipment firms emerged in France.[1] Often these firms drew heavily on American technical know-how (as in automobiles); and in some cases they were also linked financially to American firms (as in the case of electrical equipment). But these firms differed from their American counterparts in three important ways.

First, the French domestic market for mass-produced goods remained small; therefore, these firms had to sell 35 to 40 percent of their output abroad. Second, the French firms did not diversify, as did the Americans, by forming new divisions, closely integrated into the parent company. Instead, they followed a pattern that recalls, and may have grown out of, the *système Motte* (it also anticipates a Japanese pattern of organization, which we will examine: they formed subsidiaries of the parent firm that were linked by financial ties that might loosen in time, eventually giving autonomy to the new firm).

The third way that the early-twentieth-century French firms differed from the American firms was their belated discovery of the logic of fixed costs. The rise of the new firms in France coincided with a period of almost unbroken prosperity, stretching from the mid-1890s to the end of the 1920s; corporations operating in the emergent mass-production economy had therefore not elaborated techniques of microregulation before the 1930s. Whereas the American downturn of 1920–21 prompted U.S. firms to consider strategies for matching average expected supply to demand, French firms continued to be preoccupied with the technical organization of production throughout the 1920s.

Despite these three differences, however, there were two respects in which early-twentieth-century French firms resembled their American counterparts. First, like American industrialists in this period, French managers were free of all but the most minimal state control. Not that the French state was as administratively fragmented and legally restricted as its American counterpart: France had inherited from the ancien régime and Napoleon a public service composed of corps of highly trained engineers, jurists, and financial experts. But France's economic liberalism and the political weight of its peasantry and small-scale capital forestalled the use of these public-service corps in forced-draft industrialization. Apart from the economic modernization in the 1830s, the railroad construction forty years later, and the rationalization of the munitions industry during World War I, these public-service corps and the state they incarnated did little to reorganize industry.[2]

The second broad similarity between early-twentieth-century French and American firms was their freedom from the interference of unions. In this regard, too, the autonomy of French managers had a long history. Before the first world war, labor organization in France had developed rapidly. But except for a few groups with extraordinary power in the labor market, unions had little influence at the work place. One reason was management's use of blacklists and other reprisals against union sympathizers. Another was the continuing influence of the Proudhonist tradition of craft mutualism, in which not the plant but the regional community of skilled workers was the locus of organization. This tradition was kept alive through *bourses du travail* (labor exchanges similar to American construction's union hiring halls); these labor exchanges were partly financed by national and municipal governments anxious to conciliate—but also to control—the emergent working class. The system encouraged workers to believe in their self-sufficiency as a class and the irrelevance of organization within the factory or the national parliament; it thus excused the empty union treasuries and diverted attention from labor's impotence in the face of management. The pattern was temporarily reversed during World War I, when French unions (like labor unions in all the warring countries) were accorded rights to organize in return for collaboration in the war effort.[3] By 1919, however, the French state withdrew its protection; employers returned, successfully, to the attack; and mass-production industry easily kept the labor movement at bay during the 1920s.[4]

But in the 1930s the large French firms were unable to organize economic recovery—attempting to conquer foreign markets by cutting prices,[5] Citroën went bankrupt installing the latest mass-production equipment. This corporate incapacity reopened the question of the state's role in macroeconomic stabilization, and drew—briefly—labor organization from the periphery of politics and factory life to the center of both. The French tried two experiments, which recalled, in reverse order, the two periods of the American New Deal.

The first experiment was initiated by the Popular Front government, which came to power after the elections of May 1936; the experiment was inspired by an underconsumptionist view of the crisis. Its centerpiece was a policy of reinflation through wage increases, combined with a program of work sharing, through a reduction in the workweek and a legislative guarantee of annual paid vacations. But instead of hiring more workers, as the government had hoped, employers ran their factories fewer hours per week and raised prices to compensate for higher hourly wages and reduced output. Not all factories reduced output by equivalent amounts, of course; cutbacks in some sectors led to shortages in others—which further reduced productivity. The wage increases that were not nullified by the resulting inflation were spent on food (whose price had been increased, partly through government subsidies to agriculture), not industrial goods. As the failure of the reforms became evident, France drifted to the Right. Firms took back much of what they had earlier conceded, even though fragments of the Popular Front program were eventually incorporated into the postwar system of macroeconomic regulation.[6]

The second wave of French economic experimentation came under the Vichy government, during World War II, after Germany's defeat of France. This time the state aimed to create a system of self-governing industrial communities or corporations reminiscent of those envisaged in the NIRA. But whereas the U.S. committees that assembled to write industry codes included representatives of labor, the Vichy *comités d'organisation* were composed exclusively of businessmen, who often simply reconstituted existing trusts or trade associations under a new name.[7]

These arrangements were as confused and inconclusive as the earlier reforms; yet they, too, helped create the preconditions for the postwar reorganization of the French economy. For one thing, collaboration between the state and industry brought the elite bureaucratic corps into economic affairs and created a network of well-informed persons disposed to increase state direction of the economy:[8] thus these Vichy institutions functioned in form—though certainly not in substance—like the American war labor boards to educate the personnel who would administer a new system of regulation. The Vichy system also helped clear the way for postwar organization because petty capital supported the collaborationist government and therefore was discredited by its fall. This political collapse of the workshop economy removed a potential obstacle to state programs favoring industrial concentration.[9]

The French postwar synthesis was formalized in a series of plans for national economic growth, called the *économie concertée*. Politically it was (as Andrew Schonfield describes it) "an act of voluntary collusion between senior civil servants and the senior managers of big business." The political parties were largely excluded from power; so were the labor unions—divided and weakened by the postwar collapse of the hopes for transformation that had been nurtured by the collective resistance against the fascists. The "conspiracy in the public interest" succeeded because nationalization of important banks, utilities, and industrial firms (such as Renault) gave the government enough control over the economy to command the respect of big business; and big business wanted a stable economic environment that, in this period, only state action could provide.[10]

On the level of microregulation, the *économie concertée* meant the state's encouragement of modernization cartels. Such encouragement came first through the rationing of credit to the promising firms, and then through tax exemptions for capital gains from mergers and through the provision of medium- and long-term credit for fusions. Small firms fused with one another or with larger firms to form more efficient units; larger firms formed giant conglomerates, on the American model. The aim of this merger movement—which continued until the late 1960s—was to create internationally competitive corporations: "national champions," capable of profiting from economies of scale in mass production.[11]

Once these cartels began to dominate the French economy, they worked to complete what the state had begun. Large firms such as Renault formed vast networks of dependent suppliers—sometimes by buying up parts manufacturers, sometimes by decentralizing labor-intensive operations to low-wage rural areas in the south and west of France. Where domestic labor reserves were inadequate, firms recruited immigrants, mainly from Francophone Africa and Portugal. Vertical links between parent firms with headquarters in Paris replaced horizontal links among firms with complementary specialties in a given region: one result, to which we referred earlier, was to tear the tissue of human and commercial relations that were crucial to the resilience of such region economies as Lyon.[12] Another consequence of these developments was that the internal structure of the largest French firms came to resemble the American divisional pattern, rather than the system of financial federation observed in the 1920s.[13]

On the level of macroregulation, the *économie concertée* also borrowed from American experience; but here, too, the state played a much larger role in France than in the United States, and labor played a more subordinate part. Throughout the 1950s, the French economy was relatively sheltered from international competition, by trade barriers and by the focus of potential competitors on domestic reconstruction. France in this period exported and imported a smaller fraction of its gross national product than did any other major European country; and if the figures are adjusted to exclude exchanges with the Saar region (which returned to Germany in 1957) and countries using the French franc, France was only slightly more exposed to the world economy than was the United States: both French and American exports in the mid-1950s were roughly 5 percent of gross national product; French imports were roughly 7.5 percent of GNP, and American imports were 5 percent. This insulation from the world market allowed the French government to raise the level of demand enough to encourage growth despite high (for then) rates of inflation.[14]

Effective demand was maintained in several ways: by offering investment credit to selected firms at favorable rates; by direct purchases of goods and services; and by the, albeit hesitant, recognition (encouraged by American advisers) of the need to keep wages rising in order to absorb increased output and to overcome workers' resistance to technological change.[15]

The government controlled wages by two means. The first was simply to raise the minimum wage, which after 1952 was explicitly indexed to the cost of living: because the wage structure was formalized through industrywide job classifications, increases in the minimum wage generally resulted in corresponding increases at higher levels, as better-paid workers fought to reestablish differentials.[16] The second means by which the government controlled wages was pattern-setting contracts in state-owned firms (for example, the two-year agreement at Renault in 1955, which was plainly modeled on the UAW-GM contracts). Such agreements were spread to the rest of the economy through sectoral collective bargaining, in which the state decreed that agreements reached in one firm were binding on other firms in the same industry.[17]

This expansionary strategy had to be modified, however, after the Treaty of Rome, in 1957, which created the prospects of a European common market in industrial goods. The consequent foreseeable increase in France's exposure to world markets[18] meant that its relatively high inflation rate was a long-term threat to the economy's international competitiveness. To encourage growth under the new circumstances, the franc was therefore devalued by 20 percent in 1957, and by an additional 14.5 percent the next year, when de Gaulle inaugurated the Fifth Republic. The new government also abolished wage indexing and used its control of the tax code and of the allocation of credit to shift expenditure of the national income from consumption to investment.[19] This combination of limiting the domestic demand and price increases while encouraging internationally competitive industries defined the official French macroeconomic policy until the wave of strikes and factory occupations in May 1968.

Yet despite these declarations of intent in the 1950s and '60s, French macroeconomic regulation continued much as it had been in the earlier postwar period. This persistence was due to several factors: the urging of the Keynesian planners; the prompting of officials who were convinced that expansion depended on labor's participation in decision making; and popular pressure. Thus, the French state not only tolerated the continuation of wage indexing in various guises but also created a system of unemployment insurance that helped maintain purchasing power despite downturns in the economy.[20] Looking back on the 1950s and '60s, econometricians have found that wage increases in France were strikingly similar across industries, and except during 1958–59, they were independent of changes in the unemployment rate.[21] It was only after the strikes of May 1968 that principle and practice coincided: the minimum wage was again indexed to the cost of living, unemployment insurance was increased, wage differentials between regions and between skill levels were reduced, and the freedom of firms to lay off workers was limited.[22]

In the years following May 1968, the newly formalized macroregulation seemed consistent with a high level of economic performance. The government offset the increase in wages by generous fiscal and credit concessions to business, whose confidence was further restored by impressive Gaullist electoral victories only a year after the strikes. In August 1969 a devaluation canceled the effect of domestic inflation on France's position in world markets, opening the way to an export boom similar to the one in the early 1960s.[23] In the years before the first oil crisis, in 1973, it seemed that France had overcome its history and created an economy of corporations and wage-determining institutions that applied American principles of organization—even more self-consciously than they were applied in the United States.

The same, finally, can be said of the French system of shop-floor control. In France as in the United States, the rise of mass production meant the subversion of craft practices in the economy as a whole. This was partly the result of the deliberate destruction of the remnants of the workshop economy by the partisans of the *économie concertée*. But, more important, it was the result of the failure of the French labor movement from the end of the nineteenth century through the 1970s to take root in mass-production industry.

Owing to labor's defeats following both world wars, French managers were able to impose organizational principles that are as obstructive of the acquisition of craft knowledge as are the narrow American job structures. Firms in France carefully separate conception from the execution of tasks, translating each job into a set of detailed instructions. This approach requires (as seen in comparisons of technologically matched pairs of French and German factories) many layers of bureaucracy whose function is to do the translating and supervise its application.[24]

To an American, this system appears to be a textbook example of the Taylorist principles preached, if not always practiced, by U.S. managers. But in the United States the contemporary forms of shop-floor control grew out of the failure of a more flexible system of welfare capitalism and the decline of managerial authority in the 1930s. In France, by contrast, such shop-floor control was deliberately introduced into industry by the engineer and administrator Henri Fayol, in the early decades of this century. Fayol, unlike Taylor, was not concerned with finding the one best way to organize the flow of production among allegedly stupid and habit-ridden workers. Fayol's system of control was instead based on theories—rooted in the long history of the French public service—of how to organize an administrative apparatus.[25] The consequent bureaucratization of the French work place, combined with the absence of strong work-place unions, explains why French firms seem both to have much discretion in dealing with labor and to have none at all. In chapter 9 we will see that this bureaucratization—along with features of economic organization that are more directly borrowed from the United States—may well prove to be liabilities in the changed competitive environment of the 1980s.

Germany

Of the major industrial powers, Germany was where the craft paradigm of production remained most central to the national economy. This was true throughout the century that spanned the incipient second industrial revolution of the 1870s and the oil shocks of the 1970s. During that time, Germany was primarily a supplier of customized capital goods to world markets. And just as the need for a machine-tool industry keeps alive the practice of craft organization in a national economy dominated by mass-production, so Germany's role in the international division of labor has depended on and reinforced the dominance of the craft paradigm within the nation's industry as a whole.

The origins of Germany's vocation for craft production lie in the collaboration between nineteenth-century regional workshop economies, similar to those in France, and aggressively efficient state authorities. But the French state in this period did not attempt to control the direction of industrialization. By contrast, the German states had taken a lesson from Napoleon's victory at Jena and their ensuing success at meeting efficiency standards imposed by their revolutionary neighbor: they saw the geopolitical significance of industrialization early on. Thus, even before the unification of the German *Reich*, in 1870–71, the German states actively directed industrialization. They promoted the construction of extensive railroad and telegraph systems, they built technical schools at the service of industry, and they sponsored new firms in the emergent electromechanical and chemical industries by contracting for their products.[26] The Germans' easy victories over Austria in 1866 and France in 1870 demonstrated the strength of the industrial base of their military technology.

The organization of the German economy took form under the impact of two blows: first, the twenty-year depression that began in the *Reich* in 1873, and, soon thereafter, the arrival of American grain at prices that could not be met by the large East Elbian estates. The consequent economic downturn touched off a frantic scramble to stabilize markets through the creation of cartels, especially (as in the American experience) among producers of such standard items as steel, fertilizer, coal, and chemicals. Many of these cartels (whose legality was established by a court ruling in 1897) moved from price fixing to the imposition of production quotas to the creation of syndicates or joint-marketing organizations. Demand then grew, slowly in the 1870s and '80s, more rapidly in the boom between the mid-1890s and the outbreak of World War I (between 1873 and 1913, industrial production increased at the average annual rate of 3.7 percent). With this growth, the stabilization of market shares in product-specific technologies was introduced in the cartelized sectors, although not across the range of food-processing and engineering industries, which in the United States had shifted to mass-production technologies.[27]

The reasons for the limited success of mass production in Germany had to do with Germany's protectionist response to American grain imports and the associated reorganization of its home market. In the late 1870s, for domestic political reasons, Bismarck brokered a marriage of iron and rye: from 1879 on, tariffs protected the distressed heavy industry of the German west and the beleaguered agriculture of the German east. By increasing the price of food, these tariffs reduced the purchasing power of the working classes, thus limiting the extent of emergent mass markets for consumer durables. In addition, the political alliance ratified by the tariffs increased the power of groups at court and within industry who saw a massive arms buildup as the way to stimulate economic growth and establish national power: a vast program of fleet construction thus tied heavy industry, and its subcontractors in the engineering sector, to the state—instead of to consumer-goods mass production.[28]

German industry's craft orientation was reinforced by other factors, as well. Late-nineteenth-century programs of urban electrification created markets for large, often semicustomized electromechanical equipment that German firms—with their access to technical universities, their own research laboratories, and their reserves of skilled labor—were well positioned to exploit. And the seven large joint-stock banks that financed the major industrial concerns—through long-term loans and the underwriting of stock issues—encouraged expansion into these new sectors (especially when payment was guaranteed by the customer's access to tax revenues); by doing so these banks protected their investments.[29]

The results of this line of development stand out in contrast to the production strategies of American firms before World War I. Except for manufacturers of electrical machinery, the American engineering sector mass-produced office machines, sewing machines, agricultural implements, and automobiles—as well as standardized pumps, elevators, boilers, and the like. German manufacturers made heavier equipment, usually to customers' specifications. Whereas the Americans stressed marketing skills and services, the Germans stressed technical virtuosity. Similarly, whereas American petrochemical firms produced kerosene for lamps and gasoline for automobiles, German chemical firms dominated world markets for sophisticated aniline dyes.[30]

The craft system of production in Germany was associated with a pattern of shop-floor control and a labor movement that respectively encouraged and challenged this system. On the one hand, welfare capitalism, similar to the American form, grew up with the first large German firms. In Germany, however, the early industrial magnates modeled themselves on the odd—to American eyes—combination of feudal baron and modern welfare-state bureaucrat. The Germans' predisposition to take care of their employees perhaps made it easier for them than for their American counterparts to recognize how the provision of housing and insurance served immediate economic interests. In any case, the Germans viewed the firm as a community, governed by norms of solidarity—however distorted this view may have been by the employers' paternalist pretensions. This view implied both the collaboration of capital and labor and the substantive resolution of disputes—two key elements of the craft paradigm.[31]

The counterinfluence on this craft orientation was the German labor movement. The late-nineteenth-century Social Democratic labor movement was the most powerful and ideologically militant in Europe. By outlawing the Social Democratic Party from 1878 to 1890, Bismarck willy-nilly encouraged all workers to think of themselves as members of a single class; and by forming powerful industrywide coalitions just as the antisocialist laws were repealed, employers terrorized workers into forming industrial, rather than craft, unions.[32]

Thus, by the turn of the century, a class-conscious party allied to militant industrial unions coexisted with plant-based craft communities. Skilled workers whose trust in work-place solidarity made possible flexible production were also the members of organizations that denied capitalism any capacity for solidarity.

Improbably, defeat in World War I and the ensuing political and economic dislocations strengthened the position of the producers'-goods industry in the German economy. Moreover, an agreement was institutionalized among the plant communities, the labor movement, and the state, which safeguarded the flexibility of production and which became the matrix for German shop-floor organization in the second postwar period.

The inflation of the early 1920s reinforced the earlier pattern of German industrial development. It destroyed the savings of the middle classes; but it also canceled the indebtedness of the industrial firms, and it encouraged investment in the productive assets that would be needed in the next upturn. When American capital began to flow into the country in the mid-1920s—as part of a program of international financial restabilization—German steel, chemical, and machinery firms geared up to repay their new debts, by expanding into world markets that were expected to grow at prewar rates.

In the last half of the decade, this strategy was arguably a success. The German chemical, electronics, electrical-equipment and machine-tool industries—with their high-quality specialized products—regained dominant positions in world markets.[33] But steel was an exception. Rushing to replace production capacity annexed by the French, and ignoring the fixed-costs burden of integrated equipment, German steel producers overinvested in new plants. After 1925, the industry used cartels, fusions, and a rebate system for domestic customers with foreign markets, in order to keep domestic steel prices high. The steel firms also demanded wage cuts to make their products internationally competitive. But despite these measures, steel's problems during this period resulted more from strategic miscalculations than from a fundamental fragility of the economy.[34] A single statistic captures the continuing difference in orientation of German and American production: in 1930 in the United States, automobiles—symbol of the mass-production-mass-consumption economy—accounted for 34 percent of industrial exports; in Germany, they accounted for 2 percent.[35]

Germany's reconstitution of its export sector was accompanied by two major events: the amalgamation of the labor movement into the larger political community and the reconciliation of the industrial trade unions and the plant communities.

During World War I, the trade unions had been drawn into the national government by the promise of official recognition in exchange for their support for the militarized economy. But as defeat neared and the working classes became discontented with the costs of war, shop-steward movements (dominated by skilled workers in the Berlin armaments factories) emerged in opposition to the national labor movement.[36] When these shop stewards formed factory councils in November 1918, it seemed briefly that plant communities under worker control would be the structuring units of the labor movement and of the society as a whole: indeed, the Weimar constitution recognized these factory councils. But the limited coordinating capacity of the council movement soon became evident; the middle classes and national labor movement reestablished joint control of the economy; and a division of labor emerged between the national unions and the Social Democratic Party on the one hand, and the chastened councils on the other. The unions and the party then took responsibility for setting industrywide and national standards of pay and social-welfare benefits, either through collective bargaining or, increasingly, through legislation and binding state arbitration of the wage disputes. The factory councils applied and supplemented these standards through plant-level agreements.[37]

This situation meant that the integrity of the plant community was preserved, and the skilled workers became the representatives of the work force in factory-level negotiations with management. In the larger context of national collective-bargaining agreements and legislation, disputes could be composed according to principles of equity, without resort to the rules associated with industrial unionism in the United States. An unforeseeable balance of power emerged among parts of the labor movement and between capital and labor as a whole: this balance served as a framework within which the craft paradigm of production, consistent with the general orientation of the economy, was protected.

The collapse of world trade in the early 1930s, however, revealed the fragility of the system, and opened a brutal parenthesis in the country's industrial history. Under Hitler's leadership, all industry now rallied to a program that had seemed unthinkable when power was in the hands of liberals and Social Democrats dedicated to an open world order and repayment of reparations: this new program was autarky and imperialist expansion.[38] German liberals and Social Democrats had rejected plans (put forward by the trade unions, among others) to create jobs by reflating the domestic economy—they saw these plans as incompatible with international financial discipline. But Hitler quickly adopted expansionary policies, and imposed exchange controls to shield the economy from foreign interference.[39]

The stillbirth in the 1920s of a domestically oriented German automobile industry had been the negative image of the economy's dependence on the export of producers' goods (a wave of American-inspired rationalization and overexpansion in automobile mass production was followed by mass layoffs and contractions). And so the shift to an aggressive military form of Keynesianism was symbolized by the new Volkswagen: this workingman's car (purchased in weekly installments, supervised by the government) could also be modified into a military vehicle—together with the expansion of the highway system, it was to play a crucial role in the German campaign to create jobs.[40]

But, once more, military defeat unexpectedly renewed the predominance of the export-oriented industries in the German economy. Partition of Germany into the Federal Republic (controlled by the United States, Britain, and France) and the Democratic Republic (controlled by the Soviet Union) separated the industry of the German west from much of its prewar domestic market in the east. The size of the market within West Germany was also reduced, by currency stabilization in 1948 that, as in 1920, favored holders of productive assets over savers. Moreover, every plan of Keynesian demand stimulation was tainted by association with the Nazis' autarky policies and therefore excluded from discussion by Adenauer's neo-liberal minister of economics, Ludwig Erhard. In addition, the influx of 12 million often skilled East German refugees (a quarter of the West German population) kept wages down; and undervaluation of the deutsche mark, despite growing trade surpluses, redoubled the competitive advantage of low domestic production costs. All these factors combined—along with the Korean War boom for investment goods—to create an early post–World War II success in the world markets. Industrialists and public authorities thus were convinced that they were on the right track.[41]

Under the circumstances, it was not surprising that by the end of the 1950s West Germany emerged as a major exporter of capital equipment. Exports as a share of industrial production rose from 8.3 percent in 1950 to 15.1 percent in 1960; 70 percent of the foreign sales of the ten largest exporting industries were capital goods; and West Germany's share of world trade rose from 3.5 percent in 1950 to 7.3 percent in 1957 to 10.9 percent in 1965.[42]

Nor was it astounding that there was no macroregulatory system for the stabilization of wages. Wages, negotiated annually by region and by industry, were similar from sector to sector; but the average around which they clustered was plainly determined by the market: a report (prepared for the Organization for Economic Cooperation and Development) on the relationship between collective bargaining and inflation found that between 1953 and 1960 "one of the most striking features of the development of wages in Germany has been the responsiveness of the rate of advance of negotiated wage rates to variations in the demand situation."[43] The Bundesbank, moreover, stood careful watch over the economy, ready to tighten credit at the first sign of inflation; and given the extraordinary concentration of West German financial markets (as before World War II, a few commercial banks dominated industry, and there was no significant securities market), the central bankers' actions, or threatened actions, carried huge weight.

By an equally circuitous route the Weimar system of shop-floor control was reestablished in the second postwar period. Improbably enough, events from the Nazi seizure of power to the early 1950s repeated in broad outline the events from the 1890s to the 1920s. The fascists destroyed the national labor movement, but they defended the idea of the plant community—seen again through the paternalistic lens with which it had been viewed before World War I. Military defeat again discredited capital; and when it did, workers—once more isolated from any national movement—formed factory councils and demanded legal recognition of their rights. Finally, as capital regrouped, the priority of regional and national bargaining and legislation was reasserted; the weak support for the Left was exposed (in the 1953 elections, the Social Democrats received 28.8 percent of the vote, as against the Christian Democrats' 45.2 percent); and the labor movement revived, under the control of repatriated Social Democratic émigrés, backed by the occupying powers. As in the Weimar period, the result was a system of industrial relations in which—depending on each industry's circumstances and the condition of the economy as a whole—the unions could be viewed as federations of factory councils, or the factory councils as subordinate extensions of the unions.[44]

In the 1960s, however, economic success began to change the character of German production, macroregulation, and shop-floor control. Increasingly, firms followed the technological trajectory of mass production; and tentative steps were taken toward a system of Keynesian macroregulation. These shifts in turn menaced the organization of the shop floor along craft lines—an organization that, since the late nineteenth century, had played a key role in the success of the investment-goods sector.

The reorganization of German production was the joint result of new market opportunities and a change in the makeup of the labor market. From the early 1960s on, growing national income and the expansion of trade in Europe opened possibilities for German expansion into markets for mass-production consumer goods. At the same time, the labor market was tightening as the last reserves of skilled East German refugees were being absorbed. This combination of opportunities and obstacles seemed to dictate a single strategic choice: German firms began to recruit native-born women and foreigners (the immigrant *Gastarbeiter*) to work on American-style assembly lines at jobs presupposing no knowledge of manufacturing.[45]

This emergence of a mass-production–mass-consumption society was interpreted within the Federal Republic as requiring a reorientation of macroeconomic regulation. The government's economic advisers—as well as economic experts among the Social Democrats—believed that inflation was likely to result from the booming export market, the scarcity of labor, and (due partly to the latter) an increasingly assertive labor movement. These experts predicted that the Bundesbank would respond by tightening credit, thereby slowing growth and imposing needless costs to the economy in lost jobs and bankrupt firms. As an alternative, these economists elaborated a program that took account of the special features of West Germany's labor relations, its place in world trade, and the advances of Keynesian demand management, as advertised by the United States.[46]

The central idea was to control the domestic price level, through an incomes policy, and then to reward labor for its restraint in wage negotiations by revaluing the deutsche mark (thus increasing and using state intervention to maintain full employment). The plan was for the leaders of labor and management to meet under government auspices (they had already begun to do so in the early 1960s); they would then agree to wage increases that allowed labor to benefit from productivity gains without undermining the international position of export industry. It was assumed that the central confederation of unions would be able to hold its member associations to this agreement. As the economy prospered, the undervalued currency would be revalued enough to allow labor to benefit from cheaper imports, but not so much as to endanger exports. Moreover, whenever the international business cycle threatened domestic stability, the government would use monetary and fiscal policy, as well as public spending, to keep the economy on an even level.

The Keynesian technocrats got their chance during the recession of 1966–67. This recession, growing out of the central bank's tight money policies, was the most severe in the postwar period to that time. Alarmed at the economic situation, the reigning Christian Democrats abandoned their coalition with the small Free Democratic Party and—anxious to share the blame for the crisis if they could not master it—allied with the Social Democrats.

The new government immediately announced programs to increase state expenditures and subsidize investment; got labor and capital to agree to wage restraint; and passed the Stability and Growth Law. This law called for better budget planning, coordination of public spending at all levels of government, and annual economic forecasts to facilitate decision making. Above all, the law gave the government authority to alter tax rates and depreciation schedules, as well as to block expenditures on short notice without parliamentary approval. The architect of the legislation was the minister of economics, Karl Schiller; he defended his work in a lecture whose title reflects the intellectual climate of the time: "Business-Cycle Policy on the Way to an Affluent Society" (*Konjunkturpolitik auf dem Weg zu einer Affluent Society*).[47] The new policy never quite operated according to plan. During the abrupt recovery, increases in wages lagged behind increases in profits. In September 1969 workers reacted with wildcat strikes to the disparity between their sacrifices and capital's gains. These strikes disrupted the patterns of labor relations and led to wage increases well above the planners' goals.[48] Nevertheless, at least until 1973, the West German variant of Keynesianism appeared to work. Although firms increased their prices to cover higher wages, this proved a harmless maneuver, owing to conditions on world markets and the ability of West German exports to command a premium because of their high quality. In the early 1970s, therefore, the new arrangement, however flawed, seemed an appropriate apparatus of macroregulation.

On the microlevel, the reorganization of production inside the plants began to undermine the factory community. So long as the work force was skilled, job ladders long, and chances of promotion real, craft domination of the factory council had seemed a natural expression of the organization of production. But as the work became deskilled, the units of production came to be dominated by marginal groups, more interested in high wages than climbing (now narrow) career ladders. At this point the factory council seemed more like the crafts' instrument for defending their interests than a committee of worker representatives: in 1973 a wave of wildcat strikes supported by unskilled immigrant workers and opposed (sometimes violently) by skilled Germans revealed the tensions within the work force.[49] Meanwhile, the crafts themselves were threatened, both by the subdividing of tasks and by university-educated engineers, trained in new technologies, who were taking posts traditionally held by skilled workers, promoted step by step from the shop floor.[50]

Thus, in the early 1970s, the contours of the German production system began to blur. The market strategy, production setup, use of labor, and macroregulation associated with the American mass-production–mass-consumption economy were being superimposed on a system that had been formed by custom production for export. The confusion of the two models produced strains just as external events were about to reveal their incoherence.

Italy

The political preconditions of Italy's unification made almost impossible even a belated imitation of the American paradigm of mass production and mass consumption. Only briefly before and after World War I and in the early 1960s did an Italian version of American-style economic success seem close at hand. Most of the time over the last hundred years, disjointed efforts have been made to deploy mass-production technology without a corresponding armature of micro- and macroregulation. These efforts have led to one economic and political dislocation after another. Above all, the piecemeal installation of a mass-production regime has prevented Italian industry from reaching any lasting accommodation with labor. Periods of compromise that might have produced American- or French-style regulation of work-place relations have given way to ferocious attacks on labor's control of production and paralyzing counterattacks on managerial authority. The result has been the expulsion of skilled labor from the large mass-production firms, as well as its subordination to semiskilled hierarchies. Thus the Italian craft sector has had to survive outside the large firms.

Italy began to industrialize in the 1880s, two decades after its unification. It followed the Germans' footprints: agricultural-estate owners in the south allied with industrialists in the north to create a national market; this market was sheltered by the tariffs of 1887 against both cheap American grain and the manufactured goods of Italy's more advanced competitors.[51] Thus, large-scale mechanization was possible, but at the price of dependence on a newly formed state more notable for respect for privilege than for technologically sophisticated esprit de corps. The peasants footed the bill for state industrial subsidies—either through land taxes (avoided by the wealthy) or, in the case of millions of emigrants working abroad, through remittances to those who stayed behind.

This compromise resulted in interlocking but sometimes feuding firms that produced steel, ships, armaments, and railroad equipment. These firms were so inefficiently organized that—despite occasional technological bravura—they never outgrew dependence on the state. The Ilva steel and armor-plate mills; the Ansaldo shipyards, locomotive works, and heavy-equipment shops; and the Breda heavy-engineering works are famous examples. These firms were the chief industrial proponents of Italian imperialism until World War II—and they stumbled from crisis to crisis, flush with military orders one year, near bankruptcy the next.

Despite their ultimate failures, however, these heavy industries contributed to the rise of a more dynamic set of firms in pre–World War I Italy. They did this by introducing foreign technology and by schooling generations of craftsmen and engineers in its use. Two of these new, consumer-goods firms were Olivetti, founded in 1907, and FIAT, founded in 1899 (and financed by Turinese boosters when the Banca Commerciale shunned a venture not protected by the state). These new firms matched or exceeded international standards of technological sophistication; and their products, unlike those of the state-sponsored firms, succeeded abroad.[52]

The prosperity of this new sector was accompanied by other changes in pre–World War I Italian society—changes that might have produced a strong mass-production economy based on consumer durables and the home market. At the plant level, reformist socialists and (then) progressive industrialists (such as Giovanni Angelli of FIAT) began to bargain collectively. Prime Minister Giovanni Giolitti's liberal regime was eager to integrate the working class into the national policy by recognizing trade unions and instituting social-welfare schemes. Thus—unlike Germany and Great Britain, where industry had become conservative and imperialist—in Italy, economic advance was regarded as compatible with "orderly social progress" (ordinato progresso sociale).[53]

World War I buried this possibility of a mass-production economy, by destroying the incipient collaboration between capital and labor. Tight wartime labor markets allowed labor to increase its control over production. And workers were radicalized by a sharp fall in the standard of living and their fears regarding the consequences of forced-draft rationalization and postwar reconversion to civilian production. The example of the Russian Revolution and the emergence of factory councils in Germany, Hungary, Austria, and elsewhere led to a general strike in Piedmont and occupation of Turinese factories, both unsuccessful.

These uprisings were more a desperate defense against regrouping opponents than a revolutionary offensive.[54] Nevertheless, together with growing militance in the countryside, they provoked violent reprisals. Industrialists, landowners (especially in the Po Valley, where the agrarian wing of the Socialist Party had its greatest following), and the royal court sponsored or tolerated attacks by armed bands of demobilized soldiers; these soldiers had enrolled in the new Fascist movement out of bitterness at Italy's and their own treatment in World War I. Giolitti's attempts to assert control (by confiscating the gains of war profiteers and imposing taxes on wealth) combined in 1921 with the bankruptcy of the Ansaldo steel trust and the Banca Italiana di Sconto to draw Fascist and industrial interests closer together. In 1922 Mussolini's followers marched on Rome; three years later, the socialist labor movement had been outlawed and destroyed in the factories.[55]

The Fascists eliminated organized resistance to drastic wage cuts, and thereby invited deflationary adjustments to international economic pressure. These adjustments had profound consequences (not immediately apparent) for the development of Italian industry. In the years following the march on Rome, Italy participated in the international boom. But the domestic price level rose, and trade deficits accumulated. Mussolini responded to the deteriorating economy by revaluing the currency, restricting the supply of domestic credit, and ordering wage cuts. This action choked off a construction boom and stopped growth in the automobile industry.

Nor, when international markets collapsed, did the government make any sustained effort to stimulate mass production; the great steel and armaments combines that went bankrupt came under public control, as did those parts of the banking system that provided long-term credit to industry.[56] Wherever possible, the state encouraged substitution of domestic products for imports; but this policy of autarky had little success. Wages were cut to reduce the burden on firms, although the state did guarantee a subsistence income to workers with large families, and supplemented the wages of those who were working shortened weeks. It also instituted a system of piece-rate bargaining at the plant level, which may have kept alive traditions of local negotiation. During

World War II the workers were at least nominally protected against the effects of inflation through cost-of-living allowances.[57] Thus, although production increased during the 1930s, the workers' share in national income declined and the industrial system came to resemble the late-nineteenth-century world of inefficient trusts, utterly dependent on state protection—firms that Giolitti had tried to reform.

For a brief moment after Italy's liberation from Fascism, it seemed that labor would secure power: power enough in politics and on the shop floor to block the repressive low-wage strategies of the 1920s and '30s, and to encourage a mass-consumption economy.[58] But the Christian Democrats' victory in the parliamentary election of 1948; the Left's incapacity to organize extra-parliamentary opposition (following the unsuccessful attempt on the life of Palmiro Togliatti, the Communist leader); and then the ideological splintering of the trade-union movement cleared the way for management's counterthrust. Under attack were the remnants of the culture of skilled, socialist workers who had led the shop-floor resistance to Fascism and had experienced fleeting glory following liberation. Many of these workers were expelled from the factories; they became independent but politically isolated subcontractors. Those who stayed in the factories were often segregated from the other workers, who were increasingly intimidated. As in the years after 1925, capital had substantial freedom to reorganize the economy by its own lights.

The emergent system aimed at fostering technologically advanced consumer-durables industries, which were export-oriented. The system depended on a combination of deflationary macroeconomic policies and the accelerated introduction of mass-production technology. The consequent tight credit and reduction of government spending—especially subsidies to marginal producers—bankrupted many small firms and farms; thus unemployment went up and wages down. The low wages made Italian goods competitive on world markets—markets that had, in any case, been violently decongested by the war. With American advice, Italy had initial success, which in turn encouraged investment in product-specific technologies, typically financed by American loans and purchased in the United States.

Industrial expansion then increased both the demand for and the supply of labor: the growing sales of mass-produced consumer goods and cheap farm machinery in Italy threw thousands of artisans and agricultural laborers out of work and into the labor market. Productivity increases in the mass-production sector allowed managers to pay wages in excess of the low minimums fixed by the centralized collective-bargaining system, some of whose principles (cost-of-living allowances, family bonuses, wage differentiation according to geographic zone) had survived since the war. The high wages in such firms as FIAT—attracting hundreds of thousands of rural workers to the industrial north—helped guarantee labor peace. By the end of the 1950s, the Italians were celebrating an economic miracle.

A few years later, however, this pattern of development was disrupted—by the most sustained and widespread outbreak of labor militance seen in the post–World War II West. The masses of peasants (many of them southern) and artisans who had come to the northern plants were new to factory life; judging it against the traditional standards of their home communities, they were dismayed by the conditions of the plants and cities of the north. They absorbed and transformed the old socialism of the skilled workers into a militant egalitarianism, reflecting both their current situation and their earlier communitarian experiences in their native villages. The craftsmen were driven closer to the unskilled workers by the absence of trade-union defense against the introduction of mass-production equipment. The creation in 1960 of a high court to judge the constitutionality of the state's acts and the abolition of Fascist restrictions on internal migration (which had condemned newly arrived workers to a semilegal existence) raised hopes of institutional reform in favor of the working class. In addition, with the depletion in the reserves of young, mobile workers who could stand the killing pace of the assembly lines, labor markets were tightening; this situation increased labor's militance. In 1962 a wave of strikes dominated by the unskilled gave an indication of what was to come.

The large private firms (such as FIAT and Olivetti) and the leading state enterprises toyed with introducing American-style collective bargaining, under the auspices of the Center-Left, a coalition of Christian Democrats and Socialists that had come to power in the mid-1960s. But neither the managers in these firms nor the Christian Democrats (still beholden to small capital) could agree on a strategy; and the fundamental problem of shop-floor regulation remained unsolved. At the next economic upturn, the strikes began again, culminating in the hot autumn of 1969.

As at the end of World War I, production-line workers in the late 1960s took control of the factories. They minutely regulated and limited the pace of work, as well as management's right to hire, fire, and promote. Elected shop stewards (*delegati*) sprang up, and factory life was supervised by the plantwide councils they organized. The *Statuto dei Lavoratori,* modeled on the American Wagner Act, was passed in 1970 to guarantee the rights of these new representatives and the labor movement's access to the plants; this was done in the hopes of transforming ideological passion into concern for narrow material gains. But the act's effect was to entrench a militant rank-and-file movement with at once vague revolutionary goals and an extremely sophisticated understanding of how to control a mass-production factory.

The employers' reaction to their loss of control was immediate and decisive. From the early 1970s on, they decentralized production. Whole units were transferred to small, physically separated firms. This decentralization created work for various enterprises: the traditional artisans; the shops founded by the skilled workers who in the 1950s had been expelled, for political reasons, from the large factories; and new enterprises, many of which had been founded by middle-level managers from, and with the help of, the large firms. This decentralization was facilitated by the exodus of skilled craftsmen from the large firms. As it became clear that labor's control of the shop floor would not mean either political power (for example, through Communist participation in government) or control of industrial investment and strategy, the craftsmen came to resent the leveling of wage hierarchies and the destruction (by the *delegati*) of traditional skill ladders; they were thus lured by the prospect of high earnings in small runaway shops.

In sum, the failure to solve the problem of shop-floor relations by the mid-1970s had called into question the viability of the mass-production paradigm in Italy. More and more work, and more and more of it skilled, was occurring in the rapidly growing sector of small firms— firms that in the mass-production model would have played a subordinate role to the large assembly-line factories. The assembly-line factories that persisted were under the control of militant shop stewards. As in the early 1920s, economic progress seemed to depend on reestablishing capitalist order in the large factories.

Japan

Japan's economic success after World War II is so exceptional that one might think the Japanese institutions, if not the technology, that contributed to that success must be radically different from their Western analogues. Yet since the 1920s the Japanese economy has been built of pieces closely related to those found in Western countries: the

Japanese corporate form recalls the federation of specialized firms known in France as the *système Motte;* the Japanese system of labor control resembles the American system of the 1920s and the plant communities in Germany; and the Japanese stimulation of domestic demand is similar to American Keynesianism, although the Japanese techniques of control are closer to French than American practice. But Japan is unique in its history: it is the peculiarities of Japanese history— the nation's place in the world order, the timing of its economic development, its cultural ideas, and its vicissitudes of war—that fused characteristics shared by other nations into a distinct Japanese economic character. This character is adapted to the needs of mass production yet organized around many of the principles of the craft paradigm.

As in Germany, and Italy in the nineteenth century, industrialization in Japan was fostered by the state and explicitly linked to the assertion of national power. Japanese industrialization dates from 1868; in that year a movement for national regeneration and defense against technologically superior foreigners deposed the Tokugawa family of military shoguns (in power since the beginning of the seventeenth century) and placed the legitimate ruler, the young Meiji, on the imperial throne. In the following decade, the government built harbors, telegraph systems, and railroads; expanded the shipyards, mines, and engineering works inherited from the Tokugawa regime; reformed the legal system; and established plants in the cement, cotton-spinning, and silk-filature industries. As constructed under the shogunate, the excellent schools, the highly developed trading-and-commercial network of merchant houses, and the efficient agricultural sector and fiscal system were indispensable to the new order's success. State subsidies of industry were financed largely by a land tax on peasants, whose productivity had dramatically improved during the preceding two centuries, and whose cottage industries (especially silk weaving) supplied export earnings that covered part of the cost of imported technology.[59]

Beginning in the 1880s, however, the Japanese state began to withdraw from direct intervention in the economy. Hence a looser pattern of state collaboration with private interests—which would characterize the modern economy—took shape. The industrialization campaign produced large deficits in the state budget. The value of paper money fell; the price of rice rose; and, encouraged by the liberalism then dominating Western thought, the state sold off many of its industrial assets to private investors. Except for a brief period at the turn of the century— when railroads were nationalized and a publicly owned steel mill was established—the Japanese government promoted industrialization by granting contracts and tax exemptions to private entrepreneurs in control of large, diversified empires.

These industrial empires took the form of *zaibatsu:* confederations of about a dozen large firms—trading, insurance, and trust companies—grouped around a bank and holding company in the hands of the family that had founded the whole combine. The firms typically specialized in complementary activities, such as coal mining, shipping, warehousing, the merchandising of exports, and shipbuilding, and they held one another's stock. Yet each of the associated firms retained substantial operating independence. Thus the *zaibatsu* can be seen as a giant, capital-intensive version of the firms in the nineteenth-century French workshop economy federated according to the principles of the *système Motte.* Like the *système Motte* entrepreneurs, the founders of the *zaibatsu* often expanded by endowing sons of the traditional merchant house—the *ie*—with capital for new ventures, or by adopting trusted employees into the family for this purpose. And the connections among the member companies became, if anything, more marked as time went on.[60]

From the 1890s, the *zaibatsu* moved into industries associated with the second industrial revolution. Engineering began to become an important element of industry at the turn of the century. The chemical, steel, and electromechanical industries all developed rapidly during World War I in response to military demands and the possibility of import substitution. Despite a drop in private consumption, wartime overexpansion, and the volatility of world markets, the growth of these industries continued during the 1920s—largely because of local government spending on electrification and urban infrastructure in general.[61]

But despite the consolidation of a heavy-industry complex based on hydroelectric power, there were fluctuations in employment. These fluctuations combined with long-term shifts in the character of the work force and in management ideology to create two institutional features that became persistent, though not always dominant, motifs of Japanese industrial organization. The first institutional feature was lifetime (or at least long-term) employment guarantees for workers in large, often export-oriented firms. The second institutional feature was industrial dualism along the lines suggested in the discussion of fixed costs: a radical distinction between the large firms and the small, unstable firms that served as subcontractors and bore the brunt of business-cycle fluctuations.

Until 1890, when silk reeling and cotton spinning were the major factory industries, plants rarely employed more than thirty or forty workers. Most of the workers were young women off the farm, so it was easy for management to utilize paternalistic labor control (including, for example, the construction of dormatories and the provision of lessons in the ancient Japanese feminine graces), inspired or at least legitimated by the practice of the traditional merchant house. Growth was steady and employment levels increased regularly. But as engineering became more important and skilled male workers appeared in appreciable (though still insufficient) numbers, the situation changed. Managers began to offer employment guarantees to craftsmen, especially in shipyards, to lower labor turnover and ensure the necessary reserves of skill. The craftsmen, increasingly aware of their bargaining power, began to join the equivalent of British friendly or mutual-aid societies. The inflation and unemployment that immediately followed World War I, however, abruptly changed the character of labor organization, leading to the formation, in 1919, of a true labor federation, with unforeseeably radical aims.[62]

The firms, in the meantime, were increasingly in the hands of university-trained managers. These managers were anxious to live up to what they saw as international standards of correct behavior (and equally anxious to demonstrate that they, more than their predecessors, were unquestionably servants of the public good). Moved by some combination of moral concern, strategic calculation, and past practice, these managers responded to the economic and political disruption by extending the shipyard solution of employment guarantees to other sectors of industry. This action, of course, made craft labor a fixed cost, and in the unstable market environment of the 1920s, firms kept their core work force to a minimum; they met increased demand by drawing on the pool of unemployed or by subcontracting for what they could not produce themselves. The result was a dual structure, composed of high-wage, stable firms employing craft workers paid according to skill level (which typically corresponded to their seniority) and low-wage subcontractors.[63]

This pattern became further engrained in the Japanese economy in the 1930s; after momentary hesitation, the government redoubled its efforts to maintain the aggregate levels of demand and employment. Between 1929 and 1931 the country adopted a deflationary policy similar to the one Mussolini applied in 1927: tight credit and cost-cutting rationalization were to reduce the domestic price level and permit a return to the gold standard at an internationally respectable parity. But as the disruptive effects of the policy and the depth of the Depression became clear, a new finance minister, Takahashi, reversed course: he devalued the yen by 40 percent, increased government expenditures (particularly in rural areas), and imposed foreign-exchange controls to gain room for domestic maneuver.

Increased export revenues, state contracts, and the uncertain environment encouraged investment and cartels, as heavy industry moved both to exploit the possibilities for expansion and to protect itself against the fragility of the boom. "New" *zaibatsu* (Nissan, Hitachi, Toyota, among others) took commanding positions in such growing industries as automobiles, aircraft, and electrochemicals. By 1936, however, inflation and budgetary deficits were forcing Takahashi to moderate his program; but he was assassinated in 1936, during a putsch that grew out of the widespread conviction (paired with disdain for the "old," nineteenth-century *zaibatsu*) in military circles that Japan could weather the crisis only by imperial expansion. From 1937, therefore, military expenditures grew and the course was set for a clash between Japanese and American interests in the Pacific.[64]

Developments in postwar Japan were a traumatic reprise of the disruptions following World War I. As in Germany, military defeat and occupation led to the reemergence of prewar economic structures— above all, the reinforcement of a system of production and labor control based on largely autonomous plant communities. The original intention of the American occupiers of Japan between 1945 and 1952 was to break up the *zaibatsu* and establish national trade unions—thereby excluding those forces that had sponsored imperialist expansion. But the Americans quickly discovered that to change the Japanese economy and society, they had to rely on, and thus recognize, the Japanese state. Moreover, once the cold war began, the *zaibatsu*'s industrial experience made these combines seem necessary allies to the United States, whereas the left-wing politics of the trade unions made the unions seem potential American enemies. The Americans' half-hearted, contradictory attempts at reform thus allowed the old alliance between industry and the state to coalesce again in a program of export-led reconstruction. This alliance blocked the creation of a powerful national labor movement and allowed a system of flexible shop-floor control to emerge through collective bargaining in export-oriented plants.[65]

Although there were restrictions on the exchange of equity among federated firms, a loosely knit variant of the *zaibatsu* system was nonetheless functioning again by 1965. Firms in each group specialized in a narrow range of products and judged their performance by comparison with similar firms operating in industries defined by the same assortment of products. To move into new, complementary areas, firms formed subsidiaries; the autonomy of these subsidiaries was demonstrated by their capacity to outgrow their founders (in time, a parent firm might become nothing more than a minor stockholder in its offspring).[66] The stability of the key firms, which employed only a third of the Japanese work force, was protected by well-coordinated inter- and intra-company strategies: within firms, distinction between the conception and the execution of tasks was deliberately blurred. Large companies formed consultative boards in which labor and management exchanged information and discussed problems, but did not formally bargain. Foremen, chosen from among the most experienced workers on the shop floor, were encouraged (as in Germany) to regard themselves as the work team's representative to management, rather than vice versa (as in the United States in the postwar period).[67]

These developments were facilitated by two measures: the institutionalization of long-term employment guarantees, and extensive job rotation to familiarize workers with the context of their work and to increase their flexibility. Both were probably responses to the shortage of skilled workers after the war. The current *nenko* system of payment by length of service seems to have grown out of early postwar efforts (similar to those in France and Italy) to guarantee subsistence wage levels regardless of skill level; but since skill and seniority increased together, as a result of the general operation of the system, and older workers (who retired in their mid-fifties) could be dispatched to subsidiaries, it was integrated into the model. Finally, once the work force was multiskilled, used to consulting with management, and committed to the firm, it was easy to introduce, in the 1960s, "quality circles," in which labor-management teams improved the phases of production for which they were responsible.[68]

The Japanese government encouraged the reformation of a variant of the *zaibatsu* system by promoting sectoral-growth cartels. In Japan, as in France, most long-term investment capital is supplied to industry through banks, not the open securities market; and the Japanese authorities, like the French, were able to use control of the Bank of Japan (part of the ministry of finance and the perpetual creditor of large "city" banks with direct connection to industry) as a way of funneling cheap credit to favored sectors and firms. Import controls were used to protect infant industries against foreign competition; to channel foreign technology to rationalizing sectors; and to prevent inflows of speculative capital. Export controls were used to prevent Japanese firms from expatriating capital (except to invest in sources of raw materials); tax subsidies were used to encourage exports; and accelerated depreciation allowances were used to promote investment in new equipment. The yen was not allowed to appreciate enough to imperil the international competitive position of Japanese goods.[69]

It is difficult to estimate how much the Japanese industrial structure of the late 1960s was the direct, intended result of all these policies—rather than an unforeseen outcome of the interplay of official measures and counterstrategies pursued by private industry allied with subordinate government departments. On the one hand, it is clear that the Ministry for Industry and Trade helped underwrite highly integrated producers of such intermediate goods as steel and chemicals—whose low production costs gave their customers (in, for example, the automobile industry) cost advantages of their own.[70] But on the other hand, the fact that the Liberal Democratic Party—which has governed without interruption since the end of the war—has protected its electoral clients in agriculture and small industry may have been an indispensable precondition of success: by subsidizing the rice price, the Liberal Democrats kept the bulk of the farming population on the land, where it had to supplement its agricultural income by working in the subsidiaries of large industries established in the countryside.[71] Similarly, programs of technical assistance for small subcontractors allowed them to meet the quality standards set by the large firms, and even to develop innovative products of their own.[72]

In any case, by some combination of long-term strategy and narrow political calculation, the Japanese, by the end of the 1960s, had created an industrial structure flexible enough to move rapidly from the mass production of one high-quality good to that of another. Such mass production was due, paradoxically, to a production and labor-control system built largely on craft principles.

Genus and Species

This chapter's review of economic developments in France, Germany, Italy, and Japan shows that even if capitalist industrial societies are all of a genus, they are distinct species. Partly because these countries mechanized production in the same world but at different times; partly because some elements of the mass-production model can be substituted for others without impairing the core, these economies possess distinctive features. The features reflect both the shared characteristics of a common system and the countries' individual histories. Thus, despite strong similarities, to know one of these societies is not to know them all; nor is it possible to know any of them without considering the others. Four points stand out in the interplay of commonality and diversity that marks the industrial progress of these countries.

The first point is their common embrace of the technology of mass production. Sooner (as in Japan) or later (as in France), the elite in each country saw the commercial and military potential of a mass-production economy as indispensable to national survival. Each country therefore forsook a distinctive national form of mechanization in order to introduce machines that had been pioneered in the United States or Great Britain. Just as Westerners are now awed by Japanese breakthroughs in work organization, so Europeans and Japanese were awed by American mass-production machinery. The result was that by the late 1960s, all four of these advanced industrial countries followed the same technological trajectory.

The second point is that, like the American pioneers, mass producers in all four countries learned by bitter experience that the product-specific use of resources pays off only when market stability is ensured. The point is obvious in retrospect; but each country had to discover it under conditions of great uncertainty about the capacities of firms, states, domestic markets, and international trading regimes. There was a brief period in the 1960s when international trade was booming, the prewar monetary system was reconstituted, and domestic investment in mass-production technology surged: it then seemed that depression, autarky, war, and reconstruction had finally taught these leading industrial nations how to use the corporation, the wage system, the state, and even the fixed-exchange-rate system to create an open world economy of separate yet increasingly similar affluent societies.

But the third point is that in these four countries, the state played a dominant role in creating and stabilizing the mass-production markets—a role that was conspicuously different from the state's role in the United States. In the United States, mass markets seemed to result from technological progress, symbolized by the railroad; the state's role (in coordinating industrial activities) seemed only to complement the activities of the firms, whose autonomy was established without any exercise of public authority. In the four countries under discussion, mass-production firms and their markets were deliberately shaped by the state: the state's protection of certain domestic interests, sponsorship of alliances, and mediating role within the world economic order defined what would be produced, by which kind of firms, and for whom.

The fourth point in the interplay of commonality and diversity is that although all four countries moved in the same direction, there was at least one place where their paths did not converge: workers running equipment that was the same throughout the four countries were organized in different ways. These ways were dictated by compromises reached amidst each country's experience of war, inflation, and the threat of economic collapse. In Germany and Japan, the idea of the plant as community structured shop-floor relations even in the mass-production firms. In France, management imposed a bureaucratic organization on the shop floor, creating a system in many ways as rigid as the New Deal resolution of industrial relations. In Italy, no compromise held; the mutability of shop-floor control that is seen only in the early industrial history of more stable countries has there been a fact of daily experience.

It is the points of commonality of these four economies that, since World War II, have held the attention of theorists and practitioners—not the points of diversity. The convergent use of technology and regulatory institutions has seemed more significant to most observers than the distinctiveness of development paths and labor-control systems. The pursuit of efficiency seems to leave room for only a culturally satisfying but economically inconsequential view of tradition. Yet in chapter 9, we shall see that as the technological trajectory and regulatory institutions of mass production break apart, it is the seemingly insignificant traditions—and not least of all the labor-control systems—that determine how each economy responds to the crisis. Just as two old buildings look similar until an earthquake reveals their different structures, so the similarity of the industrial societies was in part an illusion, encouraged by a world that did not test their differences.

CHAPTER

7

The Mass-Production Economy in Crisis

FOR THE FIRST two decades after World War II, the economic structures discussed so far produced great prosperity and social stability. The industrial countries grew rapidly and, compared with earlier periods, steadily. Inflation was moderate. Unemployment was generally low, and in some places negligible. The fruits of economic expansion were widely dispersed. There was a general feeling of well-being.

No more. Starting in the late 1960s, the industrial world entered a time of troubles. One economic disruption succeeded another. As the conviction spread that events could not be explained—much less reversed—by the theories and policies of the preceding epoch, the economic disruptions merged in the public mind into a general crisis of the industrial system.

The crisis began with widespread expressions of discontent and social unrest; then came raw-material shortages, followed by rapid inflation, rising unemployment, and finally economic stagnation. In the United States and elsewhere, these signs of crisis raised questions about the fundamental social and economic institutions. There were halting attempts to reconstruct corporations, unions, and the state. But the crisis remained an unsolved puzzle: How could the institutions that had generated stability and prosperity suddenly cause inflation, unemployment, stagnation, and social unrest?

There are two ways to answer this question. One focuses on external shocks to the economic system, the way these shocks further disrupted economic activity through their effects on macroregulatory institutions, and how political responses to these disruptions—based on a false or incomplete understanding of the endangered institutions—further undermined the macroeconomic stability and aggravated the crisis. The bulk of this chapter is written from this point of view; it traces the history of the crisis as a chain of accidents compounded by mistakes.

The second answer to the puzzling turnabout of institutional performance connects the crisis to limits of development in the postwar economic system. In this view, presented in the latter part of this chapter, the crisis results from the incapacity of the late-1960s institutional structure to accommodate the spread of mass-production technology. This second explanation is consistent with an important implication of the first: that the 1970s crisis could have been avoided, or its effects much reduced, either by a manipulation of the institutions or by their reformation along the lines of their principles. But it also differs from the first explanation. The second explanation implies that, sooner or later, given the international economic order and the prevailing domestic techniques of industrial stabilization, continued prosperity would depend on a basic rearrangement of the institutional structure: enlightened crisis management might have spared the world the crisis, but not the need for critical reforms.

The Crisis as Accident and Mistake: Five Critical Episodes

Looked at as the result of external shocks rendered more disruptive by policymakers' mistakes, the crisis divides into five overlapping episodes. The first episode was the social unrest of the late 1960s and early 1970s. The second was the United States' abandonment of its commitment to exchange dollars for gold at a fixed rate, and the resulting shift, in 1971, of the international monetary system to a regime of floating exchange rates. The third and fourth episodes began with huge increases in oil prices: the first increase, accompanied by food shortages, dominated 1973 to 1979; the second increase, a result of the Iranian revolution, shaped events from 1979 to 1983. The fifth episode, beginning in 1980, was marked by the deep worldwide economic downturn produced by prolonged high U.S. interest rates.[1]

1. SOCIAL UNREST

In the United States, the social unrest of the late 1960s was associated with student protests against the war in Vietnam and with the civil-rights movement. The latter was primarily a protest movement of blacks, but their demands for equal treatment on and off the job were eventually adopted by other disadvantaged groups. In Western Europe, social unrest was more diffuse: it included students and such minorities as immigrant workers; but native-born blue-collar workers—and, in France and Italy, some white-collar workers—also seemed on the verge of revolt against the economic order. The goals of the protest were also more diffuse in Europe; these goals provoked debate about the ends and means of industrial society. In the United States, such debate was subordinated to concerns about economic opportunity and the war.

There is still no theory that convincingly explains both the simultaneity of these protest movements and their heterogeneity. A common interpretation assumes that the social stability of the preceding decades had rested on the collective self-restraint of the working masses, which was a cumulative result of preindustrial deprivation and deference, reinforced by market discipline and the suffering of the 1930s.[2] The argument is that postwar macroregulation removed the market discipline; and that as a new generation matured in the postwar prosperity, without memories of the Great Depression or the flux that preceded it, the freedom from such constraints encouraged protest against the remaining ones. A radical interpretation along similar lines sees the protests as an extension to the work place of the democratic rights of political participation.[3]

There is, however, an alternative view of the working-class unrest in the United States and Western Europe. This view focuses not on changes in the workers' environment but on the changing attitudes of the workers; the view connects these latter changes to the structure of macroeconomic regulation as we have presented it.[4] Because of the rigid wage structure in the United States and the labor shortages in Europe as the economy moved toward mass production, there was, as we saw, a need for reserves of labor available on call to industry at the prevailing wage. In the early postwar decades in the United States, these reserves consisted largely of blacks from the rural South, women, and youths. In Europe, the reserves consisted of agricultural workers, women, and youths, augmented by immigrants.

The smooth operation of the labor market, and of the fixed-price allocative system as a whole, depended on the willingness of these reserves to move in and out of the factory labor force on demand. Such conditions of employment were acceptable so long as these marginal groups saw themselves as outsiders to industrial society, and their industrial income as a means of establishing or defending their place in the extra-industrial world. Rural blacks in the United States and immigrant workers in Europe wanted money from the factory to support rural life and to buy or enlarge farms at home; women wanted factory money to pay off a mortgage, and then they would return full-time to homemaking; young people wanted factory money for college or simply for the apparently endless pleasures of adolescence. Given this situation, these workers were not interested in acquiring factory skills—skills that were irrelevant to their long-range plans. Nor were they determined to win job security—during downturns, farmers could go back to the farm, women to the home, young people to their parents.

Nevertheless, as the example of the southern Italians in the last chapter showed, these workers were drawn into full participation in industry. This evolution had important consequences for their self-conception and, hence, their labor-market behavior. The more these people saw themselves as permanent members of the industrial work force—dependent on factory work—the more they aspired to stable, high-status, well-paying factory jobs. At the same time, the conditions that they had tolerated when they considered themselves marginal to the labor force came to be viewed as confining and unjust. This view has been documented in studies of southern Italians in Turin and Milan, blacks in Detroit, Portuguese immigrants and native-born former agricultural workers in France, and Turkish immigrants in West Germany.[5]

This alternative interpretation is consistent with the protesters' demands and the changes to which these demands led (even though it is difficult to trace a direct connection between shop-floor militancy and institutional reform). In the United States, the chief effect of the protests was to bring the disaffected groups under the institutional protections from which they had been excluded. For example, large agricultural employers were obliged to pay minimum wages. By tying the wages of the rural labor reserve to the national wage structure, this extension of coverage ensured that all wages would rise—however belatedly and underproportionally—with the rise in the minimum wage. Another series of reforms extended the system of income maintenance to previously marginal workers. This was done through modest changes in the unemployment and social-security systems and a dramatic increase in the provision of relief to indigents.

In Western Europe, Marxism provided the axial principles for debate among leftist parties and trade unions. The protests here were thus interpreted as signs of an incipient social transformation—the beginning of the transition from capitalism to socialism?—rather than as demands for the extension of constitutional rights. But despite all the talk of revolt against capitalism and industrial society (and even experiments with new forms of production that were later to prove significant), the protests brought reforms that moved the European economies closer to the American type of macroregulation. In France, as we saw in the last chapter, wages were indexed to the cost of living, and job security and unemployment-insurance benefits increased. In Italy, the *Statuto dei Lavoratori* was only the first in a series of reforms, including wage indexing, that made pay levels and purchasing power independent of the situation on the labor market. And the same holds for the *Arbeitsförderungsgesetz* (Work-Encouragement Law) of 1969 in West Germany.

The price of all these changes was to make each national economy more vulnerable to wage inflation. Such wage inflation arose from either labor shortages or trade-union demands, backed by shop-floor militancy, for a greater share of national income. But in the early 1970s, employers took countermeasures. In the United States, they hired young people, illegal immigrants from Latin America and the Caribbean, and an increased number of women—none of whom demanded inflated wages. In France, firms found ways around the new employment guarantees by hiring workers from temporary-help agencies and introducing short-term employment contracts.[6] In Italy, as we saw, large corporations subcontracted work to small firms. And in West Germany, employers were able to shed surplus labor when necessary because employment guarantees were not buttressed through legislation and because divisions within the work force blocked the unions from protecting the jobs of unskilled immigrants as tenaciously as the jobs of skilled Germans. Similarly, the example of the American grievance procedure suggested that union strength on the plant level was compatible with rapid economic growth, provided that the contest for power in the shop was subject to appropriate rules.

In the United States, the reforms of the early 1970s were seen as a natural extension of the existing system; in Europe, the reforms were seen as an acceleration of the modernization (Americanization) of society. Moreover, the costs of change seemed bearable to those who had to pay them. For these reasons, this first episode of the crisis was seen as a continuation of postwar developments, as much as the first crack in the system. Thus, the protests had indeed scotched the belief (widespread since the early 1960s, even within the European Left) that economic progress made protest obsolete; but the persistence of the institutions and the direction of the reform suggested that further progress down familiar paths might vindicate that earlier belief. Even as this hope gathered strength, however, in the early 1970s, other changes in the system forestalled its realization.

2. FLOATING EXCHANGE RATES

In the wake of the social unrest of the 1960s, the international monetary system underwent a major change: the abandonment of fixed exchange rates and the shift to a system of floating currencies. This shift was not widely perceived as a critical episode in the development of the capitalist industrial world—at least not in the sense of the social unrest that preceded or the oil-price shocks that followed it. To the average person in the industrial countries, it passed as a technicality, beyond immediate understanding or concern. But it was an important technicality. It was compelled by the European countries' response to the social unrest of the late 1960s and, in its turn, it compelled much of the global response to subsequent events.

The immediate cause of the change in the international monetary system was the rapid deterioration in the late 1960s in the United States' competitive position in international markets. The loss of competitiveness was due largely to domestic inflation, touched off by President Johnson's unwillingness to raise taxes to pay for the Vietnam war.[7] By mid-1971, the surplus in the balance of payments on goods, services, and remittances had fallen from a high of 7.6 billion dollars in 1964 to near zero. The change in the balance of merchandise trade alone was even more dramatic.[8] Because the dollar's role as the international reserve currency was, as we saw in chapter 5, already precarious, this development opened the way for international speculation and panic. To defend the dollar's privileged place in the Bretton Woods system of fixed exchange rates, the United States would have had to abandon its freedom to set domestic economic policy, and instead tailor its actions at home to the needs of safeguarding industrial competitiveness abroad. Faced with this prospect, President Nixon in 1971 instead sacrificed the American commitment to convert foreign currencies to dollars and dollars to gold at fixed rates. The dollar was first devalued and then—although monetary authorities continued to intervene in currency markets—allowed to float in value relative to other currencies over an increasingly wide range.[9]

170

But even without the deterioration in the U.S. trade position, Western Europe's institutional response to the social unrest of the late 1960s made the change in the exchange system inevitable. Whereas the fixed rates freed the United States from international constraints, they forced other nations, as we have seen, to subordinate domestic economic policy to the requirements of balance-of-payments equilibrium. Once the European countries committed themselves to maintain domestic purchasing power through demand management and (as in France and Italy) linked the wage structure to the cost of living, shortfalls in current accounts could not easily be corrected by adjustment of the domestic price level. Hence trade imbalances created pressure in the European countries to free their currencies from the burden of maintaining a fixed rate under the prevailing rules of the International Monetary Fund.

But if a major reform in the international monetary system had by 1971 become inevitable, the decision to adopt floating exchange rates had not. The corrective for the deficit in the U.S. balance of payments— the proximate cause of the exchange crisis—was devaluation. Devaluation could have been accomplished by realigning currency values within a fixed-rate system. Devaluation of the dollar would not by itself overcome the unwillingness of both the United States and other major trading countries to make their short-term domestic policy dependent on their international competitive position. But this problem could have been solved by returning to one of the plans rejected at Bretton Woods: providing the international monetary system with enough liquidity to allow any country to sustain a balance-of-payments deficit in the medium term. A persistent deficit would eventually have to be corrected, for a deficit implies that a country is living off the exports of the rest of the world, and other countries—despite their desire to accumulate foreign exchange—will not tolerate this situation indefinitely. But an expansion of liquidity, as our earlier discussion suggested, enables the structural adjustments needed to eliminate such a deficit to be made over a relatively long period of time. A system of fixed exchange rates capable of absorbing some of the shocks of structural change might have been preserved; this could have been done either by creating a new international-payments instrument—distributed so as to expand the trading countries' reserves—or by equipping the IMF or some other international agency to lend funds on easy terms to deficit-ridden countries.[10]

Instead, the system of floating exchange rates that was created was the composite result of political expediency, the prevailing economic theory, and sheer accident. Pressure on the dollar under the old system increased so rapidly that there was no time for the multilateral negotiations required to install what would be a supra-national bank. An agreement upon a new set of relatively fixed rates was reached only in 1972, and it was not supplemented by the institutional reforms that might have made it effective. A system of floating rates thus emerged, seemingly by default. But, beyond this, there was a strong preference for flexible rates among influential American economists. That preference led them to see a virtue in what would soon become a necessity, and to discourage efforts to negotiate another solution.

The economists' preference for floating rates is partly due to the aesthetics of their profession. Floating rates fit more naturally into the kinds of auction markets that neoclassical economists typically analyze than do fixed rates. But insofar as it rested on a considered theoretical judgment, the preference for letting the dollar float was based on two arguments. First, in a system of fixed rates, adjustments in currency values must be corrected by adjustments in the prices of individual commodities. Hence, a shift to flexible rates means that the adjustment of a single price replaces the adjustments of hundreds of thousands of prices—the price of the currency changes, not the price of all the individual tradables. One price change is simpler, more efficient, and less subject to random disturbance than many price changes. The second argument for floating the dollar was that flexible exchange rates would insulate each economy from the home-market policies of the others; thus all the economies would be freed from the constraints of international trade.[11]

But these arguments neglected an important aspect of the use of money, as well as fundamental features of the micro- and macroregulatory systems of the postwar economies. These oversights explain why it was impossible to reap the promised benefits of the new system. They also explain why the shift to floating rates became an obstacle to subsequent attempts at stabilization.[12]

To begin with, the first argument for floating rates was irrelevant. This was because, as we have seen, the internal wage-price structure in a Keynesian system of macroeconomic regulation is relatively rigid. All wages and prices in a national system move up and down together, as if indexed to a single base. Under these circumstances, it does not make much difference whether the exchange rate or the domestic price level changes. Either way, only one adjustment is required.

The second argument, regarding the insulating capacities of a floating-rate system, was also wide of the mark. This was owing, again, to the rigidity of the production system. When a major trading nation went into a recession, its demand for the goods of its partners fell off. In the neoclassical view, changes, caused by the recession, in the relative prices of traded goods would, under a floating-rate regime, return the demand for foreign products to its original level. But under the conditions of the 1970s, economic activity in many major trading countries had become so dependent on domestic conditions that once an economy went into recession, modest increases in exports did not produce the burst of investment and consumption necessary to restore demand for imports: neo-Keynesianism had taken hold enough so that domestic policy was necessary for domestic recovery, but not so much that economic conditions in one country had no influence on conditions in its trading partners. The net result was that, despite the change to floating exchange rates, major trading countries were still hostage to one another's actions—not through the impersonal mechanisms of the international monetary regime, but, more directly, through the effect of one nation's expansionary or restrictive policies on the markets of the others. Thus, the move to floating rates did not solve the problem of international economic interdependence any more than it simplified corporate bookkeeping.

Furthermore, because an important function of money was not considered, the shift to the new system did not shore up disrupted international commerce but, rather, weakened its foundations. Money, as any elementary text will tell you, has three functions: it serves as a unit of account that expresses the value of different commodities relative to one another; it serves as a medium of exchange; and it serves as a store of value. The case for flexible exchange rates was derived from the first two of these functions. But in addition to using money in these two ways, people hold money—particular currencies—because they think it a safe means of storing value—safer than alternative assets. The demand for a particular currency can shift radically, according, for example, to investors' beliefs about the prospects for political stability in one country or one area of the world. Under a fixed-exchange regime, a shift in demand for a country's currency will not affect the world-market price of that country's products. But under a variable-exchange regime, a shift in demand for a currency does affect the price of tradables. Changing views of the safest store of value—the safest currency—are probably the most important reason for the wide fluctuations in the value of the dollar since 1971.[13] This means that the shift to floating exchange rates made the price of goods in international trade

hostage to forces only distantly connected to national economic performance—and almost impossible to forecast and control.

These unpredictable exchange-rate fluctuations, in turn, wreak havoc
with a mass-production economy; they also produce political reactions
that threaten the whole open-trading system. That would not be so in
the world envisaged in neoclassical economics. Neoclassical theory
depicts international exchange as a set of extremely flexible relationships,
in which demand shifts easily among countries and commodities. But
in mass production, as we have repeatedly emphasized, producers make
long-term commitments to certain production techniques. Once these
commitments are made, it is difficult, if not impossible, to shift to
different techniques. For example, the Japanese entry into the U.S.
automobile market required changes in product design and the creation
of a network of dealers and repair facilities. These are long-term
investments, and the Japanese might not have made them had they
expected wide fluctuations in the value of the dollar relative to the yen.
But having made these investments, they were unlikely to abandon
them simply because the dollar's value changed temporarily. On the
contrary, the Japanese—and all others in such situations—were much
more likely to defend existing markets by searching for some administered solution (barter deals, contingents, etc.) to the problem of market
fluctuations. Such solutions, however, undercut the reigning free-trade
principles. Thus, the unexpected, increasing volatility of exchange
rates—due to the hunt for a safe store of value—created two more
obstacles to a return to business-as-usual under the existing regulatory
regime: it discouraged investment in mass production, and it encouraged
the formation of major trade blocs (as, for example, the system of fixed
rates within the European Economic Community, which raised fears of
a return to autarky).

In sum, the change to a system of floating exchange rates solved
immediate problems both for the United States and for its major trading
partners; but its long-term effect was to increase the confusion and
instability of world markets. The value of the dollar fluctuated widely
with respect to other major currencies, and in a fashion that could not
be explained by trade flows, or differences in interest and inflation rates.
Consequently, the variation in the price of the dollar was impossible to
predict.[14] This variation was especially marked in the early 1980s, as
shown in table 7.1. Although it is difficult to assess its effects on
economic activity, it is clear that this variation (like the two changes
in the postwar order that are discussed next) weakened the stability on
which mass production was based.

TABLE 7.1
Effective Exchange Rate of the U.S. Dollar*
(1975 = 100)

1970	118.6
1971	115.7
1972	107.4
1973	98.5
1974	101.0
1975	100.0
1976	105.2
1977	104.7
1978	95.7
1979	93.7
1980	93.9
1981	105.7
1982	118.1

SOURCE: International Monetary Fund, *International Financial Statistics Yearbook*, vol. 24 (Washington, D.C.: IMF, 1983).
* This index measures changes in the effective exchange rate. It combines the exchange rate between the U.S. dollar and other major currencies with weights derived from the International Monetary Fund's Multilateral Exchange Rate Model (MERM). Each weight represents the model's estimate of the effect on a given country's trade balance of a change of one percent in the domestic currency price of one of the other currencies.

3. THE FIRST OIL SHOCK AND THE RUSSIAN WHEAT DEAL

In 1973, the Western world was still dominated by memories of the 1960s protests, and it still did not suspect the full impact of floating exchange rates. At that point, two events marked the beginning of the next episode of the postwar industrial crisis: the Arab oil embargo and the Soviet wheat deal. Neither was a direct result of economic developments in the advanced capitalist countries. The wheat deal was triggered by a chain of poor harvests in the Soviet Union, which forced the Soviets to turn to Western markets to overcome the shortages. The oil embargo was a political reaction of the Arab states to Western support for Israel in the Arab-Israeli war of 1973. But regardless of their origin, both events increased the instability of national economic systems that were predicated on rigid wages and prices and hence vulnerable to shortages in basic inputs and raw materials.

Surplus agricultural stocks had been accumulated in the United States as a buffer: to stabilize agricultural prices according to analogous principles in the industrial sector. These surplus stocks had kept world agricultural prices within a narrow range, despite wide annual variations in growing conditions. But the Soviet wheat deal exhausted the stocks, so—for the first time in the postwar period—a change in demand was reflected directly in prices.[15] The reduction in the supply of oil caused by the Arab embargo had the same effect on prices as the increase in Soviet demand for wheat. The will and capacity of the Arab world to expand production on demand had provided an oil buffer comparable to the U.S. grain stocks; when this buffer was removed, oil prices, too, reflected variations in scarcity.

The wheat deal and the oil embargo posed exactly the same threat to the regulatory systems of the advanced countries as had the protests of the marginal work force in the 1960s. But if the threat was the same, the advanced countries' ability to counter it was not: whereas corporations had quickly found new labor reserves, there was no quick way to replenish the depleted stocks of grain and oil. Shortages of food and fuel thus led rapidly to higher prices in the market. Given the rigid wages and prices central to the system of macroeconomic regulation, price increases in these crucial markets levered all wages and prices upward. This rise set off an unprecedented wave of inflation in virtually all the industrial countries. Everything that made for stability in times of plenty increased instability in times of want.

The inflation was, however, only one effect of this depletion of buffer stocks. Another was an enormous increase in uncertainty. The uncertainty regarding food was limited, because the United States could control Soviet access to Western markets, which it quickly did. But regarding fuel, the uncertainty was great: the Arabs' ability to ration oil and thus drive up its price was not readily controlled; and despite the increase in the general price level, the restraints on supply resulted in changes in the price and availability of oil relative to other goods. A sudden, one-time shift in relative prices would have been disruptive enough. But the actual situation was much worse, because it was never clear whether the changes in relative price and availability were permanent (in fact, in the years following the embargo, the relative price of oil dropped).

This was exactly the kind of uncertainty that mass producers—with their long-term investment in high-fixed-cost, specialized assets—found most difficult to manage. Should they plan production on the assumption of low energy prices or high ones? The dilemma is illustrated by the fluctuations in the demand for fuel-efficient cars: demand rose from 9.3 percent of the U.S. market before the crisis, in 1967, to 32.4 percent in 1975; and then it fell, by 1978, to 26.4 percent.[16] Such uncertainty about the product was compounded by uncertainty about the operating costs of the production equipment. Together, these uncertainties meant a quantum leap in the cost of mass production relative to that of craft production. The reduction of the efficiency advantage of mass production was equivalent to a once-and-for-all reduction in the size of the market.

Along with the inflation and the uncertainty was a third effect of these shocks: a shift in the objective of economic policy in the industrial world. The shift was from expansion to restraint. Virtually all industrial economies made this shift in response to the rise of prices, though some countries were slower to do so than others. The Japanese moved first. They had not experienced the social upheavals of the 1960s, and because they were the most dependent on imported energy, they experienced the most pronounced inflationary response (the Japanese consumer price index rose seventeen percentage points in 1973–74 and eleven more in 1974–75).[17] The United States—where unemployment was becoming an all-purpose "cure" for economic problems—also reacted quickly. The shift was slowest in Western Europe: there the memory of the upheavals of the 1960s was sharpest, and the fear of rekindling protest, by a restrictive policy, the greatest. Germany, with its institutionalized horror of inflation, adopted a more rigorous policy than France or Italy. But despite all these differences in timing and rigor, as one economy after another deflated, the interdependencies of international trade took their toll: all the industrial world went into recession. As it did, social protest did not—as feared—increase; this encouraged the political leaders to persevere in the deflationary policies. The result was that the growth of mass markets—already retarded by the uncertainty of oil prices and of exchange rates—was further slowed by the decline in demand.

The final result of the first oil shock was to move the epicenter of economic expansion from the developed world to the developing world. During the 1950s and '60s, economic output had grown more rapidly within the developed than within the developing world, and trade among developed countries had increased much faster than trade between them and the developing countries. But after 1973, the rate of growth of the industrial world slowed considerably. The U.S. slowdown, from 2 percent for 1965–70 to 1.4 percent for 1970–75, was actually the least severe among the major industrial countries. In Japan, the average annual growth rate of per-capita gross domestic product fell at this time from 10.5 to 3.4 percent. In Germany, it fell from 3.7 to 1.6 percent; in France, from 4.4 to 3.2 percent; in Italy, from 5.2 to 1.6 percent; and in the United Kingdom, from 2.2 to 1.6 percent.[18]

The impact of the oil crisis was much less severe on the growth rates of the developing countries. The continuing expansion in this part of the world economy had several causes. In some cases, of course, the growth was attributable to the increase in oil revenues. In Southeast Asia, growth was maintained by capturing a share of the developed world's market for the low-wage mass production of consumer goods—especially textiles, garments, and electronic components. Other economies, such as Brazil and Poland, kept growing through extensive foreign borrowing.[19] The large revenues accumulated by the oil-exporting countries and deposited in the banks of the industrial nations facilitated this last strategy; because of these petrodollar reserves, interest rates were relatively low and the banks willing to lend.

The upshot of this shift in the epicenter of economic growth was that from 1971 to 1974, manufactured exports from the developing countries increased at an average annual rate of 25.6 percent; in the developed countries, the rate was 11.2 percent. The developing countries' share in the growing world market rose from 5.8 percent in 1968 to 8 percent in 1976; and the share of three of the newly industrialized economies—Hong Kong, Korea, and Singapore—doubled during the period, from 1.5 to 3 percent of world exports.[20] In particular industries, the growing role of the third world was even more pronounced. Thus in 1980, cars, trucks, and buses produced in Mexico and Brazil together accounted for 4.2 percent of new-vehicle sales worldwide; and their output was equal to almost 15 percent of the new vehicles sold in the whole U.S. market. If Argentina is included in the calculation, the Latin American automobile market for that year equaled 17 percent of the U.S. market.[21]

The shift in the locus of world trade served further to destabilize and confuse industrial producers. It was undoubtedly a factor in deterring mass production and favoring more specialized technologies. Who could know which industry would next come under attack from the newly industrializing countries—and when?

4. THE SECOND OIL SHOCK

The fourth episode in the calendar of crisis was the second oil shock. This shock was produced by the Iranian revolution of 1979. Even by the standards of the 1970s, it was a very shocking shock. For it came just as the advanced capitalist countries were convincing themselves that they had a good chance of recovering from the preceding disturbances with their institutions and ideas of economic policy intact. Just before the upheaval in Iran, the West Germans had taken expansionary domestic measures, and they were encouraging their trading partners to do the same. The International Monetary Fund—influenced by expansionary impulses in Washington—was considering easy-credit policies toward third-world debtors; such policies, if coordinated with private banks' lending programs, might have led to an expansion of world purchasing power. But the second oil shock destroyed confidence in the system of international adjustment—at precisely the moment when the resilience of that system was encouraging experimentation that might have led to major reform.

Again, oil prices rose dramatically. This time, however, the impact of the increased oil prices on the internal price structures of the developed countries was more varied. In the United States, France, Great Britain, and Italy, it produced a rapid price inflation, as it had done in 1974 (the national-income deflator—a measure of the inflation rate—rose in these countries, respectively, 8.5, 10.6, 16.1, and 17.1 percent). By contrast, in Germany and Japan inflation was extremely moderate (4.3 and 2.8 percent—much below the 1968–78 rates of 5.1 and 7.4 percent).[22]

The inflation forced the Western economies to restrain demand; led by the United States, they slipped by 1980 into a recession. In that year, GNP declined, or stagnated, in all Western countries but Italy. But Japanese GNP expanded by 5.5 percent—about the same rate as the year before, and almost 2 percentage points above the rate of expansion in the years following the first OPEC shock.

The recession in the industrial world, the inflation, and the huge OPEC earnings—recycled through the world banking system—made real interest rates low if not negative (the real interest rate is the difference between the rate at which money can be borrowed from banks and the rate at which it is losing value because of inflation). In other words, it could cost next to nothing to borrow money at one year's interest rates and pay it back with the next year's inflated earnings. An effect of these low interest rates was further to encourage borrowing in the developing nations. Another effect was the increased difficulty for the United States of containing the inflation.

The recession of 1980 was slow in coming and relatively shallow; policymakers were unsure how severe it was. The American economy stagnated; unemployment rose slightly; productivity declined. But inflation continued. Ultimately, the Federal Reserve Board responded by driving up real interest rates to unprecedented levels. The Federal Reserve discount rate—the price banks pay for money when their own reserves do not cover their needs—rose more than 7 percentage points during this period, from 5.5 percent in 1977 to 13.4 percent in 1981. The prime rate charged by banks surged from 6.8 to 18.9 percent. The real interest rate (adjusted for inflation) rose from near zero in 1979 to 9.4 percent in 1981.[23]

5. HIGH INTEREST RATES, WORLD RECESSION, AND THE DEBT CRISIS

These unprecedented interest rates produced the fifth episode in the economic crisis. With these rates, the industrial world was finally driven into a deep, prolonged recession. And, in contrast to the earlier years of the crisis, the developing world was now forced to follow. Moreover, the developing nations had to refinance—at astronomically high rates— the debts that they had contracted at relatively low interest rates in the 1970s; they had to do this in the context of depressed world trade, which limited their ability to earn foreign exchange. In addition, many of these countries had contracted the debts to finance development programs on the assumption that world markets would expand as they had done in the early postwar period; the changed economic environment made many of these plans unworkable and thus jeopardized the debtors' ability to pay off their loans.

The problems this pattern of lending has produced could be resolved if the International Monetary Fund and the U.S. monetary authorities were willing to defend the liquidity of the world banking system. But the United States has been reluctant to provide the kind of funding for the world monetary system that would make the resolution of these problems systematic and automatic. As a result, each refunding has prompted bargaining among the monetary authorities, the creditor banks, and the debtor governments; this haggling has created a climate of anxiety about the state and direction of world markets.

Given the U.S. stakes in the world banking system, it is unlikely (although not impossible) that the United States will allow the world monetary system to collapse. But the United States and the IMF have used the recurrent negotiations to try to impose a "disciplined" national economic policy on the debtors; and the contentious refinancing has unsettled markets and confused business decisions in debtor nations regarding production and sales. These effects are compounded by the difficulty of assessing how the economic programs imposed by foreign lenders affect the domestic politics and social stability of the borrowers. No one knows what to expect.

Finally, the imposition of austerity programs aggravates even further the world depression. Austerity can, at most, be justified as buttressing the financial integrity of any one country; if each country were indeed acting alone, austerity just might serve both the interests of the international creditors and domestic interests. But applied as a general policy, austerity reduces world trade—offsetting any benefits to single national economies or the world financial system.

Together with long-term energy conservation, the recession has produced a sharp drop in the demand for oil. The declining oil revenues have, in turn, forced the energy producers to join the rest of the world in recession. Moreover, some producer countries have attempted to make up for the declining revenues by expanding oil production, thereby exceeding the OPEC production quotas and thus straining the structure of the cartel—to the point that it was in danger of collapse. This danger further added to the volatility of world markets, for it menaced the international banking system and generated more uncertainty about the nature of demand for individual commodities.

A SHIFT IN PUBLIC POLICY

By the end of the 1970s, the world economy was in a state of confusion owing to the second oil-price shock, the high U.S. interest rates, and the worldwide recession. This confusion was aggravated by a shift in the attitude of policymakers toward economic institutions. Policy during the first two critical episodes (the social unrest and the floating exchange rates) had been the application of Keynesian logic; policy during the following three episodes (the two oil shocks and the high interest rates) was an attack on the institutions that had made that logic workable. This turnabout was not seen as a radical break: rather, it was seen as a corrective (costly but necessary) to the "excesses" of the preceding period. Because it was understood in this narrow way, policymakers never considered the coherence of the overall system, or the implications of the social changes that they now sought.

In the United States, the burden of the new policy was to restore the pressure of the market on wage and price decisions. This was done by eliminating government institutions that had restricted entry to markets and had controlled prices and the provision of services within markets. This shift in policy is plainly seen in the markets for oil and other forms of energy where regulation had been extensive. Whereas, in the first oil crisis, price controls had been imposed (leading to rationing and misallocation of resources), these controls were eliminated in the second oil crisis (freeing the price of heating oil and gasoline to vary according to market conditions).

The "decontrol" of petroleum prices was part of a general effort to restore the free play of market forces. Government regulation was amended or eliminated when it blocked competition in the banking, airlines, and trucking industries; the telephone and telegraph service; and radio and television broadcasting. There was also an attempt to eliminate state measures that reinforced the rigid wage structure.

181

Although these last efforts were not generally successful, changes in the level and scope of regulations exposed more of the work force to market pressures. Thus, for example, the effective minimum-wage rate was lowered, and previously covered employers were exempted through changes in administration of the program. Similarly, the interpretation of the Davis-Bacon Act—which since the 1930s had tied wages for federal construction to local union wages—was relaxed to allow employment of cheaper construction labor. Also weakened was the enforcement of restrictions on industrial piecework done at home. And so on.

These changes combined with the pressure of the recession to produce a major break in the postwar system of wage determination. In sharp contrast to the recent past, industries (and within industries, individual companies) began to sign collective-bargaining agreements that reflected their individual competitive positions in world markets and that suspended the wage-determination rules central to the postwar regulatory structure (a point to which we will return in chapter 9).

Outside the United States, European and Japanese politicians also affirmed a commitment to the market as regulator of economic activity. But this commitment was not strong, nor did it strongly influence economic activity. France, Japan, and, to a lesser extent, West Germany, as we saw, had industrial policies that had been formed by the state together with corporations and financial institutions. The market in these countries was seen, at least partly, as an instrument with which to benefit industries that state planners championed, and to penalize industries that they had decided to sacrifice; but the market did *not* serve as a forum for the determination of the goals of economic development. Nonetheless, a new willingness to shift some of the burden of regulating the economy from the state to the market represented a shift in policy, especially in France and Japan. And in some countries (France, again, is a notable example), the government's action in the labor market paralleled efforts in the United States to increase the play of competitive pressures on wages and unemployment.

These efforts at governmental "deregulation" were an attack on the institutions that had created and maintained the stability presupposed by mass production. Their effect, in the short run, was to exacerbate the confusion introduced by the economic crisis—penalizing mass production yet again and pushing industry toward more flexible production and marketing strategies. Increased competition undoubtedly lowered some prices, at least temporarily. But by pushing industries into unfamiliar situations and promoting radical restructurings, deregulation also lowered productivity, and it may have raised unemployment.

182

THE CRISIS AS CRITICAL EPISODES: AN OVERVIEW

Seen as accidents and mistakes, the economic disorder began as a crisis of *supply* and then (owing to responses of the regulatory system and of the government) turned into a crisis of *demand*.

There were three critical supply shocks: the labor shortages produced by the revolt of the marginal labor force; the food shortages occasioned by the poor Soviet harvests; and the oil shortages of 1973 and 1979. Given the rigid wage-price structures of postwar macroregulation, these shortages set off an inflationary spiral. This spiral was the first symptom of the crisis.

The subsequent symptoms were slow growth, low productivity gains, and rising unemployment. These symptoms were produced by the crisis of demand. The demand crisis had both a familiar and a novel aspect. It was familiar in that it was a classic deficiency of aggregate demand: policymakers' efforts to control inflation through monetary and fiscal restraints produced recessions in 1974, 1980, and 1982–83. The novel aspect of the demand crisis was its association (part cause, part effect) with growing confusion about the level and composition of demand in individual markets, and about the price and availability of resource inputs.

This confusion led to the breakup of mass markets for standardized products. It did so by reducing the portion of demand that employers saw as sufficiently long-term to justify the long-term fixed-cost investments of mass production. Because mass production was the engine of growth in the postwar period—indeed, throughout most of industrial history—the breakup of mass markets led to a decline in the rate of productivity increases and thus to slower growth. The desire to maintain flexibility also discouraged firms from long-term hirings. During upticks in the economy, companies typically preferred to employ current workers for longer hours rather than to hire additional ones. This and other practices—especially the use of part-time and temporary workers—increased the level of unemployment associated with a given level of employment or aggregate demand. The initial supply shocks alone would have produced some of these effects, because they introduced uncertainty about the availability of various inputs; they also, in the critical automobile industry, raised unanswerable questions about the composition of demand. But the responses of public policymakers aggravated the situation. Their efforts to control inflation and to enhance price and wage flexibility caused the fluctuations in demand that intensified the confusion.

THE SECOND INDUSTRIAL DIVIDE

The Crisis as Limitations of the System

Viewed as in the preceding description, the economic crisis seems the product of fortuitous, historically contingent events. But there were also long-term trends at work that made a crisis in the postwar regulatory system extremely likely. Analysis of these trends suggests a more fundamental explanation of the economic history of the last decade.

THE SATURATION OF INDUSTRIAL MARKETS

The most consequential and long-term postwar development was the saturation of consumer-goods markets in the industrial countries, and the consequent interpenetration—through trade—of the industrialized economies. By the late 1960s, domestic consumption of the goods that had led the postwar expansion had begun to reach its limits. This saturation was especially true in the United States, where in 1979 there was one car for every two residents, compared with one for every four in the early 1950s.[24] Ninety-nine percent of American households had television sets in 1970, compared with 47 percent in 1953. Similarly, more than 99 percent of households had refrigerators, radios, and electric irons, and more than 90 percent had automatic clothes washers, toasters, and vacuum cleaners.[25]

Because of this saturation, it became more and more difficult to increase economies of mass production through the expansion of domestic markets alone. Further development along the trajectory of mass production thus brought the major industrial economies into direct competition for one another's markets and for those of the developing world. It also exposed the limits of the postwar regulatory system.

That system—as elaborated in the United States and institutionalized to varying degrees elsewhere—had been designed to promote economic expansion within the borders of discrete nations. The adjustments to the social crises of the late 1960s and the shift to flexible exchange rates had reaffirmed the idea of regulation as a domestic matter. On a global scale there were no mechanisms (analogous, say, to the UAW-GM contract) to ensure that the world economy would grow at the rate required to justify new investment in increased productivity capacity. Sooner or later, therefore, a shortfall in demand would occur, accompanied by trade conflicts that arise from competition for larger shares of limited markets.

184

TABLE 7.2

Exports and Imports as a Percentage of GNP

	1950	1955	1960	1965	1970	1975	1980
			Exports of Goods/Services as Percentage of GNP				
U.S.A.	4.9	5.0	5.5	5.7	6.4	9.6	12.9
Japan	12.5	11.0	11.5	11.0	11.0	13.5	15.0
Germany	11.0	20.0	20.0	19.0	22.0	26.0	28.5
France	16.0	15.0	14.0	12.5	15.0	18.5	21.0
U.K.	22.0	21.5	20.0	18.5	22.0	25.5	28.0
Italy	12.0	11.0	13.0	15.0	17.0	21.0	23.0
			Imports of Goods/Services as Percentage of GNP				
U.S.A.	4.2	4.5	4.6	4.7	6.0	8.3	12.0
Japan	11.5	10.5	11.0	10.0	10.0	14.0	16.0
Germany	13.0	17.5	17.0	19.0	20.0	23.5	29.0
France	15.0	13.0	11.0	11.5	15.0	18.0	21.0
U.K.	23.0	23.0	21.5	19.5	21.5	27.5	26.0
Italy	13.0	12.0	15.0	14.0	18.0	22.0	27.0

SOURCE: United States: United States Department of Commerce, *Survey of Current Business* for the years cited.
OTHER COUNTRIES: International Monetary Fund publications for the years cited.

The drive into foreign markets, as engendered by the exhaustion of domestic demand, is documented in table 7.2. The table shows exports and imports as a percentage of GNP for the major industrial countries. The shares for all countries are fairly stable in the early postwar period, but begin to expand after 1965. The expansion is particularly marked in 1970–80.

Conventional economic theory does not explain these developments. It envisages a system in which nations gain from trade to the extent that they produce goods from resources with which they are most richly endowed. The more different the endowments of two countries, in this theory, the greater the potential gains from and hence the greater likelihood of trade. If the theory were correct, trade would have expanded between the developed and the developing world—the latter exporting raw materials and manufactured goods intensive in unskilled labor in exchange for sophisticated industrial products, made by capital- and skill-intensive methods in the developed world. As the income of the developing countries rose, in this reading, they would have increased the market for mass-consumption goods, thus solving the problem of saturation in the developed countries.

But the trade expansion that occurred after World War II did not follow this pattern. Rather than a trade among radically different partners, the trade that developed occurred among producers that were most alike: the trade was among the industrialized countries; and among those countries, it was within industries, rather than among industries.[26] Thus, for example, between 1960 and 1973, the income of the developed countries' economies grew at an average annual rate of 5 percent, but their manufacturing exports and imports grew at 9 percent. Similarly, manufacturing production in these countries grew at 6 percent, but manufacturing exports grew at 10 percent, and imports at 11 percent. In the developing countries, by contrast, exports and imports grew at about the same rate as production, with only manufacturing exports exceeding the growth of the economy as a whole.[27]

The figures for the distribution of trade tell a similar story. In 1963–73, manufacturing trade among industrial countries grew at an average annual rate of 12 percent, while sales of manufacturing goods of the industrial world to the developing world grew at 7 percent.[28] The percentage of manufacturing exports going to the industrial world rose between 1963 and 1973 from 61 to 70 percent for North America, from 71 to 78 percent for Western Europe, and from 41 to 46 percent for Japan.[29]

This trade pattern could be explained in two contrasting ways. First, it might result from an effort to combine the mass-production economies of scale with increased product differentiation.[30] The industrialized countries might each have been concentrating on a different version of the same generic product and thus sharing one another's markets in a way that makes such differentiation efficient. For example, the United States produced large cars and the European countries, small ones, and then these two groups exchanged their output. The alternative explanation for the trade pattern is that the trade occurred primarily in specialized commodities; that is, luxury items and the specialized capital goods used as inputs in mass production. This trade, as we have seen, is responsive to quality and performance, rather than to price, so presumably users of capital goods and lovers of luxury looked for the best they could find anywhere in the world, regardless of cost.

The data are not arranged in a way that enables us to distinguish between these alternative explanations. Both types of industrial trade were going on. But it is likely that their relative weight changed over time. In the early postwar period, when the European economies were still recovering from the war, trade between the United States and Europe consisted of capital goods exported from the United States and very high- or very low-quality consumer goods exported from Europe.

But as the Europeans recovered, the United States began also to seek specialized producers' goods from European manufacturers.

At the same time, as we saw in chapter 6, the Europeans moved into mass production—slowly at first, and then with increasing clarity of purpose by the 1960s. The creation of the European Economic Community, for one thing, was motivated by a desire to obtain in Europe markets comparable in size and scope to those of the United States; its formation, in 1957, and subsequent expansion promoted trade among member nations in mass-produced goods. Nonetheless, trade interpenetration as predicted by the theory of product differentiation was not much in evidence before the middle 1960s. The U.S. automobile market was dominated by the American firms, General Motors, Ford, and Chrysler, all producing the same types of cars; the German market was dominated by the German firm Volkswagen; the French, by the French firms Renault and Peugeot; and the Italian, by the Italian firm FIAT. The same was true for other major commodities. Even in the European coal and steel community—a forerunner of the Common Market—international trade was largely in specialty alloys, rather than in mass-produced carbon steel.

By the end of the 1960s, however, the interpenetration of mass markets was clearly observable. In the U.S. automobile market, the share of imports jumped from 6 percent in 1965 to 18 percent in 1975, while the total number of new cars registered annually remained roughly constant.[31] The share of non-U.S. firms grew rapidly in other markets, as well. Imported steel accounted for 1.5 percent of U.S. consumption in 1957, and 18 percent fourteen years later.[32] In the U.S. market for radios and televisions, the figures are 6 percent in 1960 and 43 percent in 1976.[33] As each major industrial country drove into the markets of the others, the result was the general increase, after 1965, of traded goods as a fraction of income or sales (as reported in table 7.2).

THE THIRD-WORLD DEVELOPMENT STRATEGIES

The saturation of industrial markets in the advanced economies was accelerated by the development strategies of many third-world countries. Not all nations outside the developed world played the role assigned to them by neoclassical trade theory and neocolonial ties to the commercial centers. Instead of limiting themselves to the export of products that reflected their endowments of primary products and unskilled labor, some countries set about changing their endowments. They trained labor, imported technology, created financial and marketing institutions, and rewrote the tax code and tariff regulations—all to encourage the growth of domestic industry.

Although these efforts were broadly comparable to the earlier industrialization drives in Europe and Japan, discussed in chapter 6, they differed in a way that directly affected the conditions of competition in the advanced world. Whereas the pre–World War I development drives had centered on producers' goods and armaments, the post–World War II strategies centered on mass-produced consumer goods, often for export. By the 1970s, two groups of countries had applied variants of this development strategy with enough success to transform their domestic economies and to raise the competitive pressure on industry in the advanced countries.

The first group consists of the East and Southeast Asian producers: South Korea, Taiwan, Hong Kong, and Singapore. These economies, poorly endowed with natural resources, imitated the model of export-led development perfected by the similarly unendowed Japanese. Like the Japanese, they began with labor-intensive, low-technology goods, and then, perfecting their skills, technology, and marketing techniques, they moved into mass-produced consumer durables. By 1978, these four economies supplied 61 percent of the manufacturing exports of the developing world.[34] These new Asian exporters are also like Japan in that they invest a much larger percentage of national income than do their Western trading partners. This means that a disproportionately large share of their export revenues are spent on specialized producers' goods, rather than on mass-consumption articles; and their international successes thus divert income from mass markets in general, even while intensifying competition in some of them.

The second major group of newly industrializing countries includes the much larger nations of Latin America. They pursued a different development strategy, but one that has already added to the saturation of markets in the industrial world. Brazil, Mexico, and Argentina all have very large domestic markets; they all have growing, consumption-minded middle classes; and they all have an abundance of natural resources, which make them less dependent on industrial exports for the foreign-currency earnings necessary to import capital equipment. These countries have therefore tried to create domestically oriented mass-production industries. To do so, they have restricted imports of competing goods from more advanced economies and required local subsidiaries of multinationals to produce an increasing percentage of the final product domestically. At the same time, whenever the capacity of a competitively efficient plant exceeds the absorptive capacity of the domestic market, they export the surplus output. And like the Asian exporters, the Latin Americans use foreign-exchange earnings to purchase specialized producers' goods in the advanced countries. In this way the Latin American successes have also contributed to the logjam of mass-production markets.[35]

The spread of mass-production technology beyond its original home-lands has thus exacerbated the problems stemming from the saturation of markets—markets whose growth defined the postwar boom. And so long as no new products emerged to stimulate demand (we will see in the next chapter that corporations have indeed searched for new avatars of mass production), all the shocks and missteps of the 1970s were amplified by a fear: that the possibilities for expansion within the existing framework were exhausted.

THE "TRENDS" TO DIVERSITY AND TO THE EXHAUSTION OF RAW MATERIALS

Two alleged long-term trends are often mentioned regarding the course of industrial society of the 1970s. Belief in them reinforced skepticism about the possibilities for continued growth along the mass-production trajectory. One of these alleged trends was an apparent shift in consumer taste in favor of diversity, even customization. The other was the apparently imminent exhaustion of world supplies of the raw materials used in manufacturing. Had there in fact been trends of these kinds, the 1970s breakup of mass markets and paralysis of the production setup would have been partly attributable to them. But these two conditions were effects, not causes. They more accurately are explained by changes in the production system, rather than serving as explanations for those changes.

The "Trend" to Diversity. The most sophisticated argument in favor of a long-term diversification of taste rests on the notion of a hierarchy of needs and wants. So long as incomes are low—this argument goes—consumers satisfy their fundamental needs for food, clothing, and shelter by purchasing the cheapest available goods, which are mass-produced. But as incomes rise, consumers can express in the market more refined wants, for more specialized goods, whose satisfaction was previously unaffordable. In this view, mass markets are a consequence of a low standard of living, and the rise of the latter contributed to the stagnation of the former.

But this essential distinction between the needs of the poor and the wants of the rich flies in the face of massive ethnographic evidence. This evidence shows that at every level of consumption, the desire for particular goods is shaped by collective, cultural ideas of what is right and what is beautiful.[36] To take extreme examples: starving Indians do not eat cows; a few pennies' worth of star-shaped cloth is a magnificent adornment in certain armies; generations of Calvinist bankers have made a point of not wearing their wealth on their sleeve; Eastern Europeans who have to wait hours in line to buy a piece of meat almost always find the time to buy flowers; Western Europeans, whose standard of living has not, until recently, been as high as that in the United States, refuse mass-produced American-style bread unless it is toasted and spread with something they like. None of this is to deny that prices make a difference and that most consumers have wants they cannot translate into possessions. The point is only that rising incomes do not necessarily translate into significantly more diversified purchases.

This view of taste as a culturally defined desire for a culturally intelligible product is consistent with the possible-worlds model of industrialization; together they suggest an alternative interpretation of the changes in consumer behavior observed in the 1970s. One reason for the early success of mass production in the United States, we argued, was the *homogeneity*—or rather the indefinition—of American taste (as, for example, documented in Nathan Rosenberg's study of American acceptance and European rejection of machine-made cutlery).[37] Conversely, one reason for the persistence of the specialized industrial districts in Europe was the *diversity* of Continental taste. This diversity of taste was perpetuated by producers' and retailers' education of consumers to appreciate the fine distinctions among products.[38]

At this level, the victory of mass production meant the redefinition of taste (through advertising) and merchandising that emphasized price, not quality. A late-nineteenth-century example is the British boot and shoe industry. Fearing that cheap machine-made shoes from the United States might capture the bottom of their home market, British producers followed the urgings of American shoe-machine manufacturers and launched an advertising campaign to persuade customers to buy up-to-date styles—which happened to be the ones produced with American equipment. With mass-produced goods whose forerunners were not well known (or that had no forerunners, as in electronics), the victory of the mass producers was easier.

This perspective implies that the shift in consumer tastes is best understood in social terms. Because the alternative sees a hierarchy of needs as physically wired into man's biological construction, consumption patterns change mechanically as income growth pushes people from one level in the hierarchy to another. In the social view, consumption patterns result from the interplay of culture and relative costs. In the world of mass production, consumers accepted standard goods; their acceptance facilitated the extension of the market and the reduction of prices, through increasing economies of scale; and the growing gap between the price of mass-produced goods and that of customized goods further encouraged the clustering of demand around homogeneous products.

But once mass markets began to stagnate and competition intensified, in this alternative view, a contrasting circle of causality emerged. Firms tried to woo customers by differentiating their products and reeducating the public to appreciate them; the more successful they were, the more they could invest in flexible technologies to increase their efficiency, and the faster the mass markets contracted—limiting the possibilities for further growth along the old lines; finally, the smaller the difference in productivity between mass and craft production, the smaller the difference in the selling price of customized goods, and the easier it became to attract customers away from the mass-produced goods.

This alternative view may be appealing in light of our ideas of culture and of industrial change. But there is no systematic evidence that confirms it and discredits the hypothesis—derived from the logic of needs and wants—of a tendential transformation of consumption patterns. Most readers of this book need only observe their colleagues and neighbors to find evidence that increasing salaries can lead to an ostentatious diversification of taste. On the other hand, as we will see in the next chapter, there are cases where firms—driven by competition in mass markets—have literally turned rags into fashionable garments and thus extended their markets. But the very ambiguity of the evidence is sufficient to cast doubt on the claim that the stagnation of mass markets is due to the rise of incomes—rather than to some other self-limiting mechanism within the postwar production system.

The "Trend" to the Exhaustion of Raw Materials. Similar objections can be raised against another "trend" that might account for the economic disorders of the 1970s: the exhaustion of the world's raw materials. The idea of increasing shortages and their economic disruption was the focal point of debate in the 1970s about the "limits of growth"; in various forms, this idea has played an important part in econometric explanations of the decrease in productivity.

Our analysis and hindsight suggest, however, that proponents of this view failed to distinguish between the exhaustion of supplies of raw materials and the depletion of the buffer stocks that stood between the processing of those raw materials and their sale in the market. The shortages of agricultural products, for example, disappeared as soon as the buffer stocks were rebuilt and external access to Western supplies controlled. Similarly, the fluctuations in the price of oil over the last decade are consistent with the depletion of buffer stocks. By contrast, an *exhaustion* of energy reserves would have produced a trend to rising prices. In any case, the hypothesis of the exhaustion of crucial industrial inputs was much more plausible in 1974 than a decade later. By 1984 it is clear that even at their peak, the shortages were not universal but, rather, limited to a few commodities—whose price, once the shortages passed, then decreased.

Nonetheless, the debate about the limits of growth raised questions about the stability of mass-production industry—but these questions were ignored in the rush to dispel the prospect of no more growth. The critics of the no-growth thesis argued that rising prices would signal emerging scarcities of resources, and thereby induce expansion of supply, discovery of substitutes, and shifts to less resource-intensive methods of production. But if our characterization of the postwar industrial system is correct, this system does not adjust easily to major changes in its environment. The interesting question, therefore, is not: What happens when resources are exhausted? Rather, it is: What happens to industrial structures when supplies of resources become erratic and their prices fluctuate unpredictably? To the extent (hard to measure) that firms in this situation are deterred from investment in mass-production technologies, then even temporary resource shortages—like shifts in taste—do limit the growth of the industrial system. But these shortages do so as the reinforcing effect of more fundamental causes.

Too Many Answers, Too Many Questions

This chapter has provided too many answers and raised too many questions. We argued that the story of the economic crisis can be convincingly told twice: once as a series of accidents aggravated by policy mistakes, and a second time as a tale of structural limits, in which one institutional block to expansion (the saturation of mass markets) was reinforced by other blocks (changes in taste, raw materials shortages). We do not know how to decide which account is more fundamental. More precisely, it is hard to imagine any proof that farsighted leaders, sensing the limitations of the regulatory system, could not have cushioned the shocks by appropriate reform—except, perhaps, for the following. Given the previous successes of the postwar system and the encrustation of interests that slowed its working parts, it is hard to see how those in charge could have recognized the necessity of reform before it was too late to do anything about it. The decision to allow exchange rates to float is a good example.

But "proofs" of this sort prove only what the rest of this book calls into question: that the world has to be as it is. Future historians may well find that the world was closer to solving the problem of international macroregulation in the 1970s than we now think. Is it hopelessly farfetched to imagine, for example, that if the Iranian revolution and the second oil shock had occurred five years later than they did, the reflationary policies of the late 1970s could have produced a half decade of prosperity—and given world leaders the time, confidence, and resources to create international financial mechanisms for balancing supply and demand? We ourselves will argue later that past failures to find a solution along familiar lines do not exclude the possibility of finding one in the future.

And the more we examine the second, structural interpretation, the more questions are raised. Why could the large corporations not simply mass-produce new goods when the markets for existing ones showed signs of saturation? How successful have craft producers been in closing the efficiency gap between themselves and the mass producers who have defined the trajectory of technological development? What have been the effects on mass producers of an increasingly uncertain environment?

Better too many plausible answers than too many open questions. In the next two chapters, therefore, we look at the way firms, and whole national economies, have responded to the dislocations of 1970s. Our aim is not to solve once and for all the question of why those dislocations occurred. Rather, our aim is to start answering the theoretical questions raised and to sort out the practical choices posed by the fact that the dislocations did occur.

CHAPTER

8

Corporate Responses to the Crisis

THE economic crisis of the 1970s called forth two kinds of response. One was global: economic policymakers addressed worldwide unemployment and stagnation with instruments of domestic economic control. The other kind of response was individual: enterprises struggled, in their own markets and by their own means, to meet the performance standards that had been set during prosperity. The mass-production corporations sought to do this by creating harbors of stability to shelter them from the seas of the larger economy. Most of these corporate efforts came to nothing, for reasons anticipated in the last chapter: the broader structural reforms required for success were scarcely defined in international debate, let alone implemented. The story of the failures of these corporations' microregulatory strategies is our starting point here. It helps explain one of the mysteries of macroeconomic stagnation: why new industries did not emerge to replace the automobile and household-durables industries when the markets for these products in the advanced capitalist countries became saturated.

But there was also another, more successful kind of corporate response to the crisis. Often it emerged in smaller, newer firms that, unable to shelter themselves from the stormy economy, learned somehow to withstand the waves of market uncertainty that broke over them. Taken

194

separately, these firms' successes appear ad-hoc, as much the result of good fortune as of design. But underlying these various lucky accidents were common principles of organization—principles that constitute a viable alternative to the survival strategies of the mass producers. By the end of the 1970s, these principles were becoming evident to those who practiced them; in some cases, yesterday's tactical experiments were affirmed as tomorrow's strategic model. And under certain conditions, as we will see in the next chapter, even whole nations began to find their way to this alternative model of development.

Conglomeration as a Corporate Response

One response to increasing uncertainty was conglomeration: the large corporations tried to hedge risks in their primary (or original) market through diversification into others. This was done either by founding new subsidiaries or by merging with going concerns. Because it was often pursued in public-securities markets, this strategy attracted the anxious attention of investors, financial analysts, and the press.

For many commentators of the most varied political persuasions, conglomeration has been a major cause of the decline of U.S. capitalism. George Gilder, a confidant of conservative bankers, cites the conglomeration—along with speculation in real estate, antiques, and fine art— as an example of how the tax structure and government spending have distorted business decisions and undermined American entrepreneurship.[1] Robert Reich, an adviser to the Democratic Party, similarly cites the role of "paper entrepreneurialism" in the decline of the U.S. position in world markets.[2] Reich is particularly outraged by the emergence of major corporations that have no primary business at all: Gulf and Western, ITT, Litton Industries, Northwest Industries, Textron, United Technologies. But even corporations that have retained their original identity had, by the 1960s and '70s, moved into activities far beyond their primary base of operations: Du Pont and U.S. Steel acquired major oil companies; Mobil Oil acquired Montgomery Ward.

Nevertheless, it is much easier to denounce incongruous corporate matches than to demonstrate a statistical correlation between the conglomeration movement and the decline of industrial efficiency. Statistics are available only on mergers in manufacturing and mining, which constitute an analytically intractable category. This category counts mergers within a single field of activity, which may not be instances of conglomeration, and it neglects mergers between manufacturing and the service sector, which sometimes are instances of conglomeration. In short, "merger"—a linking—is not synonymous with "conglomeration"—a strategy of diversification. Data collected by the Federal Trade Commission show that the number of mergers does rise in the late 1970s; but it had already peaked in the mid-1960s, before the economic crisis had really begun.[3]

But even granting that conglomeration—as opposed to merger—has shown a marked rise in recent years, the phenomenon is best understood as a symptom, not a cause, of macroeconomic problems. As business in individual markets became riskier in this period, investors naturally sought to limit the losses they would suffer in any one line of business by diversifying their interests. The management of assets at risk is one of the things to which neoclassical economics is well suited; this school of economics has convincingly argued that in certain circumstances, diversification would have contributed to economic efficiency and growth. In light of this theory, the problem was not that conglomeration per se is a sign of decadence, but that conglomeration is an effective counter to only specific kinds of uncertainty.

Neoclassical theory shows that when investors in a decentralized economy cannot balance possible losses in one line of business against possible gains in others, they prefer to hold safe but low-yield assets. The economy as a whole then grows more slowly than when diversification occurs. To be sure, there is no theoretical reason why risk spreading can be accomplished only through conglomeration: the large corporations might, for instance, have returned their investment reserves to their stockholders, who could have used the cash to diversify their own financial portfolios (the fact that U.S. corporations chose conglomeration reflects their historical propensity to accumulate retained earnings—a propensity strengthened by the tax code). But neither is there a theoretical reason to believe that individual portfolio management is a better form of risk diversification than corporate conglomeration.

Conversely, there are grounds not only to believe that conglomeration can do some good, but also to doubt the arguments purporting to show that it is necessarily bad. By itself, the conglomeration movement can explain neither the level nor the composition of real investment. Although conglomeration redistributes entitlements to the proceeds of economic activity, the entitlements themselves are not altered in the process. For example, in the form of the proceeds from the sale of stock, they are still available for investment in productive activities. When U.S. Steel invests in Marathon Oil, the owners of Marathon acquire financial reserves; they or their bankers could invest in steel projects if they found them attractive enough. The problem of explaining why there is so little investment in the American steel industry thus remains even after conglomeration is taken into account. Indeed, it can even be argued that investment in steel might be encouraged by the U.S. Steel–Marathon Oil merger, because U.S. Steel has become a less risky business.

Nor can it be plausibly argued that conglomeration is ruinous because it drains the energies of corporate talent—energies that would otherwise go into productive tasks. Any effort to diversify risk requires the gathering of information, careful analysis, and informed decision making. All of these activities absorb talent. But they absorb no more of the total available talent when done in conglomerates than when done in government bureaucracies, investment banks, or brokerage houses.

The real shortcoming of the conglomeration movement (and the reason that—beyond outraging many people—it disappointed its architects) was that the risks it sought to contain could not be reduced through diversification. For the risks arose not from business accidents, randomly distributed across markets, but from shocks to the economy as a whole. The result was a strong correlation among the problems of individual markets. Thus, risks in different markets were cumulative, not offsetting: it is no use betting on three horses of different colors if they are all lame in the same leg. In short, to reduce the economic risk in the environment of the 1970s, corporations would have had to insulate their markets from the macroeconomic shocks that disrupted the economy in each of its parts. And some mass-production firms—intuiting the fallacy of conglomeration—tried to do just that. A major such effort was the strategy of multinationalization.

Multinationalization as a Corporate Response

Multinationalization is a microeconomic substitute for macroeconomic efforts to resolve the crisis of macroeconomic stability by strengthening national institutions of neo-Keynesian regulation. Multinationalization seeks to achieve economies of scale no longer obtainable through the

.on of the domestic market by producing a good that can be sold
ıany national markets simultaneously.

Multinationalization is typified by the American automobile firms'
strategy of the world car. This strategy is a projection on a global scale
of Sloan's GM strategy of the 1920s and '30s. But whereas Sloan's
strategy was to spread superficial variations on a single model across
the price range, the world-car strategy is to spread them across countries.
As one of GM's economists, Marina von Neumann Whitman, put it:

[W]e have multinational companies which must reap efficiences of specialization
and resource allocation and of scale economies if they are to keep costs down
and compete in world markets. ... Instead of having totally different vehicles,
each with its own design and engineering features to meet the demands of
different markets, there is a variety of vehicles, all of them adaptable with some
modification to many different geographic areas. ... [Y]ou can't really make a
car in one place and ship it to another. Government regulations and requirements
are not yet standardized for all countries. Nevertheless, you can do a lot off a
common base.[4]

This strategy required the corporations to extend their operations
into at least some parts of the developing world, while defending their
position in metropolitan markets. The developing countries would
provide the expanding margin of demand necessary to achieve further
economies of scale, but the new demand would only do this if the level
of demand already created in the advanced countries was sustained.

Two developments pushed the American automobile industry to apply
the world-car strategy. One was the oil crisis. The high price of gasoline
forced numerous Americans to abandon their preference for large cars,
in favor of the small, fuel-efficient ones popular in the rest of the world.
This Whitman calls "the convergence of consumer preferences in
various countries."

The second development that encouraged the world-car strategy was
the mesh between the development strategies of the newly industrializing
countries and the cost-cutting strategies of major producers. As we saw,
many developing nations (especially those with the largest and fastest
growing automobile markets, Brazil and Mexico) had imposed regulations
to foster domestic production of consumer goods and to discourage their
importation. Firms that wanted to sell in these markets therefore had
to produce what they sold there. In practice, American companies found
it profitable to locate their labor-intensive production of components in
the developing countries to exploit the low labor costs and apparent
docility of the workers. The host country then earned foreign exchange

by exporting these components, which compensated that country for the fact that only part of the automobile was produced there. This arrangement served both parties, but only on the condition that cars sold throughout the world were built largely of the same components, as dictated by the world-car strategy.

The American world car is the clearest example of the projection of the mass-production paradigm from a national to a multinational scale. But other industries in other countries pursued similar, if less articulated, strategies. The French steel industry (reorganized after 1966 into two groups, Usinor and Sacilor)—as urged and financially helped by the state—built massive facilities on the southern coast, near Marsailles, and the northern coast, at Dunkerque. As with the world car, this strategy was motivated by the prospect of supplying new markets and cutting production costs. The new facilities produced for the domestic mass market, but their locations facilitated the export of carbon steel in great quantities. Moreover, their locations allowed the use of cheap Mauretanian iron ore and other imported raw materials in place of the expensive materials from the depleted French sources. As a bonus, the move permitted the industry to escape the rule-bound, militant workers of the traditional steel-making areas.[5]

The Japanese in the 1960s were faced with a shortage of scrap metal, which they needed for the electric-arc furnaces they used to make steel. They seized the opportunity of a reduction in shipping costs to pursue a strategy similar to the world car. They too built giant coastal plants, charged their blast furnaces with imported raw materials, and exported the finished steel.[6] During the oil crisis they also organized "depression cartels" in several industries to eliminate redundant operations and to reduce capacity by closing down the smaller, less efficient units. Japanese energy-intensive industries built facilities in oil-exporting countries (such as Iran and Saudi Arabia), both to reduce energy costs—by being close to cheap supplies—and to make the host countries technologically dependent on Japan. This way Japan hoped to ensure for itself both a supply of raw materials and a market for its industrial products.

But none of these strategies fared well. On one level this was because of a disjuncture between the prevailing macroregulation and the micro-regulation of individual markets. More fundamentally, the failure was due to the disjuncture, discussed in the last chapter, between the mass-production technological trajectory and the regulatory regime taken as a whole.

Continued expansion along the mass-production trajectory required, as we saw, the creation of transnational markets that joined the saturated markets of the developed countries with the expanding markets of the developing countries. But the postwar regimes of domestic macroregulation were not designed to ensure the expansion of multinational economic entities: underdeveloped regions were ignored except insofar as they provided the labor and raw materials required by the rigid allocative systems of the metropolitan economy. The institutional responses to the crisis, we saw, only exacerbated the problem.

Thus the shift from a fixed- to a floating-exchange system—to recall the clearest example—broke the one solid link among the principal industrial economies. In theory the shift gave individual countries freedom to disregard their current account balances and to concentrate on the regulation of their domestic economies. But this freedom was illusory. And it destroyed the incentive for any nation—alone or with others—to demand institutions of international coordination and control. Moreover, the floating-rate system introduced a major new element of uncertainty, as the relative price of different currencies—and hence of production in different areas—was allowed to vary radically from moment to moment.

Seen against this backdrop, the world-car and similar strategies were corporate substitutes for failed international coordination: the corporations tried to use their productive apparatus to create the kind of stable world that international macroregulation could have achieved through new financial and trading arrangements. The problem was that the manufacturing systems built by the corporations had enormous hidden costs. Four of these costs soon came to light in the case of the world car.

THE FIRST HIDDEN COST

The price the corporations paid to integrate the developing economies into a transnational market was the dispersion of production. But in the early 1970s, this dispersion seemed more a benefit than a cost: production in the developing countries avoided both the labor unrest (considered the main threat to economic stability) and the higher wages of the developed countries. In the course of the decade, however, labor strife and broader social upheavals proved by no means to be confined to mature, industrial countries: workers new to assembly lines could (as Italian employers had learned) turn discontented and demanding, if not politically radical, almost overnight;[7] states that promised the moon in order to attract the subsidiary of a multinational made very earthly claims on the subsidiary's revenues and development policy once it was built.[8] The corporations could defend themselves by building identical plants in different countries ("multiple sourcing") and playing one off against another; but this was expensive insurance because the more the corporation multiplied its sources, the less it was able to take advantage of the economies of scale of global production.

THE SECOND HIDDEN COST

The inventory and quality-control costs of the world-car strategy proved extraordinarily high when compared with the Japanese *kanban*, or just-in-time, system of organizing the flow of components. In the *kanban* system (named for the routing slips attached to each piece in transit), suppliers are grouped closely around the final assembly plant so that the parts they supply arrive literally minutes before they are needed. In this way, the final producer is spared the costs of inventory, and defective components are spotted immediately. By contrast, in the geographically dispersed "global sourcing" system of the world-car strategy, firms must hedge against the interruptions of supply by maintaining large inventories; these large inventories mean that a supplier may turn out batch after batch of defective parts which will not be discovered until much later, when the first bad batch is finally drawn from inventory.

By the early 1980s, the advantages of the just-in-time system were so evident that American firms embraced it. They announced plans to recentralize production of many components in the Midwest, and to enter into long-term contracts with favored suppliers.[9]

THE THIRD HIDDEN COST

It turned out to be much more difficult than the world-car strategists had imagined to consolidate the market around a standard, transnational design for a car. Again, the macroregulatory regime was incapable of sustaining the conditions required for this kind of stability. Demand in the critical U.S. market fluctuated widely between small and large cars, according to the price of gasoline and the general economic conditions: when gasoline prices and interest rates rose, cost-conscious buyers (those who purchased small cars) were forced out of the market, making high-income, luxury consumers (who purchased large cars) the dominant element.

THE FOURTH HIDDEN COST

Finally, fluctuations in the exchange rate and the general international instability made the impact of foreign competition and the level of world demand hard to predict.[10] On the days that the world-car strategy worked, everyone made money hand over fist. But unpredictable labor unrest, state regulation, interruptions of supply, and changes in demand made it hard to say just when those days would be.

Mass Production in New Product Markets

The difficulty of creating and sustaining a mass market in the 1970s was not confined to older products; nor was it attributable to the problems peculiar to multinational production and marketing. A very similar difficulty was evident in the U.S. computer industry—and in the home-entertainment industry.

COMPUTERS

The market for computers at the beginning of the 1960s resembled the automobile market at the turn of the century, when Henry Ford began work on the forerunners of the Model T.[11] The computer was sold to a limited number of users and tailored to their individual needs. Not every computer was unique—there were broad scientific and commercial categories—but these categories were subdivided into many segments, and to use a product designed for one segment in another application required a supplementary program, which was cumbersome and expensive.

Technological developments and customers' habits, however, favored the integration of markets. As commercial customers became more experienced, business applications of computers became as sophisticated as scientific applications; and as technicians became more experienced, conversion of machines from one use to another became less expensive. In 1961, as these trends emerged, IBM decided to make a single product that would integrate the whole market and open the way to the economies of mass production.

The new, all-encompassing product was called the 360, for all the degrees of the compass. It was meant to be a machine for everyone and everything. The hardware of a computer is a package of related parts, ranging from the core memory and computational equipment, to the peripherals that store information outside the core, print out results, and allow the introduction of data and commands; the software is a library of programs that direct computations and thus adapt the hardware to one use or another. The 360 bundled all, or virtually all, of these different pieces into a single package or commodity. It was clearly meant to be the Model T of the computer industry.

The IBM 360 made money. But its success did not ensure the long-term triumph of the strategy it embodied. It proved impossible to concentrate demand for a single, integrated computer system. Just how quickly the market fragmented is hard to say, because as it fragmented its boundaries became debatable. The ball-park estimates of the trade press gave IBM 70 percent of the market in 1967, and its share gradually declined in the following decade. But what is certain—and what makes the story of IBM and the computer industry different from the story of Ford and the automobile industry—is that the decline of the dominant producer's market share came not from the intrusion of another mass producer, but from the internal disintegration of the mass market itself.

One cause of the market's disintegration was the capacity of specialized producers to supply substitutes for pieces of the 360 bundle. These substitutes were cheaper, better suited to particular uses, or technically more advanced than IBM's model. Another cause of market disintegration was other producers' ability to provide complete alternative systems, which either did something the IBM system could not (for example, perform at extraordinary speed) or else did only some of what the IBM system did, but more cheaply (as did mini- and micro-, or home, computers). It was as if the Model T could be assembled at home with pieces—not just the tires, but also the clutch and the brakes—from several manufacturers, or as if Ford's prospective customer could find a go-cart that was good for nine-tenths of the trips that the Model T could make.

The disintegration of IBM's market did not occur overnight, however. And IBM was able to follow the 360 with other profitable models designed on similar assumptions. But gradually IBM had to alter its marketing strategy. By the time it entered the microcomputer market, in 1982, the corporation had turned its strategy almost 180 degrees.

The home computer, of course, performs much more slowly, and at a correspondingly reduced cost, all the calculating operations of larger machines. Its invention, in 1977 (when the pioneer, Apple Computer, was founded), depended on dramatic decreases in the cost of semiconductors. By 1981 there was a 1.6-billion-dollar market for micro computers, for homes and workplaces; by 1983, sales of the machines had reached 5.4 billion dollars.[12] Thus, a specialty item that had first seemed a curiosity or hobbyist's plaything in a few years became a potential mass market for an unsuspected consumer durable.

IBM's entry into this market reflected the lessons of its experience with the 360. Instead of supplying a self-contained system—and maximizing the difficulty of attaching foreign components—IBM designed and marketed its home computer so that all producers could attach their hardware and software to it. IBM thus became not the manufacturer of a single integrated device but rather the organizing center of a community of computer companies, which collectively supplies the consumer with the parts to build a customized system. In this way it no longer attempts to define the final product—as General Motors did through its integrated model line and annual model change. Instead, IBM makes its mark by being the infrastructure of the home-computer industry, rather than the industry itself.[13] Put another way, the key to IBM's extraordinary success in this enterprise (it holds a market share of about 20 percent)[14] is a policy of self-limitation: the way to obtain high-volume sales is to avoid classic mass production.

HOME-ENTERTAINMENT PRODUCTS

The second new industry that might have become a late-twentieth-century replacement for the automobile as a growth sector is the "home-entertainment" industry. That industry, however, never even passed through the mass-market era defined for computers by the IBM 360. In fact, the home-entertainment industry, as a branch of economic activity, has been defined by the popular press, not by the success of a single company or an identifiable product. In press descriptions, the industry makes a range of hardware, extending from stereo and video systems and games to cable television and home computers; its software consists of video-cassette movies, video games, records, and tape recordings.

Whereas the mass market for computers disintegrated when the computer came unbundled, the home-entertainment sector has not become an industry—let alone a mass-production industry—because it has *not* bundled its product. The elements always fall apart. Even within a stereo system, the speakers, turntables, styluses, audio-cassette players, amplifiers, and preamplifiers have always been sold separately by their manufacturers. Consumers who liked rock music bought speakers from California; those who liked classical music bought speakers from Europe. Today this lack of unity in a "home-entertainment center" seems inevitable: a single product that appealed to devotees of Bach, pornography, video games, and computer-controlled weaving (and whose price was not undercut by specialized products) has an air of absurdity about it.

But, in fact, the notion of this kind of pleasure machine is no more absurd than Ford's vision of a car industry, Swift's vision of a Chicago-based national meat industry, Edison's vision of an electric-light industry, or even Bell's vision of a telephone network. Indeed, the trade journalists who speak of the home-entertainment product as though it existed are so convinced that this "industry" will go the way of these other industries that they fail to see that it is not doing so.

This contrast between the success of earlier visions and the failure of current ones raises questions about industrial development in our time. Perhaps it is not the peculiarities of home entertainment that explain the disappointed expectations. If changes in technology and the relationship between consumers and products are undoing mass-produced packages (such as the IBM 360), then it is understandable that it is harder nowadays to package parts in the first place.

This conclusion is suggested by changes at the periphery of the traditional smokestack industries. Despite the picture of stagnation presented by these industries, there are, in each of them, pockets of prosperity. And in these pockets, the structure of markets and the evolution of technology closely resemble those in the computer industry. Analysis of these successes sheds new light on the failures of those corporate strategies that followed the mass-production trajectory. It also suggests one answer to another of the questions left hanging in the last chapter: How can firms turn the trick of reducing production costs while maintaining the flexibility necessary to thrive (often at the expense of mass producers) in economic uncertainty?

Exceptional Success: The Reemergence of the Craft Paradigm amidst the Crisis

Even within industries that had begun in the nineteenth century, certain firms and products found markets and grew during the economic crisis. Whole regions escaped the stagnation of mass production. Some of the success stories, of course, were easily explained: firms in developing countries or in backward parts of developed countries took advantage of low wages and docile labor to capture a share of the metropolitan mass markets. But some of the most prosperous companies were in mature industrial areas: the "Third Italy," which stretches from the

Venetian provinces through the center of the country to the Adriatic Marches; in Austria, the area around Salzburg; and in West Germany, parts of Baden-Württemberg. These regional economies created new products and processes to build markets in specialty steel, precision machine tools, specialty chemicals, luxury shoes, medium-priced textiles, motorbikes, ceramic building materials, furniture, and industrial instrumentation. Unlike the successes of the newly developing regions—or the islands of "postindustrial" society that grew up around the computer-based industries—the prosperity of the older industrial areas cannot be explained as either a simple affirmation or rejection of existing models. Nor did that prosperity appear, even to its beneficiaries, the result of strategy. Industrial winners seemed to emerge by accident; success was surprising to the successful. In many cases, firms that had stood precariously on the edge of their industry—dependent on subcontracts from large companies—suddenly enjoyed a prosperity that eluded their erstwhile benefactors.

This view of success as luck was common at first: a good guess on the coming style in a high-fashion industry or a chance variation in materials happened to match the momentary needs of rapidly shifting markets. But as success led to success, it became apparent that entire regions and whole segments of industries were flourishing together. Individual, temporary triumphs came to be recognized as the enduring achievement of a district in the world economy. The participants began to understand the underlying principles of their work well enough to see how they could reproduce their successes. By the end of the 1970s, these principles had become a model of industrial development in certain regions and even, in the case of West Germany and Japan, in whole nations.

This model stands the regnant paradigm of production on its head. Dominant sectors of the established system were subordinated, subordinate ones dominated. As in any revolution, it was this reversal of roles—and the revelation of surprises in familiar structures—that disconcerted participants and observers.

The structure and history of mass production had, of course, hinted at the possibility of this reversal of roles. Mass production, we saw in chapter 2, has always necessitated its mirror image: craft production. During the high noon of mass production, craft production was used by firms operating in markets too narrow and fluctuating to repay the specialized use of resources of mass production. Craft production supplied luxury goods, experimental products, the specialized equipment used in mass production, and the standardized goods for which the demand was too unstable to make the use of dedicated equipment profitable. Craft production thus appeared either as a residual category—taking up the markets rejected by mass production—or (in the case of the capital-goods industry) as a limit on the pace of the introduction of mass-production equipment. The idea that flexible machinery could be made ever more productive seemed utopian in light of the enormous productivity increases of mass production.

From the second industrial revolution at the end of the nineteenth century to the present, economic downturns have periodically enlarged the craft periphery with respect to the mass-production core—but without altering their relationship. Slowdowns in growth cast doubt on subsequent expansion; in an uncertain environment, firms either defer mass-production investments or else switch to craft-production techniques, which allow rapid entry into whatever markets open up. The most straightforward example is the drift toward an industrial-subsistence, or -repair, economy: as markets stagnate, the interval between replacements of sold goods lengthens. This lengthened interval increases the demand for spare parts and maintenance services, which are supplied only by flexibly organized firms, using general-purpose equipment. The 1930s craftsman with a tool kit going door to door in search of odd jobs symbolizes the decreased division of labor that accompanies economic retrocession: the return to craft methods.

What is distinctive about the current crisis is that the shift toward greater flexibility is provoking technological sophistication—rather than regression to simple techniques. As firms have faced the need to redesign products and methods to address rising costs and growing competition, they have found new ways to cut the costs of customized production. And the more they have narrowed the gap in cost between mass and craft production, the easier it has become to draw customers away from the formerly cheaper mass-produced goods. Technological dynamism has thus allowed a shift from a purely reactive strategy, aimed at survival, to an expansive strategy, which has threatened to cut ground away from mass production. In short, craft has challenged mass production as the paradigm.

These developments have been common to the manufacture of goods as diverse as ceramic tiles, agricultural implements, and hiking boots. But what is most striking is their occurrence in two very different *types* of producers: in apparently mature mass producers (in such industries as steel, chemicals, and textiles), and in the machine-tool industry, which seemed frozen by definition in the perpetual adolescence of craft inefficiency. Because these two types are so different—yet have experienced similar developments—it is worthwhile examining them. The remainder of this chapter therefore looks first at the rejuvenation of the first type and then at the redirection and maturation of the second.

Specialty Steel and Mini-mills

In 1960 the developing countries produced 6 percent of the world's crude steel. A decade later, their share in world production had risen only one percentage point. But by 1980, their share had almost doubled, to 13 percent, and it was predicted to reach 20 percent in 1990.[15] Developing-country steel exports grew by just under 23 percent a year between 1960 and 1973, and by 13 percent annually between 1973 and 1978. By the late 1970s, there were more than fifty nations competing in the world steel market.

As competition from new steel exporters increased, the struggle for market shares among established producers increased. Producers tried desperately to amortize substantial investments made in the optimistic early 1970s. For example, in 1970 the Japanese operated at close to full capacity and planned to produce 160 million tons of crude steel by 1975; but by 1980 they were only producing 110 million tons and operating at 70-percent capacity. Under these circumstances, steel firms abandoned plants; they shifted from the production of steel to the sale of steel-making technology; they cut labor costs; and they called for tariff protection, government subsidies, and the formation of price-fixing cartels. But they also began to experiment with new products and more flexible equipment and systems of shop-floor control.

Standard steel is an amalgam that is 98 percent iron and about 2 percent carbon, with traces of phosphorus, silicon, and sulfur. It is called carbon steel. Typically it is mass-produced in integrated, or tonnage, mills, by the basic oxygen process. First, iron ore is heated with limestone and coke (baked coal) in a giant blast furnace to reduce its oxygen content.[16] This molten metal (pig iron) is then fed into a second furnace, where impurities (including excess carbon) are removed; this is done by blowing a supersonic jet of oxygen onto the surface of the molten-metal bath. The resulting steel is then poured into molds, cooled, reheated, and rolled into final shape. The system is extremely efficient when operating at full capacity; but it is also extremely inflexible, because of the high cost of cooling and reheating furnaces whenever production is interrupted for want of orders. No wonder steel makers are always tempted in downturns to dump their output abroad at prices that at least recover a fraction of the fixed costs.

During the 1970s firms increasingly distinguished their products from standard carbon steel in one or some combination of three ways. First, they started to improve the reliability of existing products. The more carbon there is in steel, the harder it gets. By controlling the carbon content in the steel more accurately, therefore, firms could guarantee its degree of hardness.[17] Second, they introduced new shapes (such as wide-diameter pipes) and new alloys, to define and satisfy emergent demand. These alloys are made by adding such metals as chromium, vanadium, or tungsten to carbon steel. This renders it especially resistant to changes in temperature, corrosive chemicals, high pressure, and the like. The alloy developed by Thyssen—the West German specialty producer—for a rustproof car is typical.[18] Such customized products command high prices: a ton of alloy steel for high-speed cutting tools can cost thirty times more than a ton of carbon-steel rods used to reinforce concrete.[19] The third way in which firms distinguished their output was by gearing production to the unstable margin of demand for standard goods—filling small rush orders for a range of products that mass producers can profitably supply only in large lots.[20]

Integrated producers—particularly in Japan and Western Europe—have tailored their setup to exploit these possible modifications. Computerized process-control equipment, for example, allows firms to regulate the carbon content of steel more precisely and to add a sequence of different alloys without interrupting the flow of production.[21] Continuous casters (giant Liebig condensers that cool the stream of molten steel into a continuous strip, or slab, as it issues from the furnace) eliminate the need for molds.[22] Together with computer-controlled cutting-and-rolling equipment, these innovations facilitate the changeover from one product to another; they save energy; and they reduce the material wasted in the transformation from molten metal to marketable shape.

An alternative way to increase flexibility was to eliminate the conversion of iron ore to pig iron in the blast furnace through the construction of mini-mills. The heart of the mini-mill is an electric-arc furnace in which the metal bath is heated by passing an electric charge through it; impurities are removed by the injection of oxygen. Since an electric-arc furnace can process ferrous scrap (whose price, moreover, is often lower than that of iron ore), the flexibility of the system is no longer limited by a need to keep a blast furnace in continuous operation.

209

Mini-mills have been very successful. By using continuous casting and advanced process controls, and by locating near expanding markets, mini-mills have been able to capture a growing share of the U.S. steel market. Between 1960 and 1982, mini-mill raw-steel output grew at an annual compound rate of almost 10 percent; its market share rose from 3 to 18 percent.[23] It seems likely, furthermore, that mini-mills will produce high-quality alloy steels, as well as the tin sheet and auto plate that are just now coming within their technical reach. They are also likely to reduce their dependence on scrap (whose availability will decrease with the spread of mini-mills), by charging the electric-arc furnaces with iron ore reduced without the use of a blast furnace. The Congressional Office of Technology Assessment estimates that they will hold at least 25 percent of the national market by 1990.[24] The mini-mills' success is already forcing integrated mills to abandon blast for electric-arc furnaces and to adopt continuous casting.[25]

But whether integrated or not, specialty steel producers are alike in using craft principles of shop-floor organization. In West German plants, for example, the need to change products and production processes more quickly, to meet higher quality standards, and to operate increasingly delicate and expensive equipment has led to a fundamental reorganization of worker training. Traditionally, West German steelworkers followed the practice (widespread in the industry) of acquiring their skills on the job and then passing from job to slightly more demanding job over many years. Now workers are given basic courses in metallurgy and plant operation and are briefly apprenticed in all the mill's operating units before they receive intensive theoretical and practical instruction in the area in which they will eventually work. Workers trained in this way are formally regarded as craftsmen, rather than semiskilled production workers.[26] In the United States, labor practices in the mini-mills seem radical viewed against the backdrop of the system of narrow jobs in big steel. In many ways they recall the labor-relations pattern of the 1920s: plants are often not unionized; workers—broadly skilled and organized in teams—are given a share of the profits; and foremen both work in production and, with their teams, help redesign the plant (the tendency is to eliminate industrial engineers as a distinct group from the organization).[27]

By the late 1970s there were many indications that firms intending to stay in the steel business would have to respond to fluctuating markets with flexible techniques. In the United States between 1972 and 1976, the average annual return on equity for a mini-mill was 15.8 percent; for integrated, or tonnage, producers it was 9.1 percent. Between

1977 and 1981 the mini-mills returned an average of 17 percent annually; the integrated producers returned 5.6 percent.[28] In Italy, the mini-mills in the Lombard province of Brescia weathered the crisis much better than integrated competitors.[29] In Austria, the state-owned firms moved aggressively to acquire and develop mini-mill technology.[30] Everywhere in the steel industry, rationalization and increasing flexibility seemed to require, rather than to exclude, each other.

Chemicals

A similar drift from mass to specialty production was detectable in the chemical industry in the advanced industrial countries in the 1970s. Basic plastics and artificial fibers—products so standardized that the industry calls them commodities—were by then produced in Eastern Europe and the newly industrializing nations (many of them oil-rich); production occurred in self-contained "black box" manufacturing units, available from many vendors on the world market.[31] These producers threatened the established firms with ruinous price competition. Many established producers therefore began to invest in specialty chemicals, such as insecticides, herbicides keyed to specific ecologies, high-performance plastics and fibers that can substitute for ceramics and alloys, pharmaceuticals, and genetically engineered microorganisms. Like alloy steels, these specialized products are difficult to imitate on short notice, and they command high prices per unit because of their great utility to a restricted group of customers.

By the late 1970s, specialty chemical firms were generally recognized as more profitable than those in the commodity business; many of the industry's leaders publicized a new strategic interest in customized goods.[32] Du Pont, the largest American chemical firm, faced stagnating sales of some of its commodities—nylon, Orlon, and Dacron; the company responded by announcing plans to reinvest the proceeds from other, still profitable commodities in technologically more sophisticated and specialized products.[33] When Dow, the second largest U.S. chemical firm—and more dependent on commodity production than Du Pont—announced similar plans, an investment analyst called the decision "an absolutely necessary strategy."[34] In the 1980s, major European firms—such as Rhône-Poulenc in France, Solvay in Belgium, and Imperial

Chemical in Great Britain—also moved into specialized chemical products: high-fashion yarns, engineering plastics, agrichemicals, catalysts, and pharmaceutical intermediaries.

"Large chemical companies," a trade journal remarked in 1981, seem to be "tumbling over one another in the rush to get into specialties."[35] Two years later, an article headlined "New Chemical Business Recovery May Be Very Different" reported:

the idea that the commodity sector is mature or maturing, that the huge export market for many chemicals is contracting, and that producers are moving inexorably into specialties is accepted so widely it is in danger of becoming a truism. Around the industry, producers echo the line that companies must position themselves in those markets—or "niches," in the new sense of narrowly defined opportunities—in which they will be most competitive.[36]

W. R. Grace, the world's largest producer of specialty chemicals, was thought to be entering a golden age.[37]

And as with specialty steel, the strategic reorientation of the successful chemical firms has entailed more flexible deployment of people and machines. New factories are being designed to manufacture a diversity of products, using a wide range of starting materials (feedstocks).[38] Whereas the typical petrochemical plant—like the integrated steel mill—is constructed to minimize the cost of producing a few products by one process, the new plants are very different. As described by the director of Polaroid's specialty-chemicals division, a specialty-chemicals plant is like a set of "giant test tubes, arranged as in a huge laboratory to let you make whatever you want."[39] And, just as in steel, the use of more flexible equipment grows out of and requires a more flexible use of labor: the reorganization of training in the West German steel industry is matched in the country's chemical industry by a new training system modeled on craft practices.[40] And in the United States, some large chemical firms have resisted unionization and are operating a version of the American Plan, which officially died during the Great Depression.

The chemicals division of Eastman Kodak, for example, has worked to keep layoffs to a minimum as it adjusts to the changing competitive environment by building flexible plants and looking for market niches. The techniques are familiar from American practice of the 1920s and the current system of Japanese shop-floor control: workers are shifted from products with slumping sales to ones that are doing better; subcontracting is reduced; the workweek is shortened; and attrition and early retirement buttress these other measures.[41] Here, too, a plant community of multiskilled workers seems a precondition for agile maneuvering in a hostile world.

Textiles

The most mature of the mature industries is textiles. If the open-hearth furnace symbolizes the second industrial revolution, the giant cotton mill symbolizes the first. From the early nineteenth century to the present, the construction of a textile industry has provided industrializing regions everywhere with an apprenticeship in mechanical production. Because the mass-production of textiles can be done with large amounts of unskilled labor and small amounts of capital equipment, upstart manufacturers have regularly displaced established ones. Eastern European, Far Eastern, and Latin American countries that after World War II entered the textile market exploited the same features of the industry that had allowed the American South after 1880 to lure textile firms away from the North.[42]

But some textile producers have withstood the new competition and even—despite the apparently fatal disadvantage of high labor costs— expanded. These successes are sometimes attributable to customers' allegiance to a cloth that would not be considered authentic if not produced in a particular area (for example, Austrian loden and Scottish plaids), or to customers' indifference to price (in the case of luxury fabrics). But there are other producers that do not make traditional or luxurious cloth that have also expanded: even while paying ever higher wages, these producers have used craft methods of production to grow in medium- and low-price markets.

An example is the textile district of Prato, a group of towns in the provinces of Florence and Pistoia in central Italy. Between 1966 and 1976, employment in the Western European textile industry was generally declining—by about 25 percent in France and West Germany, and by more than 35 percent in Great Britain. But employment in Pratese textiles remained steady (at about 45,000 workers, distributed in roughly 10,000 firms), and exports boomed. By 1977 Pratese exports totaled about 820 million current dollars, roughly 60 percent of output and in 1982 the value of exports had risen to about 1.5 billion dollars, equal to 75 percent of total production.[43]

Prato's success rests on two factors: a long-term shift from standard to fashionable fabrics, and a corresponding reorganization of production from large integrated mills to technologically sophisticated shops specializing in various phases of production—a modern *système Motte*.

At the end of the nineteenth century, Prato was established as a major center of woolens production. It used regenerated wool (*lana meccanica*), produced by recycling rags and remnants as a raw material. Large factories united spinning, weaving, and finishing under one roof. The industry competed successfully with cheap British woolens in the international market (particularly in developing countries) and with worsteds from Piedmont in the domestic market. The Pratese industry continued to expand in these product lines through the 1930s, thanks largely to low wages.[44]

The reorientation of Prato's industry began in the 1950s, when the Pratese became vulnerable to competition from lower-cost woolen producers in Japan and Eastern Europe. In response, local manufacturers came up with *tessuti fantasia:* "fantasy" fabrics, woven of different-colored reconstituted threads, combined according to the designer's imagination and fashion's whims. Despite these fabrics' higher style, they did not cost much more to produce than standard fabrics because the cloth did not have to be dyed once woven. From the late 1950s on, the addition of artificial fibers to the fantasy yarns made it possible to work them on faster, more sophisticated looms; this development both rendered the cloth more durable and allowed the industry to exploit a new cheap raw material. With constant experimentation with the finishing of the cloth (*rifinitura*), the Pratese achieved a variety of textures and finishes that give products "born poor" the appearance of luxury.[45]

This shift toward more flexible markets both grew out of and hastened the decomposition of the large integrated firms. In 1927 just under 80 percent of the 11,560 persons employed in Prato's textile sector worked in large integrated mills. The pattern changed during the 1930s Depression when—despite expansion—firms laid off workers and sold or rented to them equipment for subcontracting work; the firms did this to convert fixed to variable costs. In this way, former employees now had to bear the risks—as dependent subcontractors—that the firm would otherwise have borne. The large firms reacted to the crisis of the 1950s in the same way. Thus an already fragmented industrial structure was pulverized. In its place emerged a vast network of small shops, employing one to twenty workers (often members of a single extended family) who possessed an intimate knowledge of materials and machines.[46]

While these small shops were springing up they needed to be formed into a network. To combine them into a flexible production system, and to reduce their dependence on the large firms, it was necessary to coordinate their separate skills in autonomous federations—federations that attended to the currents of fashion. Such coordination became, as of the late 1950s, the function of the *impannatore*.[47] A descendant of the medieval merchant and the early-modern *Verleger* (putter-outer), the *impannatore* had survived during the period of mass production as an important, though secondary, figure on the edge of the integrated mills. This person purchased raw materials, organized a network of small shops to produce cloth according to well-known specifications, and then brought the product to market or sold it to a merchant. But as markets for standardized products became inaccessible, the *impannatore* became more important: he or she became a designer, responsible for shaping and responding to fashion, as well as for organizing production. The *impannatore* urged the firms to experiment with materials and processes; and the firms' successes, in turn, fanned the creativity of the *impannatore*, making him or her still more demanding. In this way, the small firms coalesced into a network, and this network expanded—at the expense of the integrated firms. Today the integrated firm is all but extinct: precisely one survives, employing a few hundred workers.[48]

The Pratese made a habit of quickly adopting the latest textile technology. In the early 1970s, the area's 13,000 old looms were being replaced by automatic models—costing 100,000 dollars or more—at the rate of 1,000 per year. The Pratese also prided themselves on their ability to modify new machines to perform unsuspected tricks. Their efforts at innovation led naturally to the introduction of numerically controlled looms, which appeared in small shops by the late 1970s. All of this technological flexibility allowed a firm that had guessed wrong about this year's fashion to serve as a subcontractor for a luckier competitor that had an overflow of orders; and next year the roles might very well be reversed. According to a local saying, "There is always someone who botches a pattern book, but always someone else with swatches that do better than expected."[49]

In sum, technological innovation, constant subcontracting rearrangements, and the search for new products became the structuring elements of a resilient regional economy. The vitality of this flexible industry was reflected in the way it was perceived by academic observers and by the Pratese themselves. In the early 1960s—when the transition away from mass production was well under way—observers predicted that prosperity would lead back to a reconcentration of production in the large factories; this would mean the end of the "inefficiencies" of decentralized production.[50] But twenty years later, observers described Prato's innovative cottage industry as a viable manufacturing system. More significant, the local banks, trade unions, and artists' and industrialists' associations collaborated in a vast project: they began to devise computer-based technologies to increase the flexibility of the links among the firms, as well as the efficiency of each production unit. The expectation was that technology could be suited to the region's vocation as a collective specialist rather than adapting regional structures to the technology used in advanced mass-production firms.[51] A system that had begun as an expedient—accidentally discovered—gave birth to a distinctive technology—and vital economy.

Machine Tools

There were two dramatic, and apparently contradictory, success stories in the machine-tool industry of the 1970s. One was the experience of the West German makers of precision, special-purpose machines. The other was the experience of the Japanese makers of general-purpose, numerically controlled machine tools for small shops.

At least until 1980, when the situation began to change, the prosperity of the West German machine-tool industry reflected the application of mass-production techniques to new areas, as well as rationalization along existing lines in the industrial metropoles. By contrast, the explosion since 1970 of the Japanese machine-tool industry reflects the search for alternatives to mass production—a search touched off by the crisis of the 1970s. The Japanese success is due to a transformation of the metalworking sector that parallels the transformations in specialty steel, chemicals, and textiles.

Given Germany's historical vocation for producers' goods (as described in chapter 6), there is nothing surprising about the prodigious performance of its machine-tool industry in the 1970s. In this decade there was increased demand for machine tools. The new wealth of the oil-exporting countries and the aggressive industrialization of Eastern Europe, South Korea, and Taiwan increased the world demand for capital goods; this demand was especially for "turnkey" factories: complete manufacturing installations, which the purchaser need only switch on to set in motion. Meanwhile, the growing competition in the market for sophisticated mass-produced goods forced core industrial countries to modernize their plants, which increased the demand for special-purpose machinery. As the world's largest exporter of machine tools (from 1970 to the present West Germany has accounted for 25 percent of annual world trade in the industry—double the share of its nearest competitor), the West Germans were well positioned to supply both sectors of the market. Through the 1970s and early 1980s, therefore, the machine-tool sector maintained its traditional place as Germany's largest industrial employer—ahead of both the chemical and transportation industries. It was the country's largest exporter, as well. In 1979, more than a million persons worked in the machine-tool industry, which accounted for 15 percent of all industrial employment; and the industry's trade surplus (37 billion deutsche marks) was more than one-and-a-half times larger than the *nation's* trade surplus (22 billion marks).[52]

The predictability of the Germans' success contrasts with the unexpected success of the Japanese. The Japanese machine-tool industry caught all the established competitors off guard. In part this surprise was due to the speed with which the Japanese made space for themselves in the world market. Between 1960 and 1970 Japanese machine-tool production expanded sevenfold, but only a fraction of the output was sold abroad—the Japanese share of the world market in 1970 was only 3.6 percent. By 1980, however, the Japanese were exporting 55 percent of what had become a much larger output; and they held 12.4 percent of the world market—a share second only to West Germany's.[53]

But what made the Japanese success remarkable was not so much its speed as its revelation of a widespread demand for a new kind of machine tool: numerically controlled general-purpose equipment that is easily programmed and suited for the thousands of small and medium-sized job shops that do much of the batch production in metalworking. Until the mid-1970s, U.S. practice suggested that computer-controlled machine tools could be economically deployed only in large firms (typically in the aerospace industry); in these firms such tools were programmed, by mathematically sophisticated technicians, to manufacture complex components. But advances in the 1970s in semiconductor and computer technology made it possible to build a new generation of machine tools: numerically controlled (NC) or computer-numerical-control (CNC) equipment. NC equipment could easily be programmed to perform the wide range of simple tasks that make up the majority of machining jobs. The equipment's built-in microcomputers allowed a skilled metalworker to teach the machine a sequence of cuts simply by performing them once, or by translating his or her knowledge into a program through straightforward commands entered via a keyboard located on the shop floor.[54]

A few American firms (such as Dana Corporation's Summit product center in Bozeman, Montana) realized the potential of the new technology and experimented with the production of job-shop NC machine tools in the late 1970s. But it was Japanese industry that shifted abruptly toward production of cheap, small NC equipment: Japanese production of numerically controlled lathes increased tenfold between 1970 and 1979, as did its production of numerically controlled machining centers (whose programmable tool changers allow a single piece of equipment to perform a variety of boring and cutting operations traditionally associated with distinct types of machine tools). By 1980, small and medium-sized Japanese firms bought 64 percent of the industry's output of numerically controlled machines (as against 28 percent in 1970). And the Japanese also dominated the growing market for small NC equipment in the United States—where numerical control had been pioneered. U.S. imports of small NC machining centers from Japan totalled 91 million dollars in 1981, roughly half the dollar value of all imported Japanese NC machining centers, and about three times the total value of American exports of this class of machine tool. As late as 1982— when U.S. manufacturers had decided to enter the small-shop market in earnest—the Japanese companies offered a far wider range of low-horsepower equipment for small producers in their competitors' home market than did the new entrants.[55]

The Japanese success with NC equipment was strong evidence that parts suppliers in metalworking were reacting to the 1970s crisis in much the same way as the mini-mills and Pratese textile firms. As subcontractors of larger firms, the parts suppliers felt the effects of the increasing volatility of their clients' markets; in response, they adopted techniques that reduced the time and money involved in shifting from product to product, and that also increased the sophistication and quality of the output. The Japanese certainly viewed the explosive demand for NC equipment as a result of the changed economic environment of the late 1970s, and they saw a corresponding need to increase the efficiency of the subcontracting network. A crucial development was the appreciation of the yen, in 1977,[56] which threatened the competitive position of export firms. When this occurred, the executive director of the Japan Machine Builders Association wrote:

attempts were made to overcome the recessions by means of rationalization. This led to a change in the production set-up. Replacement demand was stimulated mainly in the small and medium enterprises. This resulted in a rush of orders for NC machine tools which are very effective in reducing labor and promoting rationalization. The situation in Western industrialized countries was the same as in Japan, but other machine tool makers made little effort towards development of NC tools. This increased the demand for Japan's machine tools.[57]

Furthermore, just as in the specialty steel and chemical producers and the Prato textile industry, the use of the new equipment went hand in hand with a revival of craft skills. When NC machine tools are used in the production of a short series of parts, the machine operator has a say in writing, or at the least correcting, the program: in the same way the Pratese weaver knows, through long observation of his or her machine at work, how best to adapt it to new tasks, so the skilled metalworker is able to put his or her craft skill to work in optimizing a program for a new part.[58]

Finally, the very production of the Japanese NC machine tools draws on elements of the craft paradigm. This is not, however, apparent at first glance. Production runs in the Japanese machine-tool industry are long by Western standards—so long that trade journals reporting monthly data often underscore that they have not mistakenly printed an annual total. And the Japanese make such lavish use of robots and other automatic equipment in the production of machine tools that they are regarded as the pioneers of mass-production techniques in the industry. Indeed, looked at from this perspective, the Japanese have stood the Fordist paradigm on its head: instead of using general-purpose equipment to produce special-purpose machines, they are doing the reverse—using special-purpose equipment to produce general-purpose machines to fill the craft needs of the rest of the metalworking industry.[59]

But this view overlooks three important features of the Japanese machine-tool industry that this industry—like all Japanese industry—shares with the *système Motte*.[60] First, with only one major exception (Okuna, which accounts for only 9 percent of NC sales), the Japanese firms are not vertically integrated. Most of them subcontract the production of various mechanical components, and they buy the micro-processor-based control devices from one firm, Fujitsu-Fanuc, which

219

specializes in their production (Fujitsu-Fanuc supplies three-quarters of the Japanese market and earns almost 90 percent of its gross revenues from these units). Second, most of the machine builders specialize in a narrow range of products (Mori Seiki makes NC lathes, Osaka Kiko makes machining centers, etc.); and the specialist producers tend to cluster around a major producer of traditional machine tools (such as Amada), which created and nurtured the specialists before granting their independence. Third, the firms are able to shift from one line of products to another extremely quickly, owing to their policy of broadly training employees (engineers and production workers) on the gamut of equipment that the company might one day produce or use.[61]

Thus, the Japanese NC machine-tool makers may appear to be mass producers when seen against the backdrop of an industry in which products are often one-of-a-kind. But the techniques these firms use are actually similar to those associated with the new craft sectors of mass-production industries. If the Japanese experience reverses the classic relationship between the machine-tool industry and its clients, it also blurs the distinction between the two. It demonstrates that in a changed environment, machine tools can be built and used by the same logic.

History, Practice, and National Strategies

THE STORIES of the American mini-mills, the Italian textile firms, and the West German and Japanese machine-tool makers stand out: they are exceptional instances of prosperity in a survey of the bleak prospects for traditional industry in the advanced economies. But some of these success stories in fact are not so exceptional: within the context of their national economy, they reflect a trend that is similarly reshaping a range of domestic industries. In other words, some countries regularly produce industries that— because of their craft principles of organization—are strikingly successful in comparison with other countries' economic performance.

In Italy, for example, the story of the Prato textiles can be retold for many industries: the mini-mill steel industry of Brescia; the ceramic building-materials industry of Sassuolo; the shoe industry around Ancona; the high-fashion silk industry of Como; the farm-machinery industry of Reggio-Emilia; and the special-machinery and motorbike industries of Bologna. In West Germany, the move to specialty steel and chemical production is echoed in attempts to increase the flexibility of the automobile industry and (under the impact of Japanese competition) the machine-tool industry. And in Japan, the domestic success of the machine-tool industry both symbolizes and results from a reorganization that was economywide.

Success stories in the United States and France, however, do appear anomolous even in their national economic settings. The prosperous American mini-mills were founded often in opposition to the organizing principles of the integrated mills, by executives who had left the large companies in disagreement with their practices. Perhaps more revealing, French industrial success in the 1970s came from mass production (for example, in the automobile sector), and from the armaments and nuclear-power industries—not from application of the native *système Motte,* whose vitality was being demonstrated outside France.

An economy's propensity to react to the 1970s crisis by adopting the craft paradigm was clearly related to the way it had previously adopted mass production. As we saw in chapter 6, the manufacturing sector in each capitalist industrial country adopted the mass-production model in a nationally specific form, shaped by the manufacturers' relation to the world market, to the state, and to the postwar labor movement. In doing so, some economies conserved more elements of the alternative craft production than others. These national differences seemed either superficial variations on one structure or functionally equivalent solutions to common problems. So long as domestic mass markets expanded, investment in American-inspired technology remained profitable, and techniques of stabilizing demand at the sectoral and national levels remained effective, these national differences seemed inconsequential.

But as firms groped their way in the uncertainty of the 1970s, these apparently inconsequential national differences—the residual craft elements—began to play a large role in shaping responses to the crisis. There was never a deliberate application of craft principles as part of any national conversion to more flexible methods of production; rather, the craft residues influenced industrial development toward customization. For the presence, if unacknowledged, of these craft elements served to obstruct potential solutions based on elaboration of the mass-production model; it also foreshadowed—in a limited, intuitively if not yet theoretically comprehensible way—the possibilities of an alternative form of organization. Indeed, the discovery procedures that firms and national economies applied to the search for a solution were largely the institutionalized result of historical developments. Thus, any country's residual barriers to wholesale Americanization served to guide local efforts at economic survival. Like the nocturnal drunkard who searches for his lost keys under a streetlight because that is where they are easiest to see, so national economies looked for solutions to their problems in the areas illuminated by their past practices.

Where historical experience lit a way—as in Italy, Germany, and Japan—fumbling hunches were rewarded with success. This success, in turn, encouraged further exploration of the same route—now accelerated by an increasingly clear view of it. Conversely, where historical experience led to a dead end—as in the United States and France—attempts at reorganization stalled. In some cases, these attempts became desperate efforts of trial and error or else mechanical imitation of success—uninformed by any strategic conception of its foundations. The leaders' conception of industrial organizations—the distribution of authority at the work place and among firms—and the example of daily practice made it hard to comprehend what the competition was doing better.

But it is revealing that when change did occur under these unpropitious circumstances, it was change in the direction of accommodation to splintering markets. Even in the United States, there was evidence in the early 1980s of a hesitant shift toward flexible specialization. This suggests that the same market pressures seen in the survey of industrial successes will also be seen in a survey of national reactions to the problem of industrial reorganization. But whereas the survey of industrial successes indicates a generic strategy of response to the crisis, the survey of national reactions indicates some of the conditions under which that strategy is likely to be discovered, and the variety of ways it can be applied.

Japan

As evidenced by Japan's great success with NC equipment, the key to the reorientation of the Japanese economy was probably the rationalization of small suppliers across the industrial spectrum. This campaign began in the mid-1950s. Such forced-draft rationalization, we saw in chapter 6, had two complementary sources. The first was the desire of the Liberal Democratic Party—in power since the end of World War II—to protect its small-business clients. This desire led to, among many other measures, the creation of some 180 state-subsidized local research centers.[1] These research centers collaborated with nearby universities and national technical institutes to develop new products and processes and to facilitate their diffusion among small firms. One of these centers might, for example, demonstrate the use of a new machine and plan its introduction into a particular firm; or it might sponsor research on promising new industrial techniques (for example, electrolytic polishing in the flatware industry in Tsubame City, or vacuum-mold casting in Nagano Prefecture).[2]

The second spur to industrywide rationalization was the desire of the large firms in the export sector to create a federation of efficient suppliers on the *système Motte,* or *zaibatsu,* model. These suppliers would be linked to the final assembler—the exporting firm—yet independent enough to initiate responses to changing market conditions. To this end, industrial engineers and subcontracting managers in the exporting firms undertook a program of permanent collaboration with their suppliers. Thus they identified suppliers that would be willing to innovate; suggested and demonstrated new shop layouts; and carefully rewarded those suppliers that learned the fastest.

The methodical character of this rationalization program, and its scrupulous balance between the large firm's authority and the small firm's autonomy, are revealed in an account by the director of purchasing at the Nissan Motor Company of changes that took place in his division in 1956.

    a. The buyers were assembled and taken to visit all the manufacturers in chartered buses. In the bus, any dubious points about the prices of the manufacturers' products, high-lights and major features of the factories were explained. On the way back, various aspects that could be improved, as well as an evaluation and grading of the factory, were considered.

    b. The principle of the same price for the same product was laid down so that there would be no more cases of manufacturers taking a loss after rationalization.

    c. Guidance on order placement was given so that the subcontractors could concentrate on their strong points and withdraw from their weak fields.

    d. Order placement control was effectuated by advising the firms which relied 100 percent on our company to buy their whole output to lower this level to 70 percent and to sell to others.

    e. The term gaichu-kigyo (outside-order firm) was to replace the existing term shita-uke (subcontractor).

    f. Calling the head of the firm oyaji (the old man, in the sense of one's father) was strictly forbidden. He should be referred to as the president. He was told to feel free to come by car in his business suit.

    g. When meetings ran into the lunch hour, a private room was made ready for the president and a meal was served.[3]

The next year, in response to a recession, Nissan hired university graduates to work in the subcontracting firms, where they eventually rose to prominent positions. Still later, the company conducted a series of "Sunday experiments," in which every Sunday for two years subcontractors—prompted and supervised by Nissan's representatives—rehearsed new layouts of machinery and sequences of operations.

Nissan clearly recognized the continuing need for at least some specialty producers. But the main goal of this constant reorganization was to produce, as fast as possible, a core of American-style subcontractors, geared to mass production (by 1960 Nissan was encouraging fourteen selected firms to meet a production standard of 100,000 units per month, turned out at a six-second tact). Rapid change abbreviated the necessary phases of growth. In the mid-1950s, the director of purchasing recalled, Nissan's strategy was

to start at the stage that had been reached in the United States some forty years earlier, and in Europe twenty-five years ago, and to move ahead rapidly to catch up with them. Theoretically, if we carried out a change in layout three times a year, this was the same as accomplishing three years of progress in a single year.[4]

But an unintended though perhaps more profound effect was to create among the subcontractors a tradition of permanent innovation and organizational plasticity. The lesson they learned from collaboration with the large firms was not only how to become mass producers, but also how to adapt rapidly to changing economic and technological circumstances.[5] The import of that lesson, however, became clear only in the late 1970s, through two developments: the maturation of the NC-machine-tool industry and the increasing volatility of mass markets.

The first of these developments, the emergence of a strong NC industry, (we argued earlier) followed the typical pattern of Japanese economic advance: the government protected the domestic market (by charging the same high tariffs on NC equipment as on imported computers) and encouraged the foundation of research cartels; and private industry regularized production (by accepting Fujitsu-Fanuc controllers as the industry standard), thereby allowing all firms to benefit from economies of scale for a key component, while distinguishing their products along other dimensions.[6] On the other hand, the second development of the late 1970s, increasing market volatility, caught the Japanese as much off guard as everyone else.

Together with the catechism of self-transformation that the suppliers had learned in the preceding decades—as well as the mechanisms familiar from the American plan and the *zaibatsu* of shifting labor from declining to expanding sectors—these changes produced the reorientation of the Japanese economy we observed earlier. The small and medium-

225

sized firms that produced the components in the *zaibatsu* system simply rationalized production, as they had done many times before. And the experience of reorganization itself was so familiar that (as suggested by chapter 8's matter-of-fact remarks of the director of the Japan Machine Builders Association) the Japanese were baffled by the inability of other nations to break in this last round of rationalization with the habits of mass production mastered in the preceding ones.

Italy

Italian developments reversed in crucial ways the Japanese pattern. Yet these developments produced a surprisingly similar result: a flexible network of small and medium-sized firms, using more and more NC technology to adapt to rapidly shifting markets. But whereas the Japanese suppliers had been encouraged to exercise their autonomy and by the mass producers they served, the Italian small producers turned to forced-draft innovation largely to escape the domination of mass producers that wanted the dependence of the small firms.

Italian employers responded to the strike waves of the 1960s, we saw in chapter 6, with a strategy familiar from the Pratese example: radical decentralization of production. There is no indication in the early commentary that this response was conceived as anything but a short-term expedient for regaining control of production and biding time; once the worker militancy had passed, operations were to be regrouped in the large factories. The new shops used rudimentary technologies; evaded taxes and payments to the social-security system; ignored health-and-safety regulations; and, when the market demanded it, insisted on brutally long working hours. Trade unionists were not wrong to analogize these runaway plants to turn-of-the-century sweatshops.[7]

What happened next caught managers, trade unions, workers, and government officials by surprise, although it had been foreshadowed in Prato and elsewhere: dependent subcontractors began to federate. They used their collective capacities to devise innovative products and processes that gave them increasingly independent access to markets. The Brescian mini-mills, for example, moved at least as fast as their American counterparts in continuous casting; the farm- and construction-equipment industry in Emilia-Romagna got into production of sophisticated hydraulic-control devices; the Sassuolo ceramic makers devised new clay mixtures, tunnel ovens, and microprocessor-based devices for sorting output by subtle differences in the hues of each tile.[8]

From the mid-1970s on, these changes were caught in the wide-meshed net of Italian statistics. Wage levels in areas such as Emilia-Romagna (where there were virtually no large firms and a proliferation of small shops) drew even with the levels in Piedmont, the most industrialized Italian region. Similarly, unemployment rates fell: in 1966 the rate was 4 percent for Italy, 4.3 percent for Emilia-Romagna, and 2.5 percent for Piedmont; in 1976 the rates in both Emilia-Romagna and Piedmont were 2.8 percent, three-quarters of the national average. A dramatic sign of the prosperity of the new small-firm sector was the rise of Modena—the capital of the decentralized economy—in the rank list of provincial wealth: in 1970 it had only the seventeenth per-capita income of the Italian provinces, but in 1979 it had the second highest (after the Val d'Aosta, a center of luxury tourism). Statistics on regional trade suggest that firms in decentralized industries were increasingly selling their output directly to foreign customers, rather than to large Italian firms for subsequent export.[9]

This transformation of the supplier sector was also reflected in changes in the Italian machine-tool industry. As in Japan, the growing demand for flexible equipment led to a boom in production of NC equipment for (and often by) small shops: at the end of the 1970s, Italy ranked behind West Germany but well ahead of France and Great Britain as West Europe's second largest producer of NC equipment.[10] Turin became a center of small industrial-automation and robotics firms, often serving the needs of the small-shop sector.[11] Dozens of consultancies sprang up around Bologna to adapt large-firm technology to the needs of small shops, and to help automate artisanal processes (such as firing ceramics and annealing metals) to allow for subsequent modification of product and process.[12] Leading American equipment makers began to market Italian shoe machinery because of its flexibility;[13] and Italian ceramic-production machinery appeared on world markets.[14]

Four coincident factors were crucial to this innovative turn: the Italian extended family; the view of artisan work as a distinct type of economic activity; the existence of merchant traditions connecting the Italian provinces to world markets; and the willingness of municipal and regional governments (often allied to the labor movement) to help create the infrastructure that the firms required but could not themselves provide. In the context of technological advance and market reorientation suggested by the earlier survey of industrial successes, these four

227

conditions turned what might have been a regression in the industrial division of labor into an advance in the new direction.[15]

The tradition of familialism—the use of kinship relations as the structuring principles of industrial organization—and the existence of a distinct category of "artisan" firms facilitated the accumulation of capital in the early stages of decentralization. A great many of the new firms were family operations; husbands, wives, and children were expected to, and did, put in long hours at low wages to meet deadlines and pay installments on the first pieces of machinery. Self-exploitation—legitimated (though in the case of child labor, usually limited) by a traditional sense of obligation to the family—may well have been crucial to the survival of many of the firms in their vulnerable youth. The same holds for the exemption under Italian law of artisan firms (essentially those employing no more than fifteen persons) from many provisions of the tax code and the *Statuto dei Lavoratori*. Originally introduced by the Fascists to separate the petty bourgeoisie from the working classes, the artisan-firm category was defended by the ruling Christian Democrats as a favor to their small-business clients; and in the early 1970s it helped secure the survival of the new shops, by reducing their payments to social-welfare funds and increasing the capacity, for example, to schedule work loads flexibly.[16]

Whereas familialism and the artisan-category exemption protected the small shops in their infancy, mercantile traditions and local-government intervention helped them grow. The mercantile tradition of the Pratese *impannatore* appeared in various decentralized industries: these figures provided the essential link between shifting, long-distance markets and emergent federations of specialist firms. The scrap dealers of Brescia who contributed to the mini-mill industry are a well-studied example.[17] Further research is likely to turn up a complex web of connections among bankers, petty traders, and small producers dating back to medieval patterns of production, yet vital enough today to facilitate the new firms' autonomy.

Local government played a double role. On the one hand, municipal and regional governments constructed industrial parks for the small producers (equipped, for instance, with common dining halls); improved roads; opened vocational schools (when these were not provided by the associations of artisans and industrialists themselves); and in some cases (as in the knitwear region around Carpi) operated regional research centers, along Japanese lines. In areas dominated by the Communists (such as Emilia-Romagna), government intervention was motivated not by a vision of a new industrial order; rather, it was motivated by a determination to secure if not the allegiance at least the neutrality of small business, and so to counter a reemergence of the Fascist bloc of petty bourgeoisie and big capital, as had existed in the 1920s.[18] In the areas dominated by the Christian Democrats (such as the Venetian provinces), the motive behind government intervention was to continue a century-old policy of promoting industrialization in the hinterland as a means of preventing migration to the cities and the consequent decomposition of the rural parishes on which the party depended.

The government's second role in helping the small shops become established was to act as an agent of community sentiment in limiting the violations of health and safety standards in the new shops. Although the Italians themselves referred to the new shops as the underground economy in the 1970s, the practices of nearly every firm were common knowledge in its home community. Employers were often the ex-workmates, the kin, the political comilitants, or the coreligionists of their employees. But if these ties did not check the shops' temptation to reject community standards of decency, the trade unions or the church—in concert with the local government—would remind them of their responsibilities. Thus, while local government helped create the literal space for innovative expansion, it also blocked money-making through the exploitation of labor.[19]

So ingrained are our notions of the orderly progress of economic development that it is hard to believe any structure formed by such contingent forces could long stand—let alone represent new principles of efficiency. Yet by 1983, careful observers of the decentralization movement (such as Arnaldo Bagnasco and Sebastiano Brusco, who early underscored its abusive character) were agreed that much of this sweatshop sector had become innovative. Moreover, this new form of industrial organization proved more resistant to economic crisis than the rest of the Italian economy.[20] In the national trade-union confederations, the role of labor in the industrial districts became a topic of increasing interest.[21] Indeed, the Italians, like the Japanese, began to treat the new system matter-of-factly—but only after it had become a matter of fact.

West Germany

Compared with Italy and Japan, the reorientation of West Germany toward craft production is proceeding so quietly as to be almost unnoticed. Moreover, in West Germany the changes are often centered in the large firms, rather than in the network of their suppliers. West German firms are decentralizing internally, instead of dissolving into their supplier networks (the limiting case in Italy) or functioning as assemblers of customized components (the limiting case in Japan). And the government in West Germany—whether national or local—has been far more a witness to than an instigator of transformation. The Italian and Japanese shift toward custom production was the unintended result of a state-supported effort to create a system of mass production; by contrast, the West German shift toward custom production was the industries' revival—under pressure of events—of a system that had begun to pass out of practice—before its utility was rediscovered.

As we saw in chapter 6, West Germany had started to blur its traditional focus on producers' goods during the boom years following the Treaty of Rome, in 1957. The country was forming a new industrial system, based on expansion into consumer-durables markets, the recruitment of foreign workers, and the redesign of work to suit any unskilled labor force. Its economic prospects seemed assured by the American example.

But the fragility of the system was already showing by the early 1970s. Continued trade surpluses had led to revaluation of the Deutsche Mark. This had little effect on the sale of producers' goods (where customization and service justify premium prices); but it reduced the competitiveness of mass-produced goods. Wage settlements in the vast, heterogeneous metalworking sector were pegged to the profits of the machine builders and manufacturers of luxury automobiles and then applied (through a variant of pattern bargaining) to less fortunate consumer-durables firms, which were competing in increasingly saturated markets.[22] Even if this arrangement had not resulted from the fact that both types of firms were organized by the same union (IG Metall), the 1973 wildcat strikes of the *Gastarbeiter* were so intense as to make it hard for any union to neglect them.[23]

West German economists recorded these strains in the mid-1970s with a special clarity. This clarity reflected both their nation's long experience with international markets and their discipline's mercantilist tradition; this tradition, since Friedrich List, has connected domestic prosperity with world-market success. Study after study (mostly conducted by the Institut für Weltwirtschaft at Kiel) showed that in the most diverse industries, standard goods made by semiskilled assembly-line workers were succumbing to foreign competition: everything—from light bulbs to vehicle parts to simple machine tools to switch gears—was under attack.[24] The obvious answer, formulated with an eye to the

American and Japanese experience, seemed to be a move toward production of more "intelligent" products: customized goods using sophisticated microprocessor technologies beyond the grasp of the competition. The historic success of the producers'-goods industry was to be extended to the economy as a whole.[25]

In the late 1970s, however, much of West German industry seemed stuck in its ways. It continued to succeed in areas of traditional strength such as machine tools; yet it missed opportunities to strengthen such vulnerable sectors as consumer electronics or household appliances through innovative use of microprocessor technology. This paralysis was partly due to the continuance of standard operating procedures defined during the earlier prosperity: organizations that had just recently come to think of themselves as mass producers could not overnight abandon their new-found methods of marketing, product development, and labor control. In addition, the immobility resulted from the government's inability to orchestrate industrial renovation. The limits of the state's action were demonstrated by its bumbling efforts to coordinate reduction of excess and superannuated steel capacity.[26] More crucially, it failed to promote a viable domestic computer industry—the sector that seemed key to success in all others.

The West German state is a powerful administrative machine. Its inability in recent decades to conduct large-scale economic transformations is primarily the result of a political stalemate. The dominant corporations—and behind them the commercial banks—were unwilling to cede decisions on the economy's future to a Social Democratic government. The Social Democrats tried to make the German Ministry of Technology and Research an instrument for structural reform. But they were unable to establish it as a central bureau for coordinating industrial policy—like, for example, the French ministry of finance or the Japanese Ministry for Industry and Trade (although the power of these latter is exaggerated by Americans who bemoan the absence of such institutions in their own country). Thus, in West Germany the Ministry of Research and Technology must compete with the ministries of finance (clearly allied to industry), education, and defense—all of which advocate separate, often cross-cutting policies.[27] To make matters worse, agreement is almost impossible between the regional governments (*Länder*) and the federal state (*Bund*) on any reorientation plan—since any plan will inevitably favor some firms and regions over others.[28]

Had the West German consumer-electronics industry been less fragmented or the electromechanical industry less tied to traditional technologies, the government's lack of leadership might have been inconsequential: either an innovative, fast-growing consumer-electronics industry or a technologically aggressive electromechanical industry might have financed a drive into semiconductors and computers—a drive that would have been fueled by its appeal to other industries. But these industries did not have the capacity for self-transformation, so the state's role was critical. Moreover, public policy did nothing to reverse—and may have reinforced—the market's confusion: such giants as Telefunken were given large sums to develop equipment that had little commercial application, and that—imposed on universities and government offices—retarded the spread of computers by some years. A clear illustration of West Germany's failure to develop a computer industry was Siemens's decision to buy a 6-percent stake in Fujitsu-Fanuc (the Japanese maker of machine-tool controllers), rather than to continue its efforts to establish a place in this key sector.

But despite these rigidities and failures, there were many signs by the early 1980s that West Germany was regaining its footing and shifting—ever more deliberately—toward flexible production. This progress went beyond that of the steel and chemical industries noted earlier. Preambles to new government programs, journal articles on new technologies, and academic studies of reorganization all reveal a striking consensus: mass markets were breaking up, and domestic industry had the capacity to apply microprocessor technologies (often based on imported components) to a particularized demand.[29] These new writings did not just describe the weaknesses in the current system; rather, they outlined an emergent alternative. The program to foster new manufacturing technology, sponsored by the Ministry of Research and Technology, for example, opened with a general statement of the economic situation that captured the prevailing view. In the past, the Ministry announced,

[P]rogress in manufacturing technology and increases in labor productivity were frequently associated with the decomposition and standardization of tasks. Because of new information technologies, a reorientation of production technology has become not only imaginable but visible. This new orientation is characterized by greater elasticity with respect to customers' demands and less monotony at the work place. Flexibility and productivity need no longer be contradictory characteristics of equipment for the production of high-quality goods.[30]

At the company level, this new consensus was reflected in the internal decentralization of the factory—or the return to the workshop as the basic unit of production. German observers note that in the traditionally flexible industries (such as machine tools), the new form of automation was at first threatening: programming NC machines off the shop floor, for example, disrupted established workplace relations.[31] But as the NC machines proved to be compatible with the high skill level of the workers and the de-facto decentralization of production these industries accepted such automation. Studies show that these German firms are in fact more likely to take advantage of the shop-floor programming possibilities than such firms in other countries. "Companies, particularly in Germany," the sociologist Gert Hartmann and his collaborators write,

are increasingly seeing the merits of stressing craft skills as a viable option when implementing the new technology. This is not because it is a necessary consequence, but because CNC has been developed in a context which links economic success with this process. There is a striking kinship between the increasing use of CNC and the renewed interest by companies in training and employing skilled workers.[32]

As the new technology spread, its use led to a reconceptualization of the relationship between the shop and the manufacturing process as a whole. Technical journals wrote, for example, about the creation in large plants of "technology centers": units that group machines by general type (lathe, machining center, etc.), as in an Italian or Japanese small shop specializing in one phase of manufacturing. This grouping is done as an alternative to placing heterogeneous machines together in a sequence defined by the steps of production—as in mass-production assembly lines.[33] The aim is to facilitate production of constantly varying families of parts, rather than to facilitate speed of assembly of just those parts required for current output. Similarly, the coordination of several machine tools from one computer ("direct numerical control," or DNC) is being conceived, to make the workshop—not the factory— the locus of design: hence a spate of articles on *Werkstatt* (workshop) DNC.[34] These efforts at redefinition of the work unit were complemented by developments in the systems that control the flow of workpieces from unit to unit.[35] Finally, wage systems (even in the industries that had gone furthest toward narrow, American-style, job definition) were reformed to reflect flexible redeployment and multiskilled workers. The best example is the Volkswagen *Lohndifferenzierungsvertrag* (Wage Differential Contract) of 1980, which created extremely broad job definitions; it also put a premium on ease of future reorganization in the initial regrouping of tasks.[36]

Meanwhile, small West German firms have begun to rationalize, along the lines marked out by the Italians and Japanese. They have been aided by developments at large firms such as Bosch, but also by changes in state policy. The Social Democrats (allied with export-oriented industry) fell from power just as they were discovering the significance of flexible parts suppliers in the changing economy; the Christian Democrats (allied with small business) succeeded them, and they have been quick to promise aid to clients whose economic centrality has been affirmed by international experience. New programs of state aid to technological innovation will certainly be a centerpiece of the industrial policy articulated by the new government.[37]

Thus—between the internal decentralization of the large firms and the technological revitalization of the small suppliers—West Germany may well be on the verge of claiming the legacy of its craft history. What labor's place in the emerging system will be, however, no one could say. The only certainty is that employers have been anxious to bargain with workers plant by plant; they will concede whatever is necessary to increase flexibility at the work place, and avoid regional or industrywide agreements that limit their local freedom of maneuver. How the unions—organized as a federation of factory councils—will respond to this attempt to break them into their parts is anyone's guess. This last question is perhaps the major imponderable in any assessment of West Germany's chances for recovery.[38]

France

French policy in the first half of the 1970s was dominated by memories of May 1968. In 1968 it seemed that society itself would be dashed apart by waves of strikes and occupations of factories and schools. Therefore, when Giscard d'Estaing became president, in 1974, his Center-Right government responded to the oil crisis and the recession with a contradictory mixture of policies: some aimed to contain inflation, and others aimed not to antagonize the working class. Thus, the deflationary Plan Fourcade—named after the minister of economics and finance—was followed the next year by a second Plan Fourcade, which encouraged expansion. Meanwhile, the government—honoring concessions made to labor during the Events of May—made it harder for firms to lay off workers, and it increased benefits to the unemployed.

But when unemployment subsequently increased and did not provoke more social unrest, the government was emboldened. It embraced business interests and pursued deflationary policies. The turn was marked by the appointment of Raymond Barre as prime minister in 1976. An advocate of competition and market rule, Barre echoed theories then prominent in the United States and Germany. To all appearances, his appointment was the repudiation of the French *dirigiste* tradition of enlightened bureaucratic supervision of the economy.[39]

There was, however, a fundamental difference between the liberalism of Paris and the liberalism of Washington, London, and Bonn. In these latter capitals, there was a new belief that a restoration of market forces would allow firms to find a way to adapt efficiently to changed conditions of competition. By contrast, the French in Barre's camp did not see the restoration of competition as a means of finding the best solution to economic problems; rather, they saw it as an instrument for achieving a known end: the creation of a network of giant world-class corporations. The Barre government favored the market because it thought the market would favor these large corporations at the expense of the smaller, inefficient producers—those that the government had worked to eliminate since the end of World War II.

The restoration of the market was thus in large measure the French leaders' answer to the limitations of *dirigisme*—limitations that resulted from the very transformations of the industrial structure that the planners had encouraged. Among these limitations on the state's ability either to shape the economy or to let the market do its dirty work, two stand out. They help explain why, despite Barre's intentions, the government was often forced to override market decisions that it favored.

The first, most crucial limitation was imposed by the political countermovement of those businesses that were disadvantaged by the national program of concentration (the *économie concertée*).[40] These small shopkeepers and manufacturers had turned increasingly to their parliamentary representatives for protection against the alliance of state planners and large firms. The narrowness of Giscard's election in 1974 (he beat the candidate of the united Left, François Mitterand, with 50.3 to 49.7 percent of the vote) meant that the new government could not ignore discontent. At the same time, however, Giscard could not run the risk of so antagonizing the working class that it protested—thus calling into question his guarantee of social peace. Therefore—though his hand was strengthened enough by the 1978 legislative elections to reduce protection of temporary workers—Giscard still did not want to leave triage to the market if the potential victims defended themselves too forcefully. Thus, when in 1979 steelworkers in Lorraine protested a mill closing, the government pressured French automobile firms to establish subsidiaries in the area.[41] Similarly, the state was forced to aid workers who had lost their jobs through the failure of new firms that the government had encouraged in an effort to spread labor-intensive mass production to low-wage rural areas.[42]

The second limitation on the state's ability to shape the economy or let the market do so was the transformation of the bureaucracy, and its relations with industry. This transformation resulted from the administration of the *économie concertée*. Under de Gaulle's stabilization plan of 1958 the planners' interest in long-term expansion conflicted with the finance ministry's interest in short-term stability. The conflict was resolved in the 1960s by allowing the finance ministry to act as the arbiter of investment projects approved by planners in other bureaus. One effect of this shift of responsibility was to change the role of the planners, from that of chief conspirators in the creation of modernization cartels to that of advocates of the industrial groups they had supervised. Another, related effect was to encourage firms to advance their interests through bargaining with the finance ministry or, when that failed, through sympathetic parliamentarians. And, of course, the more openly state agencies pressed the cause of certain firms, the more those disadvantaged by state policy claimed that planning was a screen for privilege—and, finally, the more disorganized, inefficient, and uncontrollable the results of government intervention appeared to those at the highest levels of command.[43]

But even when it was not obliged to do so by political pressure and administrative entanglements, the French state continued to aid industry. The most obvious form of continuing public intervention was the state's promotion of export industry. Before the first oil shock, France sold 70 percent of its exports in markets within a radius of 1,500 kilometers of Paris. But beginning in 1974, the government supported an export drive into industrializing countries, oil-rich or not: it insured exporters against various risks; it forgave taxes on goods sold abroad; and after 1976, it granted low-interest loans to firms enlarging their capacity for export production. At the same time, the government advocated a reorganization of the international monetary system, to be discussed in later chapters, which would have generally enlarged the advanced countries' market for exports.

The appeal for reform of the world-trade regime went unheeded, but the export drive was a success. Between 1973 and 1978, the dollar value of French exports to developing countries increased by 191 percent, as against an increase of 99 percent in the value of exports to advanced countries—and this despite a 12-percent appreciation of the franc against the dollar, and a rate of inflation above that of many of France's competitors. France was notably successful in selling mass-produced goods ranging from pumps and centrifuges to transportation equipment; but its telecommunications and power-generating equipment, as well as ships, armaments, and aircraft, were also marketed.[44] A comparison of the industries that showed a net gain from government transfers with the industries favored under the then-current plan for economic development suggests that the government was more interested in subsidizing industries that promised high near-term export revenues than it was in investing in structural transformations that would pay off only in the distant future.[45] The success of this export drive—together with the fitful application of expansionary domestic policies—helps explain why, between 1973 and 1978, the average annual growth rate of the French gross national product was above that of West Germany and the United States (the rates were, respectively, 2.8, 1.9, and 2.3 percent).[46]

While Giscard's government was abandoning attempts to restructure the economy—in favor of market triage and mercantilist promotion of exports—a new generation of technocrats came into play. They were considering how best to reform the mechanisms of planning and state control of the economy. Typically, this new generation had grown up with the économie concertée. Their education in the elite corps of civil servants and their apprenticeship with the architects of postwar industrialization disposed them to believe that the French economy required guidance from above. However much they appreciated the elegance of neoclassical economics, these young technocrats viewed the policies it suggested as inappropriate to the France they knew. But they saw, too, that the older forms of planning led to inefficiency and admitted pressure groups of every sort into the antechambers of power. Thus, if they could not accept the neo-liberalism of Barre, neither could they defend the dirigisme of the older generation of planners. The problem for the young technocrats was therefore to invent a system of planning that would elude the control of the market, yet profit from the lessons of the competitive struggle.

Their quasi-official resolution of the problem (presented by Christian Stoffaës in the widely read book, La grande menace industrielle)[47] was to revive collaboration between the state and the large firms, but in a new form. Stoffaës pictured French industry as caught in a pincer movement: the Americans, West Germans, and Japanese were crowding the French out of both the high-technology market and the capital-equipment market. France was only the eighth largest producer of machine tools in the world, but it was the second largest importer—after the Soviet Union. Simultaneously, the French production of less sophisticated goods (ranging from shoes to carbon steel) was coming under increasing competition from the developing countries.

Stoffaës was convinced that French industry was not "mature" enough to surmount this double crisis. Rather, the economy's best chance was to renew the partnership between the state and the large firms created during the concentration movement of the 1960s. This was to be done through an elaborate system of "growth contracts."[48] Using various legal instruments, the state was to subsidize selected firms on the condition that the firms undertook to meet certain growth targets. In case they failed, the subsidies had to be repaid. The plan was justified by a sophisticated discussion of the need to reduce the risks associated with innovation. But the real idea was that the state was competent to identify the leading firms in the crucial sectors, while the firms were the best judge of strategy in their own markets. The planners—chastened by inefficiency of conglomerates formed in the 1960s—had lost faith in their capacity to envisage in detail the future form of French industry; they were still confident of their capacity to identify those who could.

Had Giscard's government remained in power, some version of this scheme might have served as the blueprint for the reconstruction of the planning machinery. But the Center-Right lost the presidential and legislative elections of 1981 (as much because of its political missteps as its economic policies), and power passed to the Left. The historic irony—and the measure of how much France's economic future is mortgaged to the successes of the past—is that the young Socialist technocrats who now took control held ideas about industrial reorganization that were similar to those of the technocrats they had displaced. They, too, were committed to expansion along the mass-production trajectory.

But there was a dramatic shift in the means by which that end was pursued: the new program of nationalization. This program gave the French state control of economic developments that is unmatched in any nominally capitalistic country save, perhaps, Austria. Today, French state-controlled firms produce 80 percent of the nation's steel, 63 percent of its nonferrous metals, 75 percent of its artificial fibers, 54 percent of its basic chemicals, 36 percent of its office equipment and computers, and 84 percent of its aircraft. Just under one-half of the manufacturers employing more than 2,000 people were in the hands of the state; all important banks were also nationalized. This program of nationalization substituted direct coordination by the state for the market discipline of the Barre regime. Nevertheless, Socialist strategies shared their right-wing predecessors' belief that the future of French industry depended on a group of giant firms' maintaining dominant positions in world markets.[49]

In questions of macroeconomic policy, too, the new government pursued some of the goals of the Giscardists, but, again, by different means. Like its predecessor, the Socialist government pressed for coordinated expansion of international demand—and the call for a neo-Keynesian world order could now be justified not merely as good economics but also as an expression of socialist internationalism. But whereas Giscard and Barre had been determined to postpone domestic reflation until recovery began in world markets, the Socialists did the reverse. Expecting the world economy to revive soon, they reflated the domestic economy, in order to cushion France from the remainder of the international slump. Had a general recovery in fact been imminent, export revenues would soon have relieved the state of the burden of financing the expansion; and foreign competitors would have been too preoccupied with the spreading prosperity of their home markets to invade the French market.

But the recovery did not arrive on schedule. The expanding demand was captured by foreign exporters. These exporters sought outlets for the products that their reduced home markets could not absorb, and they took advantage of their lower rates of domestic inflation to undersell French producers. As the French state's deficit rose and the value of the franc declined, the Socialists were forced to revert to a policy of austerity.

The failure of many of the Socialist programs has reopened debate within the French Left over the direction of policy. A minority current in the Socialist Party (a Party made up of groups on the noncommunist Left, assembled in the early 1970s) continues to argue for some application of Proudhonist mutualism. And the government has in fact announced programs to aid small and medium-sized enterprises. But these developments seem prompted more by the potential political profits of splitting the camp of property owners than by any reconsideration of the conditions of expansion. Recent economic history seems to have influenced the new elite of Left planners as little as it influenced the planners on the Right. Those in command continue to see the nationalization of capital as a means of moving faster down the familiar path of development—rather than as an opportunity to change direction. As in so many times and places, ascent to power was seen as a warrant to do the necessary, not as the freedom to redefine it.

The United States

Until the early 1980s, the dominant response of American industry to the crisis was an un-self-conscious determination to survive by past practices. In the 1960s, American firms reacted, we saw, to the saturation of markets by diversifying into new ones. In the 1970s, their first response to the shocks was to regard them as unexpected but familiar business downturns, provoked and prolonged by political meddling in the economy. Their second response, examined in chapter 8 in connection with the world car, was to try to reestablish the competitiveness of industry by putting operations on a global scale and introducing the latest technology. All the while, they called for import restrictions in various forms and attributed their losses to the unscrupulous practices of foreign competitors, the inept economic policies of their own government, and the ruinous wage demands of their workers. One American machine-tool company claimed in court—arguing against Japanese competitors—that any system of product development that deviated from American practices and resulted in machines that outperformed American models was illegal.[50] American firms, in short, vacillated between the wishful thinking that nothing was wrong and strong-arm efforts to force the entire world to play the one game it knew how to win.

But there were other American responses as well—responses that in the brighter and steadier light of Italian, West German, and Japanese experience could be seen as the first steps toward a more flexible system of production. Some of these responses occurred outside of the large mass producers—sometimes in reaction against them. The mini-mills, often started by disgusted refugees from the major firms, are an example.[51] But there were also signs of renewed life in older sectors of craft production, which had long been subordinated to mass production. And most noticeable was the explosion of small firms using the latest technologies. Even within the dominant corporations, some factions of management interpreted the crisis as resulting from their standard operating procedures—which therefore needed changing.

Thus in the United States the crisis seemed to change everything and nothing. In Italy, Japan, and West Germany, new technologies were successfully absorbed into old industries in ways that anticipated and oriented future development. In France, those in charge were at least agreed on the fundamentals of what to say, if not what to do. But in the United States, it was unclear which successes were prophetic and which prophecies made for success. Anyone who wanted to hear a particular story about the changes in progress could find someone with facts enough to tell it plausibly. American industry was beginning to drift toward flexible specialization; but, being adrift, it was at the mercy of cross-currents, moving it in other directions as well.

A sign of the confusion regarding reform was the large corporations' incoherent attempts to redefine industrial relations—particularly the system of shop-floor control. The more American managers saw the dislocations of the 1960s as an epochal crisis, the more they saw the need to reorganize production, redefine jobs, and change the work rules and practices. But the widespread determination to change the system of shop-floor control was accompanied by equally widespread uncertainty about how to reconstruct work-place relations.

The movement for transformation of American industrial relations had two overlapping sources. One was a group of intellectuals, idealistic entrepreneurs, and forward-looking union leaders who were intent on improving the "quality of work life."[52] This group drew on American ideas of industrial psychology that aimed to create harmony in the factory by harmonizing the informal groups surrounding each work place. Typically, these ideas have been taken up during periods of worker unrest (such as after World War I, the Great Depression, and World War II); so it was historically predictable that they would be revived after the disturbances of the 1960s.[53] This time, however, the traditional notion of social-psychological pacification shaded into *marxisant* ideas—occasionally homegrown, occasionally reflecting lessons the European labor movement drew from the upheavals of the 1960s.[54] In this more radical view, the work force was becoming increasingly disaffected by mass-production work. Industrial society could therefore progress only if a way were found to "humanize" (the slogan of the West German labor movement) factory jobs: by reducing their monotony and giving the workers opportunities to exercise discretion. Experiments allowing workers to rotate among jobs and redistributing (some) authority from foremen to the work group attracted the attention of intellectuals and the press, but little came of the proselytizing of the reform group. In the late 1970s, observers sympathetic to this group's goals dismissed its efforts as a movement of academics, idealists, and industrial consultants with no constituency among the powerful industrialists. Above all, there was little evidence that reform of work organization increased efficiency. And once the "blue-collar blues" of the 1960s had been replaced by job insecurity in the 1970s, it was hard to see why tough-minded managers would bother with such reform.[55]

But, surprisingly enough, the second source of industrial-relations reform was a group of the toughest-minded managers. This group, too, was influenced by the intellectual currents of the times: articles in *The Harvard Business Review* advocating flexible styles of management; discussions of the European experiments; and so on. But this second group of reformers—identifiable by their deeds rather than writings—was motivated more by competition than by doctrine.

As markets became less stable, some managers tried to increase the flexibility of production. In doing so, they came to recognize that the system of narrow job classifications and seniority provisions—the system that both defined the unions' views of justice and gave purpose and direction to its administrative machinery—was an obstacle to progress. For this reason, what began as organizational experiments often evolved into a drive to create a "union-free" environment. The goal was to establish a flexible new form of shop control that, in new plants, would be beyond the reach of the labor movement. This drive was extensive and successful because of coordinate changes in the American political and legal environment, which we will examine in chapter 11. Here, we want only to underscore the relation among changes in the conditions of competition, attempts at internal corporate reform, and the growth of hostility to a form of shop-floor control associated in the United States with unionism.

This relation is documented in a study of industrial relations from the 1960s through the '80s, in a large corporation producing diverse goods in different plants, some unionized and some not. In the early 1960s, the corporation came under increased international competitive pressure. Management responded by inaugurating a series of experiments with new techniques of work organization. The experiments were begun in both union and nonunion plants; but the corporation found it much harder to introduce changes in the union plants. Therefore, efforts to extend the program focused on the nonunion plants; and as the experiments were elaborated, they came to presuppose an unorganized work force. Once the corporation was convinced of the new techniques' success and the desirability of applying them wherever possible, it naturally became committed to an anti-union policy: since unions and work reform apparently could not be combined, the company took care to keep unions out of the plants that it founded or acquired. As a result, the percentage of the corporation's unionized employees declined from the late 1960s on. Between 1979 and 1982 alone, the unionized portion of the work force declined from 59 to 50 percent, as the corporation started nine unorganized plants; and it cut employment in its unionized plants by roughly 25 percent.[56]

In some cases, however, unions were able to reach an accommodation with the corporations; these accommodations allowed reformers in both camps to realize part of their ambitions. The story of what the United Auto Workers called the Southern Strategy of General Motors illustrates such accommodation.[57] In the 1970s, GM opened parts plants in low-wage, traditionally anti-union areas in the South. Initially, the company's aim was to reduce its labor costs; the policy fit into the emerging world-car strategy of decentralizing labor-intensive manufacturing operations in low-wage areas. But at the same time, GM used its freedom from work-rule restrictions to experiment with flexible forms of work organization. These experiments often went far beyond anything the company had undertaken in cooperation with the unions in the North.

When the UAW tried to organize one of these Southern plants, in Louisiana, by pointing out the difference in wages paid for the same work in the North and the South, the company responded by raising wages in its Southern plants to Northern levels. But though GM was willing to meet the wages demanded by the UAW, it nonetheless continued to resist unionization of the Southern plants, in order to continue its experiments with more broadly defined tasks and job rotation. And even when the new plants were nominally opened to the union (by an agreement in 1979) between national officers of GM and the UAW, the local experiments continued—although they did not always conform to control practices of Northern plants. Finally, in the early 1980s, GM introduced the same kinds of work practices tested in the Southern—formerly nonunion—plants into new, unionized plants in the Midwest (such as its assembly plants in Orion, Pontiac, St. Louis, and Detroit).[58]

On one level, these changes in industrial relations—regardless of the unions' precise relationship to them—have a coherence that suggests a

243

new system in the making. The hallmarks of the old system were narrow jobs, defined by precise rules, constantly amended by a highly developed system of procedural justice. The emergent system is based on broader job classifications, which reduce the number of distinct jobs and facilitate the transfer of workers from one task to another. And it relies on substantive dispute resolution, reminiscent of industrial relations in Germany and Japan, or of the unionized version of the American Plan of welfare capitalism, which died aborning in the 1920s.

Thus, in the boldest experiments in which the UAW has participated, as many as sixty semiskilled production jobs have been grouped into a single classification. Craft jurisdictions have been broadened to generic categories, such as electrician or mechanic, and work is assigned either directly by management or by the work group itself, under the guidance of a team leader—a salaried employee who largely replaces the traditional foreman.[59] Workers are paid for what they know—their skills—rather than what they happen to be doing—the job at the moment. In a production unit, for example, inspectors, material handlers, and janitors are grouped into teams of ten to fifteen workers who decide—subject to the constraints of the production schedule—who does what, when. Employment security is regulated by explicit agreements to maintain the work force at stipulated levels, rather than by seniority-based job-allocation rules.

The shift from procedural to substantive resolution of disputes is reflected in the trend to "quality circles." In these and other bodies (reminiscent of modern European works councils and the plant committees of the American Plan), managers and workers discuss problems of production and management. In this way, for example, guaranteed employment for a set number of workers has been substituted for a ban on subcontracting. And when an operation is slated to be moved out of the plant, management consults with works committees on how to cut production costs in order to retain the work—or, failing that, on alternative operations that could be moved in to replace the lost jobs. The UAW has accommodated these changes by adjusting its national bargaining structure. In response to the near-bankruptcy of Chrysler, for example, the union made major wage concessions; in return, it secured the right to appoint one member of the board of directors—who would monitor progress toward solving the problems for which the concessions were a partial solution.

But an interpretation of these changes as the Europeanization of industrial relations—or even as a revival of abandoned American traditions—overlooks ambiguities in the new practices, and the intentions of those who negotiated them. First, the language in the contracts suggests that the parties—primarily the unions—are unsure whether they are breaking with the past or making temporary adjustments, during an aberrant period in the epoch of postwar expansion. The UAW, for example, has been careful to term changes in the system of shop-floor control "experiments"; wage concessions have been made by "suspending cost-of-living formulae" and "postponing" annual wage increases.[60] These expressions are not mere linguistic ploys to conceal faits accomplis: when Chrysler showed profits in 1983, the union demanded an increase in wages, to bring them closer to those of the other major producers. Thus, the postwar system of pattern bargaining by wage formula has not been abandoned for good; and its structure still influences even those negotiations whose results apparently ignore it.[61]

But even assuming that the "experiments," "suspensions," and "postponements" do mark the end of the old contract regime, it is unclear what they imply for industrial relations. Because these agreements are typically reached outside any comprehensive reorientation, they are fundamentally ambiguous: without a strategy, what does "going beyond adversarial relations" or "saving jobs through cooperation" mean? On the one hand, these agreements may clear the way for increasing efficiency, reducing the firm's vulnerability to market fluctuations, and buttressing job security—while also increasing workers' control over the work place and perhaps the firm. On the other hand, they may be nothing but declarations that plant survival amidst competition depends on wage reductions: to the affected workers, this result discredits cooperation between labor and capital—such "partnership" seems a cover for betrayal of union standards.

Often, in fact, both interpretations mingle in the same agreement. Thus, workers are asked both to participate in increasing efficiency *and* to agree to lower wages. An example was a contract negotiated in 1983 between the International Union of Electronic Workers (IUE) and GM's Packard Electric Division, a manufacturer of automobile components (some extremely labor-intensive). The settlement was the fruit of five years' collaboration between labor and management, concerning, among other things, job design. It proposed to guarantee the jobs and income of existing workers on the condition that the company be permitted to hire workers at $4.50 an hour to do what the senior workers were doing for $19 an hour. The contract was advertised by leaders of both negotiating parties as a creative solution to the competition from low-wage Mexican labor; but the rank and file rejected it in a bitter campaign that jeopardized the whole program of cooperation.[62]

The threat of such outcomes is increased by the piecemeal quality of industrial-relations reform—not only as among different companies, but also as among different plants within a company. Efforts to solve problems in one unit through collaborative reorganization can be thrown into turmoil by efforts to solve the same problems through wage concessions in another. Wage concessions produce easily calculable short-run benefits, and for that reason alone are likely to be favored by hard-pressed managers over possibly more profitable but certainly less predictable schemes that break with familiar habits. Thus, the negotiating parties face the additional problem that their efforts to decide whether the reforms are for keeps and what they ought to mean are constantly being disturbed by the uncoordinated actions of outsiders.

There is a similarly uncoordinated set of efforts to reform the corporation's internal structure and its relations with its suppliers. Again, these efforts seem to be defined by the desire to avoid past mistakes, to break with rigid habits, and to restore the freedom to respond to shifting markets—rather than by any overall vision of a flexible system. Divisions within companies, for example, are being given greater autonomy in setting and pursuing goals; and division managers are being given the kind of responsibility for new-product development that they would have if running a separate company.[63] But at the same time, internal divisions compete with one another under conditions that create pressure for short-term results—which might not influence the behavior of truly autonomous units competing only in the market for their final products. Subcontractors, as we noted in regard to the reversal of the world-car strategy and the move to the *kanban* system, are being given greater autonomy; and like the internal divisions, they are encouraged to innovate. The corporations are even buying stakes in their suppliers to facilitate long-term commitments. For example, IBM, itself a major producer of semiconductors, has a substantial interest in Intel, which makes microprocessors for its personal computer. But this decentralization of authority from corporate headquarters, too, creates new forms of divisive competition—this time between internal divisions and innovative subcontractors.[64]

And the same goes, finally, for changes in corporate-merger policy. Huge corporations, according to *Business Week,* "have learned the hard way that outright takeovers of entrepreneurial companies can extinguish the creative sparks in the acquired company"; this happens when the acquiring company imposes alien reporting procedures, personnel policies, and managers, whose effect is to disrupt the invisible social preconditions of cooperative innovation.[65] For this reason, corporations are now making limited investments in potential partners, rather than buying them out. But this tack means that internal divisions face yet another set of competitors—under conditions where measures of success are no more clearly defined than they are in comparisons of subcontractors and internal units or rival divisions.

The rejection of a system that presupposes stability and the search for an alternative are mirrored in a wave of books on managerial reform. The theme of this literature is the contrast between "mechanical pictures of organizations" and an anti-organization. This anti-organization "values arguments more highly than serenity and encourages doubt and contradiction rather than belief";[66] it is a commando team, with no fixed structure to impede instant reaction to unforeseen events. The "mechanical picture," moreover, is explicitly associated in the new management literature with the writings of Frederick Taylor and Alfred D. Chandler, Jr.; in one recent book, Rosabeth Kantor views the mechanical pictures as a historical creation of the formative period of the mass-production corporations. "In turn-of-the-century organization theory and its 'scientific management' legacy," Kantor writes,

individuals constituted not assets but sources of error. The ideal organization was designed to free itself from human error or human intervention, running automatically to turn out predictable products and predictable profits. Management was there to handle the few unexpected events that could occur.[67]

An even clearer sign of a break with past models and a tentative spirit of experimentation is the new kind of American operations manager. Operations managers are the planners and industrial engineers responsible for organizing and directing the march of production through the factory. In recent years, the career patterns and even the personality type of these managers have changed. A leading professor of operations management interviewed young managers selected by their employers as the "comers" who might soon be running the firm; he found a sharp contrast between them and the older generation they would replace:

The older ones had a long slow path to the top. They were basically engineering oriented and they came out of first-line supervision or the more professional functions and of operations management. They loved stability. They were always fighting for long runs and few product changes.

The new ones are moving up faster. The new ones are coming from the outside—from sales, from engineering, from marketing, from R&D. They're coming from the personnel department, computer programming. They're coming

247

out of human resources management and quality. They're coming out of product management experience and program management experience. These people have a much different point of view. And it's not all good. . . . But they seem to be especially effective in dealing with ambiguity and change, including changes in products. They become easily bored if there isn't enough change. . . .[68]

In this atmosphere of corporate self-doubt, disdain for past practice, and thirst for novelty—and experimentation with indeterminate results—observers of the American corporation in the early 1980s could not provide a unified account of what was happening; nor could they agree on whether it should be encouraged. A Harvard Business School expert on the automobile industry, Louis T. Wells, Jr., was convinced that after extensive innovation and reorganization, a few major firms, producing standard products, would again dominate the industry—occasionally making room for similarly organized manufacturers emerging in third-world markets.[69] By contrast, three of his colleagues, William J. Abernathy, Kim B. Clark, and Alan M. Kantrow, saw the automobile firms—the very symbols of mass production—shifting toward flexible specialization and permanent innovation.[70] John Dunlop, the most sophisticated architect of postwar American industrial relations, saw the union concessions and contract innovations of the 1980s as a temporary deviation from a fundamentally stable pattern.[71] Thomas Kochan, a close observer of the system Dunlop helped build, was convinced that the postwar bargaining regime was being fundamentally transformed.[72] Labor lawyers were perplexed by the blurring of legal lines between labor and management. Some saw the growing involvement of labor in managerial decisions as an extension of worker control, even a step toward self-managed socialism.[73] Others saw it as a return to company unionism and hence an assault on the protection of workers under the Wagner Act.[74]

Finally, some observers wondered whether developments in the small-firm sector might not prove as important for the U.S. economy as any developments in the mass producers. The most dramatic development in the small-firm sector was the explosion of companies specializing in computer-based technologies. But also in the older small firms—decayed centers of craft production—there were noteworthy developments: signs of regeneration.

The explosion of the "high-technology" firms occurred in the postwar period, around universities.[75] One such concentration was along Route 128, the Boston beltway. Another emerged near Stanford University, in what came to be called Silicon Valley. And San Antonio, Texas, and

TABLE 9.1

Employment in Selected Manufacturing Industries in Massachusetts,
1972–1979 (thousands)

	Machinery*	Metalworking Machinery	Special Industry Machinery	Weaving Mills†	Total Mfg.
1979	100.3	17.6	17.6	4.5	670.3
1978	90.4	16.4	16.4	4.4	652.4
1977	82.0	15.4	16.1	4.0	621.0
1976	74.0	14.4	15.7	3.9	539.6
1975	74.0	14.6	16.1	3.2	577.8
1974	78.5	16.1	17.7	4.3	639.3
1973	73.1	14.6	16.6	4.1	634.7
1972	66.0	12.9	16.6	3.4	610.2

SOURCE: U.S. Bureau of Labor Statistics, *Employment and Earnings, States and Areas, 1939–78,* Bulletin 1370-13, pp. 270–72; U.S. Bureau of Labor Statistics, *Supplement to Employment and Earnings, States and Areas, Data for 1978–80,* Bulletin 1370-15, p. 110.
* Except electrical
† Cotton and synthetics

Durham, North Carolina, have had some success in imitating the high-tech clusters that occurred spontaneously in Massachusetts and California.

Some of the pioneering high-tech firms have grown into large corporations and entered mass production: Wang Laboratories (word processors), Digital Equipment (medium-sized computers), Polaroid (self-developing film), and Atari (video games) are cases in point. But most firms in this branch of industry—including some of the largest—are still committed to continual innovation. And even such firms as Polaroid—which made their first fortunes through mass production of novel products—have recently come to rely on permanent innovation and small production runs of products designed to meet customers' needs.[76]

Among the more traditional small producers, developments are less noticeable. The revival of craft systems along Italian lines has been occurring, but often among just a few shops at a time, within areas that are generally decaying. Moreover, such regeneration is overlooked, because almost no one in the United States expects any such thing to happen. Nevertheless, at least in isolated areas, small firms in traditional industries in the United States reacted to the crisis in the 1970s just as such firms in Italy did: by moving toward flexible specialization.

Table 9.1 shows that in machinery, metalworking machinery, special-industry machinery, and textiles, employment increased sharply in

Massachusetts between 1972 and 1979. This increase occurred after decades of decline. It appears to reflect the growing success of specialty producers that remained in the area after the standard-goods producers had migrated to low-wage states or abroad. For example, the last textile mill in New Bedford produces specialty fabrics used in home decorations and the interiors of luxury automobiles.[77] Outside Massachusetts, too, there is evidence of this phenomenon; for example, the emergence of networks of precision-metalworking firms producing scientific and industrial instruments around Peoria, Illinois, and Pittsburgh, Pennsylvania.

In sum, the confusion of efforts at industrial reform in the United States was as notable for the social plasticity as for the social rigidity that it revealed. On the one hand, the uncoordinated, sometimes self-defeating efforts to create more flexible organizations attested to the constraining power of sheer habit: the standard operating procedures of the well-designed corporation. In France, a technocracy with a long tradition and recent successes was able, at least for a time, to shape debate about the nation's industrial future; but in the United States, debate was shaped in the almost invisible mold of past practice. On the other hand, some American firms and commentators were able to see past their habitual field of vision, to glimpse the alternative form of organization that was discovered with less exertion in countries that were historically better situated to find it. This capacity to see beyond the blindingly familiar is what (we saw in chapter 2) Thomas Kuhn describes as the precondition of scientific revolution. Thus the United States, though constrained by habit, also possessed the visionary capacity to break with the past.

But what, exactly, is this alternative form of organization that firms and nations are discovering? Is it a plausible solution to the crisis of the 1970s? Or is it, like the oasis shimmering before every parched traveler, a common delusion born of a common desperation? The aim of the next chapter is to argue that this time, at least, there is reason to believe in the substance of the hope.

CHAPTER

10

Possibilities for Prosperity: International Keynesianism and Flexible Specialization

THE REACTIONS of firms and nations to the economic dislocations of the 1970s point to two contrasting ways out of the crisis. The world-car strategy suggests that one way is multinational Keynesianism: the extension of the principles of institutional organization that gave rise to the corporation and to macroregulation. If some version of this strategy succeeds, the years following the first oil shock will resemble, in retrospect, the years after the Great Crash of 1929: a period of confused experimentation in which society discovered how to make economic use of efficiency advances in mass production.

By contrast, the spread of flexible specialization suggests that the way out of the crisis requires a shift of technological paradigm and a new system of regulation. If recovery proceeds by this path, then the 1970s and '80s will be seen in retrospect as a turning point in the history of mechanization: a time when industrial society returned to craft methods of production regarded since the nineteenth century as marginal—and proved them to be essential to prosperity.

This chapter argues that either outcome is possible, neither necessary. We claim that under some conditions, current developments could lead to a geographic extension of the mass-production system as stable and coherent as the local systems that went before. Alternatively—extrapolating from other current developments—we can imagine the creation of technologies and regulatory institutions that would make flexible specialization a crucial, perhaps dominant, sector of manufacturing in the advanced industrial countries. It is hard to see, in the current relations among machines, workers, and economic institutions, any reason to think one of these two outcomes any more probable than the other.

Once the contest is decided, however, it will be hard to escape the conviction that the outcome was the only one possible. In history, one thing does lead to the next, and the logic of the connections is always at the service of the claim that the outcome was necessary. But whatever happens, the very fact that in the mid-1980s the lines of current development clearly lead down two divergent paths is strong circumstantial evidence—the only kind available in these questions—that we are living through a second industrial divide: a time when it is difficult to say what to do about technological developments, because how technology will develop depends in a thousand ways on what we do.

Multinational Keynesianism

The first of the two potential strategies of recovery requires the construction of an international economic order based on the extension of Keynesian macroregulation. If, as we argued in chapter 7, the crisis of the last decade is a crisis of underconsumption, rooted in the saturation of core markets for consumer durables, a way out would be to increase demand for those products by raising the aggregate purchasing power of at least some nations not currently able to afford them. The world-car strategy showed that the technological and microregulatory requirements of such a solution are well understood. Although faith has been shaken in the dominant technological paradigms and forms of corporate organizations, the last chapter makes plain that in the United States, France, West Germany, and probably Japan, both would flourish under propitious circumstances.

What is required to reinvigorate them is a system of macroeconomic regulation that balances the growth of supply and demand. The reverses of the world-car strategy proved that multinational corporations cannot solve this problem by themselves. The failure of isolated efforts at reflation in large countries, such as the United States (1977–78), France (1981), and Brazil (1981), suggests that the problem cannot be solved by the uncoordinated efforts of national governments.[1] What these failures imply is that, given the continuing dominance of the mass-production paradigm, macroeconomic coordination can be achieved only by Keynesianism: an international version of the Keynesian order that governed the economies of the industrial countries earlier in the postwar period.

Such a system would be built of at least two, and probably three, related institutional mechanisms. The first is an arrangement to ensure that international demand expands at a rate equal to the expansion of productive capacity. This would require integration of the developed economies—whose large, stagnant markets would provide the bulk of demand—with those developing economies whose markets, properly encouraged, could expand fast enough to provide the margin of growth for the system as a whole. The amalgamation of markets could be achieved through the creation of regional trading blocs, in which the advanced countries would exchange sophisticated products for the raw materials and simpler manufactured goods of their less developed partners. An alternative to such benign variants of the *Grossraumwirtschaften* and co-prosperity spheres of the 1930s would be to combine markets within a unified system of world trade. This latter solution is perhaps easier to imagine, because, as we shall see, it could be realized by expanding the powers and redirecting the policies of the institutions that already oversee international commerce.

The second institutional mechanism with which to build an international Keynesian order would be a series of mechanisms for stabilizing the environment of business decisions. Put another way, these mechanisms would reduce the uncertainty that paralyzes investment in long-lived, product-specific technologies. Stabilization in this sense would require a return, if not to fixed exchange rates, at least to a system of "managed" currency exchanges, which would substantially limit short-term fluctuations in the relative values of key currencies.[2] This system, in turn, would require trading partners to maintain roughly uniform rates of inflation, to guarantee that the foreign exchange rates reflected a stable relation among the true purchasing powers of the relevant currencies. Presumably it would be easier to achieve this uniformity when all national economies are expanding together than it was when domestic stimulation of demand in some was used to compensate home industries for the shortfall in orders produced by restrictive measures abroad. Reduction of uncertainty would also entail stabilization of major commodity flows, through inventory policies that ensured purchasers a continuous supply at predictable prices, and that ensured suppliers a dependable income with which to finance the expansion of their economies.

The third institutional mechanism with which to build international Keynesianism would be a system to apportion the expansion of productive capacity among the advanced industrial countries and between them as a group and the newly industrializing countries. Without such a system to ration the available investment opportunities, a general program of expansion could tempt each firm to expand its capacity so much that the market would quickly be saturated and the problems of overcapacity would reappear at a higher level of total output.

An international Keynesian order built with these three institutional mechanisms could be realized by expanding and reorienting international economic institutions that already exist. Such institutions include principally the International Monetary Fund and the General Agreement on Tariffs and Trade. Detailed bargaining would be necessary to determine the role of other international institutions within such a system, and how authority would be distributed between the IMF (which is experienced in negotiating settlements country by country) and the GATT (which makes and oversees the application of broad rules). Although it is senseless to present a detailed organizational chart of a hypothetical Keynesian world order, it is worth looking at the scattered, partial attempts at reforming international agencies of the post-1973 period—as well as at proposals abandoned at Bretton Woods—to see the outlines of an alternative, expansionary program.

A change in IMF lending policies—as suggested in our earlier discussion of the Fund—would be the precondition for all the other reforms. The IMF could promote international economic expansion by easing the conditions under which it lends its reserves and by lengthening the term of its loans. In this way, the IMF would not force countries to improve their position in international trade by cutting state expenditures (thereby freeing up public funds to pay international debt) or reducing the level of domestic economic activity (thereby reducing the price level, making exports more and imports less attractive to potential customers); rather, the IMF would encourage long-term adjustment through economic reorganization. Because structural adjustments take time, the Fund would have to finance balance-of-payments deficits for much longer periods than its traditional policy permits. Provision of the reserves needed for long-term financing of this sort is thus the sine qua non of any reform program.

Given the appropriate reserves and mandate, and its experience in country-by-country negotiations, the Fund could also act as the super-intendent of the other parts of a new Keynesian order. For example, to ensure that structural reform results in an increase of domestic demand, the Fund could draw on domestic macroregulatory experience and insist that debtor countries respect codes promulgated by the International Labor Organization regarding minimum wages, labor standards, and the right to organize unions. To prevent countries from depressing home consumption in favor of long-term export drives, the IMF could use plans put forward by Keynes himself to tax or otherwise penalize countries showing an enduring balance-of-trade surplus.[3] Loans could be conditional on adherence to commodity-stabilization programs ne-gotiated by the United Nations Conference on Trade and Development (which convened several meetings devoted to this purpose during the 1970s), or on international agreements regulating the expansion and retirement of productive capacity. These latter agreements might be negotiated under the aegis of the GATT, whose mere presence already sets limits on the market-sharing agreements of the 1970s, as surplus capacity has become a problem in one industry after another.[4]

There are, of course, any number of potential obstacles to such a program. It is hard enough, for example, to get the advanced industrial countries to coordinate economic policy among themselves—how would they manage the additional burden of coordinating with the developing countries? Would sovereign states permit the intrusion of international macroregulatory agencies? If they did, would the staffs of these agencies—noted for their resistance to change—administer new programs in the appropriate spirit? Would efforts to stabilize commodity flows and coordinate redeployment of productive capacity be more successful in the 1980s than in the preceding decades?[5]

But several considerations suggest that such questions exaggerate the precariousness of Keynesian strategy of international economic recovery. First, the International Monetary Fund's activities are already extremely intrusive. It is hard to see how a change in policy could make them more so; opposition to its policies would come from different groups, but not necessarily more powerful ones. Second—as evidenced by the declarations of leaders in the international economic organizations—there has been substantial support in important places for key propositions of an international Keynesian order. We have already noted that between 1979 and 1981, the IMF pursued an expansionary policy of the kind just described; remarks by the Fund's managing director, J. de Larosière, (in Manila at the beginning of the period of easy credit) are clear about the Keynesian presuppositions of the lenient course:

It is paradoxical that the industrialised countries, most of which are not using their production potential to the full, are hesitating to increase their financial aid to poor countries. This is despite the fact that such aid could result in increased global demand and thus contribute to reactivation of world trade in a recovery of production. There is nothing in the present state of deflationary chain reactions in the industrialised world, stagnation feeding stagnation, which would argue against such an increase in financial aid.[6]

Third, the fragmentary character of the IMF's reform efforts, and the opposition they encountered, was largely due to the confusion, detailed in chapter 7, over how to interpret the shocks of the post-1973 period. So long as the major industrial countries saw the problem of recovery as one of protecting a fundamentally sound system from accidental disruption, they discounted third-world demands for commodity stabilization as a pretext for redistribution of wealth—rather than as part of a plan for extending macroregulation. The problems of surplus capacity in particular industries were seen as isolated exceptions in a healthy trade regime; lenient credit policies were seen as a reward for the inflationary profligacy that was exacerbating the effect of external shocks. Similarly, as long as the industrializing countries and the export sectors of the industrialized countries viewed the trade regime as inherently stable, they were tempted to take advantage of every weakness of their partners. Producers of all manner of commodities dreamed of forming another OPEC, and aggressive Japanese, French, and West German multinationals gladly invaded markets held by the United States.

But by the early 1980s, the prospects for reform began to brighten. This occurred because of both a shift in the climate of opinion regarding the crisis and a shift in the balance of power among the leading actors in the international economy. By then, the fragility and limits of the existing system had become visible. Above all, the interdependence of the advanced and developing countries was becoming generally accepted. The scramble for national or corporate advantage was checked by the intimation that selfish action could pull down the whole system. The growing tendency of multinationals to substitute joint ventures for competition was one sign of the new spirit of caution; the gingerliness with which the IMF, commercial banks, and many advanced countries went about renegotiating third-world debt was another.

More important was the renewed influence of the United States in the international economy. Because of its dominant role in the world credit system and its large markets for developing nations' goods, the United States suddenly had much more say in world economic affairs than it had in the preceding decade. With the international trading system close to collapse and with the United States' power as creditor and customer to much of the world, the United States had a chance to orchestrate the reconstruction of the international trading regime; it could do so by forcing both its allies and its competitors to choose between its plans and chaos. The chastened hegemon always has a moment of renewed strength when the potentially enormous costs of destroying the system it dominates become clear to all.

Whether the United States will make use of this power and take advantage of the favorable climate of opinion depends on the outcome of domestic political struggles. By the mid-1980s, even many conservative Republicans are willing to support some expansion of the IMF's reserves as the only alternative to an international financial collapse; but some refuse to come to the aid of what they regard as profligate debtors and imprudent creditors. Many liberals are prepared to embrace a much broader reform program, based on Keynesian ideas; but others are reluctant to commit public monies to aiding debtor countries, which would relieve private banks of the risks but not the profits of recovering outstanding loans. Some of the coalitions possible among these shifting political groups could block even those periodic, frantic refinancings of overdue loans that keep the system from collapsing. Other coalitions could clear the way for comprehensive reform and recovery, along a path of multinational Keynesianism. Assuming that neither of these polar outcomes occurs, and that the dominant order neither collapses nor rebounds strengthened from the crisis, the way is clear for another approach to the dislocations of the post-1973 epoch.

Flexible Specialization

The alternative to multinational Keynesianism as a new economic regime is flexible specialization. This second path to recovery is more difficult to visualize than the first. Not only does recent history lack a living example of a national economy built on flexible technology; history also accustoms us to the idea that such an economy, if it functioned at all, would be an inefficient deviation from the narrow track of industrial progress. To see how flexibility—until now confined to a relatively small segment within the mass-production system—could be extended throughout the economy is thus an exercise in imagination. The outline of this alternative approach to the crisis will therefore be more speculative and abstract than the outline of the approach based on an elaboration of the familiar institutions of mass production.

THE TECHNOLOGICAL PRECONDITIONS

The prejudices of experience suggest a crucial first question: Could a system of flexible specialization prove technologically dynamic enough to continually improve manufacturing efficiency? In other words, does this system constitute a genuine technological trajectory? The recent successes of flexible technologies are not by themselves proof of long-term vitality. During the reign of mass production, potential improvements in flexible technologies have undoubtedly been uncovered from time to time; yet they have remained unexploited, as managers and engineers concentrated their attention elsewhere. Do recent applications of these alternative technologies therefore simply reflect recourse to this backlog of opportunities? Or is there continual progress along a trajectory?

There are two arguments for believing that there is a trajectory: that the dynamism of flexible specialization is not transient. The first—based on the idea that there is an immanent logic of technological development—is that the application of computers to industry favors flexible systems. The second argument builds on the discussion in chapter 2 of the relation among politics, markets, and technology. It draws on evidence of the use of technologies other than the computer to support the claim that under appropriate conditions of competition, increased efficiency occurs with flexibility at *every* level of technological development. According to this argument, what we are now witnessing is not a once-in-a-lifetime burst of improvement in flexible production techniques; rather, it is movement down a development path that we

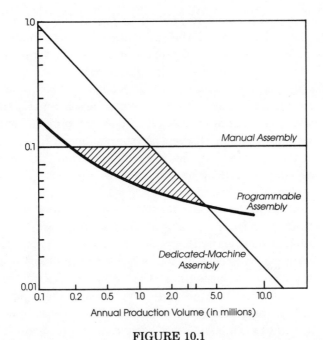

FIGURE 10.1

Comparison of Assembly Costs as a Function of Annual Volume

SOURCE: Paul Michael Lynch, "Economic-Technological Modeling and Design Criteria for Programmable Assembly Machines," (Ph.D. diss., Massachusetts Institute of Technology, 1976), figure 6.2, p. 129.

had the potential of taking earlier. From this second perspective, the use of computers in manufacturing is as much the result of shifts in the competitive environment favoring flexibility as it is of advances in computer technology.

Computers and Flexibility. The relation between computer technology and flexibility is documented in several ways. Early engineering studies indicated that the major cost advantage of computer-aided manufacturing technologies occurred in short runs. The effect of the computer, they predicted, would be to lower the costs of such batch or job-shop production, as compared with either one-of-a-kind customization or mass production. The results of one such study are reproduced in figure 10.1; it shows the relation between cost and output within the above three technologies (respectively, programmable assembly, manual assembly, and dedicated-machine assembly). The savings afforded by computer-aided manufacture (programmable assembly) are indicated by the shaded area. The effect of recent development is to expand the shaded area, by pushing the curve code downward and to the left.

The distinctive advantage of computers in batch production is easily understood in light of the earlier discussion of special- and general-purpose equipment. Efficiency in production results from adapting the equipment to the task at hand: the specialization of the equipment to the operation. With conventional technology, this adaptation is done by physical adjustments in the equipment; whenever the product is changed, the specialized machine must be rebuilt. In craft production, this means changing tools and the fixtures that position the workpiece during machining. In mass production, it means scrapping and replacing the machinery. With computer technology, the equipment (the hardware) is adapted to the operation by the computer program (the software); therefore, the equipment can be put to new uses without physical adjustments—simply by reprogramming.

This situation theoretically benefits short-run as opposed to long-run or one-of-a-kind production. When production runs are long, even substantial setup costs (incurred by replacing machinery) result in only small unit costs, so the costs of the computer-based system cannot compete with the costs of mass production. When production runs are very short (close to one-of-a-kind), *any* adaptation of the equipment—including thorough reprogramming—dramatically increases unit costs; hence, the costs of the computer-based system cannot compete with the costs of craft production, which uses tools that in the limiting case do not have to be modified at all.

The predictions of these early engineering studies have been borne out. A striking example is the spread of computer-controlled machinery in the small, flexible factories of Japan and Italy, and the reorientation of machine builders in these countries to the needs of such small enterprises. Surveys also confirm the early engineering forecasts. *Business Week,* for example, concluded on the basis of interviews in 1981 that computer-aided technology "promises to bring automation to the batch production of goods in runs of less than 50 units," and that future factories will be producing "much shorter runs."[7] Moreover, American operations managers hold these views. A recent contributor to *Operations Management Review* concluded that "job shops will be automated just like process and assembly line manufacturing systems.... Product design will be integrated with the manufacturing system.... Product life cycles will be shorter."[8] Another contributor commented, "Today, of course, a variety of new manufacturing technologies have destroyed the compelling simplicity of the job-shop–flow-shop dichotomy."[9] Writings in West German engineering journals echo these conclusions almost to the word.[10]

The connection drawn by engineers between flexibility and computers is supported by ethnographic studies of computer users—ranging from schoolchildren to sophisticated programmers (including "hackers," for whom long stints in front of the video-display terminal is the core of their life experience).[11] Whereas most machines have an independent structure to which the user must conform, the fascination of the computer—as documented in the ethnographic studies—is that the user can adapt it to his or her own purposes and habits of thought. The computer is thus a machine that meets Marx's definition of an artisan's tool: it is an instrument that responds to and extends the productive capacities of the user. It is therefore tempting to sum the observations of engineers and ethnographers to the conclusion that technology has ended the dominion of specialized machines over un- and semiskilled workers, and redirected progress down the path of craft production. The advent of the computer restores human control over the production process; machinery again is subordinated to the operator.

Markets and Flexibility. But the computer—although it has increased the flexibility of production—cannot alone explain the resurgence of craft principles. The implication of the ethnographic studies is that computers adapt to *any* environment. That the computer has been used to facilitate adjustments to shifting markets must therefore be as much a result of the character of the market environment as of the character of the technology. Had the mass markets of the 1950s and '60s endured in the 1970s, computer technology would have mirrored the rigidity of mass production. In fact, where production runs are fairly long (though not so long as to justify specialized machinery), programmable equipment is used just as automatic machinery was used in the past: a programmer (often a skilled craftsman with computer training) programs the first part; a semiskilled setup person changes tools and fixtures; and unskilled production workers load and unload the workpieces. Even when programmable equipment, such as the welding and painting robots in the automobile industry, is flexible in that it performs tasks previously requiring human dexterity, the elasticity of the machine has nothing to do with a new relationship either between workers and their instruments or between firms and their markets.

There is another weakness in the technological-determinist case for the resurgence of craft production that simultaneously strengthens the argument for the vitality of flexible specialization and connects this discussion to the earlier analysis of technological change. Not only are there many instances of computer-based technologies being put to rigid use in manufacturing; there are also many instances of the flexible use of technologies that do not depend on computers. The Jacquard loom, introduced commercially in the early nineteenth century, is a technology of this type (it operates, as we saw, by means of perforated cards, which, through springs and hammers, raise and lower the warp and hence determine the pattern of the weave). Other pre-computer flexible technologies were found in the high-fashion calico printing in Mulhouse, the specialty-steel production in Saint-Étienne, the fashionable use of artificial fibers in Lyon, and the new metalworking techniques in the Birmingham hardware trades. These all suggest that at earlier stages of technological development—under propitious market conditions—flexible technology had a vitality that defies expectations based on its relation to mass production.

In recent times, too, some of the most dramatic instances of craft production have grown out of technology that is unrelated to computers. Mini–steel mills, for example, depend on electric-arc processes, which were developed at the turn of the century by specialty producers making small batches of high-quality alloys.[12] In the 1930s, a British engineer published detailed plans for a flexible rolling mill that could achieve a higher level of capacity utilization by shifting quickly from product to product.[13] These alternative practices and visions fused in the postwar period to produce a combination of machines and organizational techniques that demonstrated competitiveness *before* the adaptation of computer technology.

There is, in sum, evidence both for the dynamism of craft production and for its independence from any particular stage of technological development. If the computer appears to be the cause of industrial flexibility, this is probably less because of its applications than because, malleable as it is, it has helped crystallize the vision of a flexible economy just as the costs of rigidity were becoming obvious. Computer technology is a kind of magic mirror, showing the economy not as it is but as some firms would like it to be—and thereby encouraging the pursuit of possibilities that otherwise would have gone unnoticed. No wonder, then, that an expert in operations management, a field that looks for connections between changes in technology and changes in industrial strategy, regarded the computer as providential. Wickham Skinner, of the Harvard Business School, writes:

We've seen shorter product life cycles, more productive proliferation, smaller order quantities. Now the new technologies, microprocessor-based, have the ability to "think," to react, to be flexible, to handle short runs, to handle product proliferation, to move an organization much more quickly. These techniques are exactly in time for and in tune with the new industrial competition.[14]

But as the rise of the corporation and macroregulation show, the life history of an industrial economy begins only once a technological paradigm is defined. The spread of flexible specialization will depend on the creation of institutions that resolve the micro- and macroeconomic problems of growth along the new technological trajectory.

MICROECONOMIC REGULATION

At first glance, a shift from mass production to flexible specialization seems to permit the kind of price-regulated economy envisaged in neoclassical economic theory. The failure of the price system as an allocative mechanism under mass production, as we saw in chapter 3, was a result of the lumpiness of investments—the increasing size of plants in relation to their markets—associated with the increasingly specialized use of equipment. Extension of the market and corresponding increases in the size and degree of specialization of efficient plants reduced the chances that price changes would lead to a rapid redeployment of resources. But in a system of flexible specialization, resources are general-purpose and hence easily redeployable. There is reason, therefore, to think that in such a system, shifts in demand would trigger price changes, and firms would simply use their existing complement of machines and labor to make the goods whose price was rising—a look at the market would redirect economic activity. But there is a crucial problem that complicates the question of microeconomic coordination in this system, and rules out the answer of the neoclassical textbooks. The problem is the maintenance of technological dynamism.

In the historical record presented in chapter 2, systems of flexible specialization run a high risk of stagnating technologically. Industrial districts producing clothing and textiles, for example, frequently limit themselves to continual but minute variations in the product—to the neglect of the improvements in design and production that define economic growth. Sometimes even such limited innovation disappears, and firms pin their fortunes to jealously guarded methods of producing a few types of, say, knives or buttons that appeal to a closed group of traditional customers.

In the worst case, even this strategy fails. Then, as the firms come under increasing pressure from mass producers or lower-wage flexible specialists, they cut production costs by sweating labor and using inferior materials. The employers take advantage of the work force any way they can, twisting whatever solidarity they have with their employees into a cover for exploitation. It is these breakdowns of innovative capacity that often make small firms a symbol of misery, not creativity.[15]

The problem of organizing continual innovation is not, of course, limited to flexible specialization. As the American steel and automobile industries have shown, technological progress can be self-blocking in mass production, as well. Once a firm has invested heavily in product-specific technology, each change in the product or process comes at the price of high retooling costs. Because the costs of innovation are easier to calculate than the potential benefits, it is easy to err on the side of caution and avoid change. Once caution has become habit, new products are designed to fit the existing setup—instead of the setup being refitted to suit the new product; and advances in the technology are limited to small refinements of existing procedures.[16] When product and production technology freeze in this way, the firm is likely to respond to competition from other mass producers by pressing down wages.

Sweating, to underscore the point, is the generic response of embattled firms—whether mass or small producers—that cannot innovate. It is not a strategy peculiar to endangered flexible specialists. The speedup is to mass production what the cut in piece rates is to customized production.

There is, however, an important difference between organizing innovation in mass production and in a system of flexible specialization. In mass production, we saw, the central problem is stabilizing and extending the market. Once this is done, the corporation as a self-contained unit has both the interest and the capacity to advance the division of labor through the simplification of tasks and the creation of special-purpose machines—thereby lowering production costs and setting the stage for further growth. In a system of flexible specialization, by contrast, the problem of organizing innovation just begins with the creation of a market. There are two reasons for this.

First, once a specialty firm has found its market, by identifying some special need or desire, there is always the temptation to remain there. Because its product appeals to only a limited number of customers, there is no presumption that cuts in production costs will substantially increase the market. Nor, in the absence of competition, is there reason to think that life in another market will be more lucrative.

The second reason why innovation is hard to organize in specialty firms is that flexible specialists face characteristic problems in coordinating innovative activity. The very fluidity of resources that makes the system flexible paradoxically also makes it necessary to create institutions that facilitate cooperation within and among firms without jeopardizing their future redeployment.

Microregulation in a system of flexible specialization is—as Proudhon foresaw—a question of finding compatible institutional answers to the problems of instigating and coordinating innovation. Competition of the wrong kind undermines the necessary coordination; misdirected coordination undermines competition. The prior discussion of historical and contemporary cases of craft production contained many examples of the practical reconciliation of these apparently antagonistic principles. Such reconciliation occurs in four settings: regional conglomerations of small, independent enterprises; federated groups of large, loosely allied enterprises; "solar" firms, holding smaller enterprises in steady orbits; and internally decentralized workshop factories. A review of the operation of each setting will provide the empirical clues to the principles of microregulatory institutions in flexible specialization. It will also distinguish these institutions from the analogous ones of mass production.

THE FOUR FACES OF FLEXIBLE SPECIALIZATION

1. Regional Conglomerations. Examples of regional conglomeration are the specialized industrial districts of northern and central Italy, the New York City garment district, and the construction industry in any number of U.S. cities. In the past, such examples include the European regional centers of Birmingham, Solingen, and Lyon, and the U.S. centers of Philadelphia, Pawtucket (Rhode Island), and the Connecticut Valley (of Vermont). Each of these industrial districts is, or was, composed of a core of more-or-less equal small enterprises bound in a complex web of competition and cooperation.

In this model, none of the enterprises is permanently dominant, and the arrangements among them are defined by a series of relatively short-term contracts, in which the roles of the parties are always shifting. Within these industrial districts there are also institutions that facilitate the recombination of the productive enterprises: trade associations; unions; guilds; and cooperatives for purchasing materials, marketing regional products, securing credit on favorable terms for members, and supplying semifinished products whose manufacture permits economies of scale.

But no single institution formally links the productive units as a group. The cohesion of the industry rests on a more fundamental sense of community, of which the various institutional forms of cooperation are more the result than the cause. In the New York City garment industry, we saw, the community has been based primarily on ethnic ties—first among Jews and Italians, more recently among Chinese and Hispanic groups. Both the employers' associations and the unions are active in their members' ethnic communities. Thus, Jews attend and contribute to fund drives for Italian orphanages, and Italians help out with the United Jewish Appeal; such activities reinforce the cohesion of the community in which the industry is rooted. Similarly, ethnically oriented family occasions—weddings, christenings, bar mitzvahs, funerals—provide further opportunities to assert the unity of the community and its identity with the industry. This effort for the greater community tempers competition within the community: manufacturers and union leaders are always present at the public rituals in the families of their competitors, as well as their colleagues. This carefully nurtured solidarity also makes possible—and is reinforced by—institutions that serve the whole industry: for example, the Liberal Party, the Fashion Institute of Technology (a public school that trains designers for the multitude of small firms), and the zoning regulations protecting the manufacturers' loft spaces from residential and commercial competition.

In the Third Italy of the small firms, shared politics and religion play the same role that ethnicity plays in New York City. In the communist areas, such as Emilia-Romagna and Tuscany, many of the workers and entrepreneurs are craftsmen who opposed first the Fascists and then the reassertion of employer dominance in the large shops. Many of the small factories that benefited from the wave of decentralization in the 1970s were, in fact, founded by left-wing militants who had been purged from the large factories in the 1950s and used their severance pay to start their own businesses. The role of the Left among the entrepreneurs has been reinforced, we noted earlier, by the determination of the Communist Party to bind the petite bourgeoisie into an alliance, making it inaccessible to fascism. Analogous themes in the Christian Democratic Party—reflecting the ambition of the Catholic church to put its parishioners beyond the reach of working-class organizations—encourage similar bonds between workers and managers in Christian-Democratic rural areas, such as the Venetian provinces.[17] The structures and operation of employee associations and unions in the Third Italy are thus similar to those in New York City, with the difference that the Italian municipal governments play a greater role in providing the industrial infrastructure.

To judge by these cases, it is doubtful whether regional conglomerations can survive without community ties, be they ethnic, political, or religious. Although manufacturers and contractors as a group have, we noted earlier, a common interest in stabilizing wages and working conditions, as individuals, each is tempted to cheat on the standard; and no producer can afford to adhere to a standard if his or her competitors do not. But in a regional conglomeration, a breach of the standard violates not only an economic contract, but also deeply held community mores. Moreover, the fear of punishment by exclusion from the community is probably critical to the success of the explicit constraints on competition.

2. *Federated Enterprises.* The second form of flexible specialization has been discussed in connection with the *système Motte,* the prewar Japanese *zaibatsu,* and the looser postwar federations of Japanese enterprises. Here again, the association must be defined both economically and socially. It is defined economically by interlocking personnel and financial agreements. The federated enterprises hold one another's stocks and have interlocking boards of directors. Frequently, the managers of a going enterprise in the federation are dispatched to serve in a new one. Sometimes the firms share financial and marketing facilities. But the group is not as integrated as the mass-production corporation, and member firms are not hierarchically arranged. On the other hand, their sense of common identity is much sharper than that of firms in regional conglomerations.

Socially, federations of this type depend on the family—understood as an organizing principle, rather than a biological entity. In the case of the *système Motte,* we saw, each of the enterprises was founded by one family member working with a skilled employee from outside the lineage; outsiders were in effect adopted by the family, through close association and a lifetime of demonstrated loyalty. The *zaibatsu* originally expanded out of family-run merchant houses, and workers were literally adopted into the bloodline. The modern Japanese federation does not attempt to establish legal family ties with its work force; but employees continue to think of their relation to the organization as familial.

3 and 4. "Solar" Firms and Workshop Factories. The third and fourth forms of flexible specialization are the firm with the solar-system model of orbiting suppliers and its close cousin, the workshop factory. In chapter 2 we referred to these patterns of organization as welfare capitalism and paternalism. Examples from the past are the specialty-steel plants in Saint-Étienne, the largest textile producers in Lyon, the calico-printing firms in Mulhouse, and J. S. Henckels's Solingen cutlery firm. Modern examples can be found in the American and West German economies; but these are more difficult to identify, because outwardly they resemble the major mass-production corporations. But unlike the mass producers, these firms do not produce long runs of standardized products; and their size results from the high capital requirements of their products—not economies of scale, as in mass production. Internally, the works are organized, like their nineteenth-century counterparts, as a collection of workshops.

Despite their large size, the modern "solar" and workshop firms frequently treat external suppliers as collaborators, not subordinates. Subcontractors retain considerable autonomy; and unlike the mass producer, the solar firm depends on subcontractors for advice in solving design and production problems, because it generally does not produce in-house what it subcontracts. An example is the Boeing Company, which does not produce either the engines that power its airplanes or much of the avionic equipment that holds them on course. Other examples are the farm-equipment and construction-machinery firms in the American Midwest, many of which do not make such critical parts as the link track needed for traversing rough terrain. Parts of General Electric also function according to these principles.

These firms are large and central enough to their respective industries to supply internally many of the services that in a regional conglomeration would be supplied by the community. But firms in this category often cooperate with community institutions—as seen in the complex of research, educational, and welfare institutions financed by the Mulhouse calico firms but supervised by the municipal council. In the United States, the large firms' provision of community services has been more limited, partly because welfare capitalism is here associated with the abuse of worker trust. But it is nonetheless common for such firms as General Electric and the aerospace companies to provide equipment to vocational high schools and community colleges; to lend their supervisory staff and skilled craftsmen as instructors; and to encourage their executives to sit on the advisory boards of these institutions. Computer firms have begun to donate expensive equipment to financially hard-pressed universities, and they even contribute funds for the creation of new faculty positions.

MICROREGULATION IN THE FOUR FORMS

Underneath the diversity of the four organizational forms of flexible specialization, it is possible to discern a single model of microeconomic regulation. These four organizational forms share basic characteristics that distinguish them from the worlds pictured in neoclassical price theory, on the one hand, and our earlier account of the allocative institutions created by the mass-production corporation, on the other. Listing these characteristics separately underscores the complementarity of competition and cooperation in flexible production; it also focuses subsequent analysis of the role of wages and prices in these systems.

Flexibility plus Specialization. The first, obvious characteristic of these different organizational forms is their combination of flexibility and specialization. Flexibility—as compared with the twentieth-century

American corporation—is their salient feature: the capacity continually to reshape the productive process through the rearrangement of its components. But they are also specialized, in that the set of possible arrangements is bounded and the aim of redeployment limited. One limit is the participants' shared sense of what kind of products "their" industry makes. IBM produces computers; Boeing, airplanes; Motte, textiles. There is an identifiable Milanese style in clothing, a Japanese feel in machine tools.

But the limits are also physical. Members of a Japanese federation may move away from their home district and product lines, shifting more and more of their business to firms they have engendered; yet they view provision of their line of products as a service to the community, and they gauge their performance against that of others burdened with the same troubles or blessed with the same opportunities— thus they cannot simply pull out of the industry. Similarly, an Italian firm can depart from a regional conglomeration only by long-term growth. A New York City garment firm may die out with a family, and an individual entrepreneur may drop back for a time into the ranks of the employees, but cultural and family ties make it unlikely that anyone who has begun working in the industry will leave it.

This dedication of individuals and firms to a specialized task and attachment to a well-defined industry is possible only on the condition that—except when the community as a whole is under severe external pressure—each reorganization of production puts all the available re-sources to use. No firm or individual has a right to any particular place within the community, but all have a claim to some place within it. IBM executives may move rapidly up and down the corporate hierarchy in the continual feudal jousting that is their pride and inexhaustible complaint; but they are never laid off. The Japanese firm has obligations to carry not only its own labor force but also that of its major subcontractors. It is no coincidence that the garment and construction unions even in the United States prefer work sharing to layoffs. Unemployment insurance, which is criticized by American conservatives for keeping workers within a particular industry, is used under flexible specialization to produce precisely this effect.[18] Saint-Étienne, it will be recalled, tolerated a rate of municipal taxation among the highest in nineteenth-century France in order to finance unemployment assistance to this end.

Limited Entry. A second characteristic of these organizations of flexible specialization is that they limit entry. This follows from the fact that the communities are bounded, and the boundaries identify those with claims to the provision of social welfare. Once social-welfare services are available, outsiders—even if they are qualified to work in the community's industry—cannot be permitted to lay claim to these services, or the system will become overburdened. Many (though not all) of the restrictions to entry are informal: getting a job depends on whom you know, and whom you know depends on who you are. Such limitations, in turn, reduce the incentive for outsiders to acquire skills that might benefit the whole community. Barriers to entry are thus an important factor (though certainly not the only one) in jeopardizing the reproduction of communal resources.

The Encouragement of Competition. A third characteristic of successful systems of flexible specialization is their encouragement—or at least tolerance—of competition that promotes innovation. Competitive pressure arises both internally and externally. Internal pressure results from competition among firms for a favored position in the commonly acknowledged hierarchy. This flows from the point just made: the recognition of common interests and mutual obligations does not guarantee that all members of the community are treated equally. Whereas everyone is guaranteed some place within the community, no one is guaranteed a particular place. In the construction and garment industries, a successful entrepreneur can always find a job in someone's shop; but he or she will not necessarily find a contract for his or her own company. A manufacturer of a component for the IBM personal computer knows that if the market grows too large, IBM will manufacture that component in-house; he or she will therefore have to shift attention to some other piece of equipment—unless it proves possible to outrun the giant competitor in the race for cost-cutting innovations.

External pressures come from competing communities of flexible specialization. In garments, Milan and Paris put pressure on New York; in high tech, Silicon Valley is a goad to Route 128 in Massachusetts; in computers, Apple (or AT&T) and the Japanese firms challenge IBM; in civil aviation, Airbus and McDonnell Douglas keep Boeing on its toes. The result in all cases is innovation.

Limits on Competition. A fourth characteristic of successful flexible-specialization complexes is that they prohibit the kind of competition that distracts from permanent innovation. Each of the different models of flexible specialization limits competition—particularly competition over wages and working conditions—whose effect is simply to drive down factor costs. In the U.S. garment and construction industries, these limits are imposed by unions, which aim to standardize wages and other terms of employment in each local market. Worker organization is also critical to standardizing competitive conditions in the American aerospace and shipbuilding industries. IBM, which prizes its nonunion tradition, blocks unwanted forms of competition through its internal personnel policies. And although the expansion of the small-business sector in the Third Italy was a reaction to union control in large enterprises, the ability of small businesses to compete through sweating was doubly limited: by organizations of employers and workers in the artisan sector, and by the state and municipalities, which made it difficult for small firms to resort permanently to illegal homework, tax evasion, child labor, and the like. Conversely, the examples of Sheffield and Birmingham discussed in chapter 2 show that when communities did not limit wage competition, they lost their dynamism and fell into a spiral of decline by responding to competition with sweating.

Another indication of the connection between limits to competition and technological dynamism is the link between shop-floor control and innovation in flexible systems. Some bargaining regimes encourage experimentation with process, and hence process innovation; others serve to limit experimentation to new products. The New York garment industry, for example, attempted to control wage competition through a detailed piecework system that assigned a fixed rate to each manufacturing operation. Collective bargaining focused on fixing these prices, which bound not only manufacturers but also their subcontractors. The result was to standardize labor costs and eliminate all incentive for process innovation, by allowing the labor force to capture the proceeds of technological advance through the piece-rate system. But once the centralized wage-determination system was relaxed, in the late 1970s, the pace of technological change in the New York garment industry quickened.

An approach to limiting competition without discouraging innovation is the bonus system. This incentive system is typical in Japan and common in such U.S. enterprises as IBM. In both cases, as we have noted, employment is guaranteed and wages stabilized, so as to limit the enterprises' capacity to respond to competition with wage reductions. But large Japanese firms pay their employees substantial bonuses if the firm does well; and IBM gives prizes and dramatic promotions for employees' innovative contributions.

Corporate limits on labor exploitation are important not only in making competition a spur to innovation, but also in maintaining the organizational cohesion required for flexibility. Without restrictions on placing the costs of readjustment on the weakest groups (the lowest-level workers), the sense of community among workers and employers would be threatened; the vital collaboration across different levels of the official hierarchy would then be improbable. Hence, employment-security arrangements that build trust can be as important as wage systems in fostering innovation. But, as in the case of wages, some forms of employment security are more likely to encourage process innovation than others. Job guarantees and universal work sharing, combined with broad job classifications, favor the introduction of new techniques; by contrast, job guarantees combined with narrow job classifications increase the risk of stagnation: recall the narrowly organized Sheffield cutlers, who lost out to the broadly organized workers of Solingen, and the difficulties of U.S. construction workers in the face of technological change.

PRICES AND IDENTITY

The foregoing characteristics describing the microregulation of flexible specialization point to the limited role of price as an allocative mechanism within innovative craft production. Because innovation is fostered by removing wages and labor conditions from competition, and by establishing an ethos of interdependence among producers in the same market, flexible specialization succeeds only by moderating price fluctuations. In this regard, it is surprisingly like mass production. But the rationale for sticky prices and the nature of the resulting rigidities differ sharply in the two systems of production.

In mass production, price rigidities result from a firm's efforts to stabilize its economic environment. These efforts extend beyond wage stabilizations to all other input markets, often increasing the vertical integration of production. In flexible specialization, price rigidities result from a productive community's efforts to secure labor's place in the community, as well as the need to stabilize relations among federated firms. These workers and managers, as groups, and these firms, as productive units, must deal with one another over long periods, and depend on their partners' willingness to help solve unforeseeable problems; therefore, the prices of the goods and services exchanged reflect not momentary market circumstances but a mutually agreed-upon rate of fair return. This is not to say, however, that all input costs are rigid or that wages are completely inflexible. Craft production is compatible, as we have seen, with incentive systems that reward individual initiative, but do not undermine the sense of community indispensible to the constant redefinition of the product and production.

Nevertheless, prices in both mass production and flexible specialization are too rigid to direct the deployment of resources—most crucially, those required for the perpetuation of the system as a whole. In both cases, other allocative mechanisms are required. In mass production, it is the firm that organizes research, recruits labor, and guarantees the flow of supplies and credit. In flexible specialization, it is community institutions—the community itself—that are responsible for these tasks.

An example of the differences in the two systems is their respective training of labor. The extensive division of labor in mass production—reflected in both the break between the conception and execution of tasks, and the highly specialized character of almost all production jobs—makes it possible to rely on two separate institutions for training employees: the formal education system and the firm itself.[19] The formal education system is well adapted to providing potential employees with an abstract understanding of products and production; on the job, their lack of practical experience results in mistakes that are not costly when distributed over the long mass-production runs. The firm, for its part, is willing to pay for the training of the fraction of the work force that needs skills beyond those acquired by progressing up the job hierarchy. Because training required under these circumstances is so specialized, the firm need not fear that workers will take knowledge acquired at the firm's expense and apply it elsewhere. Put the other way around, there is small danger of the firm's failing to capture the return on its investment in plant-specific knowledge.

Flexible specialization, by contrast, cannot rely on these training mechanisms. Production runs are too short to spend time debugging products designed by inexperienced technicians. Designers must be so broadly qualified that they can envision product and production together; book learning alone does not teach this ability. Production workers must be so broadly skilled that they can shift rapidly from one job to another; even more important, they must be able to collaborate with designers to solve the problems that inevitably arise in execution. And the more broadly skilled the work force, the greater the danger that firms will economize on training costs—either in the hope that they can hire individuals who learned their craft at another firm's expense, or out of fear that their competitors will do just that to them.

Here, too, it is tempting to think that a return to competitive markets would resolve the allocative predicaments of flexible specialization. It is plausible to expect, after all, that as the firm's incentive to invest in training declines, the incentive for institutions and individuals outside the firm to make such an investment correspondingly increases. In theory, as skills become more generally useful, more and more employers will compete to hire the well-rounded workers. This competition will drive up the latter's wages, creating an incentive for other, less skilled workers to pay for more training for themselves.

The obstacles to this solution have to do with the bounded, communitarian character of flexible specialization. Even when craft-production skills can be employed in a variety of ways, they are fully productive only when integrated into a community of closely collaborating workers and enterprises. Entry into a community specialized in this sense depends on a socialization process so daunting that outsiders might be reluctant to pay for training, even if they could calculate the potential return on their investment. And for all the reasons discussed above, the community may well be sufficiently closed that outsiders are too ignorant of it even to consider working there in the first place.

Organizations based on flexible specialization solve this problem by linking the acquisition of skill to acquisition of membership in the community of the skilled. Craft workers are bred, not born; and the formation of their identity as persons is bound up with their admittance into a group of producers, on the one hand, and their mastery of productive knowledge, on the other. Because everyone is encouraged to seek the pride of place, this is an honor system with a vengeance. Wages are more the counters in the game of success than the inducements to action.

In northern Italy and analogous sectors of U.S. industry, the family has been used to solve the joint problem of skill transmission and socialization. The first generation of entrepreneurs typically are skilled workers with scanty formal education. They start their businesses relatively late in life, using savings or, in Italy especially, severance pay as a grubstake. These first-generation businesses are also the least likely to devise innovative products and processes, and the most likely to operate as dependent subcontractors. The second generation of entrepreneurs combine formal technical education with the experience of working after school and summers in the family firm; these second-generation businesses are more likely to form the innovative core of the regional industry.

Countries such as Japan and West Germany have institutional methods for providing the combination of education and experience that in Italy and the United States is provided by the family firm. Nevertheless, these systems resemble the family-based ones in that they, too, entwine the acquisition of knowledge with the initiation into a productive community.[20] In all cases, becoming skilled is part of a larger process of taking on a certain identity.

In Japan, the large companies hire highly educated managerial trainees and give them extensive on-the-job training in production. This procedure may not afford the fresh graduates enough shop-floor experience to anticipate practical problems in design and innovation. But since the Japanese treat the firm like a family and expect cooperation across hierarchical lines, the graduates communicate readily with skilled workers, who help with the practical problems. The German system is the opposite. It uses a highly specialized apprenticeship system to supply a skilled blue-collar work force with enough conceptual understanding of their work either to progress via formal education into managerial positions, or to communicate easily with managers who come directly from the university. Here, it is pride in the craft as a collectivity that underlies collaboration among skilled workers and their self-confidence in collaborating with others. Thus, both in the informal family training system of Italy and the United States and in the formal enterprise-based training system of Japan and Germany, versatile labor is trained through participation in the production process. In this way, incentives signaled by the market are of secondary importance.

The problem of microregulation in flexible specialization consists, in sum, of a double dilemma with a single solution. The first part of the dilemma is the reconciliation of competition and cooperation. The second is the regeneration of resources required by the collectivity but not produced by the individual units of which it is composed. The common solution is the fusion of productive activity, in the narrow sense, with the larger life of the community. The same experiences that teach people who they are teach them which skills to acquire; how to collaborate; and what they may not do in their competition for honor in the community.

Put another way, flexible specialization works by violating one of the assumptions of classical political economy: that the economy is separate from society. Markets and hierarchies—the two categories that dominate contemporary theory and practical reflection on the organization of industry—both presuppose the firm to be an independent entity. In market models, the firm is linked by exchange relations to other units; in hierarchy models, the firm is so autonomous as almost to constitute an industry in itself. By contrast, in flexible specialization it is hard to tell where society (in the form of family and school ties or community celebrations of ethnic and political identity) ends, and where economic organization begins. Among the ironies of the resurgence of craft production is that its deployment of modern technology depends on its reinvigoration of affiliations that are associated with the preindustrial past.

THE MACROECONOMICS OF FLEXIBLE SPECIALIZATION

Whereas the microeconomic organization of flexible specialization seems complex and difficult to achieve, macroeconomic stabilization is much easier to treat with familiar categories. A shift away from mass production would restore the neoclassical equilibrating mechanisms that (to the extent they have functioned at all) were probably most prominent in the early-nineteenth-century American economy.

Thus, if resources become more flexible, investment decisions will be less dependent on forecasts regarding the demand for any single good, and the risks of investment will be generally reduced. If economies of scale become less important, units of production will become smaller, and the numbers of young, middle-aged, and old plants will be approximately equal. A roughly constant portion of the capital stock will therefore normally be retired every year, and minor imbalances between supply and demand will be corrected by attrition and replacement, as well as by the migration of resources among alternative uses.

Such changes would make investment decisions more sensitive to the cost of funds—the interest rate—and less sensitive to variations in aggregate demand. The economy would consequently be more responsive to truly internal stabilizing mechanisms and less dependent on the panoply of macroregulatory institutions characteristic of the postwar mass-production regimes. As economic activity declined under these conditions, the demand for investment capital would sink, pulling down the interest rate and whetting the appetite of entrepreneurs who were hesitant to go forward when the costs of borrowing were higher. Because relative wage rates, as well as returns to other cooperating producers, must be taken out of competition in order to preserve the community in which flexible production is embedded, the economic system would not be as stable as the world pictured in models of a competitive economy. It would also require, for purposes of microregulatory solidarity, social-welfare institutions related to those justified in the postwar period by a Keynesian logic. But it would be possible to maintain full employment largely through monetary policy, without resorting to wage-determination systems linking purchasing power to the rate of increase of productive capacity, the automatic stabilizing features of the welfare state, and discretionary fiscal policy. Since wages and social-welfare payments need no longer be tied to purchasing power or tightly integrated across different sectors—as they were in the U.S. system of macroeconomic regulation after World War II—there would be much less danger of shocks to the economy touching off inflationary surges, as in the 1970s.

Flexible specialization also imposes fewer constraints than mass production on the scope and character of the international economic system. It could operate effectively in a large, open world economy; but it does not need the markets that such an economy would provide. The more technological development renders economies of scale irrelevant and raw materials substitutable, the more likely each nation would produce a wide range of products on its own. Similarly, flexible specialization is better able to accommodate fluctuations in exchange rates and commodity prices than is a regime of mass production. Fluctuations might slow growth by distracting attention from improvements in the process and product; but they would not paralyze investment, as they do in mass production by disrupting the calculus of investment decisions.

Choosing

Which of these possible worlds should we try to realize? This is not merely a question of economic reorganization. It invites debate as well about the just distribution of power in industrial society—a debate complicated by the fact that it is not clear which world would benefit which groups most.

As seen in the emergence of American shop-floor control, the creation of an economic system under particular historical circumstances freezes some distribution of political power for a long period; and that distribution is not determined by the economic institutions alone. Labor had much more power than did capital in the postwar United States, as compared with, for example, postwar France—although the economic institutions of the two countries had many similar properties. American labor's postwar power was also greater than it had been before 1930, despite many similarities of economic organization in the two periods.

The balance of power between labor and capital under either flexible specialization or multinational Keynesianism will thus have to be fought out country by country. It seems likely, for instance, that the spread of flexible specialization in the United States would weaken the labor movement—unless some widely acceptable flexible, unionized system of shop-floor control suddenly emerges from one of the innumerable industrial-relations experiments now under way in American plants. Conversely, a move toward multinational Keynesianism would probably revalidate much of the institutional structure created under the New Deal, thus augmenting the power of American unions. If you are concerned, as we are, about what would happen to American society without the presence of a strong organized force to protect the vulnerable, then this calculation might lead to preference for multinational Keynesianism over flexible specialization.

Alternatively, flexible specialization opens up long-term prospects for improvement in the condition of working life—regardless of this system's effect on the balance of power between currently existing organizations of capital and labor. Mass production is least attractive on the shop floor. Even when shop-floor control is based on broad job classifications and substantive dispute resolution, mass production still invites an adversarial, hierarchical relation between workers and managers, and among the different units of an organization. Mass production's extreme division of labor routinizes and thereby trivializes work to a degree that often degrades the people who perform it. By contrast, flexible specialization is predicated on collaboration. And the frequent changes in the production process put a premium on craft skills. Thus the production worker's intellectual participation in the work process is enhanced—and his or her role revitalized. Moreover, craft production depends on solidarity and communitarianism. Given these conditions of working life in craft production, there is a case for preferring it to mass production, regardless of the place accorded to unions within craft production.

But choosing between the two systems is not so simple as picking the one most propitious to the side you favor in the contest between labor and capital. The two systems can both be instantiated in more or less comprehensive forms, so their relative attraction, to us at least, depends on whom they include and exclude.

The macroeconomic logic of multinational Keynesianism, for example, gives all participants in the system a collective interest in prosperity. The expansion of demand means the expansion of industry. The crucial question is how such a regime is established: whether by linking a few efficient manufacturing centers in the metropoles with the most prosperous third-world markets (to the exclusion of badly situated workers in the advanced countries, and the impoverished nations in the developing world), or by redistributing purchasing power and skills so that the circle of privilege becomes so large that it is difficult to speak of privilege at all.

Similarly, it is possible to imagine two kinds of regimes of flexible specialization. In a restricted regime, isolated communities of producers would seek their fortune in disregard of the fate of their rivals—be they citizens of the same country, coinhabitants of the advanced world, or inhabitants of the third world, sunk—so it would seem—in their primitive needs. Such a regime could resemble the old Bourbon kingdom of Naples, where an island of craftsmen, producing luxury goods for the court, was surrounded by a subproletarian sea of misery.

In the other kind of flexible-specialization regime, the local community structures would be coordinated by national social-welfare regulation, and the provision (or at least supervision) of research facilities and training would be partly a public responsibility. The Austrian trade-union movement, for example, has made this variant of flexible specialization a key part of its plan for national economic reorganization.[21] In such a regime, it might also be possible to modernize the burgeoning craft sector of third-world countries along the lines of flexible specialization—rather than urging these countries to imitate the mass-production history of the advanced countries.[22] This alternative regime of flexible specialization would look more like the artisans' republic envisioned by Rousseau and Proudhon than the court paradise of Bourbon Naples.

This chapter began with a discussion of the fateful choices confronting the industrialized and industrializing worlds. It ends with the hopeful suggestion that we may not have to choose at all: that the two proposed systems might, under some conditions, prove not contradictory but compatible. Not that they could be combined through simple addition: if flexible specialization and mass production operated side by side within each industry, the flexible producers would chip away at the markets for standard goods, thereby undermining the capacity of the mass producers to obtain the necessary economies of scale and the rates of expansion required for progress along their technological trajectory. To survive, the mass producers would have to control the expansion of the flexible specialists.

But it is conceivable that flexible specialization and mass production could be combined in a unified *international* economy. In this system, the old mass-production industries might migrate to the underdeveloped world, leaving behind in the industrialized world the high-tech industries and the traditional dispersed conglomerations in machine tools, garments, footwear, textiles, and the like—all revitalized through the fusion of traditional skills and high technology. Such a system would have to be created in much the same way as a multinational Keynesian order: and it would require many Keynesian institutional features to maintain economic prosperity and ensure macroeconomic stability.

To the underdeveloped world, this hybrid system would provide industrialization. To the developed world, it would provide a chance to moderate the decline of mass production and its de-facto emigration from its homelands. Such a system would not last forever—any more than the corporate economy or the world of domestic macroregulation has proved immortal. But a hybrid of mass and flexible production would for a time create a universal interest in two basic goals: worldwide prosperity and a transnational welfare state.

But despite the appeal of this hypothesized system, in the United States it does not hold much promise for a better future. For here, the decline of mass-production industries is proceeding more rapidly than the spread of flexible specialization. It is to the origins and resolution of this dilemma that we turn next.

CHAPTER

11

The United States and Flexible Specialization

THERE IS no hidden dynamic of historical evolution. No law of motion of capitalist development makes the spread of flexible specialization the inevitable outcome of the crisis of the past decade. The last chapter showed that it is easy both to imagine more comprehensive institutions that could relaunch growth on the established model, and to discern (even in the confusion of public purposes) the political means for emplacing them. But whether such a solution in fact emerges depends on a thousand imponderables of international politics. If it does, it will revalidate many American institutions and predispositions; the United States could then possibly resume its preeminence in the world economic order.

Such an international solution, however, seems unlikely to emerge soon, if it emerges at all. Meanwhile, the drift and disorganization in international economic policy will continue to drive companies toward a strategy of permanent innovation. National economies that encourage the shift to flexible specialization will have an easier time—and an increasingly commanding place—in the world economy that emerges from the companies' strategic choices. Eventually, a few of these economies could, if they choose, substantially reduce their dependence on world trade altogether.

Adjustment to a world of flexible specialization is thus the probable challenge for the U.S. economy. We therefore focus on it in this last chapter. As the pioneer of mass production, the American economy seems confounded by current developments: it is moved by the force of events and the example of others' success to experiment with flexible specialization—yet because of its history, it is apparently unable to grasp the logic connecting the pieces of the alternative strategy. We will see that if historical success has made the United States' future hostage to its past, then the buried treasure of forgone possibilities is the ransom to set it free.

Openings and Obstacles for Flexible Specialization in the United States

To continue the discussion in chapter 9, flexible specialization might be emerging in the United States in two ways. First, mass-production corporations are flattening their hierarchies and giving lower-level supervisors more authority, in order to speed adjustment to shifting markets and to lower the cost of producing small lots. Second, nuclei of small firms are forming, recalling the nineteenth-century industrial districts of flexible workshops: some of these modern industrial districts exist in traditional industries, ranging from metalworking to women's garments; others are exploiting technologies so new that they have given rise to only a handful of salable products. These two broad developments, inside and outside the large corporation, might eventually crystallize a flexible-specialization economy by realigning the behavior of the widening circles of innovators' clients and suppliers. But thus far, neither the reform of the large corporation nor the reemergence of the industrial district has resulted in institutions and practices that assure the survival of flexible forms of production where they now exist—to say nothing of their propagation throughout the economy.

1. THE REFORM OF THE CORPORATION

The paradox of the American movement toward flexible specialization is this: The same competitive pressures that drive firms to flexible organization could also block the communitarian ethos that—the last chapter argued—craft production requires, in order to survive market shocks. Undisciplined by community institutions that define fair ways for firms to compete, all-out competition can destroy the firms' capacity to respond to volatile markets by rapidly developing new products. In countries where collaboration is the natural response to adversity (as determined by systems of shop-floor control, forms of corporate organization, and the larger balance of political power), an economy that has started down the path of flexible specialization will probably accelerate its advance as competition grows. But in the United States, where collaboration is not a natural response, firms that have started toward flexible specialization may well, under competitive pressure, turn back.

At first glance, there is not much danger of such a turnabout in the decentralization of the mass-production corporations. For the corporation itself defines a kind of community, and it has vast experience in financing collaborative internal activities. But the current reorganization within mass producers is confusing the relationship between corporate headquarters and the productive units that it coordinates. There is a chance that efforts to break with mass-production patterns of control will produce chaos, rather than a system of coordination for flexible specialization.

This danger that corporate reforms could end in chaos is increased by the potentially contradictory nature of the reforms. On the one hand, the corporation is trying to reconstitute itself as a congeries of autonomous units: it is giving its divisions greater autonomy; establishing competing units to race one another to a common goal; and taking financial stakes in (though not acquiring) outside firms whose products both complement and compete with those of the corporation. On the other hand, the corporation is reconcentrating operations: it is abandoning divisions that are unrelated to the corporation's main line of work, and it is establishing closer and more collaborative relations with suppliers. This second effort can mean, as the discussion of the *kanban* system suggested, establishing long-term contractual relationships with a small group of select subcontractors—rather than inviting bids from a large number of subcontractors; in the limiting case, the corporation buys a stake in a supplier with which it has previously had only arm's-length dealings.

If you have in mind the *zaibatsu,* the *système Motte,* or the Italian industrial districts, both kinds of corporate reform express a single theme: the need for collaboration in which all the parties share a goal—so that they all profit from complementary innovations—but they are not so tightly integrated as to lose the competitive spirit to innovate. From this perspective, it is clear that inciting ferocious competition among subcontractors is doubly disastrous: it either discourages them from entering bids or forces them to bid so low that they must cut quality, to reduce production costs and to increase (at the expense of their client's reputation) sales of replacements.[1] It is also obvious that innovation can be throttled by the same tight integration that allows the use of standard parts and procedures in a variety of products, for economies of scale. For example, because the General Motors J Cars were designed by the same engineers who had designed the established cars, what was meant to be a radically new car was in fact a product of modified parts. This (as Sloan realized in the 1920s when he assigned construction of the Pontiac to Chrysler engineers) was the cheapest way to design each part, but clearly no way to design a radically new vehicle. The result was a variant on old themes, rather than the breakthrough GM proclaimed it.[2] It took a design disaster to remind Sloan's heirs of the secret of his success, and to open their eyes to the possibility that his times and theirs might truly be different.

But if these various corporate reforms are not conceived like the *zaibatsu, système Motte,* or Italian industrial districts—as a comprehensive shift to flexible specialization—they will not necessarily be executed in a way that contributes to a new synthesis. On the contrary, they will probably be executed confusedly, with a bureaucratic clumsiness that jeopardizes their success. A recent survey of automobile-industry managers on the future of their industry illustrates the disjointed approach to reform: parts suppliers (with whom purchasing agents were still haggling down prices) saw the move to a *kanban* system as an exploitative attempt to shift inventory costs to them; major producers (giving voice to their hopes) saw it as an important step towards a cooperative industrial structure.[3]

Under these conditions, the reform efforts may undercut rather than reinforce one another. Without a unifying vision of craft production, how long will it be before corporate divisions—struggling against internal and external rivals—pare expenditures for training and long-range development programs? Indeed, to what extent have the recent productivity gains of the corporate sector been achieved in just this way?[4] And if the corporation—having loosened its internal controls and shifted responsibility to its external collaborators—no longer provides such services, who will?

It is hard to know whether American corporate leaders have thought these problems through to a solution: managers in a crisis play their cards even closer to the vest than usual. But the hunger for books on managerial reform described in chapter 9 suggests that there is no generally accepted solution to the problems of U.S. industry. That literature, we saw, focuses more on condemnation of past practices than on recommendation of alternatives. Moreover, the recommendations of managers that are documented in the literature point to detours and dead ends. And these conflicting recommendations both reflect and contribute to the confusion of strategic action in the corporations.

Much of the new literature, for example, accuses the corporations of shortsighted neglect of long-term goals. Put more sympathetically, it portrays them as victims of unthinking stockholders who demand high profits every financial quarter, at the sacrifice of long-range development. But as we saw in chapter 3, the corporation was built largely to make planning possible; and presumably American mass producers, like foreign mass producers, still have the capacity to plan. After all, such West German corporations as AEG and Bauknecht—both under the control of presumably farsighted bankers rather than dividend-crazed Wall Street money managers—have fallen victim to many of the same problems as their American counterparts. The real difficulty has not been addressed in the literature, although it has been in some programs of reform. It is not a failure to plan; rather, it is the assumption that planning can always be based on the same conditions of competition.

Meanwhile, the new literature also reveals and encourages confusion about the strategy of investing in—rather than merging with—outside collaborators. One reason for recommending investment over merging is not to endanger the smaller firms' creativity by subjecting it to the accounting procedures and personnel practices of the larger firms. Another is not to saddle the smaller firms with the overhead charges and high labor costs of the larger ones. But how can corporate divisions be asked to bear all these charges when they must compete with outsiders that do not? How long will it be before those who feel stifled by the large firms' practices jump ship to the new acquisitions? And who—given decentralization and the need to reduce costs—will advocate expensive corporatewide training programs and uniform employee benefits, to reduce internal migration by employees?

The reform of labor relations, as chapter 9 suggested, is no more coherent. It is seen by many managers (particularly at lower levels), observers, union leaders, and workers as part of an effort to lower wage costs and break the power of unions. Others see it as a chance to shift to a collaborative system of shop-floor control; in this system, the union would play a role similar to the one it plays in Japan and West Germany and might have played in the United States, had a progressive variant of welfare capitalism emerged from the 1930s Depression.

Confusion in each of these areas of reform, finally, compounds the dilemmas that arise in adjacent ones. The inability to decide whether investment in outside collaborators is a way of increasing flexibility or preventing the spread of costly personnel practices makes it harder to decide whether the reform of industrial relations is primarily a way of increasing the flexibility of labor or instead, a way of reducing wages. The absence of coherent long-term planning makes it impossible to establish a policy on the allocation of overhead and training costs—a policy that might help stabilize the relations between corporate head-quarters, corporate divisions, outside collaborators, and the work forces both within and outside the corporation. Plainly, the reform of the corporation might serve as the point of crystallization of an economy of flexible specialization; but then again, it might not.

2. THE REEMERGENCE OF THE INDUSTRIAL DISTRICT

The second potential route to flexible specialization in the United States passes through the nuclei of small firms that form industrial districts: the traditional centers of the garment, textile, shoe, and metalworking industries, on the one hand, and the new high-technology startups, on the other. The traditional industrial districts contributed to and were strengthened by community institutions that are now breaking down, partly owing to their disruption by mass-production industry. The nuclei of high-tech industry grew up in communities whose integrity is being undermined by the industry's very expansion. As with the large corporation, there is no guarantee that the pressures of competition will lead the industrial districts to institutionalize innovation as their survival strategy. Here, too, it is as though a master builder had ordered all the structural elements for erecting flexible specialization, and then misplaced the blueprint diagramming the connection between the parts.

The High-Technology Industrial Districts. The most prominent industrial districts in high-tech industry are located—as we saw—around Boston and Palo Alto, California. Firms in both of these areas grew out of the local university communities. The founding entrepreneurs came from the faculty and research staffs of Harvard, M.I.T., and Stanford. They drew on technological breakthroughs achieved (often under military sponsorship) in university laboratories; and their initial products were sometimes also developed there. In addition, the universities have played a continuing role in the technical development of the industry, as a source of both professional employees and innovation through research.[5]

More important, however, the universities have served as the organizing center of intellectual communities for the employees in this industry. Here engineers and scientists employed in separate, often competing enterprises can share ideas, seek advice, and come to respect one another for the creativity and elegance of their innovations. Because they went to school together and conceive of their business activities as an extension of their university work, the high-tech professionals have not only a common language, which accelerates the diffusion of ideas, but also a common set of standards—perhaps even an aesthetic—regarding the "right" way to make money applying technology in the market. Thus, the university campus is like the corner café where Italian artisans solve one another's problems and share—or steal—one another's ideas: a place where Proudhon might have taken Marx to show him where cooperation and competition meet.[6]

The enormous success of the silicon-chip, computer, and software firms in these high-technology industrial districts has extended their boundaries to encompass new geographical areas and social classes. As they have expanded their production facilities and labor force, the new industries have turned to local and state government for lower-level vocational training and other employment services; for financial and tax aid; and occasionally for public transportation, communication networks, and other physical facilities.

The high-tech enterprises around Boston have converted abandoned factories—especially old textile mills—to house the new manufacturing operations. The Massachusetts Employment Service inaugurated a program to assist small and medium-sized high-tech firms in recruiting the labor they need. The state government has even provided venture capital for new high-tech firms with risky futures. All of these efforts have been encouraged and partly coordinated by a consortium of some 150 firms called the Massachusetts High Technology Council. The Council portrays high-tech industry as the mainspring of prosperity— indeed, the only force capable of reversing the region's economic decline and physical deterioration following the departure of traditional industries after World War II. This group has had some success in getting the region to identify its future with the future of high-technology and to bend local institutions to the industry's requirements.[7]

But despite these developments, Massachusetts industry refuses to commit itself to a long-term alliance with the larger community—even as its leaders solicit it. Although these firms are rooted in a particular geographic area and their success depends—to an extent that industry leaders themselves probably cannot assess—on its location, they are constantly threatening to leave if their various demands are not met. Thus, the promise of a mutually beneficial community—a true industrial district—is undercut by the possibility of selfish desertion. This aspect of the high-tech firms' relation to the economy comes to light in their dealings with the state and local governments, on which they depend for services, and in their treatment of their blue-collar workers.

The high-tech industrialists have, for example, pressed hard for reductions in state taxes and burdens imposed by other programs and regulations originally sponsored by the labor movement. And they have heavy-handedly suggested that if their demands are not met, they will move their firms to states with a more favorable business climate—a threat that borders on industrial blackmail.[8]

This form of bargaining makes it impossible to say what will happen when, as is inevitable, the industry encounters some setback in the market. Will it look to the larger community for help, only to be spurned because of its past bullying? Or will it pull up stakes and move, thereby destroying the social ligaments that support its flexibility?

The same kinds of questions apply to the relation between the industry and its labor force, particularly its blue-collar workers. The new firms are largely unorganized; in the absence of unions, the firms unilaterally establish working conditions and wages. The industry's success and the competition for highly qualified labor have made it necessary for firms to be openhanded in order to get and keep workers. But their generosity is not institutionally guaranteed. Should times turn bad, the firms might well shift the burden of adjustment to the production workers, the most vulnerable and easily replaced part of the labor force; in this way, the cooperative industrial relations that now prevail in the shop would be destroyed overnight. Under such conditions, disputes are likely to be particularly acrimonious, because the larger community will feel that its original contribution to the growth of the firms has been ignored.

If events take this turn, the industry might suddenly face the kind of reaction that produced industrial unionism when the mass-production corporations abandoned their commitment to welfare capitalism during the Depression. But because in flexible specialization the cooperation of the labor force is so critical, and because the industry depends on the community for its interstitial structure, such a reaction would be even more disruptive than it was to mass production. Moreover, flexible specialists continually face competitive pressures that mass producers encounter only in deep downturns, so the chances are increased that such a crisis of confidence in the high-tech firms will occur sooner rather than later.[9]

There is another reason to think that the community structures of high-technology in Massachusetts—and California—will soon be tested. It is that a number of communities in other states are trying to imitate the success of these two areas. These communities are creating university-based institutions to serve as the intellectual centers of high-tech industrial districts; these institutions are provided with high-level personnel and the kind of physical plant, venture capital, and employment and training services that were provided by governments to the original high-tech centers.[10] It is too early to tell whether the newer areas will prosper. And if they grow, will it be by developing new firms or by attracting established firms from the older high-tech areas? Many of the new areas—particularly those in the South and Southwest—have historically grown by luring "runaway" shops away from mature industrial regions, so they are tempted to revert to a familiar strategy. And the established high-tech firms—confronted with skyrocketing housing costs, clogged highways, and no space for expansion—are tempted by the lure. They perhaps even see migration as a natural stage of industrial growth.[11]

If the right kind of bait is in fact offered, the resulting dispersion of production will damage the communitarian supports of the firms in two ways. First, firms that relocate will be, at least for a time, resident in but not part of a new and largely alien community. Second, when firms expand to new locations but maintain their home bases, the existence of distant subsidiaries will weaken management's attachment to the home base—and its commitment to it and its work force in times of economic adversity. The failure to cooperate in the past will jeopardize the possibility of cooperation in the future; and once more, an incipient productive community will be threatened by the failure to appreciate the role of community in an emergent form of production.

The Traditional Industrial Districts. To see what the high-tech industrial districts might become if their communitarian supports crumble, one need only look at the decaying industrial districts in the traditional industries. But the success of the American steel mini-mills and the halting revival, discussed in chapter 9, of traditional metalworking districts in New England suggest that there are also countertendencies at work in the United States. Certainly the rapid spread of computer technologies to traditional industrial districts in Japan, Italy, West Germany, and Austria is evidence that under the right conditions, the networks of small shops in the industrial heartlands of the United States could become nuclei of flexible specialization.

But there is another side to the story. Many of the shops around Detroit, for example, recall the end of the last century, rather than anticipating the end of this one. Instead of devising new products, they scurry to remake those old ones that are not worth the attention of better-equipped manufacturers; instead of investing in new machines, they specialize in rescuing old ones from the scrap heap. To repeat what is now a refrain: the only thing that is sure is that the transformation to flexible specialization will not occur automatically.

The deterioration of the industrial districts that survived into the 1970s has two causes. One is related to the shifting strategies of the mass producers. The other concerns disruptions of the communities on which the districts depended.

The first cause is illustrated by the experience of the Detroit metalworking industry. The deterioration of that industry began in the late 1950s, when the large automobile producers started taking direct control of the manufacture of tools and dies, by establishing or purchasing "captive shops." The automobile producers initially conceived of this integration of production as a means of guaranteeing their sources of supply during periods of peak demand, and of protecting the secrecy of styling changes in automobile skins. But the more they expanded their own facilities, the more they used the threat of producing tools and dies internally as a club to beat down the prices demanded by the independent shops; and as lower profit margins forced more independent shops out of business, the large firms hedged still further against future shortages by expanding the captive shops—setting the stage for another round of threats, bankruptcies, and concentrations of control. By the mid-1970s, the independent shops that attempted to meet the pressure on costs through modernization and numerical control got (unlike their counterparts in Japan) no help from their customers, and went out of business.[12]

The American automobile industry's shift to the *kanban* system in the early 1980s made things worse. As the large firms noticed the defects of the world-car strategy and the advantages of the *kanban* system, they moved to reduce the circle of their outside suppliers. This meant casting off many subcontractors that had been dependent on the mass producers for direction; and this rewiring of commercial circuits disrupted the regional economic machinery. Banks that aggregated funds from subcontractors, for example, were suddenly reluctant to provide working capital that might have served to open new markets. Long-standing methods of blue-collar training were also jeopardized. In the Detroit area (as in similar regions), it was common for young workers to start out in a large assembly operation; move to a shop that made odd parts or specialized machines, in order to learn a craft; and then either move into the maintenance-and-repair department of the larger company or start a small specialty shop of their own. Once the subcontractor relationship is broken, however, the subcontractor loses the contacts that permit this movement, and the accumulation of skills and the exchange of knowledge—on which both partners depend—is arrested.[13]

The second cause of the deterioration of traditional industrial districts has come from the difficulty of transmitting skills and family businesses from generation to generation.[14] Many of the industrial districts in the United States grew out of and sustained the identity of a single ethnic group. The ethnic group earned its living in a given industry, and the prosperity of the industry allowed the group to build institutions that reinforced its integrity. Many of these communities sedimented out of the late-nineteenth-century streams of immigration to the United States. As with the Turks, Portuguese, North Africans, and southern Italians who went to work on Western European assembly lines in the postwar period, most of the late-nineteenth-century immigrants to the United States remained attached to their place of origin and had little interest in a long-term industrial career far from home.

But when the freedom to move in and out of the United States was blocked (first by World War I, then by legislation in the 1920s), the ethnic communities' attachments to the United States became stronger. Many upwardly mobile second-generation immigrants became owners or supervisors of shops where their parents had worked. As this occurred, those immigrants from established ethnic groups who were allowed into the country under the family-reunification provisions of the immigration legislation replenished the lower grades of the work force.

In the post–World War II period, however, the ethnic communities began to disperse. Immigration from traditional areas of Europe slowed or ceased. The children and grandchildren of the original immigrants climbed educational ladders out of the industry and into the professional classes. And as the ethnic communities disintegrated, the industrial infrastructures embedded in them began to collapse.

The New York City garment industry exemplifies the connection between the decline of the community and the disruption of the industry.[15] This connection was difficult to detect in the 1950s and '60s, because the industry was migrating out of the city. It appeared that the demand for labor was contracting more rapidly than the supply; and when spot labor shortages did develop, they were easily met by recruiting blacks and Puerto Ricans, who moved into the lowest jobs in the skill hierarchy.

But stop-gap solutions to what seemed minor problems masked longer-term transformations. The acquisition of skill in the garment industry depends on the instruction that experienced workers give to novices on the job. Since earnings in the industry, as we have seen, are based on piece rates, the instructors must make substantial monetary sacrifices in order to pass on their knowledge; they are likely to bear this cost of training only if they are bound by kin or ethnic ties to the entering generation of workers. Given this situation, the Jews and Italians who had long been employed in the industry were unwilling to transmit their skills to the new black and Puerto Rican employees. And because these latter received little training, their earnings remained so low that at the first prospect of better work they left the industry. The upshot was that when demand for women's garments finally stabilized, in the 1970s, the New York City industry faced, to its surprise, a major labor shortage.

The shortage has been met by hiring new immigrants from Latin America, the Caribbean, and Asia. But the entrance of these immigrants into the industry has divided the leaders of the contractors' associations and the unions—who are still mainly Jews and Italians—from the rank and file—who are increasingly Hispanic and Chinese. It has also widened the gap between employers—again mainly Jews and Italians— and the work force—the new immigrants—by isolating the groups in their respective community institutions. At the same time, the labor surplus that resulted first from the long period of industrial decline and then from the new immigration has insulated the industry from the pressures that in northern Italy sparked interest in new technologies. Institutions that might have promoted a technological renaissance— such as the industrial-engineering department of the International Ladies' Garment Workers Union—have atrophied.

In other traditional industrial districts, community structures are often less institutionalized than in the New York garment district, but the problems are similar. An interruption in the succession of generations leads first to a shortage of skilled labor and then to a dearth of technically versed entrepreneurs whose careers are started on the shop floor—the kind of entrepreneurs who play a crucial role in the dynamic regional conglomerations of Europe and Japan. The few remaining textile factories in New England, for example, face a shortage of loom mechanics so acute that the mill owners have begun to recruit foreign craftsmen. One employer has been indicted for illegally bringing in Colombians to fix his mill equipment. Another major mill in the region has been recruiting Portuguese with relatives who are U.S. citizens, and encouraging the new hands to exercise their rights to immigrate legally under the family-reunification provisions of the immigration legislation.

Some segments of the New England shoe industry have had a similar experience. Although parts of the industry responded to low-wage competition by computerizing the production of long runs of medium-quality shoes, others (such as L. L. Bean and Timberland) have moved into rapidly changing, sophisticated specialty markets, where production depends on traditional sewing and leather-cutting skills. Firms following this strategy have begun to move back to rural areas, where they can take advantage not only of low wages (which are still much higher than those paid in Portugal or South Korea) but also of the reservoir of traditional skills that accumulated when these areas were the centers of the nation's shoe industry.[16]

The machine-tool industry—to take a final example of the unsteady flow of skills from old to young in the industrial districts—relied on a generation of craftsmen initially trained to meet the demand created by World War II and the Korean War. In addition, it took advantage of the immigration of craftsmen from Europe to metalworking centers such as Detroit in the early 1950s.[17] The retirement of these generations of workers is creating shortages of machinists and tool-and-die makers. It is also jeopardizing the small-machine shops in such areas as Worcester, Massachusetts, New Haven, Connecticut, and Cleveland and Cincinnati, Ohio, whose proprietors have traditionally emerged from the ranks of skilled labor.[18]

In all of these industries, the problem is a result of the American success story. Skilled manual workers have used their prosperity to educate their children; and the children have used their education to move into white-collar occupations. But it is precisely the combination of a formal education, manual skills, and practical experience that is ideal for the creation of dynamic flexible enterprises. The success of the modern European industrial districts derives largely from their capacity to draw the younger generation back into their parents' industries. Thus it is no surprise that many of the fast-growing versatile machine shops in the Boston area are run by immigrants who learned their trade in West Germany, Greece, or Portugal.[19]

But there are within the traditional industrial districts regenerative as well as degenerative forces at work. These forces might revive the community structures threatened by the redeployment of mass-production industry and the erratic transmission of craft skills from generation to generation. For example, in the garment industry the union has succeeded in organizing many of the new Chinese workers.[20] An earlier effort by the Chinese contractors to secede from the contractors' association and escape union control had backfired; it angered the Chinese labor force and revealed sympathies for the union previously unsuspected by either the contractors or the union leaders. In fact, partly as a reaction to this incident, a new generation of Chinese labor activists is emerging. If these women can secure their position within the union, and the Chinese employers eventually secure theirs in the contractors' association, a whole new set of immigrant institutions could replace those of the Jews and Italians. But such a transition is still in its beginnings in Chinatown, and nothing similar is yet evident in the Hispanic community.

In some cases, state and local governments are also coming to the aid of fragile industrial districts. The governments are considering encouraging the districts' development by the same means that European and Japanese public authorities support flexible specialization in traditional industries and American public authorities aid the development of high-tech firms: providing industrial sites; underwriting the cost of training, research, and marketing; and so on. In Michigan, for instance, the state is systematically assessing its possibilities of fostering the reorganization—along the lines of flexible specialization—of those metalworking firms in the old network of automobile-parts suppliers that are excluded from the privileged circle of *kanban* subcontractors to the major producers.[21]

But these efforts at state intervention are as fitful and uncertain of success as the attempts at self-regeneration within the industrial districts. The state's ideal interlocutors, the most independent and innovative of the subcontractors, are precisely the ones likely to survive by entering long-term collaborative relationships with the reformed mass producers. The remaining shops, the ones who need help the most, may be so weakened as to be unable to take advantage of the aid that is offered. The managers of the large producers, moreover, are not eager to see the subcontractors form independent organizations, which might one day be in a position to impose business conditions on the large producers. But state and local governments naturally turn to just these captains of industry for advice when they contemplate the reorganization of small shops. In Michigan, for example, Roger Smith, chairman of General Motors, is also the chairman of a commission looking into the problems of the subcontractors—problems his firm helps create.

Thus, in the older industrial districts as in the nuclei of high-tech firms, the future of flexible specialization hangs in the balance. Just as the reform of the corporation could end in chaos, so the attempt to extend community in the high-tech zones and regenerate it in the areas of traditional industry could end in disorganization and decline. The future may be the best of worlds or the worst of worlds: our ideas of community, debated and applied through politics, will play a crucial role in deciding which.

Confusing Policies and Confused Debate

Action by the national government could have helped American firms solve some of the most serious problems of the transition from mass to flexible production. Instead, from the mid-1970s to the mid-1980s, the government exacerbated those problems. It did so by encouraging forms of competition that led firms down dead ends. More important, the public debate about the shortcomings of what the government was doing was as confused and misleading as what was being done, both privately and officially. American thought regarding the economic role of the state is trapped in a closed circle of ideas, each too credible to discard but too partial and flawed to rally broad support. Similarly, the government is burdened with institutions that seem indispensable to political order but suddenly at cross-purposes with economic efficiency.

An observer who was versed in the dilemmas just described, familiar with foreign developments, yet ignorant of American political realities, might imagine a program of minimal government intervention calculated to avoid the worst conflicts between competition and cooperation. In this vision, the national government, alone or with states and municipalities, would help reorganize decaying industrial districts, by providing technical and financial assistance to small subcontractors willing to introduce general-purpose machinery and train workers to operate it. Reorganization in the large firms would be fostered by using administrative, judicial, and legislative means to assure that more flexible forms of shop-floor control would not undermine the unions. Guarantees of this sort would encourage management to believe that work-place reorganization is possible only through compromise with the unions. The resulting managerial commitment to conciliation would reduce the likelihood of unions' resisting reforms as a cover for assaulting their existence.[22]

But, of course, the government did nothing of the sort. As the postwar regulatory system buckled under the strains of the late 1970s and early '80s, all the public and private rules and institutions that had stabilized the system came to seem, as we saw, a hodgepodge of favors to particular groups—guaranteeing them rents regardless of their contribution to national production. Union work-rule and wage-determination formulae; government regulation of telecommunications, transportation, and financial services; transfer payments of all kinds; and, symbolizing all, the level of taxation—all of these were seen as unjustifiable interferences in the market economy. The more events undermined residual confidence in the underlying coherence of the old system, the more it seemed that the choice was between capitulation to special interests, on the one hand, and deregulation—a frontal attack on the regulations encumbering economic activity—on the other.[23]

Under these circumstances, even measures that might have had a place in a program of structural readjustment were seen as ad-hoc concessions dictated by political expediency. For example, even Democrats in the Carter administration regarded training programs as an administrative device for paying political debts to minority groups—rather than as a means for developing the high-skill areas of the economy. To many of these Democrats, labor-law reform was a reward for the electoral loyalty of organized construction workers—rather than an instrument to encourage collective bargaining by strengthening the unions. And payments disbursed to workers under the Trade Adjustment Assistance Act were seen as a way to win blue-collar votes—rather than to finance the productive redeployment of labor.[24]

The Republican Reagan administration, coming to power in 1981, was far less indebted to labor than its Democratic predecessor; certainly it was less sentimentally attached to social-welfare programs and labor legislation that had originated in Roosevelt's New Deal. Hence it was far less restrained in its efforts at deregulation. In addition to such measures as reductions in the effective level and coverage of the minimum wage, referred to earlier, expenditures under the Trade Adjustment Assistance Act were cut. An illegal strike by air-traffic controllers employed by the federal government was ruthlessly crushed in a way that encouraged employers' hopes for a "union-free" environment. Deregulation of broad sectors allowed new firms paying low wages to nonunionized workers to enter markets where formerly management had acceded to high wage demands, knowing that the price-setting authorities would allow recovery of this cost through increased charges to the public; the result was to lead managers in unionized firms to confront labor by seeking reductions in wages and relaxation of work rules.

The use of tight credit to fight inflation in the early 1980s (inflation was another emblem of government meddling) had equivalent effects on the economy. High interest rates, we noted earlier, made the dollar attractive to foreign investors. This raised the dollar's value on international currency exchanges, increasing the price of American goods to foreigners and decreasing the price of foreign goods to Americans. This, in turn, exposed U.S. tradables to intense competition from imports and in world markets, encouraging managers to cut costs as quickly as possible—typically, by reducing wages. In sum, the government's macroeconomic measures induced paralyzing conflicts between labor and management—even when no attempt had been made to raise the level of competition in a particular market through deregulation.

Two core positions underlie this complex of policies; each is derived from liberal economic thought. The Democratic position, dominant in the first years of the Carter administration, is a variant of Keynesianism. It sees an active role for the state in the management of the aggregate economy, but preserves a liberal vision of microeconomic regulation: that competition among numerous independent producers ensures efficient resource allocation. Had relations among the developed countries, on the one hand, and between them as a group and the developing countries as a group, on the other, been more favorable, these Keynesians might have responded to the crisis of the 1970s by urging the internationalization of their original program. But once this solution was foreclosed, they attributed the problems to disturbances in the domestic economy: to the efforts of the state, trade unions, and large corporations to stabilize conditions in individual markets. The more outspoken they became in their criticism of all institutions that set conditions of competition, the more they resembled proponents of the second influential position: laissez-faire (especially small-business) Republicans.

To these Republicans, the restoration of market forces means a return to the ideal of politically autonomous and self-sufficient citizens: the embodiment of seventeenth- and eighteenth-century liberalism, which historians and sociologists identify as the source of that rugged individualism that has colored popular ambition and discourse in the American republic from its origins to the present.[25] What distinguished these Republicans from the Carter Keynesians was their conviction that the restoration of competitive markets would eliminate the need for almost any form of macroeconomic management.

But both of these variants of liberalism are inadequate foundations for policies fostering craft production. For flexible specialization requires a fusion of competition and cooperation that cannot occur in the model of market transactions. In the market model, economy is distinct from society, and firms are independent, competitive units. By contrast, within a system of flexible specialization, firms depend on one another for the sharing of skills, technical knowledge, information on opportunities, and definitions of standards. Structure here shades into infrastructure, competition into cooperation, and economy into society. In the liberal theory of a competitive market economy there is no space for this kind of cooperation; nor does it emerge spontaneously in practice.

Nevertheless, both of the dominant liberal positions have subsidiary traditions that address the problem of community that is central to flexible specialization. These traditions regard the large corporations, rather than the small independent producers, as the building blocks of the economy. As events called into question the dominant positions, these subsidiary traditions sparked moderate—even radical—alternatives to deregulation.

To big-business Republicans, the restoration of market forces means not the revival of a small-holder economy, but the celebration of a social-Darwinist struggle for survival: the fittest grow fastest and the size of a firm is a direct measure of its efficiency. They see the large corporation as a monument to the daring of individual entrepreneurs. Their ideas evoke the period from the 1890s to the 1920s, when the Carnegies, Fords, and Rockefellers created their giant enterprises. The future they imagine recalls the American Plan of welfare capitalism and even the industrialists' interpretation of the National Industrial Recovery Act—with trade associations licensed to carve up markets, regulate wages, and generally solve, unimpeded by labor, problems that no single company can solve.

The Democratic analogues of the big-business Republicans believe that the government should intervene in the reorganization of particular industries in order to improve the firms' capacity to compete in world markets. Advocates of such a policy have proposed measures ranging from suspension of some of the same antitrust laws to which the big-business Republicans object, to the creation of a federal investment bank to finance the reconstruction of troubled industries. But these people differ from their Republican counterparts in their two major proposals: a system of tripartite industrial planning, administered by representatives of industry, labor, and the public interest; and a plan for short-term protection from international competition, which would give industry time to regroup and would warn foreign competitors that the United States will close its borders to their products if they do not open their borders to its products.

A socialist variant of this position, finally, calls for a program of Keynesian demand stimulation (including foreign-exchange controls and trade restrictions, to shield the economy from low-wage foreign competitors and speculative reactions to reflation), and an industrial policy to revitalize the economy and extend worker control over corporate decisions. But socialists say more about slowing change and protecting communities than about reconstructing the economy in the face of changed conditions of competition.[26]

These proposals for corporate reform—especially their moderate variants—are encouraging for craft production. This is because they posit a connection between successful adaptation to changed economic conditions, the restoration of flexibility, and the regeneration of community. Moderate advocates of big-business reform—be they Republicans or Democrats—see that change of any kind requires flexibility. And they understand that flexibility depends on cooperation; cooperation, on trust; and trust, on those pledges of mutual aid that fuse bargaining parties into a community. "Industrial performance," writes Bruce R. Scott, of the Harvard Business School,

will improve when employees gain economic security through long-term commitments to productive, profitable companies. In turn, business must recognize this commitment and must adapt its strategies, organization, and personnel policies accordingly. Companies can no longer equate management with manipulation of the balance sheet, where divisions are bought and sold or plants closed and opened with little or no reference to the rights of those who work there.[27]

To moderate reformers such as Scott, the creation of community is possible only through the redirection and reinforcement of the large corporations, on the one hand, and their interlocutors in the national government, on the other. For example, Scott recommends incentives for the formation of plant-level communities through enactment of a new federal charter of incorporation: firms that incorporated under the new charter would be effectively exempt from the antitrust laws; they would be protected from stockholder takeovers (by a provision requiring employee approval of takeover bids); and they would be permitted (again subject to employee approval) to create a tax-deductible fund for investments, which would foster employment stability and hence job security. In return, such firms would have to guarantee lifetime employment to all employees with ten years of company service (except in cases of gross negligence), and the firms would have to consult with elected representatives of the work force at every level, from the shop floor to the board of directors. These measures at the corporate level (reminiscent of the welfare capitalism advocated in the 1920s) would be complemented by the recombination of federal agencies into a new Department of Industry, Trade, and Commerce. This department would consult with the reformed corporations on ways to increase American exports, through coordination of trade policy and through encouragement (by joint ventures and other means) of more competitive technologies.[28]

The logical conclusion of this line of reform is a polity composed of large, highly flexible corporate communities whose decisions are coordinated by a single national forum. In this way—suggests Robert R. Reich, of Harvard's Kennedy School of Government—firms would take responsibility for the health, day-care, social security, disability, and unemployment benefits now administered by state agencies. Corporations would "largely replace geographic jurisdictions as conduits of government support for economic and human development. Companies, rather than state and local governments, [would] be the intermediaries through which such assistance is provided."[29] Plans for major structural adjustments would be formulated in a "national bargaining arena," allowing all interested parties to arrive at consensual decisions.[30]

The problem with this line of reform is not that large corporations are constitutionally unable to serve as the organizational frame of flexible production. Examples from the Mulhouse cotton industry, the modern Japanese and German corporations in traditional industries, and such American high-technology giants as IBM show that they can. And it is plainly the success of these organizations that inspires the reformers.[31]

Rather, the problem with this line of reform is that the corporate community is only one of several ways of institutionalizing the cooperation necessary for flexible specialization; and given the history of American industry and its current problems, it is not the most promising one for the United States. The sectors of the American economy—the mature mass producers as well as small firms in traditional and high-tech industries—that most need to reform in order to compete in a world of flexible specialization are those whose structures decreasingly resemble the corporate model exemplified by IBM—or never resembled it at all. Thus large firms in mature industries that do in some ways look like IBM are in fact trying to transform themselves from self-contained corporate communities of the kind the moderates envisage into organizational centers of industrial districts; they are doing so by moving toward just-in-time production systems, which blur the distinction between inside and outside suppliers, while encouraging the spatial concentration of production. Small firms in the high-technology industrial districts, which will never reach the size of IBM, are also discovering an unsuspected need to amalgamate themselves into local communities. And small firms in the older industrial districts, which have also never been organized according to the principles of the modern corporate model, are trying to retie the human threads that hold them together before they tear beyond repair. Holding up to these firms the image of IBM—which is so preeminent that it can in fact create much of the infrastructure it needs without seeking the cooperation of other firms or the state—is to offer confusing counsel.

In our analysis, successful industrial reorganization in the United States will require reinvigoration of local and regional government—not its supersession in favor of an expansion of corporate autonomy. Industrial policy will have to be regional policy: to be effective, the coordination of training programs, industrial research, transportation networks, credit, marketing information, environmental protection, and the other elements of the infrastructure will have to be done on a regional level. In exceptional cases, large corporations could—as the moderate reformers suggest—provide their own communities. And there is—again, as these reformers argue—a need to modify the procedures (inherited from decades of American autarky) by which national policy regarding foreign trade, and its effect on domestic industry, is determined. But if uncertainty and competition push American mass producers toward flexible specialization—straining the integrity of industrial districts of all vintages—the chief problem of economic reorganization will not be finding a way to dissolve the polity into the business enterprises; the problem will be preventing those enterprises from dissolving into a political void.

A second problem with the moderates' program of reform concerns its political practicality. It is unlikely that any program of corporate reconstruction will be possible without the trade unions' cooperation. But to win the unions' assent to massive industrial reorganization, the new order will have to include a place for existing labor organizations;

THE SECOND INDUSTRIAL DIVIDE

and the moderates' vision of a cooperative economy does not do this. In the projections of the corporate reformers, trade unions lead almost as shadowy an existence as they did in the 1920s world of the American Plan. In theory, trade unions would continue to exist in order to give labor a collective voice in the "national bargaining arena." But if corporations become self-contained communities—guaranteeing lifetime employment to their members—and if all disputes between labor and management are resolved in works councils (by definition, mindful of the peculiarities of local circumstance), what would connect a national labor organization to the daily concerns of the citizens of the corporate communities? And, if there were no ties, who would want to join the unions? Most American trade-union proponents of labor-management cooperation at plant level are concerned by this train of thought; their concern—exacerbated by the contradictory managerial strategies referred to earlier—is a practical (and politically consequential) expression of the limits of the moderates' notion of productive association.

A third obstacle to the moderates' program concerns fundamental American beliefs about republican order. As opinion surveys repeatedly show, Americans profoundly mistrust not only big government and big labor but also big business. (Indeed, despite their mistrust of big government, Americans look to the state to safeguard their health and safety on and off the job, their interests as consumers, and their rights to economic self-determination.)[32] In short, concentrations of power affront political sensibilities formed by the various strands of English liberalism. There is thus no reason to suppose that Americans would welcome a further concentration of power in the corporations—whose political influence they already find alarming. Only a compelling logic of economic necessity might persuade them to put aside their misgivings. And if our analysis of the requirements of economic reform is correct, the logic of efficiency weighs against—not for—the extension of the corporate form.

In fact, if the current debate mined all the resources of our national heritage, we would be faced with a daunting shortage of possibilities for reform. We could stake everything on the market, and hope that competition would revive the corporation before wrecking it. We could stake everything on corporate reform, and hope that during the political struggles it touched off, industry and labor would come to a broader understanding of community than the reformers'. Or we could hope against hope that the socialists' vision of a regenerated working and living community would consolidate political movements that would learn how to reconcile economic flexibility and social stability. Failing all that, we might take a chance on the impossible: jumping over our national shadow and simply imitating the Japanese, or the Italians of the Third Italy, or the German craft workers.

But from the store of things we have done, might have done, and occasionally do, it is possible to draw on reserves of unused experience: the raw material from which to construct the kind of communities that do justice to both our national heritage and our economic needs. Once we begin to look, in fact, we can quickly find instructive examples. For there have been in the United States regional communities—based on flexible specialization and embodying American individualism—that make craft production seem not just an admissible but a morally appealing form of economic activity.

Yeoman Democracy

Examples from the preceding chapters show that craft community can be reconciled with American political culture. The success of industrial districts such as nineteenth-century Philadelphia is one case in point; the construction and garment industries are others. We saw, too, that under slightly different conditions, more communitarian forms of shop-floor control might have survived in large factories in the United States. And craft production survives in those shops within large plants where the organization of the work lends itself to this form of production.

A further example of a practice that is at odds with our familiar principles is the organization of much of American agriculture. The federal government provides independent farmers with detailed technical and commercial advice, just as regional technology centers in Japan and artisans' associations in Italy provide autonomous producers with the information they need to do business.[33] The American family farm (the economics textbook's favorite example of the sovereign competitive firm) could not survive without the help of an infrastructure of innovation guaranteed by the national state and administered by its local agencies.

Moreover, surprisingly, there are examples of such programs in recent American industrial history that demonstrate how the government might encourage flexible specialization in manufacturing. In 1977, during Carter's presidency, a group in the Department of Commerce took advantage of provisions in Title II of the Trade Act of 1974 to organize the Footwear Revitalization Program. This program was designed to demonstrate the possibility of restoring the competitiveness of a mature industry battered by cheap mass-produced imports.[34] To this end, consultants were recruited to help firms in New York, Boston, Philadelphia, Chicago, St. Louis, and Los Angeles to identify their problems; formulate marketing, production, training, and organizational strategies to overcome them; and assist in the preparation of applications for government loans to finance adjustment. Besides organizing the consulting network and expediting review of the loan applications, the Commerce Department group encouraged exchanges of information between manufacturers and retailers, to accelerate the industry's response to shifts in fashion. The department encouraged exports, by commissioning studies on trade regulations in potential markets; informing manufacturers of foreign opportunities; advertising American products abroad; and bringing representatives of potential foreign importers to the United States. It used its Office of Science and Technology, in collaboration with the National Bureau of Standards, to develop new technology (such as computer-controlled stitchers) to facilitate rapid change of styles and to cut production costs; and it created the American Shoe Center, in Philadelphia, to help evaluate and disseminate the new equipment. Finally—to ensure that firms would not be pushed to the wall by foreign competition before they had time to execute their new plans—the government renegotiated an orderly marketing agreement with Korea and Taiwan that limited the quantity of shoes these countries could export to the United States for four years.

Judged by several measures, the Footwear Revitalization Program was a success. Although output and employment levels in the industry held steady in the late 1970s, the value produced (and hence productivity) per person per hour increased significantly. This suggests a switch to higher-value products, which is confirmed by data on per-capita expenditures for shoes. Investment increased on average more than 20 percent annually between 1977 and 1979, suggesting that the higher productivity was associated with the use of the new, more flexible equipment. By comparison, industries that received government funds under the Trade Act but did not have a structural-reform program such as the footwear manufacturers did not show a corresponding increase in productivity. In addition, the American Shoe Center proved so valuable to the footwear firms that they were willing to assume the full financing of it. And finally, although the program was dismantled under the Reagan administration (as an "unnecessary" state intrusion into the private sector), the experience it provided with numerically controlled equipment for producing sophisticated goods seems to have helped the industry set its future course. Thus it is widely expected that many small- and medium-sized producers will take advantage of the flexibility of the new technology, by subcontracting aspects of design and production to firms that use computer-driven equipment—a pattern that recalls developments in the Third Italy.

All of these instances of flexible specialization presuppose a variant of individualism often called yeoman democracy. In a society based on market liberalism, the state is restricted to enforcing the rules of exchange; but in a yeoman democracy, the state is responsible for creating conditions conducive to a republic of small holders. Laissez-faire liberalism presumes that the state will stay out of the market unless the laws of transaction are violated;[35] yeoman democracy presumes that the state must guarantee that market transactions do not permanently advantage one group of traders—and thus undermine the balance of wealth and power that makes possible a community of producers. (Of course—as the history of American law in this century shows—the procedural liberalism of the market and the substantive liberalism of yeoman democracy shade into one another. Given the procedural liberalism of the market, the losers or potential losers in competition can expect the state to compensate them for circumstances beyond their control—the poverty of their families, the bigotry of their competitors—that will disadvantage them under the existing rules; and to the extent that the state provides redress by altering the results of previous competition, it becomes the protector of a substantive, not a procedural, order.[36])

There is another way to put the crucial distinction between market liberalism and yeoman democracy. In market liberalism, property is to be used to the maximum advantage of its possessor; in yeoman democracy, property is to be held in trust for the community—its use is subordinated to the latter's maintenance. It is this recognition of the indispensability of *community* that makes yeoman democracy—a form of collective individualism—the political analogue of the cooperative competition of craft production.[37]

The principles of yeoman democracy are a theme that runs through the newspapers and political proclamations of American artisans well into the nineteenth century;[38] the cooperative movements that rallied to Powderly's Knights of Labor;[39] the Populist rebels against the tyranny of the banks and railroads;[40] and the Debsian Socialists.[41] They reappear in modern enthographies of American craft communities in the construction, garment, and printing industries.[42] They surface, too, in the movement for worker democracy and works councils in the CIO in the 1940s and early '50s. And often the connection between earlier and later formulations has been surprisingly close: Clint Golden, a major advocate of these principles, had in fact been apprenticed as a drill tender in a mine to "Big John" Powderly, brother of the Knights' leader.[43] During the heyday of mass production—with its view of workers as collective subjects—these principles were reduced to a kind of intellectual clandestinity. But their hold on the popular imagination is seen in the modern survey-opinion findings, referred to earlier, of the mistrust in large organizations, combined with the recognition of the need for state supervision of community interests.

It is the ideal of yeoman democracy, we think, that is most likely to catalyze American efforts to rebuild the economy on the model of flexible specialization. For the idea of an economy of craft communities— some organized in large corporations; many regionally based—speaks to the American tradition of localism. And an economy that is based on skilled workers—many so versatile that alone or with a few others they can function autonomously—appeals to American individualism: the sense that entrepreneurship is the source and product of personal liberty.

The project of constructing a yeoman democracy, we believe, could win the consensus that is needed for a national shift to flexible specialization. With this consensus the state could coordinate the necessary rearrangement of relations among firms, and between labor and capital—and thereby redefine the relation between government and economy.

The Next Moves: Backward and Forward

In the end, then, if we are right, the future refers to the past. If at the second industrial divide technology veers back to the path abandoned at the first, regulatory institutions (and their correlate ideas of association) will also recall the experiments of the past. Traces of the yeoman democracy that might have been could give form to the political passions necessary to create an American yeoman democracy of the future.

But reference and recall are not repetition. The vision of an alternative past can at best inspire the vision of an alternative future. The notion that the future can replicate a history that never was is as absurd as the notion that the present can re-create the past. Should the idea of yeoman democracy become the rallying cry of economic reconstruction, it will be practicable only on the condition that truly new forms of legal, economic, and political association are invented for shaping industries into communities and communities into a nation.

Above all, it must be made clear that the ideal of yeoman democracy—like the definition of a flexible-specialization economy—does not contain any precise indication of the division of rights between capital and labor. We have seen examples of flexible specialization in which property was widely distributed and authority regarding investments broadly shared; but we have also seen examples in which the workers had autonomy at the work place, yet the managers (ultimately responsible to private investors) held control over the fundamental economic decisions. The American Plan almost worked, and there are those who would make it the matrix of flexible specialization in large firms. Employers in the Philadelphia metalworking industry in the 1920s were creating a system of shifting skilled workers from shop to shop, according to rapidly shifting needs.[44] There is no reason to think that modern American employers could not provide the training, coordination, and social insurance needed to secure labor's participation in a regionally defined craft community. Yeoman democracy could thus become another form of American capitalism—perhaps more tolerable at the work place, but in other ways indistinguishable from familiar forms of economic control.

But this need not be. If labor can shake its attachment to increasingly indefensible forms of shop-floor control; draw inspiration from its origins in craft associations; and create those political coalitions needed for the community supports of flexibility—it may well demand as the price of its boldness and initiative a voice in vocational training; government-sponsored technological development; and the permanent reorganization of the work place that is required in flexible specialization. As property rights become effectively redistributed, the new society might in time escape the old definitions of the productively possible.

We can no longer pretend that America's destiny is manifest. The more we understand of our past and present, the more we see that it was our choices that shaped our history and will shape our future. And such is the influence of the American economy that our decisions will weigh heavily on the world's.

Whether our economy is based on mass production or on flexible specialization—and what part labor will play in either—are open questions. The answers will depend in part on the capacity of nations and social classes to envision the future that they want. "What 'ought to be,' " Antonio Gramsci wrote, "is concrete. . . . It alone is history in the making and philosophy in the making, it alone is politics."

NOTES

Chapter 1

1. For the French literature on this subject, see Robert Boyer, "La crise actuelle: une mise en perspective historique," *Critique de l'économie politique*, nos. 7–8 (May 1979): pp. 5–113; idem, "Les salaires en longue période," *Économie et statistique*, no. 103 (September 1978): 28–57; idem and Jacques Mistral, *Accumulation, inflation, crises* (Paris: Presses Universitaires de France, 1978); and Michel Aglietta, *Régulation et crises du capitalisme: l'example des États-Unis* (Paris: Calmann-Lévy, 1976). For the parallel American literature, see David Gordon, "Stages of Accumulation and Long Economic Cycles," in Terence K. Hopkins and Immanuel Wallerstein, eds., *Processes of the World System* (Beverly Hills, Calif.: Sage, 1980), pp. 9–45; Samuel Bowles and Herbert Gintis, "The Crisis of Liberal Democratic Capitalism: The Case of the United States," *Politics and Society*, 11, no. 1 (1982): 51–94; Thomas Weisskopf, "The Current Economic Crisis in Historical Perspective," *Socialist Review*, no. 57 (May–June 1981): 9–54.

2. For a review of this position, see Ernst R. Berndt, "Energy Price Increases and the Productivity Slowdown in United States Manufacturing, in *The Decline of Productivity Growth*, Federal Reserve Bank of Boston Conference, Series 22 (Boston: Federal Reserve Bank of Boston, 1980), pp. 60–89.

3. Paul McCracken et al., *Towards Full Employment and Price Stability* (Paris: Organisation for Economic Co-operation and Development, 1977).

4. For a typical formulation, see Samuel Brittan, *The Economic Consequences of Democracy* (London: Maurice Temple Smith, Ltd., 1977), pp. 237–38, which contains further references. A more complicated argument incorporating many of these themes is Lester C. Thurow, *The Zero-Sum Society: Distribution and the Possibilities for Economic Change* (New York: Basic Books, 1980).

5. For an example, see Samuel P. Huntington, Michel Crozier, and Joji Watanuki, *The Crisis of Democracy: Report on the Governability of Democracies to the Trilateral Commission* (New York: New York University Press, 1975).

6. Claus Offe, "Competitive Party Democracy and the Keynesian Welfare State: Factors of Stability and Disorganization" in Thomas Ferguson and Joel Rogers, eds., *The Political Economy* (Armonk, N.Y.: M. E. Sharpe, 1984): 349–67.

7. For similar objections, see Harold L. Wilensky, "Political Legitimacy and Consensus: Missing Variables in the Assessment of Social Policy" (Reprint no. 453, Institute of Industrial Relations, University of California, Berkeley, 1983).

8. For a thorough analysis of the restrictions on layoffs in the automobile sector in West Germany and the United States—and firms' reactions to their situations—see Christoph Köhler and Werner Sengenberger, *Konjunktur und Personalanpassung: betriebliche Beschäftigungspolitik in der deutschen und amerikanischen Automobilindustrie* (Frankfurt am Main: Campus, 1983).

9. Michael J. Piore, "Convergence in Industrial Relations? The Case of France and the United States" (Department of Economics Working Paper 286, Massachusetts Institute of Technology, July 1981).

10. See John Zysman, *Government, Markets, and Growth: Financial Systems and the Politics of Industrial Change* (Ithaca: Cornell University Press, 1983).

11. Julian Gresser, Koichiro Fujikura, and Akio Morishima, *Environmental Law in Japan* (Cambridge, Mass.: MIT Press, 1981).

Notes

12. The statistics and the citation are from Berndt, "Energy Price Increases," p. 66.

13. See the data presented in William P. Nordhaus, "Policy Responses to the Productivity Slowdown," in *The Decline of Productivity Growth*, Federal Reserve Bank of Boston Conference, Series 22 (Boston: Federal Reserve Bank of Boston, 1980), figure 2, p. 150; and in the same volume, the discussion of Nordhaus's paper by Robert M. Solow, pp. 173–77.

Chapter 2

1. This chapter draws extensively on Charles F. Sabel and Jonathan Zeitlin, "Historical Alternatives to Mass Production," *Past and Present* (forthcoming). An earlier version of this article appears in *Stato e mercato*, no. 5 (August 1982): 213–58.

2. The most thorough account of the emergence of the assembly line, and its relation to earlier high-volume metalworking technologies, is David Allen Hounshell, "From the American System to Mass Production: The Development of Manufacturing Technology in the United States, 1850–1920" (Ph.D. diss., University of Delaware, 1978).

3. One-third of the 10 million Japanese employed in manufacturing between 1970 and 1977 worked in firms of fewer than 100 employees, and close to one-half worked in firms of fewer than 300. There were no signs in the 1970s of increasing concentration of employment. See Bureau of Statistics, *Japan Statistical Yearbook, 1973–74* (Tokyo: Office of the Prime Minister, 1975), pp. 182–83, and ibid. for 1980, pp. 170–73. For the statistics on Great Britain, see S. J. Prais, *The Evolution of Giant Firms in Britain: A Study of the Growth of Concentration in Manufacturing Industries in Britain* (London: Cambridge University Press, 1976), p. 156.

4. Adam Smith, *The Wealth of Nations*, ed. Edwin Cannan (Chicago: University of Chicago Press, 1976), pp. 7–16.

5. For the history of these ideas, see Maxine Berg, *The Machinery Question and the Making of Political Economy, 1815–48* (Cambridge: Cambridge University Press, 1980).

6. Karl Marx, *Capital*, 3 vols., ed. Friedrich Engels, trans. Samuel Moore and Edward Aveling (New York: International Publishers, 1967), 1:322–427. "In handcrafts and manufacture," Marx writes, "the workman makes use of a tool, in the factory, the machine makes use of him" (p. 422).

7. Smith, *Wealth of Nations*, pp. 21–25.

8. Ibid., pp. 407–45.

9. This is a reading of Marx's account of the decline of feudalism that is advanced by Maurice Dobb in *Studies in the Development of Capitalism* (New York: International Publishers, 1946), and defended in his replies to critics, reprinted in *The Transition from Feudalism to Capitalism*, ed. Rodney Hilton (London: NLB, 1976), pp. 17–67, 98–101, 165–69.

10. Smith, *Wealth of Nations*, pp. 159–81.

11. Marx, *Capital*, pp. 734–49.

12. A convincing interpretation of Marx's work (and therefore of classical political economy as a whole) as a theory of technological development is G. A. Cohen, *Karl Marx's Theory of History: A Defense* (Princeton: Princeton University Press, 1978).

13. David S. Landes, *The Unbound Prometheus* (Cambridge: Cambridge University Press, 1969). On Proto-industrialization, see Peter Kriedte, Hans Medick, and Jürgen Schlumbohm, *Industrialization before Industrialization*, trans. Beate Schempp (Cambridge: Cambridge University Press, 1981), and M. Berg, P. Hudson, and M. Sonnenscher, eds., *Manufacture in Town and Country before the Factory* (Cambridge: Cambridge University Press, 1983).

14. Alfred D. Chandler, Jr., *The Visible Hand: The Managerial Revolution in American Business* (Cambridge: Harvard University Press, 1977).

15. The estimate of the share of batch production in the output of the U.S. metalworking sector is from "Machine-tool Technology," *American Machinist* (October 1980), figure 2, p. 106.

16. See Michael J. Piore, "Dualism as a Response to Flux and Uncertainty," and

"The Technological Foundations of Dualism and Discontinuity," in Suzanne Berger and Michael J. Piore, *Dualism and Discontinuity in Industrial Societies* (Cambridge: Cambridge University Press, 1980), pp. 13–81. These refer to antecedent literature.

17. Alfred Marshall, *Industry and Trade* (London: Macmillan & Co., 1919), pp. 283–88. A detailed contemporary study of districts such as Marshall described is Philip Scranton, *Proprietary Capitalism: The Textile Manufacture at Philadelphia, 1800-1885* (Cambridge: Cambridge University Press, 1984).

18. On Proudhon, see Pierre Ansart, *Naissance de l'anarchisme* (Paris: Presses Universitaires de France, 1970), especially pages 141–68.

19. For Powderly and the Knights of Labor in connection with the cooperative movement, see Clare Anna Dahlbe Horner, "Producers' Co-operatives in the United States, 1865–89" (Ph.D. diss., University of Pittsburgh, 1978), and Paul Buhle, "The Knights of Labor in Rhode Island," *Radical History Review* 17 (Spring 1978): 39–73. For a broader view of the social and political views of the Knights, see George S. Kealey and Bryan D. Palmer, *Dreaming of What Might Be: The Knights of Labor in Ontario, 1880-1900* (Cambridge: Cambridge University Press, 1982).

20. For Schulze-Delitzsch, see Helmut Faust, *Schulze-Delitzsch und sein genossenschaftliches Werk* (Marburg/Lahn: Simons Verlag, 1949), especially pp. 16–31.

21. Proudhon argues that the mechanization of production enlarged, rather than decomposed, tasks: see his *Système des contradictions économiques, ou philosophie de la misère*, 2 vols., ed. Roger Picard (Paris: Marcel Rivière, 1923), 1:171. "Nothing is more absurd," Marx writes, "than to see in machinery the *antithesis* of the division of labor, the synthesis restoring unity to divided labor," in *The Poverty of Philosophy* (New York: International Publishers, 1971), p. 138. The editor of Proudhon's text concedes the point in a footnote: Proudhon, *Système*, n. 44, 1:171.

22. Michel Laferèrre observes that throughout its history, the Lyonese silk industry had a "double face": it was "at once servant and mistress ... so accustomed to perfectly executing the orders received that it ended up inspiring them," in *Lyon, ville industrielle* (Paris: Presses Universitaires de France, 1960), p. 235.

23. On the history of the Jacquard loom, see Dary M. Hafter, "The Programmed Brocade Loom and the 'Decline of the Drawgirl,'" in *Dynamos and Virgins Revisited: Women and Technological Change in History*, Martha Moore Trescott, ed. (Metuchen, N.J.: The Scarecrow Press, 1979), pp. 49–66; and Pierre Cayez, *Métiers jacquard et hauts fourneaux: aux origines de l'industrie lyonnaise* (Lyon: Presses Universitaires de Lyon, 1978), pp. 105–8. For its success in stimulating demand for highly patterned fabrics, see E. Pariset, *Histoire de la fabrique lyonnaise des soieries* (Lyon: A. Rey, 1901), pp. 300–302.

24. Henri Guitton, *L'industrie des rubans de soie en France* (Paris: Recueil Sirey, 1928), pp. 19–31; Maxime Perrin, *La région industrielle de Saint-Étienne* (Tours: Arrault, 1937), pp. 279–82.

25. For innovation in Lyon, see Laferèrre, *Lyon, ville industrielle*, pp. 190–241; the laboratory analogy is from page 99. For the Alsatians at Mulhouse, see Yves Schwartz, "Practiques paternalistes et travail industriel à Mulhouse au XIXe siècle," *Technologies, idéologies, et practiques* 1 (October–December 1979): 9–77.

26. For Birmingham, see Marie B. Rowlands, *Masters and Men in the West Midlands Metalware Trades before the Industrial Revolution* (Manchester: Manchester University Press, 1975), chaps. 7–8, and George C. Allen, *The Industrial Development of Birmingham and the Black Country* (London: Allen and Unwin, 1929), pp. 17–19, 43–44.

27. For Sheffield, see David G. Hey, *The Rural Metalworkers of the Sheffield Region*, Department of English Local History Occasional Papers, Series 5 (Leicester: Leicester University Press, 1972), pp. 32, 36–41; G. I. H. Lloyd, *The Cutlery Trades* (Longmans, Green and Co., 1913), p. 208; J. G. Timmins, "Concentration and Integration in the Sheffield Crucible Steel Industry, *Business History*, vol. 24, no. 1 (1982): 61–78; P. W. S. Andrews and Elizabeth Brunner, *Capital Development in Steel: A Study of the United Steel Companies Ltd.* (Oxford: Oxford University Press, 1952), pp. 107–9, 138–40. On Saint-Étienne, see Perrin, *La région industrielle de Saint Étienne*, pp. 225–39; and Jacques Schnetzler, *Les industries et les hommes dans la région stéphanoise* (Saint-Étienne: Le Feuille Blanc, 1975), pp. 95–98. On Remscheid, see Paul Legers, "Die Remscheider Werkzeug- und Eisenindustrie von der Einführung der Gewerbefreiheit bis zum Ausbruch des Weltkrieges, in Wilhelm Engels and Paul Legers, *Aus der Geschichte der Remscheider*

Notes

und Bergischen Werkzeug- und Eisenindustrie (Remscheid: Selbstverlag des Bergischen Fabrikanten-Vereins Remscheid, 1928), pp. 281–83, 313.

28. Schwartz, "Practiques paternalistes," p. 11.

29. Guitton, *L'industrie des rubans*, pp. 29–30; Perrin, *La région industrielle de Saint-Étienne*, pp. 280–82; Legers, "Die Remscheider Werkzeug- und Eisenindustrie," p. 298; Lloyd, *Cutlery Trades*, pp. 365–87.

30. For the concept of the *fabrique collective*, see Frédéric Le Play, *La réform sociale en France* (Tours: Alfred Mame et Fils, 1872) 2: 137–45; and for its application to ribbon weaving in St. Étienne, Guitton, *L'industrie des rubans*, p. 44.

31. For Sheffield examples, see Lloyd, *Cutlery Trades*, pp. 221–24, and Sidney Pollard, *A History of Labour in Sheffield* (Liverpool: Liverpool University Press, 1959), pp. 54–55. For Birmingham, see Allen, *Industrial Development of Birmingham*, p. 117–18, 159–60.

32. On the role of parole contracts in Lyon, see Laferèrre, *Lyon, ville industrielle*, p. 108. Guitton calls *intuitus personae* the "mainspring" of the *fabrique stéphanoise*, in *L'industrie des rubans*, p. 104.

33. For the *caisse de prêts*, see Guitton, *L'industrie des rubans*, pp. 242–44, 273–74; and Pariset, *Histoire de la fabrique lyonnaise*, p. 315. On the renovated Old Regime institutions, see Cayez, *Métiers jacquard et hauts fourneaux*, pp. 99–100; Perrin, *La région industrielle de Saint-Étienne*, p. 286; and Louis-Jean Gras, *Histoire de la rubanerie et des industries de la soie à Saint-Étienne et dans la région stéphanoise* (Saint-Étienne: Theolier, 1906). pp. 172–81, 234–64.

34. Guitton, *L'industrie des rubans*, pp. 225–34.

35. For Solingen, see Lloyd, *Cutlery Trades*, and his "Labour Organization in the Cutlery Trades of Solingen, *Economic Journal* 18 (1908): 373–391. In Remscheid, as the Social Democrats strengthened—following repeal of the antisocialist laws, in 1890—they wrested some control of social-insurance institutions established by the employers' association from the Liberals who had until then dominated them; see Erhard Lucas, *Arbeiterradikalismus: zwei Formen von Radikalismus in der deutschen Arbeiterbewegung* (Frankfurt am Main: Verlag Roter Stern, 1976), pp. 130–31. On mediation in Lyon, see Cayez, *Métiers jacquard et hauts fourneaux*, pp. 99–100.

36. On specialty-steel making in Saint-Étienne, see Perrin, *La région industrielle de Saint-Étienne*, p. 233. On the misleading appearance of Lyonese factories in the late nineteenth century, see Yves Lequin, "La formation du prolétariat industriel dans la région lyonnaise au XIXe siècle: approches méthodologiques et premiers résultats," *Le mouvement social* 97 (1976): 121–37, especially p. 125.

37. Heinrich Kelleter, *Geschichte der Firma J. A. Henckels*, (Solingen: Selbstverlag der Firma J. A. Henckels, 1924), pp. 189–90.

38. Schwartz, "Practiques paternalistes," p. 15.

39. The *système Motte* is described in Paul Descamps, "La famille patronale," *La science sociale* 25 (February 1910): 74–85, especially pages 82–85. For a contrasting account of factory organization in Roubaix—which focuses on psychological factors—see David Landes, "Religion and Enterprise: The Case of the French Textile Industry," in Edward C. Carter II, Robert Forster, and Joseph N. Moody, eds., *Enterprise and Entrepreneurs in Nineteenth- and Twentieth-Century France* (Baltimore: The Johns Hopkins University Press, 1976), pp. 41–86.

40. The following account comes from Laferèrre, *Lyon, ville industrielle*, pp. 162 ff.

41. The reorganization of the Lyon area has been carefully studied in a series of reports by the Centre des Recherches et des Études Sociologiques Appliquées de la Loire (CRESAL) and the Organisation d'Étude d'Aménagement de la Métropole Rhône-Alpes (OREAM Rhône-Alpes). See Jacques Roux and Étienne de Banville, "Internationalisation et région: le cas de l'industrie en Rhône-Alpes," CRESAL, June 1979, and OREAM Rhône-Alpes, "Rhône-Alpes, 1985: une région s'interroge sur son avenir industriel," La documentation française, *Études de la politique industrielle*, vol. 22 (1978).

42. In 1981 the Como silk district employed about 35,000 workers, who produced goods worth some 950 million dollars (1981 dollars). Six hundred of the 950 million dollars came from export sales. See Patricia McColl, "Spinning an Italian Yarn," *New York Times Magazine*, March 21, 1982, pp. 86, 88, 108; Unione Industriali di Como, *Como distretto tessile 1983* (Como: Edizioni Consulenze Industriale, 1983).

43. Hey, *Rural Metalworkers of the Sheffield Region*, pp. 32, 48–49; Lloyd, *Cutlery*

Trades, pp. 199–200, 348–49; Pollard, *History of Labour in Sheffield,* pp. 78–82, 159–64.

44. Lloyd, *Cutlery Trades,* pp. 110–47, 235–327; Pollard, *History of Labour in Sheffield,* pp. 65–77, 134–58.

45. Lloyd, *Cutlery Trades,* draws the comparison with Solingen, pp. 301, 392–95.

46. Allen, *Industrial Development of Birmingham,* pp. 119–21, 138–40, 197–201, 291, 369; A. E. Harrison, "The Competitiveness of the British Cycle Industry, 1890–1914," *Economic History Review,* 2nd Series, 22 (1969): 287–303.

47. See also the insightful and extensive discussion of themes in Roberto Mangabeira Unger, "False Necessity," part 1 of *Politics* (forthcoming).

48. See for the branching-tree notion, Stephen Jay Gould, "Bushes and Ladders in Human Evolution," in *Ever Since Darwin* (New York: W. W. Norton, 1979), pp. 56–62.

49. On the latitude of design decisions concerning the operating system or master program of the IBM 360 system, see Frederick Phillips Brooks, Jr., *The Mythical Man-Month: Essays on Software Engineering* (Reading, Mass.: Addison-Wesley, 1975); and for the development of the FORmula TRANslating program language, see John Backus "The History of Fortran I, II, and III," *Annals of the History of Computing* 1 (July 1979): 21–37. The authors managed the respective projects, and their discussion of the repeated discovery of alternative solutions is therefore especially revealing.

The victory of the gasoline- over the steam-powered automobile in the first decades of this century was an analogous case: see Charles C. McLaughlin, "The Stanley Steamer: A Study in Unsuccessful Innovation," in Hugh G. J. Aitken, ed., *Explorations in Enterprise,* (Cambridge: Harvard University Press, 1967), pp. 259–72. "The principal factor responsible for the demise of the steam car," McLaughlin writes, "was neither technical drawbacks nor a conspiracy of hostile interests, but rather the fact that its fate was left in the hands of small manufacturers" (p. 271).

50. A concise presentation of American economic development from this perspective is Nathan Rosenberg, *Technology and American Economic Growth* (White Plains, N.Y.: M. E. Sharpe, 1972).

51. The classic studies of French land-tenure patterns are Marc Bloch, *Les caractères originaux de l'histoire rurale française (Paris: Armand Collin, 1952),* and idem, *Seigneurie française et manoir anglais* (Paris: Armand Collin, 1967). For the vitality of corporate traditions in French industry in the nineteenth century, see William H. Sewell, Jr., *Work and Revolution in France* (Cambridge: Cambridge University Press, 1980), especially pp. 142–62. For the role of the court in stimulating innovation, see Michael Stuermer, "An Economy of Delight: Court and Artisans of the Eighteenth Century," *Business History Review,* vol. 53, no. 4 (1979). On the slow diffusion of various aristocratic tastes to the popular classes, see Theodore Zeldin, *Intellect, Taste, Anxiety,* vol. 2 of his *France, 1848–1945* (Oxford: Oxford University Press, 1977), pp. 420–23, 725–55. For the resulting specialization of French production, see Patrick O'Brien and Caglar Keyder, *Economic Growth in Britain and France, 1780–1914: Two Paths to the Twentieth Century* (London: Allen and Unwin, 1978), which summarizes earlier writing on the topic.

52. On the demand for British manufactured goods, see Landes, *Unbound Prometheus,* pp. 49–53. The precise composition and origin of that demand is, however, still controversial. On the state's role in encouraging manufacture, and its failure to control the resulting expansion of production, see Joan Thirsk, *Economic Policy and Projects: The Development of a Consumer Society in Early Modern England* (Oxford: Oxford University Press, 1978).

53. On the persistence of craft forms of organization in nineteenth-century Britain, see H. J. Habakkuk, *American and British Technology in the Nineteenth Century* (Cambridge: Cambridge University Press, 1967); Leslie Hannah, *The Rise of the Corporate Economy* (London: Methuen, 1976); and C. K. Harley, "Skilled Labour and Choice of Technique in Edwardian Industry," *Explorations in Economic History* 11 (1973–74): 391–414.

54. Nathan Rosenberg, ed., *The American System of Manufacturing* (Edinburgh: Edinburgh University Press, 1969).

55. Merritt Roe Smith, *Harpers Ferry Armory and the New Technology* (Ithaca: Cornell University Press, 1977) is a thorough account of the intellectual, political, and technical preconditions of the development of armory practice.

56. Arguments against the scarcity of labor as the determining factor in the development of mass-production technology are presented by S. B. Saul in his "Editor's Introduction"

Notes

to the collection of essays *Technological Change: The United States and Great Britain in the Nineteenth Century* (London: Methuen, 1970), pp. 1–21.

57. Paul A. David, "Labor Scarcity and the Problem of Technological Progress in Nineteenth-Century America," in his *Technical Choice, Innovation and Economic Growth* (Cambridge: Cambridge University Press, 1974), pp. 19–91.

58. Rosenberg, *American System*, p. 5.

59. *Webster's New World Dictionary of the American Language* (Cleveland: The World Publishing Company, 1957), p. 1060.

60. Thomas S. Kuhn, *The Structure of Scientific Revolutions* (Chicago: Chicago University Press, 1962).

61. For a similar application of Kuhn's theory of scientific change to the story of technological development, see Edward W. Constant II, "A Model for Technological Change Applied to the Turbojet Revolution," in *Technology and Culture* 14 (October 1973): 553–72.

62. On Ure's role as an industrial consultant and propagandist of automatic production, see Berg, *Machinery Question*, pp. 197–212.

63. Labor's continuing influence on shop-floor organization after the introduction in Great Britain of the self-acting mule is described in William Lazonick, "Industrial Relations and Technical Change: The Case of the Self-acting Mule," *Cambridge Journal of Economics,* no. 3 (1979), 231–62.

64. The new applications of skill achieved by the introduction of more advanced machinery are described in James Bavington Jeffreys, *The Story of the Engineers* (London: Lawrence and Wishart, 1946), p. 16.

65. Daniel Nelson, *Frederick W. Taylor and the Rise of Scientific Management* (Madison: The University of Wisconsin Press, 1980).

66. For the view that numerically controlled machine tools could eliminate the need for craft skill with machinery, see David F. Noble, "Social Choice in Machine Design: The Case of Automatically Controlled Machine Tools, and a Challenge to Labor," *Politics and Society* 8, nos. 3–4 (1978): 313–47. Counterarguments are presented in Charles F. Sabel, *Work and Politics* (Cambridge: Cambridge University Press, 1982), pp. 63–70. An excellent case study of the connection between a firm's market strategy and its industrial relations, on the one hand, and its use of numerical control, on the other, is Arndt Sorge, Gert Hartmann, Malcolm Warner, and Ian Nicholas, *Mikroelektronik und Arbeit in der Industrie* (Frankfurt am Main: Campus, 1982).

67. See their reports in Rosenberg, *American System*.

68. Ibid., p. 44.

69. Franz Ziegler, *Wesen und Wert kleinindustrieller Arbeit* (Berlin: Bruer und Co., 1901), pp. 445–58.

70. Franz Carl Ziegler, *Die Tendenz der Entwicklung zum Grossbetrieb der Remscheider Kleinserienindustrie* (Berlin: Klemens Reuschel, 1910). In underscoring the vitality of the small firms, Legers, writing in 1928, criticizes the analysis of Franz Carl Ziegler and praises the foresight of Franz Ziegler: see Legers, *Die Remscheider Werkzeug- und Eisenindustrie,* p. 357.

71. See the account of the French metalworker, journalist, and trade-union leader Hyacinthe Dubreuil, in Martin Fine, "Toward Corporatism: The Movement for a Capital-Labor Collaboration in France, 1914–1936" (Ph.D. diss., University of Wisconsin, 1971), pp. 278–95.

Chapter 3

1. Alfred D. Chandler, Jr., *The Visible Hand: The Managerial Revolution in American Business* (Cambridge: Harvard University Press, 1977), pp. 455–512.

2. Gardiner C. Means, *The Corporate Revolution in America: Economic Reality vs. Economic Theory* (New York: Crowell-Collier Press, 1962), pp. 78–90.

3. Alan Dawley, *Class and Community: The Industrial Revolution in Lynn* (Cambridge: Harvard University Press, 1976).

4. Alexander Keyssar, "Men Out of Work: A Social History of Unemployment in Massachusetts, 1870–1916" (Ph.D. diss., Harvard University, 1977).

5. Chandler, *Visible Hand*, p. 249.

6. Ibid., pp. 240–83.

7. Ibid., pp. 315–44.

8. Ibid., p. 442.

9. Harold C. Passer, *The Electrical Manufacturers, 1875–1900: A Study of Competition, Entrepreneurship, Technological Change, and Economic Growth* (Cambridge: Harvard University Press, 1953), pp. 126–27; and the Federal Trade Commission, *Report on the Supply of Electrical Equipment and Competitive Conditions* (Washington, D.C.: U.S. Government Printing Office, 1928).

10. Quoted in Alfred S. Eichner, *The Emergence of Oligopoly: Sugar Refining as a Case Study* (Baltimore: Johns Hopkins University Press, 1969), p. 112.

11. Quoted in Passer, *Electrical Manufacturers*, p. 109.

12. Mary Yeager Kujovich, "The Refrigerator Car and the Growth of the American Dressed Beef Industry," *Business History Review* 44 (Winter 1970): 460–82; see also Chandler, *Visible Hand*, pp. 299–302; and David Brody, *The Butcher Workmen* (Cambridge, Mass.: Harvard University Press, 1964), p. 4.

13. Chandler, *Visible Hand.*

14. Eichner, *Emergence of Oligopoly*, p. 327.

15. Kujovich, *Refrigerator Car.*

16. Passer, *Electrical Manufacturers*, p. 108.

17. Ibid., p. 118.

18. Chandler, *Visible Hand*, pp. 302–7.

19. The following account of Ford's strategy and development is based on Henry Ford, in collaboration with Samuel Crowther, *My Life and Work* (Garden City: Doubleday, Page and Company, 1923); Charles E. Sorenson with Samuel T. Williamson, *My Forty Years with Ford* (New York: W. W. Norton and Company, 1956); Alfred P. Sloan, *My Years with General Motors*, ed. John McDonald and Catharine Stevens (Garden City, N.Y.: Doubleday and Company, 1964); Allan Nevins and Frank Ernest Hill, *Ford: Expansion and Challenge, 1915–1933* (New York: Charles Scribner's Sons, 1954); idem, *Ford: The Times, the Man, and the Company* (New York: Charles Scribner's Sons, 1954); and idem, *Ford: Decline and Rebirth, 1933–1962* (New York: Charles Scribner's Sons, 1963).

20. Sloan, *My Years with General Motors*, pp. 149–68.

21. Ibid., pp. 155–58.

22. Ibid., pp. 165–68; 219–47.

23. Quoted in Alfred D. Chandler, Jr., *The Railroads, the Nation's First Big Business: Sources and Readings* (New York: Harcourt, Brace and World, 1965), p. 129.

24. Nevins and Hill, *Ford: Decline and Rebirth*, pp. 133–67.

25. Fred K. Foulkes, *Personnel Policies in Large Nonunion Companies* (Englewood Cliffs, N.J.: Prentice-Hall, 1980).

26. Brody, *Butcher Workmen*, pp. 16–18.

27. See, for example, Richard C. Overton, *Burlington Route: A History of the Burlington Lines* (New York: Alfred A. Knopf, 1965), especially pp. 199–214.

28. Faced with growing labor strife, and seeking an alternative to strikes, Congress acted in 1889: it provided that "controversies" obstructing the interstate transportation of persons and property be settled through arbitration or mediation by Presidentially selected commissioners. This was followed by the passage in 1898 of the Erdman Act, which strengthened provisions for arbitration of railroad-labor disputes and government mediation and conciliation. The Transportation Act, of 1920, established railroad boards of adjustment to deal with problems in the interpretation and administration of collective-bargaining agreements. And the 1926 Railway Labor Act required that the railroads and unions make and abide by agreements concerning rates of pay, rules, and working conditions. See Edward C. Kirkland, *Industry Comes of Age: Business, Labor and Public Policy, 1860–1897* (New York: Holt, Rinehart and Winston, 1961), and Bernard D. Meltzer, *Labor Law* (Boston: Little, Brown and Co., 1970), pp. 26–27.

29. Stephen Meyer, *The Five Dollar Day: Labor, Management, and Social Control in the Ford Motor Company* (Albany: State University of New York Press, 1981).

30. Chandler, *Visible Hand*, chap. 4.

Notes

31. The Union Pacific Railroad was completed in 1869. Its demonstration that a transcontinental railroad could be built and operated resulted in the rapid completion of the other transcontinental line, the Central Pacific, in 1883. See Carter Goodrich, *Government Promotion of American Canals and Railroads, 1800–1890* (New York: Columbia University Press, 1960).

32. This theme is developed at length in Chandler, *Visible Hand*.

33. "By the 1880s, when a well-planned railroad system was completed, France had an effective all-weather transportation network, but the anticipated expansion of the market did not materialize": Maurice Lévy-Leboyer, "The Large Corporation in Modern France," in Alfred D. Chandler, Jr., and Herman Daems, eds., *Managerial Hierarchies: Comparative Perspectives on the Rise of the Modern Industrial Enterprise* (Cambridge: Harvard University Press, 1980), pp. 117–60; citation from p. 122.

34. Allan Nevins, *Study in Power: John D. Rockefeller, Industrialist and Philanthropist* (New York: Charles Scribner's Sons, 1953), 1:276–305; see also Chandler, *Visible Hand*, p. 325; Eichner, *Emergence of Oligopoly*, pp. 195–203.

35. Goodrich, *American Canals and Railroads*.

36. See Morton J. Horowitz, *The Transformation of American Law, 1780–1860* (Cambridge: Harvard University Press, 1977), pp. 63–108, for an excellent discussion of these issues.

37. Robert Fogel, *Railroads and American Economic Growth: An Econometric History* (Baltimore: Johns Hopkins University Press, 1964); idem in Stanley Lebergott, "United States Transport and Externalities," *Journal of Economic History* 2 (December 1966): 444–46; Peter D. McClelland, "Railroads, American Growth and the New Economic History: A Critique," *Journal of Economic History* 28 (March 1968): 102–23; and Paul David, "Transportation and Economic Growth: Professor Fogel On and Off the Rails," *Economic History Review* 20 (December 1969): 507–25.

38. Chandler, *Visible Hand;* and idem, *Strategy and Structure: Chapters in the History of Enterprise* (Cambridge, Mass.: MIT Press, 1962).

39. See, for example, Passer, *Electrical Manufacturers*, pp. 335, 129–30, 78–79. Westinghouse initially worked on railroad problems (pp. 129–30); Edison's initial work was connected with the telegraph, which was itself linked to railroad needs.

40. Kujovich, "Refrigerator Car."

41. Passer, *Electrical Manufacturers*, pp. 14–40, 78–104, 129–43.

42. Sorensen with Williamson, *My Forty Years with Ford*, pp. 128–29; Monte A. Calvert, *The Mechanical Engineer in America, 1930–1910* (Baltimore: Johns Hopkins University Press, 1967); Nevins and Hill, *Ford: The Times, the Man, and the Company*, chap. 18; and Chandler, *Visible Hand*, p. 280.

43. Sloan, *My Years with General Motors*, p. 156.

44. Passer, *Electrical Manufacturers*, p. 89.

45. Ibid.

46. On this tendency toward the decomposition of highly integrated industrial pioneers, see George J. Stigler, "The Division of Labor Is Limited by the Extent of the Market," in his collection of essays, *The Organization of Industry* (Chicago: University of Chicago Press, 1983), pp. 129–41, especially pp. 135–36.

47. Chandler argues that railroads aroused less opposition in Europe because they were more closely linked to the state, so they pursued less discriminatory pricing policies than railroads in the United States. European manufacturing corporations avoided conflicts with marketing systems and small firms, either because they made producers' goods (as in Germany) or because they allied themselves with existing wholesalers (Great Britain). See Alfred D. Chandler, Jr., "Government versus Business: An American Phenomenon," in John T. Dunlop, ed., *Business and Public Policy* (Boston: Division of Research, Graduate School of Business Administration, Harvard University, 1980), pp. 1–11. On the relation between the American government and business during this period, see Stephen Skowronek, *Building a New American State: The Expansion of National Administrative Capacities, 1877–1920* (Cambridge: Cambridge University Press, 1982).

48. The following is based on William H. Becker, *The Dynamics of Business-Government Relations: Industry and Exports, 1893–1921* (Chicago: University of Chicago Press, 1982), pp. 31–47.

Chapter 4

1. Robert M. Collins, *The Business Response to Keynes, 1929–1964* (New York: Columbia University Press, 1981), pp. 116–209, and Herbert Stein, *The Fiscal Revolution in America* (Chicago: University of Chicago Press, 1969).

2. Peter Temin, *Did Monetary Forces Cause the Great Depression?* (New York: W. W. Norton and Company, 1976); Milton Friedman and Anna Schwartz, *A Monetary History of the United States 1860–1960* (Princeton: Princeton University Press, 1963); Karl Brunner, ed., *The Great Depression Revisited* (Boston: Martinus Nijhoff, 1981).

3. Alexander Keyssar, "Men Out of Work: A Social History of Unemployment in Massachusetts, 1890–1916" (Ph.D. diss., Harvard University, 1977).

4. Alan Dawley, *Class and Community: The Industrial Revolution in Lynn* (Cambridge: Harvard University Press, 1976).

5. Alfred P. Sloan, *My Years with General Motors,* ed. John McDonald and Catharine Stevens (Garden City, N.Y.: Doubleday and Company, 1964), pp. 140–48.

6. Temin, *Did Monetary Forces?,* pp. 76–83 and 138–168, and David Brody, *Workers in Industrial America: Essays on the Twentieth Century Struggle* (New York: Oxford University Press, 1980), pp. 72–76.

7. Howell John Harris, *The Right to Manage: Industrial Relations Policies of American Business in the 1940s* (Madison: University of Wisconsin Press, 1982), p. 43.

8. We are indebted to Harry C. Katz, who originally called our attention to the provisions of this agreement. He reviews it in relation to more recent developments in Harry C. Katz, *Shifting Gears: Changing Labor Relations in the U.S. Auto Industry* (Cambridge, Mass.: MIT Press, forthcoming). For an analysis of the 1948 agreement made at that time, see Frederick H. Harbison, "The General Motors–United Auto Workers Agreement of 1950," *Journal of Political Economy* 58 (December 1950): 397–411; Arthur Ross, "The General Motors Wage Agreement of 1948," *The Review of Economics and Statistics* 31 (February 1949): 1–7; and M. W. Reder, "The Significance of the 1948 General Motors Agreement," *The Review of Economics and Statistics* 31 (February 1949): 7–14.

9. This discussion of postwar wage-setting procedures draws especially on Arthur Ross, *Trade Union Wage Policy* (Berkeley: University of California Press, 1948); O. Eckstein and T. Wilson, "The Determinants of Money Wages in American Industry," *Quarterly Journal of Economics,* vol. 76, no. 3 (August 1962); H. M. Levinson, *Determining Forces in Collective Wage Bargaining* (New York: John Wiley, 1966); George W. Taylor and Frank C. Peirson, eds., *New Concepts of Wage Determination* (New York: McGraw-Hill, 1957); Michael J. Piore, *Birds of Passage: Migrant Labor and Industrial Societies* (New York: Cambridge University Press, 1979); and Peter B. Doeringer and Michael J. Piore, *Internal Labor Markets and Manpower Analysis* (Lexington, Mass.: D. C. Heath and Company, 1971), pp. 69–92.

10. N. Arnold Tolles, "American Minimum Wage Laws: Their Purposes and Results," *Industrial Relations Research Association, Proceedings* 12 (1959): 116–48; Martin Neil Baily, "Stabilization Policy and Private Economic Behavior," *Brookings Papers on Economic Activity* 1 (1978): 11–59; and Leverett S. Lyon et al., *The National Recovery Administration: An Analysis and Appraisal* (Washington, D.C.: The Brookings Institution, 1935).

11. These tables belong to a larger literature on the differential behavioral characteristics of the pre- and post–World War II American economy. Most of that literature supports the basic contention of this chapter about the difference between the two periods. See, for example, Stanley Fischer, "Relative Shocks, Relative Price Variability, and Inflation," *Brookings Papers on Economic Activity* 2 (1981): 381–431; Philip Cagan, "Changes in the Recession Behavior of Wholesale Prices in the 1920s and Post–World War II," *Explorations in Economic Research* 2 (Winter 1975): 54–104; Jeffrey Sachs, "The Changing Cyclical Behavior of Wages and Prices: 1890–1976," *American Economic Review* 70, no. 1 (March 1980): 78–90; and Baily, "Stabilization Policy."

But some analysts contend that the basic behavioral characteristics are either essentially unchanged, or unchanged along one or more of the dimensions important for our argument.

Notes

See, in this regard, Robert J. Gordon, "A Consistent Characterization of a Near-Century of Price Behavior," *American Economic Review* 70 (May 1980): 243–49, and "Price Inertia and Policy Ineffectiveness in the United States, 1890–1980," *National Bureau of Economic Research,* Working Paper 744 (September 1981). Christine Duckworth Romer finds that in several cases the apparent increase in stability from the pre- to the postwar period is explained by a change in the composition of the statistical series. For the variability of relative prices, however, these changes account for only 30 percent of the decrease in the variance. See Christine Duckworth Romer, "Spurious Variability in Historical Time Series Data" (Ph.D. diss., Massachusetts Institute of Technology, 1984), and idem, "The Decline in Relative Price Variability and its Relationship to Inflation: A Figment of the Data?" (Paper prepared for the Department of Economics, Massachusetts Institute of Technology, January 1983).

12. Doeringer and Piore, *Internal Labor Markets.*

13. Ivar Berg, *Education and Jobs, The Great Training Robbery* (New York: Praeger, 1970); Richard Freeman, *The Overeducated American* (New York: Academic Press, 1976); The Carnegie Commission on Higher Education, *College Graduates and Jobs: Adjusting to a New Labor Market Situation.* (New York: McGraw-Hill, 1973); Christopher Jencks et al., *Inequality, A Reassessment of the Effect of Family and Schooling in America* (New York: Harper & Row, 1973).

14. The metals that are bought and sold under the U.S. government's strategic stockpile program vary from year to year. Copper, cobalt, tin, tungsten, platinum, and other metals that are import-dependent (chromium, manganese, titanium) are currently stockpiled. The General Services Administration administers the purchase and sale of these metals according to goals set by the Federal Emergency Management Administration. The precise targets are published in the semiannual *Stockpile Report to the Congress* (General Services Administration, Federal Preparedness Agency, Federal Emergency Management Agency). See also *Strategic Stockpiles,* Hearings before the Subcommittee on Preparedness of the Committee on Armed Services, U.S. Senate, 97th Congress, 2nd Session, 1982 (Washington, D.C.: U.S. Government Printing Office, 1982).

15. Federal-government outlays for defense amounted to 696 million dollars in 1929, 35,630 million dollars in 1955, and 47,179 million dollars in 1965. See U.S. Bureau of the Census, *Statistical History of the United States* (New York: Basic Books, 1976).

16. The private home-financing system was restructured principally through the creation of the Federal Housing Administration (home mortgages); the Federal Home Loan Bank Board and Bank System (savings and loan industry); the Federal Deposit Insurance Corporation and the Federal Savings and Loan Insurance Corporation (insurance on deposits of commercial banks, mutual-savings banks, and savings-and-loan associations); and the Federal National Mortgage Association (secondary-mortgage market). These institutions insured the acceptability of long-term, low-down-payment, fully amortized mortgages, and they provided large flows of capital into the mortgage market. For further details, see *Housing in the Seventies,* Hearings on Housing and Community Development Legislation, Pt. 3, U.S. Senate, 93rd Congress, 1st Session, 1973 (Washington, D.C.: U.S. Government Printing Office, 1973).

17. The origins and significance of these phrases are discussed in Collins, *Business Response to Keynes,* and Stein, *Fiscal Revolution in America.*

18. For the subsequent elaboration of the disjointed legal innovations of the New Deal, see Katherine Van Wezel Stone, "The Post-War Paradigm in American Labor Law," *Yale Law Journal* 90 (June 1981): 1509–80.

19. Arthur M. Schlesinger, Jr., *The Politics of Upheaval* (Boston: Houghton Mifflin, 1960), p. 389.

20. The following draws on the excellent synthesis in Theda Skocpol and Kenneth Finegold, "State Capacity and Economic Intervention in the Early New Deal," *Political Science Quarterly* 97 (Summer 1982): 255–78.

21. The Agricultural Adjustment Act was struck down by the Supreme Court on January 6, 1936, thereby precipitating a crisis for the Department of Agriculture and the whole New Deal. Within a mere seven weeks, the AAA was legislated back into existence through the efforts of the American Farm Bureau Federation, a farmers' lobby whose welfare, and that of its members, depended on the program. For a full description of the evolution of the American Farm Bureau Federation and the transformation of agricultural

318

politics in the United States in this period, see Grant McConnell, *The Decline of Agrarian Democracy* (Berkeley: University of California Press, 1959).

22. One of the clearest statements of the sophisticated underconsumptionist concept of the NRA—and indeed the whole first New Deal—is a review of the effects of Title I of the NIRA. This review was prepared by the President's Committee of Industrial Analysis in 1937, when it was already obvious how variously the legislation had been interpreted. Title I, the committee wrote, had

> a double purpose, including immediate rescue work and more enduring improvements. Of the two, the President set the immediate rescue work ahead of the planning for the longer pull. He said, "While we shall not neglect the second, the first is an emergency job. It has the right-of-way."

The first and more immediate recovery purpose in turn had its further dual aspect: (1) Reemployment, and (2) the starting up of business in the sense of (a) increased physical production and consumption and (b) improved earnings of business. Different emphasis was laid on these aspects of the recovery objectives by different groups whose proposals played a part in the drafting of the Act. Business groups tended to lay first emphasis on business earnings; while labor groups, who accepted the Act as a substitute for the Black-Connery 30-hour bill, tended to put first emphasis upon increased employment with at least maintenance if not improvement of real wages for the individual. But the language of the Act itself, especially the utterances of the President and of high administrative authorities in the National Recovery Administration, leave no doubt that in the official attitude of the Federal authorities increased production and consumption received first emphasis, with increase of the sum total of real wages as the primary means.

Referring again to the "movements and proposals out of which the act grew" and to the "utterances of the framers of the Act and of persons prominent in the Administration in its early stages," the authors of the report argued that the NRA was intended to create the institutional preconditions for realizing four economic policies:

1. The spreading of work through reduction of hours, without corresponding reduction of weekly earnings, but instead maintaining a living wage.

2. Increasing consumer purchasing power by increasing total wage distribution and by collective bargaining as to rates above the minima.

3. Affording opportunity for industries to cooperate in (a) eliminating competitive practices similar to those already considered unfair at law, and (b) limiting ruinously severe competition as such, but without raising prices sufficiently to neutralize the workers' increased buying power, and without price limitation beyond prohibition of sales below cost, among which open price systems were explicitly contemplated and may be taken as typical, while the possibility of occasional and exceptional limitations on production was indicated in the Act itself.

4. Incidental, so far as recovery was concerned, though well worth doing in itself, was the elimination of child labor.

From the *Report of the President's Committee of Industrial Analysis*, The National Recovery Administration (Washington, D.C.: Department of Commerce, 1937), pp. 9–10, 13.

23. See the account of the experience of the cotton-textile industry during this period in Louis Galambos, *The Emergence of a National Trade Association* (Baltimore: Johns Hopkins University Press, 1966), pp. 173–259.

24. Our analysis of the origins of American social-welfare legislation follows Ann Shola Orloff and Theda Skocpol, "Why Not Equal Protection? Explaining the Politics of Public Social Welfare in Britain and the United States, 1880s–1920s" (Paper presented at the Annual Meeting of the American Sociological Association, Detroit, September 2, 1983), and Theda Skocpol and John Ikenberry, "The Political Formation of the American Welfare State in Historical and Comparative Perspective" (Paper presented at the Annual Meeting of the American Sociological Association, San Francisco, September 7, 1982). For further literature, see the comprehensive bibliographies of both papers.

25. Some historians deny that there were two significantly different New Deals; and among those historians who do see a distinction, there is disagreement on the two New Deals' fundamental characteristics. A succinct statement of positions in the debate, with appropriate references, is Robert S. McElvaine, *The Great Depression: America, 1929–*

Notes

1941 (New York: Times Books, 1984), pp. 261–63.

26.   Again, the most illuminating synthesis of the relevant literature is by Skocpol and her collaborators. See Margaret Weir and Theda Skocpol, "State Structure and Social Keynesianism: Responses to the Great Depression in Sweden and the United States," *International Journal of Comparative Sociology* (January–April 1983): 4–29.

27.   See Sidney Fine, *Sit-Down* (Ann Arbor: University of Michigan Press, 1969).

28.   See, for example, Michele I. Naples, "Industrial Conflict and Its Implications for Productivity Growth," *American Economic Review, Papers and Proceedings,* vol. 71, no. 2 (May 1981): 36–41; idem, "The Structure of Industrial Relations, Labor Militance and the Rate of Growth of Productivity: The Case of U.S. Mining and Manufacturing 1953–1977" (Ph.D. diss., University of Massachusetts at Amherst, 1982); Samuel Bowles and Herbert Gintis, "The Crisis of Liberal Democratic Capitalism," *Politics and Society* 11, no. 1 (1982): 51–94, and Samuel Bowles, David M. Gordon, and Thomas E. Weisskopf, *Beyond the Waste Land: A Democratic Alternative to Economic Decline* (Garden City, N.Y.: Anchor Press, Doubleday, 1983), p. 70.

29.   The following account is informed by many interviews and discussions with industrial-relations practitioners, trade unionists, and managers who lived through the period, as well as a broad reading of the academic and practical literature on collective bargaining. Writings that reflect a similar interpretation include: Harris, *Right to Manage;* Ronald William Schatz, *Electrical Workers: A History of Labor at General Electric and Westinghouse, 1923-1960* (Champaign, Ill.: University of Illinois, 1983); Bert Cochran, *Labor and Communism: The Conflict that Shaped American Unions* (Princeton: Princeton University Press, 1977); Walter Galenson, *The CIO Challenge to the AFL: A History of the American Labor Movement 1935-1941* (Cambridge: Harvard University Press, 1960); and Sumner H. Slichter, James J. Healy, and E. Robert Livernash, *The Impact of Collective Bargaining on Management* (Washington, D.C.: The Brookings Institution, 1960). For a perceptive analysis of the way in which industrial-relations practice is embedded in a professional culture, see Deborah M. Kolb, *The Mediators* (Cambridge, Mass.: MIT Press, 1983).

30.   Harris, *Right to Manage,* pp. 52–56.

31.   On the management-labor boards and their antecedents, see Sanford M. Jacoby, "Union-Management Cooperation in the United States, 1915–45" (Paper prepared for the Graduate School of Management, University of California, Los Angeles, 1982), especially pp. 35–50. Golden's remarks—which summarize a plan put forward by Philip Murray, chairman of the Steel Workers Organizing Committee (and later of the CIO)—are cited on page 50.

32.   Neil W. Chamberlain, *The Union Challenge of Management Control* (New York: Harper, 1948), p. 41.

33.   Harris, *Right to Manage,* pp. 139–159.

34.   For an account of the "Cow Deal," see Sune Anders Söderpalm "Social Democratic Road to Power" in Steven Koblik, ed., *Sweden's Development from Poverty to Affluence* (Minneapolis: University of Minnesota Press, 1975), pp. 258–78.

Chapter 5

1.   The following account of the postwar trading system draws on Fred L. Block, *The Origins of International Economic Disorder: A Study of United States International Policy from World War II to the Present* (Berkeley: University of California Press, 1977), pp. 1–108, and John S. Odell, *U.S. International Monetary Policy: Markets, Power and Ideas as Sources of Change* (Princeton: Princeton University Press, 1982).

2.   The GATT was constructed on the ruins of efforts to create an elaborate International Trade Organization to adjudicate national restruction on commodity exchanges. For the origins and consolidation of the GATT, see Gerard Curzon, *Multilateral Commercial Diplomacy: The General Agreement on Tariffs and Its Impact on National Commercial Policies and Techniques* (London: Michael Joseph, 1965).

3.   For a discussion of the accounting problems in the determination of the U.S.

balance-of-payments position from 1950 to 1974, see Block, *Origins of International Economic Disorder,* pp. 140–63.

4.   John A. Lapp, *How to Handle Problems of Seniority* (New York: National Foreman's Institute, 1946).

5.   See Richard Herding, *Job Control and Union Structure* (Rotterdam: North Holland Press, 1972), and Christoph Köhler, *Betrieblicher Arbeitsmarkt und Gewerkschaftspolitik: innerbetriebliche Mobilität und Arbeitsplatzrechte in der amerikanischen Automobilindustrie* (Frankfurt am Main: Campus, 1981).

6.   For a comprehensive description of American postwar industrial relations, see Sumner H. Slichter, James J. Healy, and E. Robert Livernash, *The Impact of Collective Bargaining on Management* (Washington, D.C.: The Brookings Institution, 1960). For a narrower description of the dominant system, see Peter B. Doeringer and Michael J. Piore, *Internal Labor Markets and Manpower Analysis* (Lexington, Mass.: D. C. Heath and Company, 1971), pp. 1–113.

7.   Arthur M. Ross, "Do We Have a New Industrial Feudalism?" *American Economic Review* 48, no. 5 (1958): 903–20.

8.   Daniel Quinn Mills, *Industrial Relations and Manpower in Construction* (Cambridge, Mass.: MIT Press, 1972); Clinton Bourdon and Raymond E. Levitt, "A Comparison of Wages and Labor Management Practices in Union and Nonunion Construction," *Research Report,* Department of Civil Engineering, Massachusetts Institute of Technology, vol. 78, no. 3 (March 30, 1977). An excellent ethnography of American construction work—which underscores the features of industrial organization relevant to our argument—is Herbert A. Applebaum, *Royal Blue: The Culture of Construction Workers* (New York: Holt, Rinehart and Winston, 1981). On the craft organization of work, see generally Arthur L. Stinchcombe, "Bureaucratic and Craft Administration of Production," *Administrative Science Quarterly* 4 (September 1959): 168–87; and Charles F. Sabel, *Work and Politics* (Cambridge: Cambridge University Press, 1982) pp. 82–89.

9.   Leon Stein, ed., *Out of the Sweatshop: The Struggle for Industrial Democracy* (New York: Quadrangle, The New York Times Book Company, 1977), especially pages 273–305, and Jesse Thomas Carpenter, *Competition and Collective Bargaining in the Needle Trades 1910-1967* (Ithaca: New York State School of Industrial and Labor Relations, Cornell University, 1972).

10.   Although men's fashions have traditionally been less volatile than women's, they, too, change rapidly enough so that higher-quality producers must adapt some of the flexible forms of organization discussed in chapter 8. See, for example, Donald B. Strauss on work organization in the Rochester, New York, Hickey-Freeman Company, in Clinton S. Golden and Virginia D. Parker, *Causes of Industrial Peace* (New York: Harper and Brothers, 1955), pp. 121–38.

11.   Slichter et al., *Impact of Collective Bargaining,* pp. 523–25.

12.   Ibid., n. 15, p. 355.

13.   On shop-floor control in printing, see, for example, A. J. M. Sykes, "Trade-Union Workshop Organization in the Printing Industry: The Chapel," *Sociology* 1 (May 1967): 141–63.

14.   Harley Shaiken, "Technological Change and Shop-Floor Response" (Paper prepared for the Program in Science, Technology, and Society, Massachusetts Institute of Technology, 1982).

15.   Howell John Harris, *The Right to Manage: Industrial Relations Policies of American Business in the 1940s* (Madison: University of Wisconsin Press, 1982), pp. 74–89.

16.   For a characterization of this process, see Kenneth Thomas Strand, *Jurisdictional Disputes in Construction: The Causes, the Joint Board, and the NLRB* (Pullman: Bureau of Economic and Business Research, School of Economics and Business, Washington State University, 1961), and Slichter et al., *Impact of Collective Bargaining.* See also Mills, *Industrial Relations and Manpower in Construction,* pp. 19–21.

17.   Irving Bernstein, *The Lean Years* (Boston: Houghton Mifflin, 1972), and Richard Edwards, *Contested Terrain: The Transformation of the Workplace in the Twentieth Century* (New York: Basic Books, 1979).

18.   David Brody, "The Rise and Decline of Welfare Capitalism," in idem, *Workers in Industrial America: Essays on the Twentieth Century Struggle* (New York: Oxford University Press, 1980), pp. 48–81; and in the same spirit Daniel Nelson, "The Company

Notes

Union Movement, 1900–1937: A Reexamination," *Business History Review* 3 (Autumn 1982): 335–57.

19. Ford, for example, observed that assembly-line workers in his plants constantly devised small but significant improvements in tooling. See Henry Ford, in collaboration with Samuel Crowther, *My Life and Work* (Garden City: Doubleday, Page and Company, 1923), pp. 100–101.

20. Edwards, *Contested Terrain,* pp. 105–6.

21. Brody, "Rise and Decline," p. 56.

22. Ibid., pp. 56, 58.

23. H. Feldman, *The Regularization of Employment* (New York: Harper & Row, 1925), p. 64.

24. Brody, "Rise and Decline," p. 70.

25. Feldman, *Regularization of Employment,* pp. 262–68.

26. Brody, "Rise and Decline," p. 73.

27. Ibid., p. 68.

28. David Montgomery, *Workers' Control in America* (New York: Cambridge University Press, 1979), pp. 147–48.

29. Frederick H. Harbison, "Seniority in Mass-Production Industries," *The Journal of Political Economy* 48 (February–December 1940): 851–64; citation from pp. 851–52.

30. Slichter et al., *Impact of Collective Bargaining,* pp. 100–154, especially pp. 104–5 and 150–54.

31. Jack Steiber, *The Steel Industry Wage Structure* (Cambridge: Harvard University Press, 1959).

32. Slichter et al., *Impact of Collective Bargaining,* p. 561.

33. William Green to H. Feldman, June 1923, cited in Feldman, *Regularization of Employment,* p. 287.

34. The incident is described and Swope's remarks cited in Irving Bernstein, *The Turbulent Years: A History of the American Worker, 1936–41* (Boston: Houghton Mifflin, 1970), p. 603: the reason for the labor leader's inaction was, in Bernstein's judgment, "almost certainly ... that a proposal to create an industrial union in the electrical industry raised formidable problems for the Federation that William Green was incapable of surmounting."

Chapter 6

1. The following is based on Maurice Lévy-Leboyer, "The Large Corporation in Modern France," in Alfred D. Chandler, Jr., and Herman Daems, eds., *Managerial Hierarchies: Comparative Perspectives on the Rise of the Modern Industrial Enterprise* (Cambridge: Harvard University Press, 1980), pp. 117–60. For the influence of American technology on Renault and Citroën, see p. 134; for the connection between General Electric and the French utility Thomson-Houston, see p. 124; for the narrowness of French markets for consumption goods until after World War II, see pp. 122–23 and 131–32; for exports in large-scale industry as a share of production, see p. 148; for the various legal devices for assuring that "subsidies were given the opportunity to expand their operations in an independent fashion," see p. 144; and for the failure to grasp the logic of high-fixed-cost production until the 1930s, see pp. 134–37.

2. See Richard F. Kuisel, *Capitalism and the State in Modern France: Renovation and Economic Management in the Twentieth Century* (Cambridge: Cambridge University Press, 1981), pp. 1–92.

3. Peter Schöttler, "Politique sociale ou lutte des classes: notes sur le syndicalisme 'apolitique' des bourses du travail," *Le mouvement social* (September 1981): 3–20.

4. Bertrand Abhervé, "Les origines de la grève des métallurgistes parisiens, juin 1919," *Le mouvement social* (October 1975): pp. 74–85.

5. Lévy-Leboyer, "Large Corporation in Modern France," p. 135.

6. On the aims and failure of the Popular Front reforms see Val R. Lorwin, *The*

French Labor Movement (Cambridge: Harvard University Press, 1954), pp. 72–84.

7.   Henry W. Ehrmann, *Organized Business in France* (Princeton: Princeton University Press, 1957), pp. 76–90. Collective bargaining in the Vichy system was restricted to matters of "social welfare" and conducted through "social committees," composed of representatives of the employers, the workers, and the technicians and supervisors; see ibid., pp. 91–94, and Lorwin, *French Labor Movement*, p. 89.

8.   Ehrmann, *Organized Business in France*, pp. 62–63.

9.   See Kuisel, *Capitalism and the State in Modern France*, p. 187 ff.

10.   See Andrew Schonfield, *Modern Capitalism: The Changing Balance of Public and Private Power* (New York: Oxford University Press, 1965), pp. 128–29. Both citations are from p. 128.

11.   On the merger movement, see Bela Balassa, "The French Economy under the Fifth Republic, 1958–78," in William G. Andrews and Stanley Hoffmann, eds., *The Impact of the Fifth Republic on France* (Albany: State University of New York Press, 1981), pp. 117–38, especially p. 120.

12.   See the accounts referred to in note 41 of chapter 2.

13.   Lévy-Leboyer, "Large Corporation in Modern France," p. 117.

14.   François Sellier, *Stratégie de la lutte sociale* (Paris: Les Éditions Ouvrières, 1961), pp. 121–22.

15.   For a description of the Association Française pour l'Accroissement de la Productivité and the 450 "productivity missions" it sent to the United States between 1950 and 1953, see Luc Boltanski, *Les cadres: la formation d'un groupe social* (Paris: Les Éditions de Minuit, 1982), pp. 157–64.

16.   On the politics of the French minimum wage, see Sellier, *Stratégie de la lutte sociale*, pp. 127–141. For the relation among the minimum wage, trade-union strategy, and the industrial-classification system, see Michel Brossard, "La structure de l'organisation du travail dans l'entreprise et les pouvoirs dans le système de relations industrielles," (thèse pour le doctorat de 3e cycle, Université d'Aix-Marseilles, 1977), pp. 210–310.

17.   The Renault agreement included a section entitled "Efforts to Maintain and Improve Purchasing Power," which provided for both a cost-of-living escalator and a 4-percent annual wage increase as labor's share of expected increases in productivity. See R. Jaussaud, "L'accord Renault du 15 September 1955," *Droit social* 19 (January 1956): 16–24, and Pierre Lassegue, "La situation sociale," ibid.: 35–37.

18.   French exports as a share of GNP did in fact rise from 13.9 percent in 1960 to 22 percent in 1973: Alain Cotta, *Inflation et croissance en France depuis 1962* (Paris: Presses Universitaires de France, 1974), p. 155.

19.   Officials at the ministry of industry had to outmaneuver other bureaucracies in order to keep public and private spending for investment high: James Hackett and Annie-Marie Hackett, *Economic Planning in Modern France* (London: Allen and Unwin, 1963), pp. 32–33.

20.   In 1958, during the *plan de stabilisation*, a system of unemployment insurance was created. In 1967 the prime minister—on the recommendation of an industrial-relations panel—encouraged business and labor to do the following: to consider supplementing, by collective agreements, the unemployment-insurance system, and to provide compensation for workers placed on short workweeks; to create bipartite commissions to track industrial reorganization sector by sector, particularly regarding the effects of the concentration of production; and to provide advance notification of significant layoffs. These ideas were inspired by the innovative practices of Alsatian steel firms, which provided workers substantial protection against displacement. See Yves DeLamotte, "L'accord interprofessional sur la sécurité de l'emploi du 10 février 1969," *Droit social* (September–October 1969): 498–508.

21.   Robert Boyer, "Les salaires en longue période," *Population active* (September 1978): 27–57, especially p. 47.

22.   On the post–May 1968 reforms, see Jean-Daniel Reynaud, *Les syndicats, les patrons, et l'état* (Paris: Les Éditions Ouvrières, 1978), pp. 13–42.

23.   Michele Salvati, "May 1968 and the Hot Autumn of 1969: The Responses of Two Ruling Classes," in Suzanne D. Berger, *Organizing Interests in Western Europe* (Cambridge: Cambridge University Press, 1981), pp. 329–63, especially p. 332.

Notes

24. Marc Maurice, François Sellier, and Jean-Jacques Silvestre, "La production de la hiérarchie dans l'entreprise: recherche d'un effet sociétal," *Revue française de sociologie* 20 (April 1979): 331–80.

25. M. B. Brodie, *Fayol on Administration* (London: Lyon, Grant and Green, 1967); and on Fayol's formative experience as a mining engineer and administrator, see Donald Reid, "The Origins and Genesis of *Fayolisme,*"Working Paper, Department of History, University of North Carolina, 1984.

26. A standard overview of German industrialization up to World War I is Knut Borchardt, "The Industrial Revolution in Germany, 1700–1914," in Carlo M. Cipolla, ed., *The Fontana Economic History of Europe* 4, pt. 1: 76–160.

27. See Jürgen Kocka, "The Rise of the Modern Industrial Enterprise in Germany," in Chandler and Daems, *Managerial Hierarchies,* pp. 77–116, especially p. 78 (for the prewar growth rate) and pp. 87–89 (for the legal and market preconditions of forming cartels).

28. On the marriage of iron and rye, see Alexander Gerschenkron, *Bread and Democracy in Germany* (Berkeley: University of California Press, 1943). On the naval-rearmament, see Eckart Kehr, *Schlactflottenbau und Parteipolitik, 1894–1901* (Berlin: Vaduz, Uraus, 1965).

29. Kocka, "Rise of Modern Industrial Enterprise in Germany," pp. 89–90 (on the role of the banks), and p. 95 (on the connection between industry and university science).

30. Ibid., pp. 99, 104.

31. Hans Jürgen Teutenberg, *Geschichte der Industriellen Mitbestimmung in Deutschland* (Tübingen: J. C. B. Mohr [Paul Siebeck], 1961).

32. On the changing strategies and counterstrategies of the state, labor, and capital in this period, see Klaus Schönhoven, *Expansion und Konzentration: Studien zur Entwicklung der Freien Gewerkschaften im Wilhelmischen Deutschland 1890 bis 1914* (Stuttgart: Klett-Cotta, 1980).

33. In 1928 the German share of total exports of chemicals and metal goods (machines and vehicles), among the eight most industrialized European countries and the United States, were 43 and 30 percent, respectively: see David Abraham, *The Collapse of the Weimar Republic* (Princeton: Princeton University Press, 1981), table 20, p. 149. Between 1926 and 1930, Germany was the only European country not running a trade deficit; in 1929, it was the third largest industrial exporter, behind the United States and Great Britain; and by 1931, as German industry rode out the Depression better than the competition, it achieved first place: ibid., p. 150.

34. On the German steel industry, see Bernd Weisbrod, *Schwerindustrie in der Weimarer Republik* (Wuppertal: Hammer Verlag, 1978).

35. Dietmar Petzina and Werner Abelhausen, "Zum Problem der relativen Stagnation der deutschen Wirtschaft in den zwanziger Jahren," in Hans Mommsen, Dietmar Petzina, and Bernd Weisbrod, eds., *Industrielles System und politische Entwicklung in der Weimarer Republik* (Düsseldorf: Droste Verlag, 1974), pp. 57–76; figures from page 73.

36. On the factory councils, see Peter von Oertzen, *Betriebsräte in der Novemberrevolution* (Düsseldorf: Droste Verlag, 1963).

37. See Hans-Hermann Hartwich, *Arbeitsmarkt, Verbände, und Staat* (Berlin: Walter de Gruyter and Co., 1967).

38. On the realignment of German industry, see Abraham, *Collapse of the Weimar Republik.*

39. The vicissitudes of the trade-union reflation plan are described in Robert A. Gates, "Von der Sozialpolitik zur Wirtschaftpolitik? das Dilemma der deutschen Sozialdemokratie in der Krise 1929–33," in Mommsen et al., *Industrielles System in der Weimarer Republik,* pp. 206–25, and Michael Schneider, *Das Arbeitsbeschaffungsprogramm des ADGB* (Bonn-Bad Godesberg: Verlag Neue Gesellschaft, 1975).

40. Reinhard Doleschal, "Zur geschichtlichten Entwicklung des Volkswagenkonzerns," in Reinhard Doleschal and Rainer Dombois, eds., *Wohin läuft VW? die Automobilproduktion in der Wirtschaftskrise* (Reinbek bei Hamburg: Rowohlt, 1982), pp. 18–54.

41. For the role of an undervalued currency in West Germany's postwar success, see Wilhelm Hankel, "Germany: Economic Nationalism in the International Economy," in Wilfrid L. Kohl and Giorgio Basevi, *West Germany: A European and Global Power* (Lexington, Mass.: D. C. Heath and Company, 1980), pp. 21–43.

42. These figures are reported in Josef Esser, Wolfgang Fach, and Georg Simonis, "Grenzprobleme des 'Modells Deutschland,' " *Prokla* 10, no. 3 (1980): 40–63, especially p. 43.

43. William Fellner et al., *The Problem of Rising Prices* (Paris: OECD, 1961), pp. 323–55, quotation p. 352.

44. On the consolidation of the postwar system of industrial relations, see Theo Pirker, *Die blinde Macht* (Munich: Mercator, 1960). On the relation between factory councils and trade unions, see Gernot Müller, Ulrich Rödel, Charles F. Sabel, Frank Stille, and Winfried Vogt, *Ökonomische Krisentendenzen im gegenwärtigen Kapitalismus* (Frankfurt am Main: Campus, 1978), pp. 281–321.

45. These changes in the organization of West German factory production are analyzed in a series of case studies by the Institut für Sozialwissenschaftliche Forschung in Munich. See, for example, Friedrich Weltz, Gert Schmidt, and Jürgen Sass, *Facharbeiter im Industriebetrieb* (Frankfurt am Main: Athenäum, 1974).

46. Our account of macroeconomic return follows Jeremiah Michael Riemer, "Crisis and Intervention in the West German Economy: A Political Analysis of Changes in the Policy Machinery during the 1960s and 1970s" (Ph.D. diss., Cornell University, 1983).

47. Karl Schiller, *Kieler Vorträge*, new series, n. 54, Kiel, 1968.

48. Rainer Deppe, Richard Herding, and Dietrich Hoss, "Gewerkschaftliche Organisation und politische Orientierung der Arbeiterschaft," in Rolf Ebbighausen, ed., *Bürgerlicher Staat und politische Legitimation* (Frankfurt am Main: Suhrkamp), pp. 380–410.

49. For an account of these shop-floor conflicts, see Betriebszelle Ford der Gruppe Arbeiterkampf, eds., *Arbeiterkampf: Streik bei Ford Köln* (Erlangen: Politikladen, 1973).

50. Burkart Lutz and Guido Kammerer, *Das Ende des graduierten Ingenieurs? eine empirische Analyse unerwarteter Nebenfolgen der Bildungsexpansion* (Frankfurt am Main: Europäische Verlagsanstalt, 1975).

51. On Italian industrialization up to World War I, see Richard Webster, *Industrial Imperialism in Italy* (Berkeley: University of California Press, 1975).

52. Valerio Castronovo, *Giovanni Agnelli: la FIAT dal 1899 al 1945* (Turin: Giulio Einaudi, 1977).

53. Valerio Castronovo, "La storia economica," in *Storia d'Italia* (Turin: Giulio Einaudi, 1975) 4:179.

54. Martin Clark, *Antonio Gramsci and the Revolution that Failed* (New Haven: Yale University Press, 1977).

55. For the rise of the Fascists and Mussolini's economic policies (described next), see Castronovo, "Storia," pp. 265–72.

56. M. V. Posner and S. J. Woolf, *Italian Public Enterprise* (Cambridge: Harvard University Press, 1967).

57. Daniel Horowitz, *The Italian Labor Movement* (Cambridge, Mass.: Harvard University Press, 1963).

58. The following summarizes the account of post–World War II developments in Italy that appears in Charles F. Sabel, *Work and Politics* (Cambridge University Press, 1982), pp. 145–67, which contains further references.

59. This paragraph and the next are based on Rodney Clark, *The Japanese Company* (New Haven: Yale University Press, 1979), pp. 18–21. See also Thomas C. Smith, *The Agrarian Origins of Modern Japan* (Palo Alto: Stanford University Press, 1959).

60. On the complex mixture of tradition and innovation in Japanese industrial organization in this period, see Johannes Hirschmeier and Tsunehiko Yui, *The Development of Japanese Business, 1600–1973* (Cambridge: Harvard University Press, 1975), pp. 70–144.

61. See Takafusa Nakamura, *Economic Growth in Prewar Japan*, trans. Robert A. Feldman (New Haven: Yale University Press, 1983), pp. 73, 144, and 73–93 (on the sequence of Japanese industrialization) and pp. 157–73 (on the role of government spending in stimulating demand in the 1920s).

62. Clark, *The Japanese Company*, pp. 38–41.

63. Nakamura, *Economic Growth in Prewar Japan*, pp. 220–31.

64. Ibid., pp. 232–63, traces Japanese developments in the 1930s.

65. On the creation of plant unions, see Haruo Shimada, "Perceptions and Reality of Japanese Industrial Relations: Their Role in Japan's Industrial Success" (Paper presented

to the Industrial Relations Seminar, Sloan School of Management, Massachusetts Institute of Technology, October 1982). A shorter version of this paper, entitled "Japan's Postwar Industrial Growth and Labor Management Relations," is published in the *Proceedings of the Thirty-fifth Annual Meeting of the Industrial Relations Research Association,* December 28–30, 1982, New York, pp. 241–48. For the interwar precedents of plant unions, see Taishiro Shirai, "A Theory of Enterprise Unionism," in idem, ed., *Contemporary Industrial Relations in Japan* (Madison: University of Wisconsin Press, 1983), pp. 117–43, especially pp. 121–24.

66. "Japanese firms confine their activities not simply to a particular industry but to a mere part of the process of manufacture or distribution necessary to the industry, and sub-contract the other parts of the process to specialized firms": Clark, *The Japanese Company,* p. 56. If a large firm wants to enter a new market, he continues, "it frequently does so by setting up a subsidiary company to undertake the business. Or, if the large firm does begin to make a new product or offer a new service on its own account, it commonly separates off the divisions and departments involved at an early opportunity": ibid., p. 60. But a new firm formed this way differs crucially from an American subsidiary in that it is "normally expected to achieve still greater independence of its parent company as it succeeds in the business for which it was established. As the subsidiary grows, its management becomes ever less subservient to the management of the parent": ibid., p. 61.

67. Kazuo Koike, "Internal Labor Markets: Workers in Large Firms," in Shirai, *Contemporary Industrial Relations in Japan,* pp. 29–61, especially pp. 40–50.

68. Shimada, "Perceptions and Reality of Japanese Industrial Relations," pp. 23 ff.

69. John Zysman, *Government, Markets, and Growth: Financial Systems and the Politics of Industrial Change* (Ithaca: Cornell University Press, 1983).

70. Chalmers Johnson, *MITI and the Japanese Miracle: The Growth of Industrial Policy, 1925-1975* (Palo Alto: Stanford University Press, 1983).

71. See Michael W. Donnelly, "Setting the Price of Rice: A Study in Political Decisionmaking," in T. J. Pempel, ed. *Policymaking in Contemporary Japan* (Ithaca: Cornell University Press, 1977), pp. 143–200. For the dispersion of industry to the countryside, see Ronald P. Dore, *Shinohata: A Portrait of a Japanese Village* (New York: Pantheon, 1978), p. 110.

72. For a description of these technical centers, see Houdaille Industries, Inc., "Petition to the President of the United States Through the Office of the United States Trade Representative for the Exercise of Presidential Discretion Authorized by Section 103 for the Revenue Act of 1971" (26 U.S.C. 48 [a] [7] [D], May 3, 1982).

Chapter 7

1. A view of the crisis as the product of less fundamental mistakes is developed in Alan S. Blinder, *Economic Policy and the Great Stagflation* (New York: Academic Press, 1979).

2. This argument is most clearly developed in the Samuel P. Huntington, Michel Crozier, and Joji Watanuki, *The Crisis of Democracy: Report on the Governability of Democracies to the Trilateral Commission* (New York: New York University Press, 1975). A variation on this theme is that changes in social stratification intensified social conflict. See John H. Goldthorpe, "The Current Inflation: Towards a Sociological Approach," in Fred Hirsh and John H. Goldthorpe, eds., *The Political Economy of Inflation* (Cambridge: Harvard University Press, 1978), pp. 186–214.

3. See, for example, Samuel Bowles and Herbert Gintis, "Crisis of Liberal Democratic Capitalism: The Case of the United States," *Politics and Society,* vol. 11, no. 1 (1982): 51–94. Like Huntington—who attributes the governability crisis to an "excess" of democracy—Bowles and Gintis argue that there are fundamental contradictions between liberal democracy with mass participation, on the one hand, and capitalism, on the other. But though their solutions diverge, this convergence in the analyses of both liberal and radical theorists is striking.

4. The following view is worked out in detail in Charles F. Sabel, *Work and Politics* (Cambridge: Cambridge University Press, 1982), and Michael J. Piore, *Birds of Passage* (Cambridge, Mass.: Cambridge University Press, 1979).

5. Sabel, *Work and Politics,* pp. 132–136.

6. Suzanne Berger and Michael J. Piore, *Dualism and Discontinuity in Industrial Societies* (New York: Cambridge University Press, 1980), pp. 33–41.

7. For a discussion of the events leading up to the U.S. devaluation, see Council of Economic Advisors, *Economic Report of the President and the Annual Report of the Council of Economic Advisors, 1972* (Washington, D.C.: U.S. Government Printing Office, 1972), pp. 142–75. See also the discussions of international economic policy in the reports for 1970, 1971, and 1973.

8. Ibid. 1972, pp. 149–50.

9. The abandonment of the fixed-exchange-rate system seems almost inevitable. Even in 1970, U.S. exports counted for less than 6 percent of GNP, the smallest of any of the industrial countries' shares, and considerably smaller than all but Japan's. Therefore, the decision makers believed that subordinating domestic economic policy to trade considerations was like letting the tail wag the dog. Moreover, major institutional adjustments would have been required to accommodate an international orientation of domestic policy, and it is doubtful whether such adjustments could have been made. For the wage-and-price control system that was part of the program that set the dollar afloat exempted contractual cost-of-living escalators—essential to the postwar regulatory system—and it would have been necessary to prohibit such provisions in order to maintain a fixed exchange rate. And even if the government had tried to do so, the unions would never have agreed to another vital aspect of the stabilization plan: wage controls. Such major accommodations to international pressure would have been more likely had there been a consensus that the mass-production industries under foreign attack were crucial to America's long-term growth. But there was not.

10. This expansionary alternative had strong proponents during the 1970s. In fact, according to Robert D. Putnam and Nicholas Bayne, a model of world Keynesianism was at the heart of international economic diplomacy from 1977 to 1978. At the London summit conference in 1977, the British, the Americans, and the OECD (Organization for Economic Cooperation and Development) secretariat rallied behind a program of coordinated fiscal stimulus: they proposed that Germany, Japan, and the United States be the "locomotives" for a global economic recovery. Although Japan and Germany initially opposed this alliance, they finally agreed (at Bonn in July 1978) to join the United States in implementing expansionary policies. But this experiment with global reflation was short-lived, for the United States sharply tightened its monetary policy in November 1978. The severity of the subsequent recession, deficits, and inflation in the "locomotive" countries was due more to the 1979 oil shock and high U.S. interest rates than to the modest fiscal expansion agreed upon at Bonn. See Robert D. Putnam and Nicholas Bayne, *Hanging Together: The Seven-Power Summits* (Cambridge, Mass.: Harvard University Press, 1984), pp. 67–99.

11. Milton Friedman, "The Case for Flexible Exchange Rates," in idem., *Essays in Positive Economics* (Chicago: University of Chicago Press, 1956), pp. 157–203.

12. Rudiger Dornbusch, "Equilibrium and Disequilibrium Exchange Rates," *Zeitschrift für Wirtschafts- und Sozialwissenschaften,* v. 102, n. 6 (1982): 573–99.

13. In principle, excessive movements of foreign holdings of dollars could be corrected by compensating changes in the U.S. interest rates, which of course affect the value of wealth stored in dollars. But the interest rate is a major instrument for regulating the domestic economy; and to use it to control the exchange rate would make the domestic economy hostage to foreign trade in essentially the same way that it was hostage under a regime of fixed rates and limited international liquidity.

14. Council of Economic Advisors, *Economic Report* for 1983, pp. 61–70; Rudiger Dornbusch, "Exchange Rate Economics: Where Do We Stand?" and subsequent discussion in *Brookings Papers on Economic Activity* 1 (1980): 143–207.

15. Council of Economic Advisors, *Economic Report* for 1975, pp. 160–186; and for 1980, pp. 147–55.

16. The figures given are for subcompact cars, including imports. Between 1967 and 1975, sales of standard and luxury models fell from 60 to 22 percent of the U.S. market.

Notes

By 1980, small cars (both subcompacts and compacts) accounted for 62 percent of new-car sales in the United States. See National Academy of Engineering, Committee on Technology and International Economic and Trade Issues, Auto Panel, *The Competitive Status of the U.S. Auto Industry* (Washington, D.C.: National Academy Press, 1982), pp. 65–75.

17. International Monetary Fund, *International Financial Statistics Yearbook, 1983* (Washington, D.C.: IMF, 1983), pp. 157–58.

18. William H. Branson, "Trends in International Trade and Investment Since World War II," in Martin Feldstein, ed., *The American Economy in Transition* (Chicago: University of Chicago Press, 1980), table 33, p. 188.

19. The rise of bank-debt-financed, government-led industrialization in the developing countries is examined by Jeff Frieden, "Third World Indebted Industrialization: International Finance and State Capitalism in Mexico, Brazil, Algeria, and South Korea," *International Organization*, vol. 35, no. 3 (Summer 1981): 407–31.

20. Branson, "Trends in International Trade," table 3.13, p. 194. See the following World Bank Staff Working Papers (Washington, D.C.) for further details: Hollis B. Chenery and Donald B. Keesing, "The Changing Composition of Developing Country Exports," no. 314 (January 1979), and Donald B. Keesing, "World Trade and Output of Manufactures: Structural Trends and Developing Countries' Exports," no. 316 (June 1980).

21. Motor Vehicle Manufacturers Association, *Motor Vehicle Facts and Figures*, 1981, p. 7. For details on the changing role of the automotive industry in the industrializing Latin American countries, see Rhys Owen Jenkins, *Dependent Industrialization in Latin America: the Automotive Industry in Argentina, Chile, and Mexico* (New York: Praeger Publishers, 1977).

22. GDP-deflator data from International Monetary Fund, *Yearbook, 1983.*

23. Council of Economic Advisors, *Economic Report* for 1982, table B-67. See also Organization for Economic Cooperation and Development, *Economic Surveys: The United States* (Paris: OECD, 1982), diagram 7, p. 31.

24. Motor Vehicle Manufacturers Association, *Motor Vehicle Facts and Figures*, 1981, p. 28 and 1950, p. 27. The response of automobile manufacturers to this stagnation of the U.S. market was to shift attention to the still growing European market and the potentially huge third-world markets; see "To a Global Car," *Business Week*, November 20, 1978, pp. 102–13.

25. U.S. Bureau of the Census, *Statistical Abstract of the United States: 1970*, 91st ed. (Washington, D.C.: U.S. Government Printing Office, 1970), pp. 496 (for televisions) and 687 (for other electrical appliances).

26. See Herbert Giersch, ed., *On the Economics of Intra-Industry Trade: Symposium 1978 (Institut für Weltwirtschaft an der Universität Kiel)* (Tübingen: J. C. B. Mohr [Paul Siebeck], 1979).

27. Robert Z. Lawrence, "World Manufactured Goods Trade" (Paper prepared for the Chinese Academy of Social Sciences, Brookings Institution Conference on International Economic Relations, Beijing, May 31–June 4, 1982) (mimeographed), table 1, p. 4.

28. Ibid., table 2, p. 5.

29. Ibid., table 3, p. 7.

30. This is the view of ibid., p. 6.

31. *Ward's Automotive Yearbook, 1982*, p. 112.

32. American Iron and Steel Institute, *Annual Statistical Report* (Washington, D.C.: American Iron and Steel Institute) for 1960 (pp. 100, 106, and 134), and for 1980 (p. 8); William T. Hogan, *The 1970s: Critical Years for Steel* (Lexington, Mass.: D. C. Heath and Co., 1972), table 3.3, p. 49.

33. U.S. Bureau of the Census, *U.S. Commodity Exports and Imports as Related to Output* (Washington, D.C.: U.S. Government Printing Office, 1982), p. 28.

34. Lawrence, "World Manufactured Goods Trade," table 6, p. 23.

35. Recent economic transformations in these two groups of countries have posed an analytic problem—or at least a problem in terminology—for leftist economists. Unlike neoclassical economists, and like the leaders in the industrializing world, the leftist economists believe that specialization condemns the industrializing countries to subservience to the industrial centers. They therefore believe that economic progress in the third-world

328

is possible only if the advanced countries' domination of world trade (as seen in the terms of trade for primary commodities and manufactured goods) is overthrown. The problem with this theory is that one can no longer dismiss changes in the industrializing economies as the "development of underdevelopment"—but neither can one call these countries equal partners of the advanced countries (Mexico is not telling the United States how to balance *its* budget)—let alone precursors of an advanced socialist economy of the future. Some writers refer to "dependent development"; others, to a "new bourgeoisie and the limits of dependency." The designations for this economic form proliferate, but they do not clarify this uneasy balance of autonomy and subjugation. See Peter Evans, *Dependent Development: The Alliance of Multinational, State, and Local Capital in Brazil* (Princeton: Princeton University Press, 1979), and David G. Becker, *The New Bourgeoisie* and *The Limits of Dependency: Mining, Class, and Power in "Revolutionary" Peru* (Princeton: Princeton University Press, 1983).

36. Marshall Sahlins, *Culture and Practical Reason* (Chicago: University of Chicago Press, 1976).

37. Nathan Rosenberg, "Economic Development and the Transfer of Technology: Some Historical Perspectives," in idem, *Perspectives on Technology* (Cambridge: Cambridge University Press, 1976), pp. 151–172, especially p. 158.

38. The late-nineteenth-century French department store, for example, represents an alternative to the U.S. department store, which it superficially resembles. Like Macy's, in New York, or Wanamaker's, in Philadelphia, the Parisian Bon Marché was a large bureaucratic organization that depended on high-volume, low-margin sales. But unlike its American analogue, the French department store drew on highly flexible industrial districts to produce its wares, often to its own specifications; and the Bon Marché and other *grands magasins* provided their clients with the opportunity to customize these goods still further with extensive in-store alterations. Such stores used the railroad network to make the flexible production capacities of the scattered districts more accessible to the country as a whole, rather than to homogenize the market. See Michael B. Miller, *The Bon Marché: Bourgeois Culture and the Department Store, 1968–1920* (Princeton: Princeton University Press, 1981); although this book underscores the similarities between the French and American stores, references to the locations of the Bon Marché's purchasing houses (Lyon, Roubaix, Saint-Étienne, London) and its putting-out practices suggest that the similarities masked crucial differences (see pp. 56–57). Nevertheless, as in much writing on industrialization, the book assumes that growth and technological sophistication were synonymous with standardization—as in the reference to the Alsatian cotton industry as an example of mass production (see pp. 32–33).

Chapter 8

1. George Gilder, *Wealth and Poverty* (New York: Basic Books, 1981), p. 76.

2. Robert R. Reich, *The Next American Frontier* (New York: Times Books, 1983), pp. 140–75, and Barry Bluestone and Bennett Harrison, *The Deindustrialization of America* (New York: Basic Books, 1982), pp. 40–41, 150–60.

3. Federal Trade Commission, Bureau of Economics, *Statistical Report on Mergers and Acquisitions* (Washington, D.C.: U.S. Government Printing Office, August 1980), p. 110.

4. Marina von Neuman Whitman, "Automobiles: Turning Around on a Dime?" *Challenge* 24 (May–June 1981): 37–39.

5. On the reorganization of the French steel industry, see William T. Hogan, *World Steel in the 1980s: A Case of Survival* (Lexington, Mass.: D. C. Heath and Company, 1983), pp. 27–28.

6. For the shift to giant coastal steel plants in Japan, see Kiyoshi Kawahito, *The Japanese Steel Industry* (New York: Praeger, 1972).

7. See, for example, the account of the growing militancy of automobile workers in São Paulo, in John Humphrey, *Capitalist Control and Workers' Struggle in the Brazilian Auto Industry* (Princeton: Princeton University Press, 1982).

8. Brazil, for example, led the way in Latin America in this regard. By 1962, all but 1 or 2 percent of the total weight of vehicles manufactured in the country by foreign firms consisted of locally produced parts. Argentina quickly followed suit. See Rhys Owen Jenkins, *Dependent Industrialization in Latin America: The Automobile Industry in Argentina, Chile, and Mexico* (New York: Praeger Publishers, 1977), pp. 52–53.

9. Roger Rowand, "New Just-in-Time Systems Called Boom for Midwest," *Automobile News,* October 11, 1982, pp. 1, 8; Amal Nag, "GM Is Said to Seek Long-Term Accords with Steelmakers," *The Wall Street Journal,* May 6, 1983, p. 2.

10. "Detroit Is Out of Synch with Its Market Again," *Business Week,* April 18, 1983, pp. 30–31.

11. The account of the evolution of IBM and the computer market is based on Franklin M. Fisher, John J. McGowan, and Joen E. Greenwood, *Folded, Spindled, and Mutilated: Economic Analysis and U.S. v. IBM* (Cambridge, Mass.: MIT Press, 1983), pp. 53–60 (on the merging of business and scientific markets, culminating in the development of the 360), pp. 100–130 (on alternative definitions and estimates of IBM's market share), and p. 290 (on the decision in 1961 to develop the 360).

12. Andrew Pollack, "Big I.B.M. Has Done It Again," *New York Times,* March 27, 1983, section 3, pp. 1, 28; p. 1 cites figures on the production of micro, or personal, computers.

13. "IBM's Personal Computer Spawns an Industry," *Business Week,* August 15, 1983, pp. 88–89.

14. Pollack, "Big I.B.M.," p. 1.

15. The following statistics are from *Organization for Economic Cooperation and Development, Steel in the 1980s: Paris Symposium* (Paris: OECD, 1980), p. 96 (developing country shares in world steel production); table 7, p. 91 (average annual growth rates of developing-country steel exports); p. 46 (estimate of number of world-market competitors); p. 23 (Japanese steel-production projections and actual capacity-utilization rates). An excellent survey of the steel industry, which focuses on U.S. production, is Donald F. Barnett and Louis Schorsch, *Steel: Upheaval in a Basic Industry* (Cambridge, Mass.: Ballinger Publishing Company, 1983).

16. A good survey of conventional and innovative steel-making technologies is Julian Szekely, "Radically Innovative Steelmaking Technologies," *Metallurgical Transactions (B),* 11B (September 1980): 353–71.

17. Alice M. Greene, "World Steelmakers Chase a Higher Quality Steel," *Iron Age,* December 7, 1981, p. MP-7.

18. On Thyssen's specialty steels, see David B. Tinnin, "Reforging an Old Steelmaker," *Fortune,* June 16, 1980, pp. 113–18.

19. For an illustration of the price range in 1980 of steel products, see the quotations from the Milan metal market in Istituto Regionale di Ricerc della Lombardia, *Siderurgia lombarda* (Milan: Franco Angeli, 1981), p. 103.

20. Hence the growing interest in smaller-rolling mills that make it possible to turn out a variety of products. See George J. McManus, "A New Challenge Takes Shape in Rolling Mills," *Iron Age,* September 6, 1982, pp. MP-8–MP-36.

21. Alice M. Greene, "Steelmaking Controls Give Quality, Throughput and Energy Efficiency," *Iron Age,* March 1, 1982, p. MP-7.

22. George J. McManus, "Continuous Casting: Why More Companies Are Making a Commitment," *Iron Age,* February 7, 1983, pp. MP-4–MP-20.

23. Barnett and Schorsch, *Steel: Upheaval in a Basic Industry,* p. 88.

24. Office of Technology Assessment, *Technology and Steel Industry Competitiveness* (Washington, D.C.: OTA, Congress of the United States, June, 1980), p. 256.

25. George J. McManus, "Low Costs and High Quality: The One-Two Punch of the Electric Furnace," *Iron Age,* January 3, 1983, MP-7–MP-20.

26. Ingrid Drexel and Christoph Nuber, *Qualifizierung für Industriearbeit im Umbruch: die Ablösung von Anlernung durch Ausbildung in Grossbetrieben von Stahl und Chemie* (Frankfurt am Main: Campus, 1979), especially pp. 37–94.

27. Barnett and Schorsch, *Steel: Upheaval in a Basic Industry.* p. 93, and interview with Gordon Forward, Chaparral Steel Co., Midlothian, Tex., March 23, 1981.

28. Ibid., table 4-4, p. 97.

29. Istituto Regional di Ricerca della Lombardia, *Siderurgia,* pp. 144–48, documents

the Brescian mini-mills' success in modernizing and expanding during the 1970s.

30. "Einfach geweigert," *Der Spiegel*, no.49, December 5, 1983, pp. 86–89; discussions between 1981 and 1983 with officials of the OeIAG, the holding company that controls the country's major steel-making firms.

31. *The Kline Guide to the Chemical Industry*, 3rd ed., ed. Mary K. Meegan (Fairfield, N.J.: Charles H. Kline, 1977), pp. 20–22, distinguishes *true commodities* (produced in high volume according to conventional specifications), *specialty chemicals* (low-volume custom products) and *pseudo-commodities* (custom products manufactured in large volumes).

32. James R. Hickey, "Performance Chemicals: An Overview," in *Trends in Performance Chemicals: Papers Presented at the February, 1979, Meeting of the Chemical Marketing Research Association, San Francisco* (Staten Island, N.Y.: Chemical Marketing Research Association, 1979), pp. 6–7 and tables 3 and 4, p. 16.

33. "Du Pont: Seeking a Future in Biosciences," *Business Week*, November 24, 1980, pp. 86–98; Lee Smith, "Dow vs. Du Pont: Rival Formulas for Leadership," *Fortune*, September 10, 1979, pp. 74–84.

34. Winston Williams, "Dow Broadens Product Lines," *New York Times*, February 11, 1981, p. D1.

35. The citation is from "Beware the Specialties Fad," *Chemical Week*, October 14, 1981, p. 3, and it refers to the behavior of large European producers reported in the same issue of this trade journal, pp. 40–42.

36. David Webber, "New Chemical Business Recovery May Be Very Different," *Chemical Engineering*, January 10, 1983, pp. 14–17. The citation is from page 14.

37. John C. Bolen, "Amazing Grace," *Barron's*, December 8, 1980, pp. 41–45.

38. Patricia L. Layman, "Eastman's Big Investment Drive Nears Peak," *Chemical Engineering*, November 19, 1982, pp. 9–12, reports a Kodak executive saying, "Anybody building plants now has to put flexibility into the feedstocks" (p. 10).

39. Interview with Sheldon Buckler, vice president for non-photographic products (worldwide), Polaroid Corporation, Cambridge, Mass., April 13, 1981.

40. Drexel and Nuber, *Qualifizierung für Industriearbeit im Umbruch*, especially pp. 33–37, and 95–122.

41. Layman, "Eastman's Big Investment Drive," p. 12.

42. For an analysis of the connection between the automation of textile production and its migration south, see John S. Hekman, "The Product Cycle and New England Textiles," *Quarterly Journal of Economics* (June 1980): 679–717.

43. Data on employment in the 1960s and '70s and experts for 1970 and 1977 are from Gianni Lorenzoni, *Una politica innovativa nelle piccole medie imprese* (Milan: Etas Libri, 1979), pp. 1–2 and 37, respectively. Estimates for 1982 are from Ezio Avigdor, "Il caso Prato" (Paper presented to the seminar Innovazione Tecnologica, Ruolo della Piccola Impresa ed Intervento del Governo Locale, organized by the Regione Piemonte, Turin, February 25, 1983), p. 3.

44. Lorenzoni, *Una politica innovativa*, p. 14; Avigdor, "Il caso Prato," pp. 2–3.

45. Lorenzoni, *Una politica innovativa*, pp. 16, 19–20, and, for the local phrase, 54.

46. Renzo Marchi, *Storia economica di Prato dall'unità d'Italia ad oggi* (Milan: Giuffré, 1962), and Avigdor, "Il caso Prato," p. 3; pages 154–57 of the latter describe developments in the 1930s. Lorenzoni, *Una politica innovativa*, cites figures on the concentration of the industry in 1927 (p. 43) and describes the firms' strategy of responding to crisis by obliging the workforce to bear fixed costs (pp. 44–46).

47. The history of the *impannatore* is a central theme in Ezio Avigdor, *L'industria tessile a Prato* (Milan: Feltrinelli, 1961).

48. See Lorenzoni, *Una politica innovativa*, pp. 12, 43, for the connection between the growing influence of the *impannatore* and the decline of the integrated firm.

49. Ibid., p. 34 (on the mechanics' tricks, or *furbizie*), p. 34 (on the renovation of looms), and p. 61 (the citation). The Pratese use, among other advanced technologies, water- and air-jet looms; see Danielle Mazzonis, Umberto Colombo, and Giuseppe Lanzavecchia, "The Prato System as an Example of Old and New Technologies" (manuscript, Italian National Commission for Nuclear and Alternative Energy Sources [ENEA], Rome, 1983), p. 10.

50. Marchi, *Storia economica di Prato*, p. 221.

51. The project is described in Mazzonis et al., "The Prato System." The aim is to

increase the flexibility of textile machinery, facilitate coordination among firms, and reduce energy costs. Discussion with Umberto Colombo, December 4, 1983. Colombo is the head of the ENEA, which sponsored the project.

Developments in Prato—the introduction of sophisticated technologies, the decomposition of large firms, and the switch to specialized products—are, moreover, typical of changes in the Italian textile industry as a whole. See Organisation for Economic Co-operation and Development, *Textile and Clothing Industries* (Paris: OECD, 1983), pp. 137–39.

52. Figures cited in H. Dieter Jorissen, "Innovationsfähigkeit: Chance des deutschen Maschinenbaus," *VDI-Z*, no. 1/2 (January 1981), pp. 1–4; figures are from page 1. These figures are of special-purpose production equipment, such as packaging and printing machines, as well as machine tools in the narrow sense of lathes, mills, grinders, and so on—the classic tools for making tools. Corroborating data are in Economic Commission for Europe, *Bulletin of Statistics on World Trade in Engineering Products* (New York, ECE, United Nations, 1970–80).

53. On the expansion of Japanese machine-tool production, see Shinshichi Abe, "Machine-Tool Industry Expands on Basis of NC Development," *Business Japan* (September 1980), pp. 59–70. For the industry's increasing share of world trade, see Economic Commission for Europe, *Bulletin of Statistics*.

54. For a review of these developments, see John Teresko, "Controlmakers' Challenge: Putting Computers to Work," *Industry Week*, October 15, 1979, pp. 103–9.

55. See, on the increase in production of numerically controlled lathes and machining centers, Shinshiche Abe, "Growing Demand Helps Stabilize NC Machine Industry," *Business Japan* (October 1980): 97–107; data from p. 107. The increasing share of the output of numerically controlled equipment going to small and medium-sized firms is reported in Nomura Securities Co., Ltd., *Factory Automation: Toward an Unmanned Factory* (Tokyo: Nomura Securities Co., Ltd., 1981), p. 74. For data on the share of computer-driven machining centers in total American imports of Japanese numerically controlled machine tools—as well as a comparison of Japanese and American products for small shops—see the excellent study by Paul Ong for "NC Machine Tools," in Industry and Trade Strategies, "Programmable Automation Industries (Report to the Congressional Office of Technology Assessment [contract no. 333-2840], mimeographed, Berkeley, Calif., April 1983), pp. 4, 47 (table 2). The changing composition of machine-tool production can be followed in *Machine and Tool Directory and Buyers' Guide* (Wheaton, Ill.: Hitchcock Publishing, various years).

56. According to the International Monetary Fund's index of average exchange rates, the yen appreciated 10.8 percent relative to the dollar between 1975 and 1977. By 1978 it had gained 42.3 percent over its 1975 value. See International Monetary Fund, *International Financial Statistics Yearbook* (Washington, D.C.: IMF, 1983).

57. Abe, "Machine Tool Industry," pp. 65, 70.

58. Arndt Sorge, Gert Hartmann, Malcolm Warner, and Ian Nicholas, *Mikroelektronik und Arbeit in der Industrie* (Frankfurt am Main: Campus, 1982), is to our knowledge the most careful comparative study of the use of numerical control under different market and shop-floor conditions. The introduction of CNC has touched off considerable discussion in the engineering literature of the possibilities for shop-floor programming by skilled workers. See, for example, "Programme in der Werkstatt optimiert," *VDI Nachrichten*, no. 10 (March 5, 1982), p. 12; "Programme an der Maschine erstellt," *VDI Nachrichten*, no. 9 (February 26, 1982), p. 5.

59. See the detailed account of Japanese machine-tool plants in Hermann J. Schulte, "Japans vierte Offensiv—mit Werkzeugmaschinen," *VDI-Z*, no. 3 (February 1981), pp. 59–62.

60. The following is based on data collected in Ong, "NC Machine Tools," pp. 13, 15–16.

61. Schulte, "Japans vierte Offensiv," p. 62.

Chapter 9

1. The organization, operation, and financing of these centers is described in detail in Houdaille Industries, Inc., "Petition to the President of the United States through the Office of the United States Trade Representative for the Exercise of Presidential

Discretion Authorized by Section 103 of the Revenue Act of 1971" (26 U.S.C. 48 [a] [7] [D], May 3, 1982).

2. See Keinosuke Ono, "Field Survey on Inter-Firm Technology: Flatware Industry in Tsubame City, Japan," and, on Nagano prefecture, Susumu Mishima, "Japan's Technological Transfer Promotion Policy for Small and Medium Enterprises," both in Asian Productivity Organization, *Intra-National Transfer of Technology* (Tokyo: Asian Productivity Organization, 1975), pp. 35–62 and 121–55, respectively.

3. Junzo Wada, "A Case History of Guidance and Upgrading of Subcontracting Firms," in ibid., pp. 87–119. The citation is from pp. 102–3.

4. For the "Sunday experiments" and the citation, see ibid., pp. 104, 106.

5. On the Japanese emphasis on flexibility in manufacturing as contrasted with the Western emphasis on reducing unit production costs of standard goods, see Richard J. Schonberger, *Japanese Manufacturing Techniques* (New York: The Free Press, 1982), pp. 132–55; and Koichi Shimokawa, "Product and Labor Strategies in the Contemporary Japanese Automobile Industry" (Paper presented at the International Conference on the Automobile and its Workers, Coventry, June 28–July 1, 1984.)

6. All measures that can be construed as shielding the domestic market from foreign competition and facilitating coordination of the machine-tool builders are listed in Houdaille Industries, "Petition to the President." Although this is an ex-parte document, there is little doubt that the Japanese government has encouraged growth of the industry. Whether it has been more encouraging in this regard than, say, the American Department of Defense—and what legal consequences ought to follow from its actions—are obviously separate questions.

7. For views of decentralization as economic retrogression, see Luigi Frey, "Il lavoro a domicilio in Lombardia," in Paolo Leon and Marco Marocchi eds., *Sviluppo economico italiano e forza-lavoro* (Venice: Marsilio, 1973), pp. 197–216, and P. David and E. Pottario, "Retroterra rurale e condizione operaia femminile: il settore della maglieria," *Inchiesta* 5 (October–December 1975): 9–22. A summary of the early view is Renata Livraghi, "Le ricerche sul decentramento produttivo," *Quaderni rassegna sindacale* 15 (January–April 1977): 234–39.

8. The technological aggressiveness of the Brescian mini-mills is reported in Istituto Regionale di Ricerca della Lombardia, *Siderurgia lombarda* (Milan: Franco Angeli, 1981), pp. 146–48. For a description of the agricultural-implements sector centered in Reggio-Emilia, see Vittorio Slavarani, "La domanda di forza-lavoro qualificata-specializzata: inchiesta nel comparto della meccanica agricola reggiana" (Tesi di lauria, Università degli Studi di Modena, 1979). Interviews and plant visits with Lucio Brevini (president of the Association Piccole e Medie Industrie of Reggio Emilia), in June and July 1980, underscored the role of sophisticated hydraulics in the technological progress of the area. On Sassuolo, see Margherita Russo, "La natura e le implicazioni del progresso tecnologico: una verifica empirica" (mimeographed, Modena, December 1980).

9. The wage and unemployment data are reported in Arnaldo Bagnasco and Rosella Pini, "Sviluppo economico e trasformazioni sociopolitiche dei sistemi territoriali a economia diffusa," *Quaderni fondazione Giangiacomo Feltrinelli*, no. 14 (Milan: Feltrinelli, 1981), table 4.16, p. 105, and table 4.10, p. 92. Modena's growing prosperity is recorded in Luigi Pieraccioni, ed., *Il reddito prodotto nelle province italiane nel 1979* (Rome: Unione Industria, Artigianato e Agricoltura, 1981), table 4, p. 22, and table 8, p. 39. For a discussion of trade data, see Charles F. Sabel, *Work and Politics* (Cambridge: Cambridge University Press, 1982), pp. 270–71.

10. Secondo Rolfo, "La diffusione del controllo numerico nella produzione italiana di macchine utensili," *Bolletino CERIS* 5 (September 1980): 125–36, especially pp. 126–29.

11. The origins and operations of these firms are described in M. Luisa Bianco and Adriana Luciano, *La sindrome di Archimede: tecnici e imprenditori nel settore elettronico* (Bologna: Il Mulino, 1982).

12. Various interviews with consultants in Bologna, 1980 through 1982.

13. Discussions with John A. Meuse, director of research and development, United Machinery Group, EMHART Corp., 1982.

14. "Sassuolo," *Il mondo*, November 6, 1981, pp. 61–152, especially p. 147.

15. Our discussion of these factors draws on: Bagnasco and Pini, *Sviluppo economico dei sistemi territoriali a economia diffusa,* which is the best summary of the literature on the new small firms; Sebastiano Brusco, "The Emilian Model: Productive Decentralisation and Social Integration," *Cambridge Journal of Economics* (June 1982): 167–84; Sabel,

Notes

Work and Politics, pp. 220–31; and Michael J. Piore and Charles F. Sabel, "Italian Small Business: Lessons for U.S. Industrial Policy," in John Zysman and Laura Tyson, eds., *American Industry in International Competition* (Ithaca: Cornell University Press, 1983), pp. 391–421.

16. On the political calculus behind state protection of the small-property sector, see Suzanne Berger, "The Traditional Sector in France and Italy," in Suzanne Berger and Michael J. Piore, *Dualism and Discontinuity in Industrial Societies* (Cambridge: Cambridge University Press, 1980), pp. 88–131. For a review of the legal advantages of Italian small firms, see Marco Ricolfi, "Legislazione economica e piccole imprese," in F. Ferreo and S. Scamuzzi, eds., *L'industria in Italia: la piccola impresa* (Rome: Editori Ruiniti, 1979), pp. 119–86. But keep in mind the observation—commonplace in Italy and applicable to most advanced countries—that large firms benefit from special legal provisions as much as (and sometimes more than) small. In Italy, for instance, the state periodically relieves large corporations of their obligations to contribute to various social-welfare funds, a practice referred to as *fiscalizzazione degli oneri sociali.* Thus, although the small firms profit from their legal status at a crucial stage of their development, it does not follow that their survival, and their advance into markets previously reserved for large firms, depends on legal advantages.

17. See Paul Getz Levenson, "The Metalworkers' Union and the Steel Industry in Brescia since 1945" (Senior Honors thesis, Harvard College, March, 1979), p. 24.

18. Stephen Hellman, "The PCI's Alliance and the Case of the Middle Classes," in Donald L. M. Blackmer and Sidney Tarrow, *Communism in Italy and France* (Princeton: Princeton University Press, 1975), pp. 373–419.

19. An excellent account of local institutions from this perspective is Arnaldo Bagnasco, "La costruzione sociale del mercato: strategia d'impresa e esperimenti di scala in Italia" (Paper presented to a meeting of the Social Science Research Council Joint Committee on Western Europe, Lisbon, November 1983). See also the summary of the relevant literature in Carlo Trigilia, "Sviluppo economico e trasformazioni sociopolitiche dei sistemi territoriali a economia diffusa," *Quaderni fondazione Giangiacomo Feltrinelli,* vol. 16, 1981.

20. Sebastiano Brusco, "Distretti industriali, servizi alle imprese e centri di comparto" (Paper presented to the seminar Innovazione Tecnologica, Ruolo della Piccola Imprese ed Intervento del Governo Locale, organized by the Regione Piemonte, Turin, February 25, 1983); Bagnasco, "La costruzione sociale del mercato."

21. Discussions with the staff of the Institute for Economic and Social Research of the Italian General Trade Union Confederation [IRES/CGIL], Rome, December 5, 1982.

22. Volker Hauff and Fritz W. Scharpf, *Modernisierung der Volkswirtschaft: Technologiepolitik als Strukturpolitik* (Cologne: Europäische Verlagsanstalt, 1975), p. 32, calls attention to this crucial point.

23. As an illustration of the strains to which the unions in this period were subject, see the account of a strike in an auto-parts plant in the pamphlet, Pierburg-Autorenkollektiv, *Pierburg-Neuss* (Internationale Sozialistische Publikationen: Pierburg, 1974).

24. A representative study is Rolf Dick, *Die Arbeitsteilung zwischen Industrie- und Entwicklungsländern im Maschinenbau, Kieler Studien* 168 (Tübingen: J. C. B. Mohr [Paul Siebeck], 1981). It finds that specialized products turned out in small numbers in small firms do better in world markets than longer production runs of standard machines, typical of larger plants (p. 46).

25. Here, at least, was a fundamental point of agreement between the Social Democrats (such as Hauff and Scharpf), who wanted to use the state to reshape the economy, and the more traditional mercantilists of Kiel, who would rely on the self-adjustment of the market.

26. On the mixed results of efforts to reorganize the steel industry (somewhat more successful in the Saarland than elsewhere), see Josef Esser, Wolfgang Fach, and Werner Väth, "Krisenregulierung zur politischen Durchsetzung ökonomischer Zwänge" (mimeographed, Berlin, Frankfurt am Main, and Constance, February 1983). Compare this text with the more sanguine estimate of the combined adaptive capacities of the industrialists, unions, and politicians in Josef Esser, *Gewerkschaften in der Krise* (Frankfurt am Main: Suhrkamp, 1982).

27. This stalemate is discussed in Jeremiah Michael Riemer, "Crisis and Intervention in the West German Economy: A Political Analysis of Changes in the Policy Machinery during the 1960s and 1970s" (Ph.D. diss., Cornell University, May 1983), pp. 285–423.

28. Fritz W. Scharpf, "Problemverstaatlichung und Politikverflechtung: das selbst-

blockierende System," in idem, *Politischer Immobilismus und ökonomische Krise* (Kronberg: Athenäum, 1977), pp. 104–15.

29. Not only the economic experts were reacting to the failures of the preceding years. The general public, too—alarmed by the crises in steel and shipbuilding, and the drop in exports caused by the early-1980s recession—was afraid that West Germany was becoming a second-class technological power. "Are We Sleeping Through the Future?" the news-magazine *Der Spiegel* asked its readers, in a cover headline in the December 26, 1983, issue.

30. Der Bundesminister für Forschung und Technologie, "Programm Fertigungstechnik der Bundesregierung" (Bonn: BMFT, n.d.), p. 7.

31. In the past, the introduction of automatically controlled machines has been delayed by the existence of a pool of skilled workers. Therefore, the West German machine-tool industry has developed a series of designs for machines that can be programmed in the shop: "Werkzeugmaschinenbau scheut den Wettbewerb nicht," *VDI-Nachrichten,* February 12, 1982, p. 9.

32. Arndt Sorge, Gert Hartmann, Malcolm Warner, and Ian Nicholas, *Mikroelektronik in der Industrie: Erfahrungen beim Einsatz von CNC-Maschinen in Grossbritannien und der Bundesrepublik Deutschland* (Frankfurt am Main: Campus, 1982); for the quotation, see the English precis of their argument, Gert Hartmann, Ian Nicholas, Arndt Sorge, and Malcolm Warner, "Computerized Machine Tools, Manpower Consequences, and Skill Utilization: A Study of British and West German Manufacturing Firms," *British Journal of Industrial Relations* 21, n. 2 (July 1983): 221–31; quotation p. 230.

33. Bodo Liebe, "Strategische Aspekte der Einführung neuer Produktionstechnologien," *VDI-Z,* no. 1/2 (January 1983), pp. 5–8.

34. "Programme in der Werkstatt optimiert," *VDI-Nachrichten,* no. 10 (March 5, 1982), p. 12.

35. In West Germany as elsewhere, however, there is still debate on whether the tendency is toward design of simple transfer devices, which perform a few operations at low cost or, at higher cost, design of something like a universal robot, able to manipulate many workpieces in many ways. Opinions will divide sharply so long as it is hard to assess the possibilities of the relevant technologies and the volatility of particular markets. See, for instance, Walter Everschein, Manfred Weck, Kurt Zenner, and Peter Herrmann, "Anforderungen an zeitgemässe Produktionssysteme," *VDI-Z,* no. 11 (June 1, 1981), pp. 449–57.

36. Eckart Hildebrandt, "Der VW-Tarifvertrag zur Lohndifferenzierung," in Reinhard Doleschal and Rainer Dombois, eds., *Wohin läuft VW? Die Automobilproduktion in der Wirtschaftskrise* (Reinbek bei Hamburg: Rowohlt, 1982), pp. 309–49.

37. These observations are based on discussions with Werner Sengenberger, of the Institut für Sozialwissenschaftliche Forschung, in Munich, and Fritz W. Scharpf, of the International Institute of Management, Wissenschaftszentrum, Berlin. A good statement of the major themes and positions in the emerging debate about industrial reorganization is Peter Glotz, *Die Arbeit der Zuspitzung* (Berlin: Siedler Verlag, 1984), especially pp. 132–35.

38. The best analysis of these problems is Wolfgang Streeck, "Neo-corporatist Industrial Relations and the Economic Crisis in West Germany" (Working Paper 97, European University Institute, Florence, March 1984).

39. Bela Balassa, "The French Economy under the Fifth Republic," in William G. Andrews and Stanley Hoffmann, eds., *The Impact of the Fifth Republic on France* (Albany: State University of New York Press, 1981), pp. 117–38, especially p. 128.

40. This argument follows Suzanne Berger, "Lame Ducks and National Champions: Industrial Policy in the Fifth Republic," in Andrews and Hoffmann, *The Impact of the Fifth Republic,* pp. 160–78, especially pp. 161–62.

41. For these events—the worst labor unrest in France since 1968—and the government's maneuvers to persuade Renault and Peugeot-Citroën to invest in the area, see John Ardagh, *France in the 1980s* (London: Secker and Warburg, 1982), pp. 57–60.

42. In March 1978, the unemployment rate was 9.5 percent in the south and west, and 5.1 percent in the rest of France: Berger, "Lame Ducks and National Champions," p. 171.

43. Peter A. Hall, "French Etatism versus British Pluralism" (Paper presented at the Center for European Studies, Harvard University, July 1978), and idem, "Economic Planning and the State: The Evolution of Economic Challenge and Political Response in

Notes

France," in Gösta Esping-Andersen and Roger Friedland, eds., *Political Power and Social Theory* 3 (1982), pp. 175–213.

44. Lawrence G. Franko and Sherry Stephenson, *French Export Behavior in Third World Markets* (Washington, D.C.: The Center for Strategic and International Studies, Georgetown University, 1980), pp. 3–32, 73–75.

45. Berger, "Lame Ducks and National Champions," p. 164.

46. Organization for Economic Cooperation and Development, *National Accounts* and *Economic Outlook* (Paris: OECD, various years).

47. Christian Stoffaës, *La grande menace industrielle* (Paris: Calmann-Lévy, 1978). The arguments summarized in this paragraph appear on pp. 94–96.

48. For the following, see ibid., pp. 316–45.

49. These figures are from *L'année politique, économique, et sociale en France, 1982* (Paris: Éditions du Moniteur, 1983), pp. 421, 437–39.

50. See Houdaille Industries, "Petition to the President." See also the related "Comments Submitted to the United States International Trade Commission in Investigation No. 332-149 Under U.S.C. 1332(b)," by Cravath, Swaine and Moore, attorneys for Cincinnati Milacron Inc., December 14, 1982.

51. Interview with Gordon Forward, Chaparral Steel Co., Midlothian, Tex., March 23, 1981.

52. Members of this first group—operating on the border between universities and consulting firms—include such figures as Louis Davis, Chris Argyris, and Scott Myers. See, for example, Louis E. Davis, "Design of Jobs," *Industrial Relations,* October 1966, pp. 21–45. Writers such as Richard E. Walton, of the Harvard Business School, and Irving Bluestone, of the UAW, were associated with this group, but also with the one to be described next. See, for example, Irving Bluestone, "Implementing Quality-of-Worklife Programs," *Management Review,* July 1979, pp. 43–46: he argues that although cooperation would probably produce more contented workers and higher productivity, it is often resisted by both union stewards and first-line supervisors, as a threat to their prerogatives under the existing grievance system.

53. For an excellent review of these outbreaks of interest in the humanization of work, see Charles Chevreux Heckscher, "Democracy at Work: In Whose Interests? The Politics of Worker Participation" (Ph.D. diss., Harvard University, 1981).

54. For a sophisticated (and disillusioned) retrospective of the European position, see N. Altmann, P. Binkelmann, K. Düll, R. Mendolia, and H. Stück, "Bedingungen und Probleme betrieblich initiierter Humanisierungsmassnahmen" (mimeographed, Institut für Sozialwissenschaftliche Forschung, Munich, 1980). An equally thoughtful review of the American variant of these arguments is Heckscher, "Democracy at Work: In Whose Interests?"

55. See Ivar Berg, Marcia Freedman, and Michael Freeman, *Managers and Work Reform: A Limited Engagement* (New York: The Free Press, 1978).

56. Anil Verma and Thomas A. Kochan, "The Growth of the Nonunion Sector within a Firm" (Paper presented to the MIT/Union Conference, Boston, June 19–21, 1983). Data on the unionized fraction of the work force are from table 2, p. 13.

57. For an overview of the strategy and a list of the new plants, see David Friedman, "Workers' Expectations and Labor Relations in the U.S. Auto Industry" (Senior Honors thesis, Harvard College, 1979), which draws on interviews with workers from GM plants in Alabama, Georgia, and Mississippi.

58. In the national contract settled in 1979, GM pledged to remain neutral in union-representation elections in the Southern plans. In 1982, the company agreed to recognize the UAW as the legal bargaining agent in any new plant that closely resembled an existing one. Later that year, GM agreed to waive formal elections and recognize the UAW as the bargaining agent in plants not subject to this "accreditation" clause if the relevant majority of workers signed cards authorizing the union as their representative. See Harry C. Katz, *Shifting Gears: Changing Labor Relations in the U.S. Auto Industry* (Cambridge, Mass.: MIT Press, forthcoming), chapter 4. For a glimpse of the bitter conflicts provoked by the UAW's organization drives in the South in the 1970s, see the account of the union's recognition at three Saginaw Steering Division plants near Decatur, Alabama, in September 1982, in "G.M. Plant in South Unionized without a Vote," *New York Times,* September 5, 1982, p. 28.

59. Katz, *Shifting Gears,* chapter 4, is the most thorough description of the new experiments.

60. See, for example, "Saving Jobs at GM," in the UAW magazine *Solidarity*, April 1982, pp. 5–8. The article describes the twenty-nine-month contract signed by the union and the auto maker in March 1982; it ends by quoting a worker as saying, "I'm willing to give up a few things temporarily in order to keep my job."

61. A strike at the Chrysler stamping plant in Twinsburg, Ohio, in November 1983, symbolized the workers' determination to get back what they had given up during the slump. The six-day strike at this key plant—which halted the company's car production and cost it 300 million dollars in lost revenues—resulted in the restoration of many work rules that had been suspended in the preceding year. See John Koten, "Chrysler Strike at Ohio Plant Ends after Six Days," *Wall Street Journal*, November 7, 1983, p. 3. Events at Chrysler reflected developments in the rest of the automobile industry; see "The UAW Wants a Piece of the Action," *Business Week*, August 8, 1983, pp. 20–21. A *Business Week* article from the same period noted that "Disputes are turning rancorous where concession demands jeopardize traditional bargaining patterns": "Labor: No More Mr. Nice Guy," *Business Week*, August 29, 1983, pp. 18–19, citation p. 18.

62. "The Revolutionary Wage Deal at GM's Packard Electric," *Business Week*, August 29, 1983, pp. 54–56, and John Holusha, "GM Division Workers Reject a Reduced-Pay Pact," *New York Times*, August 25, 1983, p. A13.

63. "Intrapreneurial (*sic*) Now," *The Economist*, April 17, 1982, pp. 67–72; and "Big Business Tries to Imitate the Entrepreneurial Spirit," *Business Week*, April 18, 1983, pp. 84–89.

64. "Even the most inventive of the large companies seem increasingly willing to turn to startup suppliers of innovative products when their internal development efforts are moving too slowly," *Business Week* observed, ibid., p. 88.

65. Ibid., p. 87.

66. Thomas J. Peters and Robert H. Waterman, Jr., *In Search of Excellence: Lessons from America's Best Run Companies* (New York, Harper & Row, 1982), pp. 7–8.

67. Rosabeth Moss Kantor, *The Changemasters: Innovation for Productivity in the American Corporation* (New York: Simon and Schuster, 1983), pp. 17–18.

68. Wickham Skinner, "Operations Strategy: Past Perspectives, Seven New Initiatives, and Future Opportunities," *Operations Management Review*, Summer 1983, pp. 4–10, citation pp. 9–10.

69. Louis T. Wells, Jr., "The International Product Life Cycle and United States Regulation of the Automobile Industry," in Douglas H. Ginsburg and William J. Abernathy, eds., *Government, Technology, and the Future of the Automobile* (New York: McGraw-Hill, 1980), pp. 270–92.

70. William J. Abernathy, Kim B. Clark, Alan M. Kantrow, *Industrial Renaissance: Producing a Competitive Future for America* (New York: Basic Books, 1983).

71. John T. Dunlop, "Working Toward Consensus," *Challenge* (July–August 1982): 26–34.

72. See Thomas A. Kochan's "Reply" to critics of his *Collective Bargaining and Industrial Relations* (Homewood, Ill.: Irwin, 1980) in *Industrial Relations* 21 (Winter 1982): 115–22. See also Verma and Kochan, "Growth of the Nonunion Sector," pp. 34–35.

73. Deborah Groban Olson, "Union Experiences with Worker Ownership: Legal and Practical Issues Raised by ESOPs, TRASOPs, Stock Purchases and Co-Operatives," *Wisconsin Law Review*, no. 5, 1982, pp. 729–823.

74. "Collective Bargaining as an Industrial System: Argument against Judicial Revision of Section 8(a)(2) of the National Labor Relations Act," *Harvard Law Review* 96 (May 11, 1983): 1662–82, urges courts to disallow management-sponsored employee-representation plans (typically, works councils unaffiliated with any extra-firm labor organization) even when employees have freely chosen such forms of industrial relations. The claim is that the Wagner Act established the unions' right to freedom from management subversion and management's right to limit collective bargaining to wages, hours, and working conditions. All efforts to widen the scope of bargaining—even in the interests of greater productivity and with the consent of the workers—potentially threaten the rights of either labor or management as currently defined, and therefore can be authorized only by Congress.

75. Academic observers do not agree on what to count as high-technology industry. They have alternatively defined it according to: its final product; its pace of technological innovation; its manufacturing processes; its high share of scientists and engineers in the

labor force; its research-and-development expenditures as a percentage of total sales; or its ratio of value added to total sales.

Nor do government agencies employ consistent definitions of it. Their accounting procedures are often tailored to local advertising campaigns aimed at attracting industry from "modern" sectors. At a minimum, they count as high-tech all firms making computers, semiconductors, and other electric components; aerospace and military vehicles; and advanced instrumentation. After that, lists differ. For example, the Massachusetts Department of Employment Security includes firms that produce drugs and other medicinal chemicals; ordnance, ammunition, and accessories; electrical machinery; and photographic equipment. By contrast, the Association of Bay Area Governments in California excludes such firms but includes those providing computer services and research-and-development laboratories. See Massachusetts Department of Employment Security, *High Technology Employment in Massachusetts and Selected States* (April 1981), and Association of Bay Area Governments, *Silicon Valley and Beyond* (Berkeley: ABAG, 1981).

76.   See "Polaroid Sharpens Its Focus on the Marketplace," *Business Week,* February 13, 1984, pp. 132–36.

77.   Personal communication with mill executives, Spring 1982.

Chapter 10

1.   For a list of failed attempts at Keynesian reflation, see John Williamson, "Global Macroeconomic Strategy," in Institute for International Economics, *Promoting World Recovery* (Washington, D.C.: Institute for International Economics, 1982), pp. 17–37, citation p. 30.

2.   For a discussion of this issue, see John Williamson, *The Exchange Rate System* (Washington, D.C.: Institute for International Economics, 1983).

3.   On Keynes's ideas, see Fred L. Block, *The Origins of International Economic Disorder* (Berkeley: University of California Press, 1977), pp. 48–49.

4.   See C. Fred Bergstein and William R. Cline, *Trade Policy in the 1980s* (Washington, D.C.: Institute for International Economics, 1982), especially pp. 72–73.

5.   On attempts to create the Integrated Program for Commodities within the framework of the United Nations Conference on Trade and Development negotiations, see Robert Rothstein, *Global Bargaining* (Princeton: Princeton University Press, 1979), and Jeffrey A. Hart, *The New International Economic Order* (New York: St. Martin's Press, 1983). On managing surplus capacity, see Susan Strange and Roger Tooze, eds., *The International Politics of Surplus Capacity* (London: Allen and Unwin, 1981), and the case studies of particular industries in John Zysman and Laura Tyson, eds., *American Industry in International Competition* (Ithaca: Cornell University Press, 1983).

6.   Richard Jolly, "Restructuring out of Recession," in Strange and Tooze, *International Politics of Surplus Capacity,* pp. 189–97, citation p. 195.

7.   "Spreading through the Factory," *Business Week,* August 3, 1981, pp. 60–61.

8.   David A. Collier, "The Automation of the Goods-Producing Industries: Implications for Operations Managers," *Operations Management Review* 1 (Spring 1983): 7–12, quotation pp. 10–11.

9.   William A. Fischer, "Advanced Manufacturing Technologies: Assessing the Impacts," *Operations Management Review* 1 (Summer 1983): 11–14, quotation p. 12.

10.   See, for instance, Peter Herrmann, "Fachgebiete in Jahresübersichten: flexible Fertigung," *VDI-Z* 124 (August 1982): 599–608.

11.   Sherry R. Turkle, *The Second Self: Computers and the Human Spirit* (New York: Simon and Schuster, 1984).

12.   Electric-arc furnaces were probably first used for the large-scale production of carbon steel in the 1930s, at Northwestern Steel and Wire, a manufacturer of rods, bars, and wires near Chicago. The firm wanted to integrate backwards to ensure its supply of steel. When the National Recovery Administration prohibited expansion using traditional technologies, the firm adapted electric-arc methods to its needs. It has remained a leader

Notes

in electric-arc technology. See Donald F. Barnett and Louis Schorsch, *Steel: Upheaval in a Basic Industry* (Cambridge, Mass.: Ballinger Publishing Company, 1983), p. 86.

13. George A. V. Russell, "Flexibility as a Factor in the Economic Exploitation of Rolling-Mills and Some Technical Means for Its Realization," *The Journal of the Iron and Steel Industry* 130, no. 2 (1934): 25–125, and idem, "Some Considerations Influencing Plant Facilities for Strip-Sheet Production under British Conditions," ibid. 133, no. 1 (1936): 51–93.

14. Wickham Skinner, "Operations Strategy: Past Perspectives, Seven New Initiatives, and Future Strategies," *Operations Management Review* 1 (Summer 1983): 4–10, quotation p. 8.

15. A typical case of sweating was the "Sheffield outrages"—organized sabotage of tools and materials—of the 1860s. See G. I. H. Lloyd, *The Cutlery Trades* (Longmans, Green and Co., 1913), pp. 110–47, 235–37, and Sidney Pollard, *A History of Labour in Sheffield* (Liverpool: Liverpool University Press, 1959), pp. 65–67, 134–58.

16. William J. Abernathy, *The Productivity Dilemma: Roadblock to Innovation in the Automobile Industry* (Baltimore: Johns Hopkins University Press, 1978).

17. The similarities in social structure and worker behavior between Christian Democratic and Communist areas of flexible specialization is underscored in Arnaldo Bagnasco, "La costruzione sociale del mercato: strategia d'impresa e esperimenti di scala in Italia" (Paper presented to a meeting of the Social Science Research Council Joint Committee on Western Europe, Lisbon, November 1983). On the historical origins of the Christian Democrats' strategy of rural industrialization, see Mario G. Rossi, *Le origini del partito cattolico: movimento cattolico e lotta di classe nell'Italia liberale* (Rome: Editori Riuniti, 1977).

18. Note, however, that the Amalgamated Clothing Workers union, which was rooted in the mass-production factories of the men's clothing industry, was an early advocate of unemployment insurance and many other measures that became central to the postwar regulatory system. See Steve Fraser, "Dress Rehearsal for the New Deal: Shop-Floor Insurgents, Political Elites, and Industrial Democracy in the Amalgamated Clothing Workers," in Morton H. Frisch and Daniel J. Wallcowitz, eds., *Working Class America* (Urbana, Ill.: University of Illinois Press, 1983), pp. 212–255.

19. On training in mass-production firms, see Peter B. Doeringer and Michael J. Piore, *Internal Labor Markets and Manpower Analysis* (Lexington, Mass.: D. C. Heath and Company, 1971).

20. In Japan, Rodney Clark found, "training was far more an introduction to the community than a technical course": Rodney Clark, *The Japanese Company* (New Haven: Yale University Press, 1979), p. 158. The same idea is a central theme in studies of highly skilled German workers. See, for example, Burkart Lutz and Guido Kammerer, *Das Ende des graduierten Ingenieurs? eine empirische Analyse unerwarteter Nebenfolgen der Bildungsexpansion* (Frankfurt am Main: Europäische Verlagsanstalt, 1975).

21. See Herbert Tumpel, "Wirtschaftspolitik: Vorschläge des Bundesvorstandes," Report to the 10th Federal Congress of the Austrian Trade Unions, October 3–8, 1983; and Charles F. Sabel, "Kontrollierte Flexibilität," in Anton Benya and Charles F. Sabel, *Gewerkschaftsstrategie in den achtziger Jahren* (Vienna: Verlag des Österreichischen Gewerkschaftsbundes, 1984), pp. 9–29.

22. For speculation about this possibility, see Charles F. Sabel, "Yeomen Economics and Modern Technology" (Paper presented to the Conference on Economic Development and Democracy in Honor of Albert O. Hirschman, Kellogg Institute, Notre Dame, April 15–17, 1984).

Chapter 11

1. One indication of the subaltern position of U.S. parts suppliers is the difference between the wages paid by them and those paid by the automobile manufacturers: the former pay roughly one-third the wages of the latter. In West Germany, the difference is less: parts suppliers pay about two-thirds the wages of the automobile manufacturers. See

Notes

Christoph Köhler and Werner Sengenberger, *Konjunktur und Personalanpassung* (Frankfurt am Main: Campus, 1983), p. 434.

2.   See Brock Yates, *The Decline and Fall of the American Automobile Industry* (New York: Empire Books, 1983), pp. 13–76, especially p. 55.

3.   Arthur Anderson and Co., "The Changing U.S. Auto Industry" (1983), pp. 33–42.

4.   For a case in point, see the account of recent developments at Texas Instruments in *Business Week,* September 19, 1983, p. 60.

5.   For an excellent study of the development of high-tech industry in Silicon Valley and Route 128—with special reference to the recruitment and treatment of the blue-collar work force—see Annalee Saxenian, "Silicon Valley and Route 128: Regional Prototypes or Historical Exceptions?" in Manuel Castells, ed., *Technology, Space, and Society, Urban Affairs Annual Review,* vol. 28 (forthcoming). This section of our text draws on her extensive and insightful research on these two areas.

6.   An institutionalized example of this meeting of cooperation and competition is the MIT Enterprise Forum. The Forum is an association of entrepreneurs, venture capitalists, and managers who meet to discuss one another's problems. Typically, an entrepreneur who feels he or she should be doing better presents his/her strategy to the Forum's staff; together they impanel a review board composed of other associates of the Forum. After appropriate study, the review board discusses the firm's problems with the entrepreneur— before an audience that can number in the hundreds. The entrepreneur's willingness to disclose the firm's business plans and weaknesses to the public presupposes both self-confidence and confidence in the good will of the entrepreneurial community. From an interview with Paul E. Johnson, executive director, MIT Enterprise Forum, September 26, 1983.

In Silicon Valley, certain bars and restaurants are well known as the gathering places of engineers, venture capitalists, and high-tech lawyers. For a discussion of the unwritten rules of the give-and-take in these meetings, see Everett M. Rogers and Judith K. Larsen, *Silicon Valley Fever: Growth of High-Technology Culture* (New York: Basic Books, 1984), especially pp. 79–85.

7.   See Robert Pear, "States Fostering High Technology," *New York Times,* August 17, 1983, pp. A1–A21. Often the industry association and the state cooperate closely in the administration of programs serving the high-technology firms. Under the Massachusetts Job Training and Partnership Act, for example, the High Technology Council provides initial financing for new educational programs of interest to its members, and the Bay State Skills Commission matches these funds and accredits the private firms that do the teaching. One such firm, Employment Resources, Inc., trains local residents for entry-level data-processing and computer work.

8.   The industry's demands and the angry response they have elicited are captured in an exchange in the opinion pages of the *Boston Globe,* between Howard B. Foley, president of the Massachusetts High Technology Council, and Thom Gallagher, a Democratic state representative. Under the headline "Two Issues Will Help Determine State Business Climate" (January 17, 1984, p. 48), Foley warned that unitary taxation (taxation of out-of-state corporate earnings) and mandatory prenotification (requiring firms to notify the state at least a month before closing, relocating, or laying off workers) would discourage the expansion of high-tech firms in Massachusetts. "The way in which these two issues are resolved," he concluded, "will provide either positive or negative signals for decision-makers to consider as they make expansion and location decisions that will affect job growth in Massachusetts for years to come. They may not seem important to others, but they are of utmost importance to the high-technology industry in Massachusetts. Each will be a major factor in every plant-siting decision made by high-tech company presidents in 1984."

But though most of the article simply attacked unitary taxation and mandatory prenotification—as infringements of managerial freedom—it also appealed for community cooperation in solving problems of industrial adjustment. Thus the sentence preceding the paragraph just cited reads: "Local communities should collaborate with local industries through private industry councils and the $60 million Job Training Partnership Act to retrain those who are affected by layoffs and plant closings."

Not surprisingly, Representative Gallagher—a cosponsor of the mandatory-prenotification bill—dismissed this fleeting overture in his reply (January 24, 1984, p. 43). He attacked

340

Foley for demanding that the citizens of the state appease a handful of business leaders: "After all, in just my own state representative district there are more than 35,000 people— far more than the total membership of Foley's High Technology Council. And all of them have opinions. Most of theirs, however, have more to do with how the little person generally winds up on the short end of the stick in his or her dealings with big business."

9. "High Tech Lures Union Organizers," *Business Week,* April 11, 1983, pp. 101–2 reports cases (at Honeywell and Atari) in which layoffs have encouraged unionization of blue-collar workers; it also cites a case (at Western Electric) in which management's unwillingness to discuss production changes and standards of evaluation had the same effect on engineers. See also "Union Dues: High Tech Meets Organized Labor," *Electronic Business,* December 1983, pp. 100–103.

10. One such institution is the North Carolina Microelectronics Center. Regarding this, see the debate between advocates and critics of the semiconductor industry in *N.C. Insight,* the journal of the North Carolina Center for Public Policy Research, Raleigh, 4, no. 3 (September 1981): 17–43.

11. The connection between urban-planning problems and the high-tech firms' need to disperse production is underscored in *Silicon Valley and Beyond: High Technology Growth for the San Francisco Bay Area,* Working Papers on the Region's Economy, no. 2, Association of Bay Area Governments, Berkeley, December 1981, p. 8: "Faced with some of the highest housing costs in the United States and a strained transportation and public infrastructure capacity, growing firms are now forced to make difficult decisions when they expand. Most firms would like to remain very close to their current facilities. But as labor attraction becomes difficult due to shortage of affordable housing, and labor turnover remains high due to the stiff competition for scarce skilled workers, many of the firms have decided to expand new facilities outside of Silicon Valley."

State officials eager to attract high-tech firms are well aware of the problems caused by uncoordinated expansion, and they promise newcomers that the mistakes of the past will not be repeated. For example, the governor of North Carolina wrote in a newspaper column in 1981, "We are prepared to do the kind of planning needed to ensure adequate housing, water, and so forth as a result of industry located here": Governor James B. Hunt, "Microelectronics: The Key to the Future," excerpted in *N.C. Insight,* September 1981, p. 17. Critics of the governor's policies doubt that the state will be able to exercise the kind of control over the new firms that effective planning requires: see Michael I. Luger, "Policies and Promises: The Economic Hope of the Microelectronics Industry," ibid., pp. 27–32. The debate thus mirrors the contradictions of the industrialists themselves, with state officials appealing to high-tech firms to practice what they preach, and critics pointing to what the firms actually do.

12. The foregoing is based on Harold E. Arnett and Donald N. Smith, *The Tool and Die Industry: Problems and Prospects,* Michigan Business Reports, New Series, no. 1 (Ann Arbor: Division of Research, Graduate School of Business Administration, University of Michigan, 1975), especially figure 2, p. 15 (on the decline in toolmaking activity of Detroit Trade Association companies), pp. 50–53 (on the dynamic of concentration and increasing price competition) and p. 39 (on the early use of numerical control).

13. Even the briefest canvass of Detroit-area firms reveals a pervasive doubt about the possibility of attracting talented young persons into the metalworking industry. From interviews with managers of five machine-tool and tool-and-die manufacturers in Wayne and Macomb counties, Michigan, November 16–18, 1983.

14. Regarding the following argument, see Michael J. Piore, *Birds of Passage: Migrant Labor and Industrial Societies* (Cambridge: Cambridge University Press, 1979), pp. 141–66.

15. This account follows Roger D. Waldinger, "Ethnic Enterprise and Industrial Change: A Case Study of the New York City Garment Industry" (Ph.D. diss., Harvard University, June 1983).

16. In the 1950s and '60s, Timberland—then called Abington Shoe Co. and located in South Boston—produced cheap oxfords, work boots, and work shoes. The company just barely survived the increasing competition of the mid-1960s that drove many similar manufacturers out of business; and when business revived in 1968, the owners were determined to create a distinctive product. They pioneered the use of injection molding (a process for attaching thick rubber soles to leather uppers) with high-grade hides to

Notes

create a line of rugged but fashionable footwear. In 1969, the firm moved to an old mill in Newmarket, New Hampshire, to take advantage of the skilled (and low-cost) labor still left from New England's days as a center of the shoe industry. During the next decade, the firm shifted an increasing percentage of its output from the commodity to the specialty lines, as it first profited from and then promoted the spread of what the industry calls the "outdoors" or "survival" fashions. See Lucien Rhodes, "Sole Success," *Inc.*, February 1982, pp. 44–50.

17. Sumner H. Slichter, James J. Healy, and E. Robert Livernash, *The Impact of Collective Bargaining on Management* (Washington, D.C.: The Brookings Institution, 1960), p. 660.

18. Maryellen R. Kelley, "Tasks, Skills, Training and Technology: The Machining Labor Process" (Ph.D. diss., Sloan School of Management, MIT June 1984).

19. This is a central finding of a recent report on thirty Boston-area machine shops. See Henry R. Norr, "Observations on Some New England Machine Shops," (Paper for the Program in Science, Technology, and Society, Massachusetts Institute of Technology, November, 1981).

20. Waldinger, *Ethnic Enterprise.* This account is supplemented by personal communications from Waldinger.

21. Discussions with Jack Russell and Peter Plastrik of the Governor's Cabinet Council, Michigan, 1983–84.

22. An embryonic version of such a program is presented in Arnett and Smith, *Tool and Die Industry*, pp. 77–9.

23. For surveys of the deregulation movement, see "Deregulating America," *Business Week*, November 28, 1983, pp. 80–96, and Susan J. Tolchin and Martin Tolchin, *Dismantling America: The Rush to Deregulate* (Boston: Houghton Mifflin, 1983). For a liberal's view of the limits of government regulation—which illustrates the extent to which the call for restoration of competition had become bipartisan—see Stephen Breyer, *Regulation and Its Reform* (Cambridge: Harvard University Press, 1982).

24. For example, on the use of trade-adjustment funds to secure support for the President in Democratic caucuses and primaries in 1979, see Michael Schlein, "Federal Policies toward Mature Industries: The Footwear Revitalization Program and Trade Adjustment Assistance" (Master's thesis, Department of Political Science, Massachusetts Institute of Technology, 1984), pp. 39–41.

25. Bernard Bailyn, *The Ideological Origins of the American Revolution* (Cambridge: Harvard University Press, 1967).

26. Plans for such industrial policies are rooted in the early New Deal and Roosevelt's efforts (copied from and by other leaders of the day) to shelter the American economy from the breakdown of the world-trade regime. Moderate versions recall the middle-of-the-road interpretation of the National Industrial Recovery Act as a cooperative effort to share the costs of restructuring between labor and capital. More radical versions extend the leftist interpretation of the NIRA as a means for dramatically strengthening the role of unions, raising purchasing power, and giving labor a voice in national economic planning.

27. Bruce R. Scott, "Can We Survive the Welfare State?" *Harvard Business Review* 60 (September–October 1982): 70–84, quotation p. 82.

28. Ibid.

29. Robert R. Reich, *The Next American Frontier* (New York: Times Books, 1983), p. 248.

30. Ibid., p. 276.

31. Reich cites "a few American companies producing high-technology goods" as examples in the United States of flexible enterprises that "depend on participation and thus on security and equity": ibid., p. 257.

32. See Seymour Martin Lipset and William Schneider, *The Confidence Gap: Business, Labor, and Government in the Public Mind* (New York: The Free Press, 1983).

33. For a survey of the services provided to American farmers by the government and the social movements that helped establish them—see Thomas H. Greer, *American Social Reform Movements: Their Pattern since 1865* (Westport, Conn.: Greenwood Press, 1980).

34. The following description draws on: U.S. General Accounting Office, "Slow Productivity Growth in the U.S. Footwear Industry: Can the Federal Government Help?"

(FGMSD-80-3, February 1980); Daniel Dexter, "Report on the American Non-Rubber Industry" (Master's thesis, Political Science Department, Massachusetts Institute of Technology, 1983); and, for data on productivity increases, Michael Schlein, "Federal Policies toward Mature Industries," pp. 44–88.

35. See, for example, Robert Nozick, *Anarchy, State, and Utopia* (New York: Basic Books, 1974).

36. Much American jurisprudence since the New Deal has been concerned with defining the "proper" balance between these variants of liberalism. An attempt at a philosophical synthesis that reveals—by the debates it provoked—the fundamental problems of liberalism is John Rawls, *A Theory of Justice* (Cambridge: Harvard University Press, 1971).

37. For example, William H. Sewell, Jr., argues that this idea of property informs the political rhetoric and action of French artisans up through the July Revolution of 1848. See his *Work and Revolution in France: The Language of Labor from the Old Regime to 1848* (Cambridge: Cambridge University Press, 1980).

38. See Alan Dawley, *Class and Community: The Industrial Revolution in Lynn* (Cambridge: Harvard University Press, 1976).

39. For references to the Knights' ideas, see ibid., chapter 2, n. 2-176.

40. See Lawrence Goodwyn, *The Democratic Promise: The Populist Movement in America* (Oxford: Oxford University Press, 1976).

41. Nick Salvatore, *Eugene Debs: Citizen and Socialist* (Champaign, Ill.: University of Illinois Press, 1983).

42. For example, see Seymour Martin Lipset, Martin Trow, and James Coleman, *Union Democracy: The Inside Politics of the International Typographers Union* (New York: The Free Press, 1956).

43. See Thomas R. Brooks, *Clint: A Biography of a Labor Intellectual* (New York: Atheneum, 1978), p. 17. More generally on these themes throughout the American labor movement, see Seymour Martin Lipset, "Why No Socialism in the United States," in Seweryn Bialer and Sophia Sluzar, eds., *Sources of Contemporary Radicalism* (Boulder, Colo.: Westview Press, 1977), pp. 31–149, and Maurice F. Neufeld, "The Persistence of Ideas in the American Labor Movement," *Industrial and Labor Relations Review* 35, no. 2 (January 1982): 207–20.

44. Howell John Harris, personal communications, Fall, 1982.

INDEX

Index

Index

International Labor Organization, 255
International Monetary Fund (IMF), 107–10, 171, 178, 180, 254–57
International trade, 134, 106–11; debt crisis and, 180–81; of developing countries, 178; exchange rates and, 170–74; flexible specialization and, 276–77; France and, 139, 236–37, 239; of Germany, 145–47, 150; government policies and, 297, 299; of Italy, 153; of Japan, 161; in machine tools, 217, 227; market saturation and, 184–87; in textiles, 213–14; unified system of, 253, 255; of West Germany, 230
International Union of Electronic Workers (IUE), 245
Inventory: just-in-time system of, 201; varying, 57–60
Iran, 199
Iranian revolution, 178, 193
Israel, 175
Italy, 16, 17, 133, 151–56, 164; agriculture in, 134; artisan's associations in, 303; automobile industry in, 187; competitive conditions in, 271; computer-controlled machinery in, 260; economic reorganization in, 221, 223, 226–29; exchange rates and, 171; Fascist, 153–54; flexible specialization in, 17; growth rate in, 12; industrial districts of, 284, 290; Japan compared with, 157, 161; macroeconomic regulation in, 154; nineteenth-century, 151–52; oil shocks and, 177, 179; reemergence of craft production in, 205–6; regional conglomeration in, 266, 269; shop-floor control in, 155–56; skill transmission in, 274, 275; social unrest in, 167–69; steel industry in, 211; textile industry in, 213–16; United States compared with, 240, 241, 249; West Germany compared with, 229, 230, 233; in World War I, 152–53
ITT, 195

Jacquard loom, 30, 261
J. A. Henckels (firm), 33
Japan, 3, 16, 17, 133, 156–64, 310n3; automobile industry of, 174; bonus system in, 271; computer-controlled machinery in, 260; computer industry in, 270; early twentieth-century, 159–60; economic reorganization in, 221, 223–26; federated enterprises in, 267, 269; industrial districts in, 290; industrial relations in, 16; and interpenetration of mass markets, 186; Italy compared with, 226–29; *kanban* system in, 201; machine-tool industry in, 216–20; Ministry for Industry and Trade, 231; multinationalization and, 199; nineteenth-century, 134, 157–59; oil shocks and, 177, 179; policy shift in, 182; postwar, 160; reemergence of craft production in, 206; regional conglomeration in, 292; regional technology centers in, 303; regulation of economy in, 12–13; shop-floor control in, 161, 212; small-firm sector in, 20; steel industry in, 208; textile industry in, 214; third-world development compared with, 188; training in, 274–75; unions in, 286; United States compared with, 240, 241, 244; West Germany compared with, 229–33
Japan Machine Builders Association, 219, 226
Job classification, 113–15
Johnson, General Hugh, 94
Johnson, Lyndon B., 170
Joseph and Feiss Company, 127–28
J. P. Stevens, 36
Just-in-time system; *see kanban* system

Kanban system, 201, 283, 284, 290, 294
Kantor, Rosabeth, 247
Kantrow, Alan M., 248
Keynes, John Maynard, 73
Keynesianism, 73–74, 82, 91, 94–96, 135; abandonment of, 181; of Carter administration, 297, 298; exchange rates and, 172, 173; in France, 140; in Germany, 147–50; in Japan, 157; monetarism and, 103–4; multinational, 251–57, 277–80; socialist variant of, 299
Knights of Labor, 28, 305, 306
Kochan, Thomas, 248
Korea; *see* South Korea
Korean War, 147
Kuhn, Thomas, 43, 44, 250

Labor relations, 63–65; railroads and, 68; *see also* Unions

349

Index